Institutionalizing R

MW00627811

Institutionalizing Restorative Justice

edited by Ivo Aertsen, Tom Daems
and Luc Robert

WILLAN
PUBLISHING

Published by

Willan Publishing
Culmcott House
Mill Street, Uffculme
Cullompton, Devon
EX15 3AT, UK
Tel: +44(0)1884 840337
Fax: +44(0)1884 840251
e-mail: info@willanpublishing.co.uk
website: www.willanpublishing.co.uk

Published simultaneously in the USA and Canada by

Willan Publishing
c/o ISBS, 920 NE 58th Ave, Suite 300,
Portland, Oregon 97213-3786, USA
Tel: +001(0)503 287 3093
Fax: +001(0)503 280 8832
e-mail: info@isbs.com
website: www.isbs.com

First published 2006

Paperback
ISBN-13: 978-1-84392-158-5
ISBN-10: 1-84392-158-8

Hardback
ISBN-13: 978-1-84392-159-2
ISBN-10: 1-84392-159-6

British Library Cataloguing-in-Publication Data

A catalogue record for this book is available from the British Library

Project managed by Deer Park Productions, Tavistock, Devon
Typeset by GCS, Leighton Buzzard, Beds.
Printed and bound by T.J. International, Padstow, Cornwall

Contents

Acknowledgements   vii

Notes on contributors   ix

Introduction   xiii
Ivo Aertsen, Tom Daems and Luc Robert

1 The prospects for institutionalization of restorative
   justice initiatives in western countries   1
   Michael Tonry

2 The vital context of restorative justice   25
   Hans Boutellier

3 Beyond evangelical criminology: the meaning and
   significance of restorative justice   44
   John Pratt

4 The intermediate position of restorative justice: 68
   the case of Belgium
   Ivo Aertsen

5 Institutionalizing restorative justice? Transforming
   criminal justice? A critical view on the Netherlands   93
   John Blad

6   Institutionalizing restorative youth justice in a cold,
punitive climate   120
Adam Crawford

7   The French phantoms of restorative justice:
the institutionalization of 'penal mediation'   151
Jacques Faget

8   The institutionalization of restorative justice in
Canada: effective reform or limited and
limiting add-on?   167
Kent Roach

9   The institutionalization of principles in restorative
justice – a case study from the UK   194
Robert E. Mackay

10   Risk and restorative justice: governing through the
democratic minimization of harms   216
Pat O'Malley

11   Reintegrative shaming and restorative justice:
reconciliation or divorce?   237
Roger Matthews

12   Balancing the ethical and the political:
normative reflections on the institutionalization
of restorative justice   261
Barbara Hudson

13   Epilogue   282
Ivo Aertsen, Tom Daems and Luc Robert

Index   305

Acknowledgements

First of all, we wish to express our gratitude to the authors who contributed to this edited collection. Their contributions show the complexities, conundrums and challenges of institutionalizing RJ. Without their interesting, compelling and at times controversial analyses, this collection would not be what it has become.

Eight chapters in this book are elaborated versions of papers that were first presented and discussed at an international two-day workshop on 'The Institutionalization of Restorative Justice in a Changing Society' which was organized on 5–6 November 2004 at the Department of Criminal Law and Criminology of the Katholieke Universiteit Leuven, Belgium. This workshop was set up in the framework of and with financial support from COST Action A21 'Restorative Justice Developments in Europe'[1] and the MA in European Criminology Programme of the Centre of Advanced Legal Studies of the Katholieke Universiteit Leuven. We are grateful to both organizations for providing the necessary funding. Many people helped us out during the preparation of the workshop and assisted us during the workshop itself: Stephan Parmentier, Tony Peters and Lode Walgrave (chairs of the three sessions of the workshop), Andrea Ons and Sonja Wellens (from the secretariat of the Department of Criminal Law and Criminology), Jana Arsovska and Borbala Fellegi (from the European Forum on Victim Offender Mediation and Restorative Justice) and Stefaan Viaene (student criminology). Special thanks also to Kris Vanspauwen, researcher at the Law and Society Institute, who was closely involved in the early stages of the conceptualization of the workshop and who designed the website.

Note

1   COST forms an intergovernmental framework and stands for 'European Cooperation in the Field of Scientific and Technical Research' (http://cost. cordis.lu). Concerted 'actions' on specific research topics normally run for four years.

References

Daems, T. (2004) 'Is it all right for you to talk? Restorative justice and the social analysis of penal developments', *European Journal of Crime, Criminal Law and Criminal Justice*, 2: 132–49.

Daly, K. (2004) 'Pile it on. More texts on RJ', *Theoretical Criminology*, 8(4): 499–507.

Sparks, R. (1997) 'Recent social theory and the study of crime and punishment', in M. Maguire, R. Morgan and R. Reiner (eds), *The Oxford Handbook of Criminology*, 2nd edn. Oxford: Oxford University Press, pp. 409–35.

Notes on contributors

Ivo Aertsen is Professor of Criminology at the Catholic University of Leuven, Belgium, where he teaches Victimology and Penology. His research domains are mainly victimology, mediation and restorative justice. Dr Aertsen is Vice-Chair of the European Forum for Restorative Justice and leads COST Action A21 on Restorative Justice research in Europe.

John Blad is Associate Professor in the field of criminal law sciences at the Law Faculty of Erasmus University Rotterdam. In 2000 he founded both the Dutch *Forum voor Herstelrecht* and the *Tijdschrift voor Herstelrecht* (*Forum* and *Journal for Restorative Justice*). He is editor-in-chief of the *Journal*.

Hans Boutellier has been since August 2003 Chief Executive of the Dutch Verwey-Jonker Institute. He holds an Extraordinary Professorial Chair on Police and Safety Studies at the Free University of Amsterdam. He is actively involved in studies on crime prevention and community safety and in particular is interested in the relations between social policy, criminal justice and public morality.

Adam Crawford is Professor of Criminology and Criminal Justice at the University of Leeds where he is also Director of the Centre for

Criminal Justice Studies. He has written extensively on crime prevention, criminal justice policy and restorative justice. Among other publications he is the author of *The Local Governance of Crime* (Oxford 1997), *Youth Offending and Restorative Justice* (with T. Newburn, Willan 2003), *Plural Policing* (Policy Press 2005) and *Integrating Victims into Restorative Youth Justice* (Policy Press 2005).

Tom Daems studied criminology at the Catholic University of Leuven, Belgium and the London School of Economics and Political Science, UK. He is a PhD candidate at the Department of Criminal Law and Criminology, Catholic University of Leuven where he works as a Researcher of the Fund for Scientific Research – Flanders (Belgium).

Jacques Faget is Researcher in the French National Centre of Scientific Research (CERVL) and Professor in the Institute of Political Studies of Bordeaux. Among his publications are *Médiation et action publique. La dynamique du fluide* (Presses universitaires de Bordeaux 2005), *Sociologie de la délinquance et de la justice pénale* (Erès 2002), *La médiation. Essai de politique pénale* (Erès 1997) and *Justice et travail social. Le rhizome pénal* (Erès 1992).

Barbara Hudson is Professor of Law, University of Central Lancashire, UK. Her main teaching and research interests are in philosophies of justice; penal theory and policy; race, gender and criminal justice; and poverty and punishment. Publications include *Justice through Punishment* (1987), *Penal Policy and Social Justice* (1993) and *Understanding Justice* (1996). Her latest book is *Justice in the Risk Society: Challenging and Re-affirming Justice in Late Modernity* (2003).

Robert Mackay is Youth Justice Co-ordinator with Perth and Kinross Council and Honorary Research Fellow, Perth College, UK. He has undertaken ethical-legal studies on restorative justice. A former Chair of the (UK) Restorative Justice Consortium and Board Member of the European Forum for Restorative Justice, he is a member of the COST Action A21 on Restorative Justice Research in Europe.

Roger Matthews is Professor of Criminology at London South Bank University. He received a BA Social Science degree from Middlesex University, an MA Sociology from the University of Sussex and a PhD from the University of Essex. He has edited and authored a number of books including *Doing Time: An Introduction to the Sociology of Imprisonment* (Palgrave 1999) and *Armed Robbery* (Willan 2002).

Pat O'Malley is Canada Research Chair in Criminology and Criminal Justice at Carleton University, Ottawa. He has worked in the field of risk and justice for many years, and is the author and editor of a number of books on this topic, including *Risk, Uncertainty and Government* (Glasshouse/Cavendish 2004), *Crime and the Risk Society* (Ashgate 1998) and *Governing Risks* (Ashgate forthcoming).

John Pratt is Professor of Criminology at Victoria University of Wellington, New Zealand. He has taught and lectured at universities in the United Kingdom, continental Europe, North America and Australia. He has undertaken extensive research on the history and sociology of punishment, including *Governing the Dangerous* (1998), *Punishment and Civilization* (2002) and (as co-edtior) *The New Punitiveness* (2005).

Kent Roach is Professor of Law and Criminology at the University of Toronto where he specializes in criminal justice. He is the author of eight books including *Due Process and Victims' Rights: The New Law and Politics of Criminal Justice* (1999). He also frequently represents Aboriginal Legal Services of Toronto in court, including in the landmark Gladue case decided by the Supreme Court of Canada.

Luc Robert studied criminology and social and cultural anthropology at the Catholic University of Leuven, Belgium. He is a PhD candidate at the Department of Criminal Law and Criminology, Catholic University of Leuven.

Michael Tonry is Sonosky Professor of Law and Public Policy and director of the Institute on Crime and Public Policy, University of Minnesota, and a senior fellow of the Netherlands Institute for the Study of Crime and Law Enforcement, Leiden.

Introduction

Ivo Aertsen, Tom Daems and Luc Robert

These days editing a collection of essays on Restorative Justice (hereafter: RJ) has become a tricky business. In a recent review essay with the provocative title 'Pile it on', discussing the flaws and merits of four books dealing with RJ or related topics, Kathleen Daly (2004: 500) writes: 'No other justice practice has commanded so much scholarly attention in such a short period of time.' And she continues: 'An important question for the sociology of knowledge is to ask not only what conditions have facilitated its popularity, but also why so many feel compelled to say something about it.' At the time of writing Daly mentioned that between 1994 and 2003 over 60 edited collections or book-length treatments on RJ, written in English, had been published. It should not come as a surprise that since 2003 this publication stream has far from dried up. Moreover, numerous publications in Dutch, French, German, Spanish and many other languages that are largely not accessible to the English-speaking community have seen the light of day.

Daly's implicit critique of this (one might say) 'RJ industry' puts a heavy burden on every future attempt to bring together a collection of essays on the topic. In the end, the burgeoning literature on RJ-related topics makes it far from easy to differentiate one's own collection of essays from others. Yet, if one does not manage to do this, future editors or writers open themselves to the legitimate critique of merely recycling themes and ideas that have been covered in the past, of not moving forward or, even worse, of promoting a personal agenda: at times of growing pressures to expand and embellish one's publication record in order to secure professional positions and adequate funding for research projects, (co-)editorship of a book on a hotly debated topic looks nice on any academic curriculum vitae.

We are well aware of this and we therefore realize that it is our task in this introductory chapter to spell out the distinctiveness of the book. In what follows we will clarify the thread that runs through the chapters and clarify why we think that the questions raised in this book and the (provisional) answers given by the different authors can shed yet another light on such a widely debated topic as RJ. The first section introduces the theme of the book: institutionalizing RJ. The second section provides an overview of the content of the different chapters.

Theme of the book: institutionalizing RJ

The chapters in this book deal with institutionalizing RJ: its prospects, its state of affairs, the trade-offs, the normative and analytical issues it raises, etc. In short, the book focuses on how RJ finds its way into contemporary societies and their respective criminal justice systems. This implies that readers will neither find elaborate discussions on restorative theory nor extensive presentations of results of evaluation research. Classical themes in restorative literature such as debates between maximalists and minimalists, quarrels between restorativists and retributivists, discussions of the effectiveness of restorative inter-ventions, reportage of satisfaction rates and theoretical elaborations of the restorative model are not covered in this book. This does not mean that readers will not occasionally run into fragmentary discussions of these topics. Yet it does mean that such discussions are present only in so far as the authors think it is relevant for the topic of the book: institutionalizing RJ.

Institutionalizing RJ refers to an ongoing activity in which academics often play a central role. These roles can be manifold such as *evaluator* of existing restorative practices, *participant* in expert groups and (inter-)national committees, *initiator* of new restorative projects, *disseminator* of knowledge, good practices and techniques, *organizer* of conferences and workshops, *writer* of research reports and academic manuscripts and, one might add, *editor* of a collection of essays. Yet the title of the book should not mislead the reader: this is not a practical manual for those who want to further the agenda of institutionalization.

The book does not offer ready-made recipes for restorative reform even though the careful reader will probably find hints of what 'good (or bad) practice' might look like, based on the experiences, developments and normative and theoretical issues that are discussed throughout the book.

However, the fact that this book does not directly address practical issues should not lead the reader to conclude that it deals with sterile, detached or ivory tower debates. One of our concerns as editors was to build bridges between two strands in academic debate: those who are directly or indirectly involved in processes of institutionalizing RJ on the one hand, and those who reflect on developments in the field of punishment and crime control on the other hand. To put it simply: we attempted to build bridges between what Richard Sparks once referred to as 'players' and 'floaters' (Sparks 1997). Players identify problem areas in the existing ways of dealing with crime and try to design, implement and evaluate appropriate remedies. Many RJ-minded academics fall within this category. Floaters, on the other hand, try to interpret and explain the developments they observe. In doing so, they aspire to 'float' *over* rather than to 'play' *in* the fields they study. We realize that this distinction is rather ideal-typical: players also float over the social reality they want to change, and floaters also often cannot resist the temptation to play or, at least, to point the players towards some interesting 'playgrounds'. Yet we think it is a useful distinction: too often players are unaware of what floaters are doing and vice versa. With respect to the theme of this book, we feel that the topic of institutionalizing RJ is often neglected or poorly addressed in 'floating' reflections on crime and punishment in contemporary society; similarly we often have the impression that players in the RJ movement could benefit from floating observations (see Daems 2004).

The chapters

The first three chapters of the book canvas the broad societal context in which practices of institutionalizing RJ are supposed to take place. In the first chapter Michael Tonry illustrates extensively the lack of a linear relationship between crime and punishment. Crime trends in different western societies are broadly similar, yet evolutions of prison populations tend to go in opposite directions. This observation incites Tonry to highlight the role of choice in designing and implementing penal policies: *different* reactions to *similar* crime problems are imaginable and feasible. This comparative analysis also prompts him to pose an utterly interesting question: is it possible to find determinants of penal policies which can explain the diverging penal response and, if so, is it feasible to make generalizations concerning when and why RJ initiatives are likely to occur and to be successfully implemented and institutionalized? A survey of comparative literature on penal policy and community penalties leads him to identify conditions that appear to *conduce* or *constrain* the initiation and elaboration of RJ initiatives.

In the second chapter Hans Boutellier explores the 'vital context' of RJ. Boutellier takes David Garland's *The Culture of Control* as a point of departure to understand RJ as a contemporary response to the predicament of high crime rates, widespread feelings of unsafety and the apparent failure of the criminal justice system to react swiftly and adequately. The problem of crime has come to be transformed into a safety issue that occupies a privileged position on the public agenda. The 'cry for safety', as Boutellier puts it, goes hand in hand with a lifestyle that promotes personal freedom and crossing boundaries. People are liberating themselves from the shackles of tradition and are becoming more and more responsible for their own life project. The combination of this 'vital' drive with pressing calls for more safety results in 'the safety utopia': an almost unbearable tension between a desire for maximum freedom and a longing for maximum protection. In his chapter Boutellier reflects on the place of RJ initiatives in this vital context and highlights the *moral* appeal of restorative interventions for a world that seems to be without boundaries and that has lost traditional moral anchor points.

In Chapter 3 John Pratt takes issue with *normative* understandings of RJ, i.e. those interpretations that promote RJ as a new, benevolent and superior way of reacting to crime that stands firmly in opposition to other old, malevolent and inferior ways of responding to crime. His reading of restorative theory and practice as a *social* phenomenon turns out to be a highly informative and provocative exercise that exposes a set of linkages between RJ and other past and contemporary penal developments. On the one hand, Pratt identifies a continuity between RJ and forms of criminology that he terms 'evangelical'. A crusading and evangelical fervour came to characterize earlier criminal justice reform movements such as the child savers movement in the late nineteenth century in the USA, the borstal movement in the interwar period in Britain and the alternative to custody movement in the 1980s in England and the USA. All these reform movements fell prey to the classical *adagium* of 'good intentions' turning into 'bad practices'. RJ, Pratt argues, seems to be the latest example of this evangelical criminology. On the other hand, he highlights how RJ shares the same penal DNA as other expressive, emotive and highly punitive developments. A new set of social conditions puts the old boundaries for punishment into question and pushes penal responses into widely diverging trajectories. Pratt's search for similarities and linkages conveys a crucial message for those participating in (and reflecting upon) current trends in RJ.

The next five chapters zoom in on recent processes of institutionalizing RJ in a number of different countries: Belgium, the Netherlands, England and Wales, France and Canada. In his chapter on Belgium, Ivo Aertsen highlights the variation in the Belgian RJ landscape when he points to the presence of different types of practices such as several forms of victim–offender mediation, conferencing and restorative programmes in prisons. Characteristic for the Belgian situation, so he argues, is the evolution towards a general availability of RJ programmes, i.e. both for juveniles and adults, and at all stages of the criminal justice process. Aertsen argues that institutionalization can be seen from two perspectives: 'social potential' on the one hand, and 'domination by existing structures' on the other. In his chapter he confronts the implementation of RJ with ambivalent societal developments ('participatory' versus 'regulatory'). His theoretical response emphasizes the procedural justice aspects of restorative interventions and encompasses a plea for a particular mode of local organization of RJ initiatives. Aertsen underpins the latter by means of older and newer approaches within legal pluralism which result in the concept of 'interactive settings'. This concept, which structures 'the interference of informal conflict regulation with state law', leads him to argue for an intermediate position of RJ at the institutional level.

In the following chapter John Blad explores the institutionalization of RJ in the Netherlands. Blad's account is heavily inspired by the theory of institutionalization as it is formulated by sociologists Berger and Luckmann. The chapter deals with two crucial questions: To what extent is RJ becoming institutionalized in the Netherlands and to what extent does this result in a transformation of the criminal justice system? Blad's analysis leaves the reader with a rather grim picture of RJ in the Netherlands. RJ seems to be most rapidly growing in 'informal social contexts', i.e. outside the sphere of the criminal justice system. Blad refers to restorative initiatives in neighbourhoods, schools and the workplace. In addition, he points to developments in civil and administrative law and highlights some experiments with family group conferencing in the area of youth protection law. His survey of restorative developments inside the criminal justice system is followed by a discussion of the question whether these developments amount to an institutionalization in terms of the theory of Berger and Luckmann. Blad concludes with some cultural observations on how to transform the criminal justice system in a more restorative direction.

In his chapter on England and Wales Adam Crawford situates recent initiatives of institutionalizing RJ in the field of youth justice. These are placed against the background of New Labour politics from the late 1990s onwards. Crawford focuses on the newly introduced referral orders – now the primary sentence for first-time young offenders – and youth offender panels. The referral order, Crawford argues, represents 'both a particular and a rather peculiar hybrid attempt to integrate restorative justice ideas and values into youth justice practice', and this in 'a clearly coercive context'. In an attempt to understand better the effects of local contingencies, policy ambiguities, cultural practices and institutional resistances, Crawford goes on to discuss some other questions related to the institutionalization of RJ. In doing so, he analyzes in a very concrete way how referral orders and panels are functioning in England and Wales. This in-depth look at developments 'on the ground' reveals ambivalent dynamics behind RJ policies and implementation. Several types of tensions are identified such as: a strong managerial emphasis versus restorative principles of flexibility and participation; the devolution of authority towards local institutions versus central dictates of standards and criteria; and lay involvement versus tendencies towards professionalisation.

Central to Jacques Faget's chapter is the distinction and interaction between what he calls an autonomous and a dependent institutionalization of penal mediation. The first refers to the development of 'disorderly practices' into 'stable modes of action', while the second stands for the organization of mediation programmes by existing institutions. A 'cultural conflict' stands in the way of a fully achieved autonomous institutionalization. Due to an increasing juridification of social conflicts, the criminal justice system faces an enormous 'flood of complaints', which necessitates a search for new methods to manage conflicts. It has given rise to a 'dependent institutionalisation' of penal mediation: the criminal justice system has embraced it as a form of diversion for adults. Following the institutional roots of penal mediation, Faget goes on to explore the distinctions between the two models of practice he identifies, the judicial and the restorative. The main challenge lies in the interaction between both forms of logic.

In the following chapter Kent Roach argues that since the second half of the 1990s Canada has witnessed more of a top-down political and legal institutionalization of RJ than a bottom-up actualization. At the national level, legislative initiatives have been taken in order to integrate RJ outcomes as part of sentencing. The restorative (as opposed to the punitive) purposes of sentencing have been confirmed and documented by Canadian jurisprudence. In practice, however, restorative sanctioning can be criticized because of its limited application and applicability. According to Roach, the problems of integrating restorative purposes at the level of sentencing are originating more from structural impediments than from possible shortcomings of restorative theory. Roach goes on to discuss the relationship between institutionalizing RJ and Aboriginal justice and voices some deep concerns about potential unintended negative consequences towards Aboriginal communities. Furthermore, Roach critically explores the extension of restorative approaches in sentencing to other disadvantaged groups and discusses the place of RJ with respect to extra-judicial measures in the new Youth Justice Act.

In the next chapter Robert Mackay offers a particular insider's approach to the theme of institutionalization. As a former member of a policy group in the UK, he sketches the process of developing a set of principles for RJ practices and policies. This exercise, which involved the meticulous process of reworking, rephrasing and refining principles, is presented in his chapter. Mackay highlights the need for a recognized code of ethics and principles and gives a detailed account of the group dialogue on eight critical issues. The themes that are covered in his chapter include the connection between RJ practices and the legal system, the relevance of rights, the purport of the principle of voluntariness, the meaning of the principle of proportionality and the effect on the outcome of a criminal process.

The last three chapters of the book offer a more general analysis of institutionalizing RJ. They seek to shed a different light on RJ, its theoretical basis, the way it can be aligned with risk and its vulnerability to both 'the political' and 'the ethical' in contemporary penality. In his chapter, Pat O'Malley explores the relationship between risk and RJ. He starts off by showing that risk is a very abstract technology; its use always requires a specification of the particular configuration in which it is mobilized. In most criminological analyses, the use of risk is presented as 'a profoundly negative technology'. It is suggested that in criminal justice, risk should not be narrowed down to its application in a bifurcatory actuarial justice, i.e. the incapacitation of 'high-risk offenders' and strategies of inclusion for the 'low risks'. There are other, alternative ways in which risk can be mobilized. To illustrate more constructive ways of applying risk, O'Malley draws on so-called drug harm minimization programmes in Australia and highlights their points of articulation with RJ (e.g. both are harm focused, oriented to the future). The contribution outlines an interesting exploration on how risk and RJ may come together in a reintegrative, empowering hybrid.

Roger Matthews, in the next chapter, formulates a compelling critique of the 'new generation' of RJ practices that arose in the 1990s. Evaluative studies have led to a 'major indictment' of the claims and objectives of conferencing. Yet these failings, Matthews suggests, can be traced back to the weak theoretical base of these new RJ programmes: the reintegrative shaming thesis. He goes on to examine three important aspects of the theory, namely shame, reintegration and recidivism. The centrality of shame in emotional dynamics is proven to be highly doubtful; other concepts such as trust, guilt and remorse remain undertheorized. Matthews then shows that the reintegrative shaming thesis rests on a number of false dichotomies (e.g. reintegrative versus stigmatizing shaming, retributive versus restorative justice). Moreover, the predicted effects on recidivism remain to be seen. This brings Matthews to the controversial conclusion that the marriage between reintegrative shaming and RJ practice is on the rocks.

In her chapter on the institutionalization of RJ, Barbara Hudson underscores the importance of what, in line with Derrida, is called an ideal-political dualism. In her analysis of the place of RJ in the penal landscape of today, she singles out three noteworthy themes. First of all, Hudson problematizes the move from risk management to risk control. Of particular importance is a conflation of ideas related to dangerousness and persistence. She then goes on to question the persistence of the white, male perspective in law and criminal justice. Minorities continue to suffer from an overrepresentation in the criminal justice system, while the law still falls short in protecting them from crimes. Furthermore, Hudson explores the blurred conception of community. On the one hand, criminal justice literature puts forward the view that RJ is one of the strategies to achieve community safety and community justice. On the other hand, social theory teaches us that communities are in decay. It is by no means clear today what is intended by 'the' community. Hudson concludes her paper by calling for a balancing of the ethical and the political in law and criminal justice.

In the final chapter of the book, we as editors point to a number of relevant topics and issues, which the reader might find interesting to explore further.

Chapter I

The prospects for institutionalization of restorative justice initiatives in western countries

Michael Tonry

Countries vary in their penal policies. This is obvious. One illustration is the contrast between the American imprisonment rate in excess of 700 per 100,000 population and the 60–70 per 100,000 that characterizes the four large Scandinavian countries. The death penalty, popular and used in the US and Japan but not authorized in other western democracies, is a second. The presence of 'three-strikes-and-you're-out laws' in England and the US, and their absence elsewhere is a third. The spread and scope of restorative justice initiatives in Australia, Belgium and New Zealand compared with their near absence in Scandinavia[1] is a fourth.

These differences are not random. The aim of this chapter is to examine the comparative and cross-national literature on the determinants of penal policies and practices in hopes of finding generalizations concerning when and why restorative justice initiatives are likely to occur and to be successfully implemented and institutionalized.

There is no comparative literature on national differences in receptivity to restorative justice, so I look for hypotheses in inferences that can be drawn from the nascent comparative literature on penal policy generally and from the literature on the dispersion of various community penalties.

No easy generalizations can be offered but *conducing* and *constraining* conditions can be identified. These terms are meant to parallel the concepts of 'risk' and 'protective' factors that are used in developmental psychology and criminology to characterize factors that increase or decrease an individual's likelihood of experiencing an undesirable outcome (e.g. criminality, drug abuse, school failure, teenage pregnancy).

It would be odd to refer to risk or protective factors for restorative justice, both because it is not necessarily an undesirable outcome of political processes in the same way that drug dependence or unplanned teenage pregnancy is an undesirable outcome of developmental processes, and because the terms 'risk' and 'protective' just do not seem right.

To speak, however, of political, cultural and structural conditions that *conduce* to initiation of criminal justice policies or programmes (restorative justice, drug courts, three-strikes laws) or *constrain* their initiation or elaboration does seem semantically right.

Among conditions that appear to conduce to initiation and elaboration of restorative justice initiatives are: aboriginal populations possessed of consensual dispute resolution traditions; relatively non-politicized criminal justice policy-making processes; non-partisan professional criminal justice practitioners; constitutional systems characterized by strong separation of powers traditions; and relatively parsimonious traditions of prison use. Constraining conditions include: politicized criminal justice policy-making climates; politically selected practitioners; high prison-use traditions; and highly moralized penal cultures.

Here is how this chapter is organized. The first section offers the prevailing theories in use to explain why countries adopt especially severe penal policies. One is simple – rising crime rates produce rising imprisonment rates (which I use as an indicator of severe penal policies). The other is complex – a congeries of social, economic, cultural and psychological developments of the past 30 years have produced harsh expressive policies meant primarily to reassure law-abiding citizens and to stigmatize troublesome ones and only incidentally to prevent crime.

The second section, telling the crime and punishment stories of five countries over 30 years, shows that both theories are wrong. The first is wrong because, while all western countries had rising crime rates between 1970 and 1990, imprisonment rates rose sharply only in a few. Crime does not cause punishment.

The complex story is wrong because the developments it depicts affect all western countries but imprisonment rates rose sharply in only a few.

The third section then looks at penal policy developments in three countries – the US, England and Canada – to identify particular characteristics of those countries that appear to have influenced penal policy developments.

The fourth section shifts the focus from prison-use trends to patterns of adoption of less-than-imprisonment punishments variously characterized as alternatives to imprisonment, intermediate punishments or community penalties. The permeability of particular countries to community penalties, substitutes for imprisonment, may be germane to their permeability to restorative justice as a substitute for traditional adversarial criminal justice processes.

The fifth section, finally, draws on the conducing and constraining conditions both to explain why some countries more than others have adopted restorative justice initiatives and to hypothesize where restorative justice seeds are likely to find fertile soils.

Explanations of penal policy trends

Writing on penal policy trends over the past 30 years has disproportionately focused on the United States, asking and attempting to answer the question of why penal policies and practices became much more severe (Garland 2001; Tonry 2004a). A number of explanations for recent penal policy trends have been offered but none is satisfactory.

The simplest explanation is that crime rates in the United States, and also in all other western countries, increased steadily from the late 1960s or early 1970s through the early to mid 1990s, and, directly or indirectly, penal policies became tougher, penal practices became harsher and the use of imprisonment increased.

There is a surface logic to this simple explanation. If there are more crimes, there will be more arrests, more prosecutions, more sentences and more imprisonment, and it might seem reasonable to expect a direct relationship between the size and trends of the crime problem and the size and trends of the prison population. One-to-one relationships are not likely, because criminal justice institutions have limited personnel and resources and in the face of large expansions in their caseloads inevitably must find ways to dispose of cases more quickly, more efficiently and more informally. At each stage of the process it is reasonable to expect that new ways will be found to divert cases or resolve them quickly. Citizens may report fewer cases to the police if they are less likely to be the subjects of police actions. Police are less likely to refer cases to prosecutors and prosecutors to courts if the result is to increase dismissal rates and make already overcrowded caseloads and dockets even more crowded. Prosecutors are more likely to dismiss cases, negotiate diversionary dispositions or accept guilty pleas to offences bearing less harsh sentences. Judges may be less likely

3

to send people to prison or send them to prison for shorter times. Parole authorities may be more likely to let people out earlier.

While those things might moderate the increase in the rate of imprisonment, it remains not unreasonable to expect that rate to increase substantially, even if less steeply than the crime rate.

Or rising crime rates may cause rising imprisonment rates indirectly. If rising crime rates cause people to become more apprehensive and to feel less safe, they may, as voters and citizens, demand that the state address crime more effectively. Or citizens may become more angry and resentful toward offenders, and call for and support harsher policies and harsher practices, both of which should result in harsher penalties.

The problem with the simple explanation, as the next section demonstrates in some detail, is that crime rates cannot be said directly or indirectly to cause increases in imprisonment rates for the simple reason that in most countries they did not. Although in a few countries, notably the United States (Reitz 2001) and the Netherlands (Tak 2001), imprisonment rates increased continuously from the early 1970s through the time when crime rates stabilized and began to fall in the early 1990s, and continued to increase thereafter, that is not the typical pattern. The extreme counter-examples are Finland (Lappi-Seppälä 2001) and Japan (Hamai 2001), in both of which imprisonment rates fell continuously throughout the 1970s and 1980s. The more common pattern, however, exhibited by the Scandinavian countries, Canada, Germany and England during the 1970s and 1980s, is for imprisonment rates to have remained roughly stable in the face of rapidly increasing crime rates (Tonry and Frase 2001).

If rising crime rates cause rising imprisonment rates, it should have happened everywhere. It didn't.

The intellectually sophisticated, complex and nuanced explanations of increased punitiveness take account of a large number of economic, social and other structural changes that create social and political environments in which harsh policies are more likely to be adopted. There have been a number of major writings in this tradition (Bottoms 1995; Caplow and Simon 1999; Garland 2001; Wacquant 2001). The best known and most influential is David Garland's *The Culture of Control* (2001).

Garland argues that four main developments combined to produce a harsher penal climate. First, faced by seemingly inexorably rising crime rates during the 1970s and 1980s, governments recognized and accepted that they lacked tools substantially to affect crime rates and elected, instead, to adopt expressive policies that purported to be doing something about crime but, more importantly, denounced crime and criminals, and demonstrated to citizens that government shared their resentment and hostility toward offenders.

Second, as a result of the movement of women in very large numbers into the paid workforce (meaning that many more residences were unoccupied during the day), the increased availability of valuable but portable consumer goods and rising crime rates generally, victimization was democratized. By this Garland did not mean that the burden of criminal victimization fell more equally throughout society but that crime became a 'salient social fact' in the lives of middle-class and professional elites. Previously little burdened by crime, they could afford to adopt condescending attitudes towards other citizens who could be characterized as vindictive or mean-spirited in their unwillingness to recognize the social complexities that underlay criminal activity. In the 1950s and 1960s, the middle-class elite and particularly the professional classes could adopt relatively humane attitudes and policies towards crime and criminals in part because they themselves lacked the visceral reactions to crime that victimization can produce. As the experience of victimization became more common, resentment and hostility toward offenders became more widely dispersed.

Third, what Garland calls 'conditions of late modernity' combined to produce a heightened sense of anxiety and insecurity, an elaborated sense of the riskiness of life, in the populations of democratic western states. People also became more aware of crime and the disorder associated with it, and were concerned to minimize their own exposure. In some ways, crime came to serve as a metonym for disorder more generally, a specific set of behaviours, attributable to a particular set of actors, which could be taken to symbolize all that was wrong with a rapidly changing world.

Fourth, Garland suggested that offenders came to serve as scapegoats or lightning rods for public resentments, on whom disorder could be blamed. Because offenders typically come from economically and socially disadvantaged groups, particularly visible minority groups, someone other than the majority population could be blamed. This he refers to as 'the criminology of the other'.

Taken together, these developments led to the adoption of policies not necessarily meant to be effective but meant to express hostility towards offenders which could be enforced against social groupings other than the majority middle-class.

Garland's is a plausible description of social and cultural developments of the last 30 years. The forces of globalization have been unleashed, economic restructuring has reduced the economic stability and security of large fractions of the populations of western countries, the civil rights, gay rights and women's rights movements have occurred and redistributed opportunities, populations have become more heterogeneous, and in many ways the world has become a less comfortable and predictable place. Social resentments against immigrants and members of minority groups exist in every western country. Most have fringe xenophobic right-wing political parties that attract 5–15 per cent of the vote.

As description, it is difficult to argue with Garland's analysis. As explanation, however, it falls short, for the same reason that the simple explanation – rising crime causes rising imprisonment – falls short.

In an article in the *British Journal of Criminology* in 1996, Garland offered observations about penal policy trends in England, the US, 'and elsewhere.' Hans-Jörg Albrecht (2001), some years later, challenged Garland's use of the phrase 'and elsewhere,' pointing out that penal policy trends in England and America had not been replicated elsewhere. Moreover, and this is my point not Albrecht's, penal policy trends in the United States were not mirrored even in England, in which the imprisonment rate, though it fluctuated a bit, was broadly stable for 20 years from 1970 through 1994, and has risen rapidly amid the adoption of symbolic and expressive policies not unlike some of those in the US (e.g. mandatory minimums, three-strikes laws, boot camps, sexual offender registration laws). Garland's elegant description captures some important things about secular changes in western countries in the period 1970–2000. However, they were associated with steadily rising imprisonment rates over the whole period only in the United States and the Netherlands, and in England and Wales only since 1994, in the face of widely divergent patterns elsewhere.

Why most explanations for penal policy trends are wrong

Participants in cocktail party conversations and readers of mystery novels might assume that increases in crime rates necessarily produce increases in imprisonment rates. They would be wrong, as comparison of punishment patterns in a number of western countries demonstrates. From 1970 to the present, crime patterns and trends have been broadly similar in western countries. The details have differed. For example, homicide rates typically are much higher in the US than in Western Europe, but within Western Europe the homicide rates in Finland are typically considerably higher than those elsewhere, and gun use in crime is much more pervasive in the US. Nonetheless, when changes in rates per 100,000 of violent crime and homicide are calculated for western countries, remarkably similar broad patterns hold everywhere for the period 1970 to the early 1990s (the peaks and subsequent declines vary by a year or two between countries). Homicide rates typically doubled or tripled and serious violent crime rates increased by a factor of three to five times.

As Figures 1.1 to 1.4 demonstrate, however, while crime rate trends may be very similar among western countries, imprisonment rates are very different.

Figure 1.1 shows imprisonment, violent crime and murder rates per 100,000 US population from 1960 to 1993. The murder rate has been multiplied by ten to make eyeball comparisons easier. The data end in the early 1990s because US crime rates began a steep fall in 1990–92 which continues to this date. My interest in Figure 1.1 is to compare imprisonment rate trends with crime rate trends to test the more-crime-causes-more-imprisonment hypothesis already described.

Violent crime in Figure 1.1 consists of homicide, rape, robbery and aggravated assault. The rate of violent crime, as recorded by the police, increased by nearly five times between 1960 and 1993. The homicide rate increased from about 4 per 100,000 to about 11 per 100,000, nearly three times. The imprisonment rate (here including only prisoners sentenced to state and federal institutions), though broadly stable from 1960 to 1973, increased thereafter by more than 300 per cent.

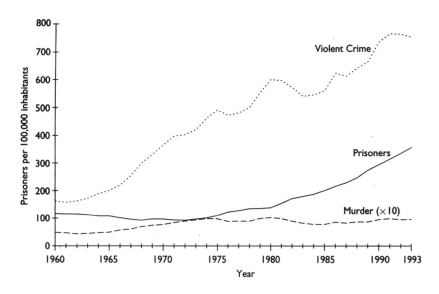

Figure 1.1 Imprisonment, violent crime and murder rates in the United States, 1960–93 (per 100,000 population).

Figure 1.1 thus tells a story in which imprisonment patterns appear to be driven by crime patterns.

Figure 1.2 however, tells a very different story. This figure also shows imprisonment rates, homicide rates and violent crime rates for a western country, Finland. As in the United States, the homicide rate (also multiplied by ten so that trends can be compared) increased by at least a factor of three, and the violent crime rate by more than three times. The violent crime rate here too is composed of homicide, rape, robbery and aggravated assault. Countries vary somewhat in precisely how they define these crimes. Finland, for example, includes attempted homicides among homicides, while the US counts only completed homicides. My interest, however, is to compare what individual countries regard as the most serious violent crimes so those counting differences are not important for my purposes. In terms of the crimes that Finland regards as its most serious violent crimes, the key point is that the rate relative to population more than tripled. The Finnish imprisonment rate, however, fell steadily from 1965, when it was around 160 per 100,000, to 1994, when it was around 60 per 100,000.

Figure 1.3, paralleling Figures 1.1 and 1.2 on the United States and Finland, shows violent crime, homicide and imprisonment rates in Germany per 100,000 population from 1961 to 1992. The homicide

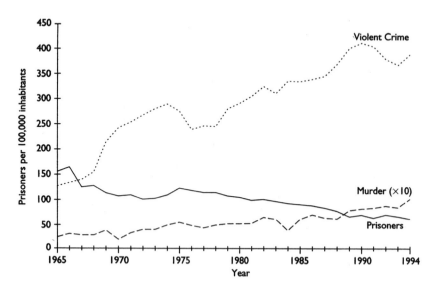

Figure 1.2 Imprisonment, violent crime and murder rates in Finland, 1965–94 (per 100,000 population).

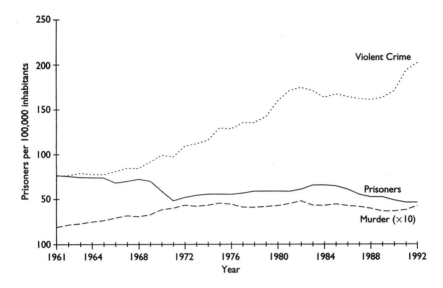

Figure 1.3 Imprisonment, violent crime and murder rates in Germany, 1961–92 (per 100,000 population).

and violent crime rate trends parallel those in the United States and Finland, but the imprisonment rate, after falling in the late 1960s and early 1970s when the use of short prison sentences became disapproved and the use of day fines was implemented, have remained more or less flat since then.

Figure 1.4 provides a fourth example, this time without crime rates. It shows incarceration rates for France from 1968 to 2002. What is striking about Figure 1.4 compared with the steady American increase in imprisonment rates, the Finnish decrease and German stability is that France's imprisonment rates have zigzagged.

How can the stark differences among the United States, Germany, Finland and France be explained?

The answer is easy. Public officials in those countries chose the penal policies that Figures 1.1 to 1.4 demonstrate. Some people might say that politicians and public officials, acting in their own perceived political interests or reflecting their own personal ideologies, made policy decisions that importantly shaped penal practices. Others might say that the character of underlying public opinion in these matters, and changes in the character of public opinion, produced changes in attitudes and political concerns that, in turn, were reflected by policy-makers and practitioners in their decisions.

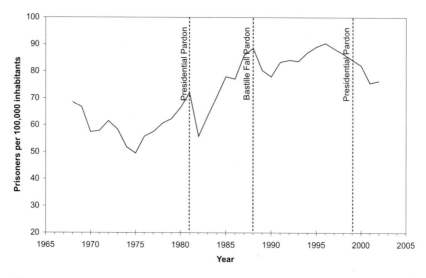

Figure 1.4 Incarceration rates in France, 1968–2002 (per 100,000 population).
Source: Kensey and Tournier (2001).

Whichever account is true (no doubt both to some degree, with the comparative balance varying between countries and over time), Figures 1.1 to 1.4 make it clear that policy drives imprisonment rates. American politicians for thirty years competed with one another to show who was tougher on crime and in a wide variety of ways – requiring mandatory prison sentences, increasing the lengths of prison sentences, paying for a many-fold increase in the size of the prison establishment, campaigning for office on 'toughness' platforms – they favoured increased severity of punishment, increased use of imprisonment and increasing imprisonment rates. The United States got what its policy-makers wanted.

By contrast, in Finland, a broad agreement was reached among policy-makers, practitioners and academics in the late 1960s that the Finnish imprisonment rate was too high and should be reduced (Lappi-Seppälä 2001). Through the beginning of the twenty-first century, over nearly four decades, Finnish policy-makers stuck to that policy goal. Enacting a wide range of new policies and practices (reducing the lengths of prison sentences, creating new alternative prison sentences, creating many diversion programmes), Finnish governments remained true to course.

The explanation typically given for the Finnish policy consensus was a shared belief in the late 1960s that the Finnish imprisonment rate, then nearly three times that of Norway, Denmark and Sweden, could not be justified morally. Finnish crime rates were then, as now, comparable to those of the other Scandinavian countries and a widely held view took hold that Finnish policies were more punitive and repressive than those of the other Scandinavian countries for no good reason and could no longer be justified in a liberal society. The somewhat different account is sometimes given that Finland, independent only since 1917, before that a Grand Duchy of Russia from 1809, wanted to be western, not eastern. The argument is that Finnish imprisonment rates, though much higher than those in the West, were only somewhat lower than those in Russia and, to some extent, could be seen as an indicator of Finland's presence in the Russian sphere of influence. By consciously emulating Scandinavian policies and imprisonment rates, thereby rejecting Russian policies and imprisonment patterns, Finland was declaring itself part of the West.

The explanation for the German trend is well known. German policy-makers in the late 1960s decided that short (under six-month) prison sentences can seldom be justified. Six months is too short for rehabilitative programmes to take hold and too short to achieve significant incapacitative effects. Concerning deterrent effects, certainty is much more important than severity, so other penalties could substitute. Six months is, however, long enough to break up a marriage and lose a person's job and possibly his home. In place of short prison sentences, day-fines and prosecutorial sanctions systems were established. In one year the number of under-six-months sentences fell from 130,000 to under 25,000 and has remained at that level ever since (Weigend 2001).

That leaves France. What is the explanation for the zigzags in Figure 1.4? They occur largely because of a French tradition of including prisoners among the beneficiaries of national celebrations (Kensey and Tournier 2001). France has adopted policy changes that could be expected to reduce the prison population, including changes in parole release policies and creation of new alternatives to imprisonment. The principal cause, however, of the occasional sharp falls in the sentenced prison population is that there are frequently amnesties, broad-based pardons and mass commutations at the time of such national French celebrations as the inauguration of a new president or the 200th anniversary of the fall of the Bastille.

If we step back for a bit and think about the four imprisonment patterns, and what they might suggest about national culture and its attitudes towards criminals, very different inferences might be drawn. French political culture clearly can accept the serendipitous good fortune of French prisoners who, unexpectedly, are released early.

In the United States and England, the political culture could not and would not countenance wholesale release of prisoners to celebrate a national holiday or a president's inauguration. Few elected politicians are likely to believe that they could survive politically were they to announce a 20 per cent reduction in the prison population or that all prisoners within six months of completion of their sentences would be released immediately or something equivalent. Likewise, in America and England, politicians could probably not successfully carry out a long-term publicized policy of reduced use of imprisonment. Public anger and resentment towards prisoners and a taste for punishment that exists in both countries make public objection and resistance likely.

What does explain penal policy trends?

The fundamental shortcoming of Garland's explanations for changes in penal policy is that while every country experienced the 'conditions of late modernity' only a few politicized their crime policies and substantially increased their prison populations. What did happen? The answers vary between countries.

United States

What explains the US changes? Four things. First, work by American historians shows that there are distinct cycles in public tolerance and intolerance of deviant behaviours in the US and that policy formulation and practical implementation vary substantially according to those cycles (Musto 1987). Concerning drug use, for example, there have been three periods of peak intolerance of drug use in the US – in the 1850s, from 1890 to 1930, and from 1970 to 2000. During periods after drug use has peaked *and begun to fall*, as happened in 1979 to 1981, policy-makers become steadily harsher and practice becomes steadily more punitive. In the US, the harshest anti-drug policies in recent times were adopted in 1986 and 1988, nearly a decade after drug use began to fall. The drug tsar was appointed in 1988. The enormous increase in imprisonment of drug offenders and steadily lengthening sentences date from the mid-1980s (Tonry 1995).

Similar cycles apply to crime and, as a result, it could have been predicted, and it happened, that the harshest anti-crime policies in the United States were adopted in the mid-1990s, well after crime rates peaked and began to fall in 1990–91 (Tonry 2004a). Moralism, intolerance and impatience with crime, the products of a period of steadily increasing rates in the 1970s and 1980s, were not counterbalanced in the mid-1990s by more traditional liberal, social-welfarist beliefs that had been influential in earlier times. As time has passed, those views have become more prevalent again, voices expressing them have become louder, and American crime policy has again become more multifaceted.

A second major explanation of American developments is that American constitutional arrangements not only do not insulate policy-makers and practitioners from shifts in raw public emotion but are designed to reflect it. Thus, unlike in Europe, where most judges and prosecutors are career civil servants, self-selecting to those roles in university and socialized into a set of professional, legal and ethical values throughout their careers, judges and prosecutors in the US are politically selected, often in partisan elections, and serve for relatively short terms. Most elections are local and candidates for prosecutors' posts and judgeships must compete with one another to demonstrate to the electorate that they reflect widely held views. If those views are angry, repressive and moralistic, they will be reflected in the beliefs, policies and actions of judges and prosecutors.

Other aspects of American constitutional arrangements and political culture tend to contrast with Europe, making policy more receptive to changes in public attitudes. There is much less confidence in the United States in elite or expert opinion, and much less acceptance of the view that on important matters experts should have a major role to play in setting policy. Instead, the United States has a constitutional system with extensive separation of powers, with legislators often elected for short terms (the federal House of Representatives for two years), the executive separately elected from the legislature and the judiciary either elected or appointed by elected officials. If politicians choose to campaign on what they see as passionate public beliefs, their opponents must typically respond in kind. If politicians campaign on toughness, their opponents are also likely to assert toughness. Once in office, it should not be surprising that repressive policies are adopted.

A third difference with Europe is that there is a strong stream of moralism in American popular culture that manifests itself in attitudes of punitiveness towards offenders. This can be seen in the findings of the International Crime Victim Survey when responses to questions concerning the punishment of hypothetical offenders are compared. Since the first ICVS in 1989, respondents in each country have been asked to indicate whether they would favour a prison sentence for a young burglar with two prior offences. Between 10 and 25 per cent of respondents in European countries (other than the United Kingdom) typically indicate that they would prefer imprisonment. Nearly 60 per cent of American respondents, in each of the successive waves of the ICVS, have indicated they prefer imprisonment (van Kesteren, Mayhew and Nieuwbeerta 2000).

A fourth speculative but creative argument has been offered by historian James Whitman (2003). Struck by what seemed to him surface differences in how German and French prisons treated inmates in comparison with the United States, Whitman looked to historical sources to try to find the origins of distinctive political cultures that might produce that difference. He was particularly struck that prisoners in French and German prisons, in a variety of ways, were treated as citizens behind bars rather than as outlaws or pariahs. For example, German and French prisoners wear their own street clothes, are allowed to vote while in prison and are generally housed in cells without observation windows (this because a right of privacy is recognized as a basic human right). German and French prison guards are career civil servants who undergo extensive, long-term training.

By contrast, in the United States, though it varies from state to state, prisoners traditionally wear stigmatising convict garb and are not allowed to vote in prison (or in many states after release). The idea that prisoners should be spared the prying eyes of their warders would generally be seen as ridiculous. Prison officers, again subject to wide variation between states and prisons, often are hired off the street, are relatively poorly educated and receive relatively little training.

How could these differences be explained? Whitman looked to the eighteenth century for an answer. He observed that persons convicted of crime were treated in very different ways in the United States, England, France and Germany. In that more inegalitarian era, privileged defendants and offenders were held in comfortable circumstances, accompanied by servants, entitled to visitors and were well-fed and well-housed, while ordinary prisoners were held in miserable conditions in overcrowded facilities promiscuously intermingling men and women, adults and children, and having to pay the local jailor for their food.

Executions provide the most dramatic form of upper- and lower-class differentiation in eighteenth-century criminal justice systems. Members of the elite typically had their heads cut off, by guillotine in France and by sword in Germany and England. Ordinary offenders were hanged or strangled. There is probably no need here to explain how the body reacts to beheading and hanging but it can fairly be said that hanging is a much more squalid and, to observers, revolting process.

All western countries have attempted in various ways to 'level' status differentiation in the treatment of offenders. According to Whitman, France and Germany levelled up and, in a non-trivial way, now treat all offenders as people deserving of concern and respect and, accordingly, as citizens behind bars, entitled to exercise the rights of citizenship other than those that are inherently denied by imprisonment. In the United States (and by implication in England) a levelling-down occurred, with all offenders being treated in the debasing, stigmatizing and unsympathetic ways that in earlier times characterized only the poor.

The United States is the quintessential levelling-down political culture. Although, of course, prison conditions vary between jurisdictions and between the custody and security levels of individual prisons, American prisoners typically are not treated as citizens behind bars.

Putting those things together, then, the United States has been at a stage in its cycles of intolerance towards crime and criminals that has made people especially susceptible to calls for repressive and punitive policies. American constitutional arrangements provide very little insulation from the influence of such calls and such policies have been adopted. American moralism, manifesting itself in punitiveness towards offenders, has created a receptivity to calls for increasing harshness of penalties.

England and Wales

England and Wales, since the early 1990s, has consciously emulated American crime control policies and the imprisonment population has nearly doubled in the past decade as a result (Tonry 2004b). If, as I argue above, Garland's general argument cannot explain enough, how are we to understand English developments?

For starters, what needs explaining is not the period 1970 to the present, but the period 1994 to the present. Before then, despite Garland's focus on the US and England in *The Culture of Control*, England was in the mainstream of Western Europe in its punishment policies, politics and practices, and there is nothing particular to explain. Since 1993, however, the Labour Party and now government have consciously emulated American crime control policies to, so far as one can tell, the satisfaction of the English electorate. Why would the English electorate have been susceptible to those appeals? There appear to be four distinctive factors (Tonry 2004b).

First, England's tabloid media are more rabid about crime issues than are mainstream newspapers anywhere else in Europe, and continually, on their front and editorial pages and in their headlines, adopt angry and punitive stances, blaming the government for insensitivity to the victims of crime and unacceptable tolerance of crime and social disorder.

Second, British crime prevention initiatives have been pervasive over the last twenty years, manifesting themselves in such things as more CCTV cameras per capita than any country in the world, more of its citizens in a DNA database used for criminal investigation purposes than anywhere else in the world, more speed cameras for traffic offenders than anywhere else in the world and a steady drumbeat of government proposals for repressive policies. One effect of this continuous concentration on crime prevention has been to raise public anxieties rather than to assuage them, making English citizens more fearful, not less, and accordingly more receptive to appeals by the tabloid newspapers and the government for harsh policies (Tonry 2004b: Chapter 3).

Third, as in the United States, there is a taste for punishment in England and Wales, a moralism that calls for much harsher penalties than the public expects in other European countries. Earlier I pointed out that, among ICVS respondents, Americans are much more punitive than Europeans except for the UK. That pattern recurred in each of the four ICVS waves. In 2000, for example, among 16 countries, US respondents were likeliest to favour a prison sentence (56 per cent) for a young recidivist burglar, compared with rates between 12 and 21 per cent among respondents from continental European countries. The three ICVS jurisdictions from the United Kingdom, however, closely resembled the United States in preferring a prison sentence: Northern Ireland (54 per cent), Scotland (52 per cent), and England (51 per cent). And, among European countries, English respondents would have imposed the longest sentences.

Fourth and finally, the current English government is highly authoritarian and operates in a constitutional framework that imposes few limits on authoritarian policy-making. England is a national constitutional system, with one legal and governmental jurisdiction, not a federal one like Germany or the US. More importantly, under the doctrine of Parliamentary Supremacy, the legislature is not constrained by a written constitution. Although Parliament has adopted legislation bringing the European Convention of Human Rights into force in England and Wales, it has done so in terms that allow courts to declare English laws incompatible with the ECHR but not to strike them down. Because the prime minister is also the leader of the majority party, and there is no effective counterweight in the legislature to executive policy preferences, accordingly, if the government decides to adopt repressive and punitive policies, there are few other centres of governmental power to oppose it. With all criminal justice agencies part of nationally administered centralized systems of police, prisons and probation, little stands in the way of the implementation of policies the government of the day prefers.

Canada

Canada is an interesting contrast to England and America because it shares a common legal system with that in the United States and England but much more recently broke away from the United Kingdom. It shares a language, educational systems and much else with the United States, and yet has radically different crime policies. Although Canadian violent crime and homicide trends have paralleled those of the United States since 1970, the Canadian imprisonment rate has been flat since 1980 and most recently has been declining. There appear to be four major explanations for the Canadian difference.

First, unlike in the United States or England, but as in Europe, there remains considerable confidence in both the appropriateness and the competence of professionals to determine policy in general, and of practitioners to make individualized decisions in individual cases.

Second, prosecutors and judges are not elected in Canada, as in the United States, but are selected in what are ideally non-partisan, selection processes, though no doubt politics creeps in around the edges. Thus, unlike America's elected practitioners, or England's bureaucratic practitioners subject to nationalized policy control, Canadian practitioners are relatively insulated from electoral politics.

Third, because of the linguistic fissure that has bedevilled Canadian politics for the past 50 years, francophonic cultural influence on criminal justice policy is powerful. Just as France's political culture happily lives with rapid rises and falls in the imprisonment population without political heads rolling, Quebec's criminal and juvenile justice policies are less punitive than those in most of anglophonic Canada. At a national level, insiders openly acknowledge the francophonic influence as a moderator of criminal justice policy.

Fourth, American oppositionalism is ever-present and very powerful. The wish, among elites, to maintain a distinctive Canadian, as opposed to American, culture and policy manifests itself in crime policy, an area in which the vengefulness and mean-spiritedness of American policy can comfortably be contrasted with the decency and liberality of the Canadian.

What the English, American and Canadian stories tell us, despite Garland's suggestion that common explanations may characterize all western countries, is that understanding of changes in penal policy and practices depends on understanding of distinct local characteristics.

Explaining the dispersion of community penalties

Before speculating about conditions that make jurisdictions more and less receptive to successful implementations of restorative justice programmes, it may be illustrative to look at ways in which various countries have and have not adopted particular community penalties. Inasmuch as community penalties are also sometimes conceptualized as 'alternatives to incarceration' or 'intermediate punishments' between prison and probation, and restorative justice programmes are meant often to displace or augment conventional criminal justice system interventions, experience with community penalties may be of some relevance.

Four short stories can be told concerning the dispersion of particular community penalties. They suggest that there may be some very stark limitations on the capacity of particular jurisdictions successfully to implement programmes that are meant to serve as replacements for traditional criminal justice system processing for non-trivial cases.

Day fines

Day fines – financial penalties scaled in their number to the seriousness of offences and in their daily amount to an offender's income and assets, variously calculated – potentially provide a meaningful system of proportionate punishments that can be scaled to the seriousness of crime and be used in place of confinement sentences (Morris and Tonry 1990). Significant experience with day fines began in Scandinavia in the 1920s and by the 1970s day fines were in particularly wide use in Sweden and Finland where they are indeed used as alternatives to imprisonment. Germany, in the early 1970s, having decided greatly to reduce the use of imprisonment sentences of six months or less, established a day-fine system which, over the ensuing 30 years, has become well-established as an appropriate sanction for both minor and moderately serious cases.

One might think that day fines would be attractive additions to the penal armamentaria of all western countries. Many European countries, including France, Portugal and Austria, have indeed adopted them to a greater or lesser extent. The English-speaking countries and Holland, however, have not. The Dutch have not tried. In both the United States and in England and Wales, extensive pilot programmes were undertaken. In England a day-fine system (called unit fines) took effect in 1992 and was repealed in 1993. In the American pilot projects, developers were unable to persuade practitioners to use day fines in place of imprisonment and, instead, they were used in place of probation sentences and as more efficient means to collect financial penalties. They had some success in increasing financial yields but no success as alternatives to incarceration (Tonry and Hamilton 1995).

The bottom line problem in England and the United States appears to have been that people did not regard fines as appropriate punishments for non-trivial cases. Their use, therefore, in place of imprisonment is simply not seen as adequately meeting appropriate punitive goals. I don't know why the Dutch, famed for their rationalistic public policies concerning crime, have not adopted day fines, but they have not. Particularly in those three countries, with their strong capitalistic and libertarian leanings, one might have expected financial penalties to be natural alternatives to imprisonment. That has not been the case.

Boot camps

Boot camps – short, intense, institutional placements, typically three to six months, typically for young offenders and characterized by arduous physical training, exercise and discipline patterned on military basic training programmes – were first adopted in the United States in the 1980s. Evaluation research quickly showed that they did not reduce the recidivism rates of offenders sent to them compared with comparable offenders sentenced in other ways, and they neither reduced prison crowding nor saved money. Nonetheless, within ten years, they had been adopted in most American states. The Australians, Canadians and English all followed suit, attempting to replicate the American experience. The Canadian and English programmes, though less rigorous and more focused on treatment interventions, were quickly abandoned. The Australian programme lasted a little longer (Freiberg 2001).

To the best of my knowledge, no continental European country adopted boot camps. How might we explain that pattern? The most likely explanation, confirmed by other data, is that citizens of Anglo-Saxon countries are more moralistic in their attitudes towards crime than citizens of other western countries, and are more punitive in their willingness to use harsh penalties. Since boot camps were targeted typically at young offenders, who in other countries are often the focus of constructive and rehabilitative interventions, they may simply have been too harsh for the sensibilities of continental Europe. On the American model even their implementation appears to have seemed too harsh to policy-makers in other English-speaking countries and in practice they have not survived.

In the United States, their numbers are declining, and their attraction is becoming less evident, but they continue in operation in many states.

Community service

This is another story, like that relating to day fines, that suggests that the United States in particular is not receptive to the use of non-imprisonment penalties for other than trivial offences. England at one time was, but that willingness has declined (Ashworth 2001). Community service in the Netherlands appears still to be going strong (Tak 2001).

The first organized community service programmes meant systematically to be used in place of short prison sentences were established on *ad hoc* bases in California in the 1960s. They were targeted particularly on welfare mothers who received fines for minor offences and, on non-payment, often were sentenced to imprisonment. That seemed excessive to California judges, who established a community service programme in which convicted offenders could do a specific number of hours of work in place of fines and on their failure to pay them, imprisonment. Thus community service was an indirect alternative to imprisonment (Morris and Tonry 1990).

The English, in the 1970s, were attracted to the idea and after consideration of its desirability by a distinguished commission and a series of pilot projects, it was implemented throughout the country. Early research suggested that about half of community service orders involved offenders who otherwise would have received prison sentences, demonstrating that they were indeed successfully being used in place of imprisonment. The Scottish government soon launched its own pilots and after them adopted community service on a national basis, with comparable evaluation results. In due course, in the early 1980s, after a series of private projects, the Dutch implemented community service nationwide and evaluators made comparable findings (Tonry and Hamilton 1995).

In the United States, by contrast, the first large-scale evaluation of community service programmes, by the Vera Institute of Justice in New York City, found that well-administered, enforced, community service programmes could retain participation by most offenders sentenced to them, that about half of sentenced offenders would otherwise have received prison sentences, and that recidivism rates of community service offenders were no better or worse than those of comparable offenders receiving other sentences (McDonald 1986).

In the United States today, and increasingly in England, community service is not used as a stand-alone sanction in its own right, particularly in place of imprisonment, but as a sentence for very minor cases, or as one among many conditions of a probation sentence. As prison alternatives, they are no longer important. This, again, alas, confirms that the Anglo-Saxon countries are not especially amenable to the use of community penalties in place of imprisonment.

House arrest with electronic monitoring/tagging

Electronic monitoring and tagging, often coupled with house arrest, 24 hours per day or intermittently, is widely used in the United States and in England with technologies and under circumstances that are increasingly evocative of George Orwell's *Nineteen Eighty-Four* and Aldous Huxley's *Brave New World*.

Electronic monitoring started in the US. Early research quickly demonstrated that judges were loathe to use community service with house arrest for serious offenders but were happy to use it for minor property offenders and for people convicted of drunk-driving offences. Since these are not typically people who are likely to present serious threats of violent or sexual offences, as an incapacitation strategy, electronic monitoring was early shown to be ineffective. It was somewhat more effective as a surveillance strategy and most effective as a stigmatizing strategy.

The English government piloted electronic monitoring programmes in the early 1990s, coming up with mixed results, and for a number of years did not proceed with their implementation. In due course, however, electronic monitoring was established, particularly in connection with an early-release home detention programme that releases some prisoners early from imprisonment under 'zero tolerance' rules that any breach of the house arrest order would meet with revocation of the early release. Since early release was typically used only for non-threatening offenders, failure rates on home detention were very low (2 or 3 per cent) suggesting, again, that the primary aim was surveillance and stigmatization rather than crime prevention.

Other countries, including Sweden and the Netherlands, have used electronic monitoring in somewhat more positive ways. They use electronic monitoring in early release programmes much as the British have but primarily for the purpose of letting people out of prison early. The Germans, at least as of a couple of years ago, have refused on principled grounds to adopt electronic monitoring programmes (Albrecht 2001). They are somewhere between rare and non-existent in Scandinavia.

Explaining the dispersion of restorative justice

Experience with community penalties suggests that prospects for restorative justice are probably not very great in jurisdictions with highly moralistic attitudes toward crime or traditions of imposition of very harsh punishments. In Sweden, for example, though sentences are typically short and though there has been success in substituting day fines for short prison sentences, there is likely to be cultural resistance to the idea that restorative justice programmes are not bound in their outcomes by strong proportionality concerns. In the United States, where prison sentences are very long by international standards, there is likely to be cultural resistance to the idea that some offenders, who in court would receive prison sentences, might have escaped any imprisonment in the agreed aftermath to a restorative conference.

In England and America, and increasingly in the Netherlands, the severity of punishments and a broad social consensus that imprisonment is the appropriate response for non-trivial crimes are likely to make those jurisdictions not very receptive to restorative justice programmes. Within the United States, however, there is a wide range of potential penal contexts and one might expect that states like Maine, Minnesota, Washington, Oregon or Vermont, with relatively low imprisonment rates and relatively progressive penal cultures, might be receptive to restorative justice programmes (and Oregon, Minnesota and Vermont are among the leaders in its implementation). It would be surprising if California, New York, Texas or Oklahoma were. The countries that would seem the prime targets would be those with relatively non-moralistic penal cultures (e.g. France, Germany, Belgium, Italy, Spain), those with relatively low imprisonment rates (much the same set of countries), and those that have demonstrated their willingness systematically to adopt new community penalties in place of imprisonment (the Netherlands, the Scandinavian countries, Germany). In addition, of course, countries with existing Aboriginal cultures that have traditionally used informal dispute resolution techniques, like Australia, New Zealand, northern Canada, and some American Indian reservations, may be promising sites.

Reverting to terms used in the introduction, the main *conducing* conditions to successful implementation of restorative justice initiatives appear to be: (1) the existence of Aboriginal cultures characterized by informal dispute resolution traditions; (2) relatively non-moralistic cultural traditions concerning punishment of offenders; (3) relatively low levels of politicization of criminal justice policy; (4) non-partisan means of selecting criminal justice practitioners; (5) relatively dispersed political authority within government and (6) a relatively modest tradition of harshness of punishment.

The *constraining* conditions are largely the opposites of the conducing conditions: moralistic cultural attitudes toward offenders, politicized crime policies, politically partisan selections of officials, especially judges and prosecutors, an authoritarian government with highly centralized political authority and high imprisonment rates.

At the end of the day, penal policies are the products of political decisions, as the figures set out in the second section clearly demonstrate. Political decisions, however, are made in particular cultural and political contexts and, as the community penalty implementation dispersion examples demonstrate, some contexts are more receptive to creative and humane penal interventions than others.

These generalizations, however, do not mean that restorative justice initiatives cannot succeed in hostile climates. They do suggest, however, that the obstacles to be overcome are comparatively high.

Note

1   Most Scandinavian countries do have mediation or victim–offender mediation programmes, but these may or may not be based on restorative justice premises. Many such programmes in the US, for example, are not.

References

Albrecht, H.-J. (2001) 'Post-adjudication dispositions in comparative perspective', in M. Tonry and R. S. Frase (eds), *Sentencing and Sanctions in Western Countries*. New York: Oxford University Press, pp. 293–330.

Ashworth, A. (2001) 'The decline of English sentencing and other stories', in M. Tonry and R. S. Frase (eds), *Sentencing and Sanctions in Western Countries*. New York: Oxford University Press, pp. 62–89.

Bottoms, A. (1995) 'The philosophy and politics of punishment and sentencing', in C. Clarkson and R. Morgan (eds), *The Politics of Sentencing Reform*. Oxford: Oxford University Press, pp. 17–49.

Caplow, T. and Simon, J. (1999) 'Understanding prison policy and population trends', in M. Tonry and J. Petersilia (eds), *Prisons, Crime and Justice*, 26. Chicago, IL: University of Chicago Press, pp. 63–120.

Freiberg, A. (2001) 'Three strikes and you're out – it's not cricket: colonization and resistance in Australian sentencing', in M. Tonry and R. S. Frase (eds), *Sentencing and Sanctions in Western Countries*. New York: Oxford University Press, pp. 29–61.

Garland, D. (1996) 'The limits of the sovereign state: strategies of crime control in contemporary society', *British Journal of Criminology*, 36(4): 445–71.

Garland, D. (2001) *The Culture of Control*. Oxford: Oxford University Press.

Hamai, K. (2001) 'Prison population in Japan stable for 30 years', in M. Tonry (ed.), *Penal Reform in Overcrowded Times*. New York: Oxford University Press, pp. 197–206.

Kensey, A. and Tournier, P. (2001) 'French prison numbers stable since 1988, but populations changing', in M. Tonry (ed.), *Penal Reform in Overcrowded Times*. New York: Oxford University Press, pp. 145–55.

Lappi-Seppälä, T. (2001) 'Sentencing and punishment in Finland: the decline of the repressive ideal', in M. Tonry and R. S. Frase (eds), *Sentencing and Sanctions in Western Countries*. New York: Oxford University Press, pp. 92–150.

McDonald, D. (1986) *Punishment Without Walls*. New Brunswick, NH: Rutgers University Press.

Morris, N. and Tonry, M. (1990) *Between Prison and Probation*. New York: Oxford University Press.

Musto, D. (1987) *The American Disease: Origins of Narcotic Control*, expanded edition (originally published 1973). New York: Oxford University Press.

Reitz, K. (2001) 'The disassembly and reassembly of US sentencing practices', in M. Tonry and R. S. Frase (eds), *Sentencing and Sanctions in Western Countries*. New York: Oxford University Press, pp. 222–58.

Tak, P. (2001) 'Sentencing and punishment in the Netherlands', in M. Tonry and R. S. Frase (eds), *Sentencing and Sanctions in Western Countries*. New York: Oxford University Press, pp. 151–87.

Tonry, M. (1995) *Malign Neglect: Race, Crime, and Punishment in America*. New York: Oxford University Press.

Tonry, M. (2001) *Penal Reform in Overcrowded Times*. New York: Oxford University Press.

Tonry, M. (2004a) *Thinking About Crime: Sense and Sensibility in American Penal Culture*. New York: Oxford University Press.

Tonry, M. (2004b) *Punishment and Politics: Evidence and Emulation in the Making of English Crime Control Policy*. Cullompton: Willan.

Tonry, M. and R. Frase (eds) (2001) *Sentencing and Sanctions in Western Countries* New York: Oxford University Press.

Tonry, M. and Hamilton, K. (eds) (1995) *Intermediate Sanctions in Overcrowded Times*. Boston, MA: Northeastern University Press.

van Kesteren, J., Mayhew, P. and Nieuwbeerta, P. (2000) *Criminal Victimisation in Seventeen Industrialised Countries*. The Hague: Ministry of Justice.

Wacquant, L. (2001) 'Deadly symbiosis: when ghetto and prison meet and merge', *Punishment and Society*, 3: 95–134.

Weigend, T. (2001) 'Sentencing and punishment in Germany', in M. Tonry and R. S. Frase (eds), *Sentencing and Sanctions in Western Countries*. New York: Oxford University Press, pp. 188–221.

Whitman, J. Q. (2003) *Harsh Justice: Criminal Punishment and the Widening Divide between American and Europe*. New York: Oxford University Press.

Chapter 2

The vital context of restorative justice

Hans Boutellier

In 2001 David Garland published his book *The Culture of Control. Crime and Social Order in Contemporary Society*. The book is widely valued as an important contribution to an understanding of the contemporary 'crime complex', the 'characteristic cluster of attitudes, beliefs and assumptions' related to crime and punishment. In his view criminal justice policy was until the 1970s dominated by 'penal-welfarism', a line of thinking that views crime as a result of some form of deprivation that can be alleviated via correction and rehabilitation. Nowadays there is no such coherent view on crime. The developments of the last decades are too complex and the reactions too divergent.

I will take Garland's book as a point of departure in my attempt to understand restorative justice as a result of wrestling today with security problems as related to crime and anti-social behaviour. In addition to Garland's analysis I would like to understand the contemporary safety issue as a result of *cultural* developments in risk society. This explains the urgency as experienced by politicians and the public to deal with the actual threats of crime to social order. And against this background we can understand why the criminal justice system is not capable of covering the crime problem in several respects.

In this perspective restorative justice can be seen as 'a solution' for the deficit of the criminal justice system. It appears as an option for politicians, a challenge for practitioners and an appealing subject for criminologists. Restorative justice is not so much an alternative as another strategy in security politics. It is not a substitution for criminal justice, but a contribution to the ongoing reshaping of social order. Restorative justice can be positioned as a way of processing anti-social behaviour that fits with contemporary multi-agency strategies in the governance of security (Johnston and Shearing 2003).

The contemporary crime complex

If something coherent could be said of the contemporary crime complex it should be – in accordance with Garland – that there is no such thing as coherence. We do not know for example what would be the proper progressive or reactionary response to the problems.

> Private prisons, victim impact statements, community notification laws, sentencing guidelines, electronic monitoring, punishments in the community, 'quality of life' policing, restorative justice – these and dozens of other developments lead us into unfamiliar territory where the ideological lines are far from clear and where the old assumptions are an unreliable guide.'(Garland 2001: 4)

This can greatly confuse anyone who confronts these problems in daily practice. It is precisely this confusion which has to be explained if we want to understand what is happening in crime control. In the introduction to his analysis, Garland cites twelve symptoms of the culture of control that I will briefly describe here. Most of them are relevant for positioning restorative justice.

The decline of the resocialization ideal

Up until 1970, it was widely believed that criminals could and should be resocialized. This belief, dominant throughout most of the twentieth century, was contested in the 1970s by progressive criticism of the unlimited power of psychologists and other therapists and subsequently by a conservative attack on the apologetic attitude supposedly inherent in this therapeutization. At the moment there is something of a revival of this ideal in the 'What Works' – approach. According to Garland, this development is not, however, an all-inclusive ideology, as was the case in the past. Instead it is subordinate to views on retribution, incapacitation and risk management. In Garland's opinion, the disappearance of the resocialization model in the 1970s was the first sign of the changing attitudes to crime.

The reappearance of punitive sanctions and expressive criminal justice

In the United States, the work of von Hirsch (1976) has been a clear starting point in the revaluation of the notion of retribution. Von Hirsch sees the rehabilitation model as mainly focusing on ethnic minorities. To improve on it, he formulates an influential model of just sentences based on an honest trial. Legal equality is represented in a system of guidelines designed to put an end to arbitrary sentencing in the criminal justice system. Quite unexpectedly, however, the effort to reform criminal law ultimately led to longer sentences. The authorities and the public alike revaluated punishment as punishment, in other words as inflicting suffering.

Changes in the emotional tone of policies on crime

There is now a dramatic undertone to whatever people say or think about crime, and fear is becoming a separate theme in this connection. Of course the media play a major role as well. It is still unwarranted, though, to blame all this on the media. In a world without coherent and universally shared worldviews, emotions do undeniably play a greater role (van Stokkom 1997). Collective rage and a call for revenge often supersede social commitment to arrive at a just and social solution to problems.

The return of the victim

Ever since the mid-1970s, the victim has been part of the crime problem. Up until then, the victim filed charges and testified in court. Nowadays, victimhood is a safety policy theme, and according to Garland it is often at the expense of the offender. In the United States and Great Britain, laws are even named after victims.[1] What is involved here is victimhood of a generalized nature. People are increasingly viewed as potential victims, which is largely what justifies the present-day safety policy (see Boutellier 2000).

The protection of the public

The protection of citizens has become the dominant crime policy theme. This aim is diametrically opposed to another public interest, the safeguarding of legal rights, designed to protect the individual from the power and possible arbitrariness of the state. It is striking that, nowadays, people do not so much demand protection *from* the state, they want protection from other people *by* the state. In this context, the attitude to privacy is very different to what it used to be.

Politicization and populism

Crime policy has been increasingly popularized. Instead of cautious and detached analyses, policy is now largely made and defended with short statements and sound bites. Expertise is valued less. No one is interested in the stories criminologists tend to tell in an effort to put things in perspective. There was also evidence of a politicization of the crime problem in the 1970s. But instead of the polarization with regard to crime evident at the time – deprivation versus control – there is now more of a populist undertone, which generates an unprecedented consensus on the importance of combating crime.

The rediscovery of the prison

In virtually all Western countries, there has been an exponential growth in the prison system since the 1980s. Garland notes that from 1973 to 1997, there was a 500 per cent rise in the United States in the number of prisoners per 100,000 residents. Shown by another measure: in the Netherlands the penitentiary capacity rose from 4,037 to 12,401 from 1970 to 2000 (Huls *et al.* 2001: 351). The belief in the prison system grew, and not because of any positive effect it might have on the convicts, but as a way to incapacitate them and satisfy the punitive sentiment. The prison system expanded into a massive and apparently indispensable component of control of the social order.

The transformation of criminological thinking

Instead of deprivation criminology, control criminology has now emerged. Welfare thinking has been replaced by disciplinary thinking. This process was accompanied by a shift from a positive to a negative image of man. In close conjunction with the control approach, theories came into fashion that view crime and the avoidance of crime as matters of everyday strategies. Crime is viewed as a rational choice or a routine activity shaped by opportunity. In this new criminology no mention is made of any deviation or deviant behaviour on the part of individuals; there is simply a normal pattern of criminal events.

The growing infrastructure of crime prevention and local safety

Following naturally from the criminology of everyday strategies, new forms of crime management have emerged. They deviate from the traditional criminal justice approach. They are focused on preventing crime, reducing the fear of crime and undoing the damage it causes.

Other parties have become involved who enter into preventative partnerships at the local level to promote a safe living environment.

Individuals and commerce

In keeping with the previous development, individuals and private parties are becoming increasingly involved in creating a safe living environment. This has led to a mushrooming of the commercial security branch, which is even larger in some countries than traditional criminal justice agencies such as the police and the courts. Private citizens are expected to play an active role in the safety issue. This can lead, for example, to the introduction of tip-off lines and the promotion of civilian surveillance.

New management styles and work forms

The criminal justice system has increasingly been influenced by the *managerialism* that became so popular in civil service circles in the 1990s. Employees think in terms of operational aims and performance indicators and in planning and control cycles in an effort to promote the efficiency and effectiveness of the criminal justice system and see to its accountability. According to Garland, all this is at the expense of the discretionary space of professionals and it confines the work forms to strictly defined implementation practices. He notes that at the same time enormous investments have been made in a detention system that can hardly be viewed as effective.

A permanent sense of crisis

Garland feels that many of the developments described above are founded on a growing awareness that the existing arrangements are no longer adequate and coherent enough to make crime management really feasible. In addition to a failure to implement and execute the necessary measures, there is a growing sense that the underlying theory no longer suffices. The system does not seem to be capable of coping with the problems it is faced with. It is now in a danger zone of constant risks, scandals and price rises where the authorities have lost the people's trust.

With this list of twelve symptoms, Garland refers to a radical change in the crime complex. Once such a complex has established itself, it is not apt to change rapidly, as is witnessed by the preceding penal welfare thinking that was dominant for so many decades. The twelve features underline the general feeling among criminologists that a new crime complex is in the making. But one may wonder if 'the culture of control' is the right characterization of this development. In evaluating Garland's twelve features, we should bear in mind that he focuses solely on the United States and Great Britain. However, this is not the reason why I view a term like 'culture of control' as being too monolithic to describe western societies.

Only two of the symptoms of the new crime complex in the making are in direct contrast with the aims of restorative justice: the reappearance of punitive sanctions and expressive criminal justice and the rediscovery of the prison. The other symptoms are not necessarily punitive in their orientation. It is also the case that they give an impetus to preventive, proactive, risk-oriented safety politics in which a favourable attitude towards restorative justice can grow. I feel the developments described above are too ambiguous and the underlying sentiments too ambivalent. I would like to discuss the question why these ambivalent changes did happen. The crime complex had to change under the pressure of changes in the cultural context.

Crime as a safety issue

During the 1990s there was increasing attention on the security problem that resulted in the symptoms of the system as described by Garland. A way of summarizing this development could be that crime was transformed into a safety issue. Security became a number one theme in many western countries (Hebberecht and Duprez 2002). In this redefinition of crime into insecurity three bridges were built. The first one is between crime and other threats and risks. Crime became registered as another risk in risk society. Although it has its own (especially moral) characteristics, a new vocabulary of risk management and control grew in the area. This development is amply studied for the police (Ericson and Haggerty 1997), criminal justice (Feeley and Simon 1994) and liberal justice (Hudson 2003).

A second bridge was built between the criminal justice system and other agencies, to begin with the local municipalities. In Great Britain this local development was strenghtened by the Crime and Disorder Act of 1998. But in other countries during the 1990s criminal policy also became more and more a multi-agency process in which the criminal justice system is a decisive partner, but no more than that. In that respect we can see a growing literature on 'governing security' (see Johnston and Shearing 2003). Especially for local authorities the challenge lies in the governance of all agencies involved in these security networks. I will return to this issue later in the chapter.

The third bridge resulting from the redefinition of the crime problem into a safety issue is the bridge between objective crime (as can be measured by police registration and surveys) and the subjective experience of crime. Fear of crime is nowadays part and parcel of (local) security policies. The meaning of either the word security or safety encloses the feelings which are related to crime. But fear of crime is a very complex concept, in which at least four layers can be detected:

- the actual fear of being victimized (this is the meaning that is generally investigated);

- a general worry about the crime problem in contemporary society (also included in most crime surveys);

- the worries of people about all kinds of social problems (from dog excrement to unemployment) (as for example shown in a Dutch study by Elffers and de Jong 2005);

- the general discontent that seems to be a characteristic of risk society (see Boutellier 2004).

So the redefinition of the crime problem into a safety problem covered at least three substantial evolutions in criminal justice policy (before 9/11): it became risk-oriented in a multi-agency approach powered by the emotional experience of victimization (Boutellier 2000). But what does this development say about our culture? Why did the security issue get such a central position in contemporary society? There are at least two reasons why this was the case.

Firstly, *crime or the threat of it has become part and parcel of everyday life.* This holds true for offending as well as for being victimized. Small social or financial offences such as fraud, hiring workers illegally, slander and traffic violations have become common practice. Shoplifting is a minor crime that is massively practised, and virtually everyone has either been the victim of some more serious offence from purse snatching to assault or knows someone who has. In the Netherlands, for example, there was a tenfold rise in registered crime from 1960 to 2000 – from about 130,000 to 1,300,000 registrations (Huls *et al.* 2001: 45). In 2004 this amounted to 1,400,000.

Next to the actual rise in crime – defined as the whole complex of acts punishable by law – there is a second evident reason for the dominance of the security issue. There seems to be an *increased significance for the state to counter the increases in crime rates.* The issue of security has traditionally been an important justification for the formation of the nation state. The nineteenth century witnessed the

Institutionalizing Restorative Justice

rise of the nightwatch state, where the government gave a certain guarantee of safety and made the necessary provisions. In exchange, the people were willing to obey its laws. In the twentieth century, notions of good and evil were embedded in the great ideological movements – Liberalism, Socialism, Christian politics – which ultimately led to the emergence of the welfare state.

The relatively low crime rates during the development of the welfare state can perhaps best be explained by the combination of a society that was still relatively highly disciplined and a rise in prosperity. In this situation, criminal justice could be used in the periphery of civil society to correct the imperfect social control mechanisms. The ideological discipline related to criminal justice prohibitions has, however, disappeared. Crime was a residual category of the successful social order, and criminal justice – the state – the ultimate remedy to deal with it. Criminal justice prohibitions are, however, no longer embedded in a more or less unambiguous moral context that guarantees their legitimacy. The state is having a harder time guaranteeing a certain extent of safety, which is why there is growing pressure on its legitimacy in the eyes of the people.

A vital culture

So the crime figures raised and states legitimacy eroded, but the question still is: what happened in western society that can explain these developments? For that question I would like to take as a starting point the concept of the risk society (Ulrich Beck), in order now to understand the lifestyle that is associated with it. To describe this lifestyle we need heavy words, like individualization, secularization, globalization and so forth. In general, however, the essence of these dynamics is that citizens live their lives in more and more loosely organized social contexts, with less social control, less prefixed social norms and many more choices to make. 'Take whatever you want – God, Nature, truth, science, technology, morality, love, marriage – modernity transformed everything into "risky freedom" (Beck and Beck-Gernsheim, quoted by Bauman 1997: 193, note 3).

In other words, life in a *Risikogesellschaft* is lived as a *Risikoleben* with all the uncertainties that this entails. Globalization, a weakening of family and neighbourhood life and the permanent danger alert conveyed by the media are all open wells of insecurity and discontent. Risky freedom leads to an overwhelming feeling of uncertainty, and even more to the fear that other people are making the wrong

32

decisions.[2] Ask young people and they will tell you: 'I can become anybody, so who should I be?' Zygmunt Bauman (2000) speaks of a liquid modernity to describe the contemporary 'postmodern' culture. So there is something to add to the observation that safety is now a universal motif in western society. The desire for safety is countered by a force I would like to define as a *vital* drive. The need for safety emerges within a context of an unprecedented and uninhibited sense of freedom.[3]

Vitality is a common denominator for numerous phenomena characteristic of contemporary society such as the dominance of the market with its emphasis on business, risk taking and competition. Or one might bear in mind the temptations of quick, expressive and visceral activities in the youth culture and the media, and the worlds of sports and popular entertainment. So the incredible paradox is that in a risk society many people, in many places experience unprecedented freedom, with little boundaries, no strict social norms, with a lifestyle of experimentation and exuberance. The non-ideological, relatively amoral risk society creates a clear field for individual interests, motives and emotions. This moral or mental state of contemporary society can be called egoism, hedonism or narcissism. However, I prefer to speak of vitality, the experience of most citizens that they have the right – and duty – to define and form their life in their own way.

This is the psychological challenge that comes with the identity politics of late modernity – according to a concept introduced by Anthony Giddens (1990). The self has evolved from a product to a project: a process that needs to be managed and monitored by the person himself (recognizable in programmes for anger management), the institutions and the state. The drive behind so many forms of crime is essentially not any different from *positive* forms of vitality. They can be viewed in fact as *negative* variants of expressiveness. Night-life violence thrives for example in an atmosphere of exuberance, like at a carnival or some other festivity (Presdee 2000). In a general sense, Van den Brink (2001) views the ego-focused articulateness that has developed since the 1970s as being responsible in part for the rising violence among youngsters in recent decades. Contemporary crime should be comprehended as emerging from a context largely focused on immediate need gratification and self-fulfilment. At the same time, though, crime puts this context to the test. Time and time again, crime explores the borders of the contemporary desire for freedom, or better yet the demand for non-intervention.

Against this background, the vitality of 'postmodern' society goes hand in hand with an obsessive desire for safety. Vitality and safety are two sides of the same coin: a liberal culture that has elevated self-fulfilment to the true art of living also has to make every effort to stipulate and maintain the limitations of individual freedom. A vital society generates a great need for safety and thus comes up against an undeniable paradox: if liberal freedom is to be unreservedly celebrated, its boundaries need to be set. In the context of a risk society where vast prosperity is accompanied by enormous fragility, a morality develops somewhere in between vague indefinable fear and boundless expressiveness.

Security politics

Theoretical reflection on safety begins by acknowledging the actual increase of the chance for citizens to get victimized, especially in public or semi-public areas like schools, soccer stadiums and entertainment districts. This basic premise is less self-evident than one might think. The evil things people do to each other and the need for a response to them are often overlooked. Intellectuals are often more interested in the structural violence of the authorities or in processes of exclusion than in the problems that generate them. This is also my basic argument with Garland who in his superb study on the culture of control spends not one section of the book on the problems that are related to the developments towards which control devices refer.

If we are to diagnose the safety issue, however, it is imperative to recognize the call for safety as an essential factor. Unsafety has become one of the major social problems of the early twenty-first century. This is evident from surveys where people list crime as one of their greatest concerns. It is similarly evident from the attention in the media and the political arena. And it is clear from the attention focused on the criminal justice system. It is simply inconceivable that politicians would not feel called upon to address the social unrest caused by rising crime rates and feelings of unsafety. After all, meeting the needs of the citizens is ultimately the most important legitimating force in a constitutional democracy.

This does not necessarily mean that the needs voiced by the people are the only factors politically affecting the legislative and law enforcement system. These needs are too widely varied and should be far more carefully considered in relation to the greater general interest of the constitutional state. For example, the reintroduction of capital punishment, even via a referendum, would be unacceptable; most European constitutional states cannot afford to have anyone's death on their conscience. But since the government, with its monopoly on violence and law enforcement, does and indeed should lead the way with regard to the safety issue, it should be able to give the people what they feel is right and just. For this reason, the cry for safety should be taken seriously, especially by criminologists.

Vitality and safety are the two extremes a human life navigates between in a risk society. When it comes down to it, we like the idea of police protection for our individual, often exuberant life project. We yearn for precisely the kind of certainty we cannot believe in. The moral discontent of our culture is consequently an unfulfillable need for certainty. In the safety issue, the borders of moral fragmentation and individualization visibly emerge. Ample individual space is accompanied, for example, by widespread criminal deviance. Freedom and risk, vitality and protection are thus two sides of the same coin. This state of affairs can be seen as an achievement of the social-liberal welfare state, but it also generates a lot of problems: psychological uncertainty, discontent about self and society, a longing for beliefs and new ideals, a lack of mutual trust, an increase in anti-social deviance, norm breaking, crime. The exuberant lifestyle is accompanied by a cry for protection against it.

On the one hand we have a vital culture that generates big egos, violations of norms and anti-social behaviour. On the other hand there is the increasing demand of citizens for safer cities, safer public transport and decency in the public sphere. These two expressions of our culture do not necessarily come from different groups. The gap between becoming a victim and becoming an offender is not that wide. Norm violation has become an everyday opportunity, just like the risk of being victimized. In any event, these two forces – a vitalist lifestyle and a demand for protection – come together in crime politics. Over the last few decades they have developed an enormous pressure on government in general and the criminal justice system in particular – a government which is sensitive to this pressure because its own legitimation is at stake.

As we all know, however, the actual amount of the crime problem addressed by the criminal justice system is very limited. I have shown elsewhere (Boutellier 2002) that there is a 'criminal justice paradox' in contemporary society: a growing demand for a supply shrinking in relative terms. Only 15 to 20 per cent of the registered crime is addressed by the criminal justice system (while in the 1960s it was about 50 per cent). However, not only in a quantitative way but, also qualitatively the criminal justice system bears – in the words of Garland – the tragic quality of punishment. People know that the need for punishment is accompanied by immanent failure for the person involved. So, in today's society there is a high level of norm violation, a cry for protection and a system with immanent shortcomings.

Given the pressure of the vital-longing-for-safety society I would like to argue that in western countries there has been a shift in position of the criminal justice system: from a peripheral position as ultimate remedy it has shifted to a central moral position. The safety utopia demands, so to speak, that the institutions of criminal justice take a central position in structuring today's society. But they lack the power – quantitative, qualitative and dogmatic – to do so. Criminal justice is doomed to get stuck in a semi-permanent crisis – as has been described by David Garland. What policy consequences arise from this situation? What kind of strategy do we search for in this situation of imbalance? How can this enormous pressure – high crime, high expectations, poor supply – be released? Logically speaking, there seem to be two possibilities: broadening the coverage of criminal justice or narrowing the top of the funnel.

In many countries you can see a two-track policy. According to Garland (2001), the state reacted in a schizoid fashion. It became stronger in the field of crime and punishment but at the same time allowed others to take more and more steps. In an effort to increase its own strength, it clung to the notion that crime control is a state matter. This strategy complies with the political logic that a government should continue to believe in its own institutions. There is even a political tendency to get lost in exaggerated rhetoric and poorly planned expansion of powers. Garland speaks in this connection of 'acting out' (2001: 131). As examples, he cites the law regulating the supervision of sex offenders, the Californian *'three strikes and you are out'* rule, prisons for juveniles, the registering of the names of paedophiles, the zero tolerance policy of various police forces and so forth.

At the same time the system adjusts itself, for example by setting priorities, making other agencies responsible, modifying its aims and developing a practical policy criminology. It is a strategy with space for other actors. It is more focused on preventive and proactive use of means. New preventive strategies and modes of cooperation develop here, with local groups related to safety and conflict management strategies. Garland refers to a strategy of preventive partnerships. So the changes do not all go in one and the same direction. The past few decades have witnessed the largest prison construction programme since the Victorian age (Garland 2001: 168). A unique development though has been the emergence of another sector next to the criminal justice system consisting of 'crime prevention organizations, public–private partnerships, community policing arrangements, and multi-agency working practices [...] local authority panels, working groups, multi-agency forums, and action committees' (Garland 2001: 170).

This new sector occupies a position between the state and the community and mediates between criminal justice agencies and the actions of individuals, local communities and companies. Crime control has become the responsibility of multifarious social and economic actors who focus on prevention, the reduction of damage and suffering, and risk management rather than on retribution, deterrence and correction (Garland 2001: 171). Community safety is becoming a major consideration, and law enforcement is more an instrument than a goal in itself. Reducing fear, damage, suffering and the various expenses accompanying them are now the primary consideration and play a larger role than the purity of the constitutional state or aspects having to do with privacy and the protection of individual rights. This leads to a situation where the criminal justice system is bigger than ever, but nonetheless occupies an increasingly restricted position *vis-à-vis* other agencies and organizations (Garland 2001: 173). The state does become more punitive, but it increasingly acknowledges its own inadequacy.

Garland notes that the crime and safety sector is structurally rearranging itself in such a way as to include new elements (the victim, prevention, restorative justice), with revised power balances (between punishment and well-being, state and commercial facilities, means and ends, the legal protection of offenders and of the public), and a change in relations between the field and the environment (the political process, public opinion and the civil society). In this new crime culture, various forms coincide. In his evaluation Garland observes that the new crime culture is more focused on exclusion than on solidarity, more on social control than on social facilities, more on the private freedom of the market than on the public freedoms of universal citizenship. This is why he speaks of a culture of control. Yet the state does not seem to be capable of adequately guaranteeing safety. An effective government can only be based on central steering and coercion to a limited extent. Instead, it should support the steering capacities of civil society's organizations together with the local forces and knowledge available there. Garland closes *Culture of Control* as follows: 'We discover – and it is not too late yet – that this also holds true for crime control' (2001: 205).

A soccer team model

It is important to bear in mind that a greater involvement on the part of other – social – institutions essentially means they will come to hold more of a normative position than they often do today. The safety goal implies more of an orientation towards behaviour that should be prevented because people – and the criminal justice system – disapprove of it. When we look at the way security is governed today we see numerous projects and possibilities at various levels. Firstly, there is the level of individual citizens and their primary spheres of life. The state can enlarge their resilience by reinforcing the social fabric. This means facilitating volunteer work, clubs and associations, advising parents on the upbringing of their children and so forth. In general, people's willingness to address the safety issue is of crucial importance. In the end, civil society should be borne by individual citizens.

At the second level, there are educational and youth and community work agencies. They are increasingly aware of their teaching role in conveying normative points of departure for daily interaction. The strengthening of the normative consciousness of these institutions cannot be forced upon them, but it can be enabled by the authorities. It would be desirable for the state to stimulate and facilitate the normative function of these institutions. Developments in the framework of the comprehensive school, cooperation between the school system and youth care agencies, and conflict mediation in neighbourhoods and at schools offer new ways for preventing crime and improving safety. The world of trade and industry can be requested to make a contribution to the integration of minorities and the sponsoring of social projects.

At the third level, there are numerous possibilities in the connection between the criminal justice system and the world of social and public policy. They focus on a contextual approach to problems from the social work as well as the criminal justice perspective. Cooperation between the police and community work can be reinforced, and connections can also be created in the cooperation between prisons, probation services, private security companies, mental health care and social work institutions. It is at this level that alternative modes of settlement in the field of mediation and restorative justice also play a role.

At the fourth level, criminal law plays a crucial role in the reaction to serious criminal behaviour. In the criminal justice response, the sense of right and wrong is confirmed but the hope of improvement is kept alive. The reintegration of ex-convicts in an effort to prevent recidivism can be promoted in penitentiary programmes and via community sanctions. In a preventive sense, efforts are needed on behalf of individual youths whose problems are accumulating and who will be part of the future hard core. Interventions for this group are planned on the basis of early indicators cited by teachers or youth workers. Special training programmes and intensive family counselling might be required.

It may be said of a number of the above-mentioned agencies that they are not the most appropriate ones to address society's safety issues. They do nonetheless often experience the negative effects of crime and the bothersome or anti-social conduct that has often come to characterize city life. These institutions should realize that if they devote more attention to safety issues now, it might open up new possibilities for their *real* work in the future. If schools can create a safer climate on their own premises, it ultimately benefits pupils' performance at school. A democratic safety policy presumes wide societal commitment. In such a policy 'the key issue for the future will not be demarcation of functions but effective coordination of networks' (Johnston and Shearing 2003: 34).

For that matter it might be useful to imagine the governance of security as a soccer team that has to play a defensive game. In goal is the criminal justice system; this goalkeeper hears the balls flying around his ears. Being in this position he coaches the defensive line in order to position the defenders in a more effective way. This defensive line is made up of institutions that deal with risks – from private security companies to youth care for children at risk and from community policing to restorative justice approaches. This defensive line has to be supportive to the midfield that consists of organizations that play a general social role like schools, business corporations and social work agencies.

The security issue forces them to take a normative stance in terms of good citizenship and promoting social behaviour and correcting anti-social behaviour before the criminal justice system has to intervene. In the front line there are the citizens and the social bonds they arrange among themselves. The soccer team has to be arranged in such a way that citizens are capable of mobilizing their social capital (Putnam 2000) in a forward-oriented way. It is a model that fits a society that seems to be in a defensive position. It is problem oriented, working from the rear to the front, backing and coaching in partnerships for safer communities. This kind of democratic security policy is in need of new vocabularies on conflict resolution, norm confirmation and restoration.

The end of a monopoly

The statement that every society gets the crime it deserves can be viewed as one of the clichés of criminology. It says everything and nothing at the same time. Contemporary culture is apparently accompanied by a serious safety issue. Many explanations have been suggested in criminology, all of which contain a grain of truth. We are familiar with the sociological discourses on the social-economic divide, materialism, ethnic minority problems, the liberal way children are brought up nowadays, the open borders, problems related to drugs and alcohol, the culture of masculinity and so forth. In crime prevention, the dominant idea at the time of writing is the life course theory that explains crime in terms of risk and protection factors.

It is characteristic of criminological explanations, which do bear a certain relevance to policy issues, that criminal behaviour is interpreted on the basis of factors outside the individual will. In so far as the individual subject plays a role in the explanations, he appears as a rational actor (the calculating citizen) who chooses the most obvious option on the basis of an internal analysis of the costs and benefits. Under some circumstances, this will be criminal behaviour. It is the image of a social-economic subject who decides without any moral deliberation. In these ways of practising criminology, the individual as a moral subject is essentially declared legally incompetent. In a sense, it is thus diametrically opposed to what is in principle the underlying assumption of criminal proceedings, that the offender or suspect acts on the basis of his own free *moral* will.

Although a criminal court judge will be willing to take the offender's personal circumstances into consideration, it is mainly the moral responsibility of the individual as legal subject that is addressed: *You did it, so you wanted to do it!* This is, I feel, an important point of departure for a realistic look at criminal behaviour today. Perhaps criminal behaviour can be explained by any number of factors, but this does not help us understand its moral significance. Criminal behaviour can mainly be interpreted as a moral act. If we are to take the offender seriously as a person who is morally competent, we can only assume there were other choices open to him. He is not just guided by the sum of costs and benefits.

Offenders themselves also often disapprove of their own conduct. Perhaps they are hoping for some measure of understanding from other people, but they are surprised when their evil acts are simply explained away. In the explanation, their internal motivation is essentially repudiated. If their guilt is disclaimed, the punishment might seem unreasonable to them.[4] In essence, to the extent that their offences are determined, they have no say in what they did. But we want to have wanted our behaviour. Acknowledging the moral subject's own responsibility can be viewed as an important legacy of the humanist tradition. This is all the more the case now the ethics of obligation has faded away as a determining framework.

If there is no longer the ideological belief that man can be shaped, we should be aware of what might be an extreme consequence.

Postmodern freedom to choose the good life for ourselves means the bad life is also viewed as a life project, albeit a wrong one. An ambiguous morality makes crime something that is interpreted as an authentic moral act and subsequently rejected. Criminal behaviour is then not so much a deviation from the norm enforced from above as a denial of a fundamental principle of a humanist culture, the recognition of the other and of the other's freedom.

This does not mean we no longer take the offender's circumstances into consideration or are no longer interested in his story. On the contrary, each individual's own motivation for the conduct he selects has even become the core of the communication with him. We accept the offender as a moral subject, but have usually good grounds for rejecting his acts. Just as we know ourselves as moral subjects who make certain choices in dilemmas involving good and evil, we hold the other, in this case the criminal offender, responsible for his choices. And thus in his pure role, the criminal court judge points us towards a central assumption of contemporary culture, i.e. that we ourselves are responsible for our own life project.

The urgent role that at the moment is attributed to criminal justice acquires a deeper significance if we bear in mind the much more fundamental desire underlying it. The call for more criminal justice is inspired by the normative simplicity of criminal justice. After all, criminal justice represents the condemnation of behaviour that causes harm to other people or makes the norms of the community secondary to the fulfilment of one's own goals. Norms defined in criminal justice terms inform us of the vulnerability of moral positions, of other people's and our own moral ambivalence.

Yet in courtroom practice, this ideal–typical function of criminal justice is frequently difficult to put into effect. What is more, there is a morally ambivalent conflict underlying many criminal acts, and it is often not so much a matter of confirming the norm as of finding or evaluating or re-evaluating the norm. Many instances of violence in schools, in clubs or in families are not characterized by the clear relation between the offender and the victim which criminal proceedings assume exists: 'One can conclude that civil society does not only need norms stiffened by punishments, but also […] an ethic of communication which can provide legitimacy for, and confirm the validity of, norms' (Mannozzi 2002: 233).

This is why in a morally complex society mediation between the various parties in a conflict that is relevant to the criminal justice system is often a better option. In restorative justice more can probably be done to address the needs of injured parties for attention, protection, compensation and so forth than in classical criminal proceedings.

Moreover, the moral appeal to the offender is stronger if he is treated as an equal moral subject. The contrast between the prominent normative function of criminal justice and its limited instrumental possibilities needs to be supplemented by other forms of conflict management. The criminal court judge has good grounds for playing a normative role, but he has no longer the sole right to do so.

Notes

1 There is, for example, Megan's Law in the United States, regulating the return of sex offenders to society.
2 Other authors such as Furedi (1997) have also noted that fear and uncertainty are central emotions in our modern-day culture.
3 I do not pursue the question here of whether it is true freedom or far more a drive to consume and blindly satisfy our needs. I view the unprecedented choices we have to lead our lives any way we wish as a condition for experiencing freedom. I develop this more in depth in another publication (Boutellier 2004: chapter 1).
4 There is some evidence that the offender will be more affected by the sanction if he has the feeling he has been fairly judged and sentenced (see, for example, Sherman 1993 and Tyler 1990).

References

Bauman, Z. (1997) *Postmodernity and its Discontents.* Cambridge: Polity Press.
Bauman, Z. (2000) *Liquid Modernity.* Cambridge: Polity Press.
Beck, U. (1986) *Risikogesellschaft: auf dem Weg in eine andere Moderne.* Frankfurt am Main: Suhrkamp.
Boutellier, H. (2000) *Crime and Morality: The Moral Significance of Criminal Justice in Postmodern Society.* Dordrecht: Kluwer Academic Publishers.
Boutellier, H. (2002) 'Victimalisation and restorative justice: moral backgrounds and political consequences', in L. Walgrave (ed.), *Restorative Justice and the Law.* Collumpton: Willan, pp. 19–30.
Boutellier, H. (2004) *The Safety Utopia: Contemporary Discontent and Desire as to Crime and Punishment.* Dordrecht: Kluwer Academic.
Crawford, A. (1997) *The Local Governance of Crime: Appeals to Community and Partnerships.* Oxford: Oxford University Press.
Elffers, H. and de Jong, W. (2005) 'Nee, ik voel me nooit onveilig: determinanten van sociale onveiligheidsgevoelens', in Raad voor Maatschappelijke Ontwikkeling (ed.) *Sociale veiligheid organiseren: Naar herkenbaarheid in de publieke ruimte* (Advies 31, Bijlage 5). Den Haag: Sdu.
Ericson, R. and Haggerty, K. (1997) *Policing the Risk Society.* Toronto: University of Toronto Press.

Feeley, M. and Simon, J. (1994) 'Actuarial justice: the emerging new criminal law', in D. Nelken (ed.), *The Futures of Criminology*. London: Sage, 173–201.

Furedi, F. (1997) *Culture of Fear. Risk Taking and the Morality of Low Expectations*. London: Cassell.

Garland, D. (2001) *Culture of Control: Crime and Social Order in Contemporary Society*. Oxford: Oxford University Press.

Giddens, A. (1990) *The Consequences of Modernity*. Cambridge: Polity Press.

Hebberecht, P. and Duprez, D. (eds) (2002) *The Prevention and Security Policies in Europe*. Brussels: VUB University Press.

Hudson, B. (2003) *Justice in the Risk Society. Challenging and Re-affirming Justice in Late Modernity*. London: Sage.

Huls, F. W. M., Schreuders, M. M., Ter Horst-van Breukelen, M. H. and van Tulder, F. P. (2001) *Criminaliteit en rechtshandhaving 2000: ontwikkelingen en samenhangen*. Den Haag: CBS/WODC.

Johnston, L. and Shearing, C. (2003) *Governing Security: Explorations in Policing and Justice*. London: Routledge.

Mannozzi, G. (2002) 'From the "Sword" to dialogue. Towards a "dialectic" basis for penal mediation', in E. G. M. Weitekamp and H.-J. Kerner (eds), *Restorative Justice. Theoretical Foundations*. Collumpton: Willan, pp. 224–46.

Presdee, M. (2000) *Cultural Criminology and the Carnival of Crime*. London: Routledge.

Putnam, R. D. (2000) *Bowling Alone: The Collapse and Revival of American Community*. New York: Touchstone.

Sherman, L. W. (1993) 'Defiance, deterrence, and irrelevance: a theory of the criminal sanction', *Journal of Research in Crime and Delinquency*, 30(4): 445–73.

Tyler, T. (1990) *Why Do People Obey the Law?* New Haven, CT: Yale University Press.

Van den Brink, G. (2001) *Geweld als uitdaging: de betekenis van agressief gedrag bij jongeren*. Utrecht: NIZW.

Van Stokkom, B. A. M. (1997) *Emotionele democratie: over morele vooruitgang*. Amsterdam: Van Gennep.

Von Hirsch, A. (1976) *Doing Justice: The Choice of Punishments*. New York: McGraw-Hill.

Chapter 3

Beyond evangelical criminology: the meaning and significance of restorative justice

John Pratt

It is undeniably true, as Mika and Zehr (2003: 135) claim, that 'the momentum of restorative justice [RJ] in the past twenty years has been breathtaking.' It is also undeniably true that RJ has assumed the status of a 'global social movement' (Braithwaite 1996), to which the bewildering expansion and diversity of projects in its name is testimony (Miers 2001). As Daly (2002: 57) writes, '[RJ] is used not only in adult and juvenile criminal matters, but also in a range of civil matters, including family welfare and child protection, and disputes in schools and workplace settings. Increasingly, one finds the term associated with the resolution of broader political conflicts such as the reconstruction of post-apartheid South Africa, post-genocide Rwanda, and post-sectarian Northern Ireland.' Clearly RJ has become something of an umbrella term, incorporating projects that are vastly different in scope and intent. Nonetheless, there do seem to be core elements running through most of the projects which bear its name thereby providing them with some sense of unity. These core elements include non-judicial processes of inquiry into criminal behaviour, with many of the formal evidential and procedural rules relaxed. These processes are likely to be facilitated by the criminal justice authorities but it is intended that victims and offenders, often in the company of their families and supporters, will be at their centre. The main purpose of such hearings is for the offender, in some way, to repair the damage they have caused (and frequently, but not necessarily, be themselves actively reintegrated into the community they have harmed (Braithwaite 1989)). This is often achieved through the delivery of an apology amid an outpouring of sentiment from all parties which it is intended will help to bring the dispute to a close (Tavuchis 1991; Bottoms 2003). Apart from anything else then, RJ is a more expressive form of justice than had previously been allowed for in the formal criminal justice system of most modern societies, allowing for an ebb and flow of human sentiment during the proceedings: that it is so is largely because it is a more 'decentred' modality of justice. That is, it is framed (in varying degrees at least) by community values and ideas of justice rather than being dominated by the bureaucratic interests of the criminal justice authorities.

What does this dramatic transition actually represent though? By posing this question I am not just referring to the importance of RJ in providing new ways of responding to crime, conflict and punishment. What I want to do in this chapter is to ascertain what this might be telling us about the broader pattern of social development that now provides for its possibility, and what the implications of this might be for current trends in RJ and its future prospects. As Rusche and Kirchheimer (1939/1968: 5) tellingly wrote long ago:

> Punishment is neither a simple consequence of crime, nor the reverse side of crime, nor a mere means which is determined by the end to be achieved. Punishment must be understood as a social phenomenon freed from both its juristic concept and its social ends. We don't deny that punishment has specific ends, but we do deny that it can be understood from its ends alone.

At present, and with some notable exceptions,[1] RJ has been understood largely on the basis of its 'ends'. In these respects, it falls prey to a kind of evangelical criminology: the fervour with which it is pursued gives it a taken-for-granted status that can blind its followers to its implications. This chapter critically examines some of the claims that have been made about RJ that have contributed to this evangelicism, going on to argue that its significance should be understood as a pointer to a more uncertain penal world characteristic of post-1970s social arrangements, with no guarantees or sure indicators of where the boundaries of contemporary punishment now lie.

New evangelicals?

For a good many RJ scholars and practitioners, RJ's place and purpose in the contemporary penal landscape is entirely clear:

> Conventional justice systems see offending primarily and often even exclusively as a violation of the interests of the state and decisions about how it should be responded to are made by professionals representing the state. In contrast, [RJ] returns decisions about how best to deal with the offence to those most affected – victims, offenders and their 'communities of care' – and gives primacy to their interests. Thus the state no longer has a monopoly over decision making: the principal decision makers are the parties themselves. (Morris 2002: 598)

Normative understandings such as this have a very clear view of the meaning and significance of RJ: it stands firmly in opposition to what is regarded as the outmoded formal processes of justice and, by implication and extension, to the 'new punitiveness' (Garland 1996, 2001; Pratt *et al.* 2005) which has emerged and taken root in many modern societies (particularly the main English-speaking countries) over the same period in which RJ has emerged. This phenomenon also allows for a considerably more expressive set of penal arrangements than had previously been the case, although of a qualitatively different kind from that to be found in RJ. Instead of RJ's emphasis on healing and forgiveness, it gives vent to much more punitive demands, such as expressions of outrage that feed their way into political demands for more and longer prison sentences, and demands for the 'right' for ordinary citizens to be informed about the release of sex offenders from prison. Sometimes it simply manifests itself in vigilante activities, where community groups take action against suspected crime or deviance in the absence of any action from the state, or what is judged to be insufficient action from the state, or, indeed, where the state has lost its legitimacy.

For most RJ advocates, its emergence in the same period as this new punitiveness seems to have been entirely coincidental: 'RJ is sometimes equated with community or popular justice, which is in turn, equated with vigilantism', writes Morris (2002: 609), who goes on to assure us that 'it is true that some forms of community justice can be repressive, retributive, hierarchical and patriarchal. But these values are fundamentally at odds with the defining values of [RJ] and cannot therefore be part of it.' Again, such normative understandings of RJ allow for no possible linkage between the concurrent emergence of these two distinct forms of expressive justice and punishment. Instead, and in fundamental opposition to such excesses, RJ stands out as a beacon of light. Indeed, in much of the RJ literature, and in many of the conventions and conferences held to discuss it, there is something of a crusading, evangelical fervour. It has taken on the identity of some inherent, self-evident, taken-for-granted 'good' – a new form of justice that acts in opposition to the inherently bad 'old justice' (Daly 2002) that it is intended to surpass and replace. We should note, though, that this is not the first time such a thing has happened in the development of modern penality. Earlier criminal justice reform movements assumed similar 'divine' qualities, with their advocates taking on evangelical roles. That is to say, their reform initiatives were projected as beyond reproach, shining out against the darkness of the unreformed areas of criminal justice they challenged; indeed, criticism is seen almost as sacrilege, put about by those on whom its light has yet to shine.

The problem is, though, that such evangelism can leave a movement's followers blind to its problems and dilemmas. Tony Platt (1969: 141) revealed these tendencies at work among the late nineteenth- century child savers in the USA. In relation to the operation of Cook County juvenile court in its first year, the claim was made that 'it has saved hundreds from lives of shame and crime; taken hundreds from homeless life or from so-called homes that were utterly unfit and placed them in institutions or the care of societies to find them suitable homes.' The belief in 'doing good' allowed such reform movements to develop practices that were coercive and controlling and informed by racial and class bias. It was thus noted that 'the [juvenile] court does not confine its attention to just the particular offence which brought the child to its notice [...] a boy who comes in for playing ball on the street may be committed to a school because he is found to have habits of loafing, stealing or gambling which cannot be corrected outside' (*ibid.*: 142).

Similarly with the rise of the borstal[2] movement in the interwar period in Britain. Magistrates and judges regularly made comments such as the following from 1929 when sentencing young offenders to be detained in such institutions: 'Borstal is not a prison at all. It is merely a teaching and training institution. These boys are no more in prison than army recruits can be said to be in prison' (quoted in Hood 1965: 31). Similarly, Head of the Prison Commission Sir Alexander Paterson (1932: 60) elegiacally wrote that borstal training

> regards a lad as a living organism, having its secret of life and
> motive-power within, adapting itself in external conduct to the

surroundings of the moment, but undergoing no permanent organic change merely as a result of outside pressure [...] the task is not to break or knead him into shape, but to stimulate some power within to regulate conduct aright, to insinuate a preference for the good and the clean, to make him use his life well, so that he himself and not others will save him from waste.

Amidst such evangelical fervour, it should not surprise us to read that

> when the Reader of Shrewsbury said he didn't believe in borstal, he was 'spoken to by the Home Office' on the subject, and criticized by the Home Secretary: 'that is a serious remark to be made by a judge in public with regard to these institutions, which with the full assent of the community are being administered in the best interests of the community'. (*ibid*.: 36)

We now know, of course, that borstal never lived up to such expectations (see Hood 1965; Bottoms and McClintock 1974; Behan 1959). At the time, however, such was the power of the evangelism surrounding it that the reality of institutionalization, the injustice of being institutionalized for several years on the basis that this would be 'good' for the individual concerned, was lost on borstal devotees.

From the 1980s, we find similar trends in relation to the growth of the alternative to custody movement in England and the United States. The promise of saving (mainly young) offenders from custody could lead to extraordinary machinations of control and surveillance as in the following English juvenile justice example from the mid-1980s:

> The scheme involves very intense surveillance of the young people, who would have to contact the project six to eight times a day. The service would be run on a twenty-four hour basis, seven days a week – there will be a centre with beds on the premises for residential stays. A contract will be entered into with the family and young person [...] the project worker will have to agree to their activities during the day [...] if the young person fails to comply with the rules laid down by the project, sanctions may be applied. This could involve compulsory recall to the unit on a residential basis. (Quoted by Pratt 1987: 157)

As Cohen (1985: 71) wrote, what was really taking place was

the development of programmes which simply recreate the institutional domains under a different name, regimes which simulate or mimic the very custodial features they set out to replace. Even when the security trade-off is less important, community treatment is often just semantic trivia for traditional programmes whose physical location in an urban area is the sole basis for identifying the programme as community based.

RJ now seems to be the latest example of this evangelical criminology. Since it emerged in the late 1980s it has tended to be a phenomenon dominated by policy and practice issues (Ashworth 2002): it has been a grass-roots movement that has gained momentum with the support of liberal intellectuals, as well as strategically placed civil servants with appeal to sections of both the indigenous rights and feminist social movements (Daly 2002). By and large, it has not been government imposed (Braithwaite 2000). It therefore assumes an 'oppositional' standing, a challenge to the status quo which has doubtless added to the crusading zeal of many of those associated with it. Not surprisingly, RJ, with its decentred framework and its emphasis on healing communities and individuals can be seen as a powerful antidote to any such counter-movements towards 'gulags Western style' (Christie 2000) that are embedded in the new punitiveness. This has meant that RJ has been largely immune from critical analysis (other than that of the 'how to make it better' kind). It has also meant that crucial questions relating to it have been focused around such matters as 'does it work?' and best- practice issues relating to how it can work even better. As such, it has come into existence and still largely remains the property of its own 'true believers'. Their faith has then been fuelled and sustained by the development of a body of knowledge relating to the historical origins of RJ, claiming that it has some natural, long-standing place in the justice arrangements of any and all societies – with differing modalities of justice thereby seen as illegitimate usurpers.

'Origin myths'

Let us examine some of these claims. Braithwaite (1999: 1), for example, writes that '[RJ] has been the dominant model of criminal justice throughout most of human history for all the world's peoples', citing as evidence for his claim 'traditions from the ancient Arab, Greek and Roman civilizations, [and] the restorative approach of the public assemblies (moots) of the Germanic peoples who swept across Europe after the fall of Rome.' This is the most grandiose of such claims, made by the foremost of RJ scholars. For others, RJ represents a replay of 'much older biblical forms of justice' (Consedine 1995), or it represents 'a reactivation of indigenous justice practices, to be found amongst a range of peoples – the Aboriginals, the Inuit, and the native Indians of North and South America' (Weitekamp 1999: 93), to which we can also throw in the South Pacific peoples as well – the New Zealand Maori and the pre-colonial inhabitants of Tonga, Fiji and Samoa (Consedine 1995).

Historical reality seems rather different, however. Let us examine, for example, the case of the Germanic peoples in the Dark Ages. It would seem that they did indeed settle their disputes in public assemblies, as the noted legal historian Berman (1983) informs us. These *prima facie* bear some resemblance to the non-judicial, community justice approach favoured in RJ. However, there seems to have been little that was restorative about these settlements. Apart from the penalties of death and outlawry (itself an effective death penalty) which they could impose, which thus seem to put them well beyond the compass of RJ, they involved offenders and their kin paying fixed financial penalties that were commensurate to the amount of harm or damage done (if we are looking for modern-day parallels, then this was a form of justice that would seem to have more to do with just deserts theory):

> So much for the loss of a leg, so much for an eye, so much if the victim was a slave, so much if he was a freeman, so much if he were a priest. The four front teeth were worth six shillings each, the teeth next to them four, the other teeth one, thumbnails, forefingers, middle fingers, ring fingers, little fingers and their respective fingernails were all distinguished, and a separate price, called a *bot*, was set for each. (*ibid.*: 56)

Criminal justice in Roman society seems to provide only the starkest of contrasts between its punishment practices and the ideals and aspirations of RJ. Not only were penalties strictly differentiated according to one's place in the social structure, but they could include being thrown to wild animals, being condemned to 'the fork' (that is being bound to 'the infertile tree' and then beaten to death or crucified), vivicombustion (being burned alive) and decapitation. Women were put to death by strangulation after those who were virgins were deflowered by their executioners. Non-capital penalties included forced labour in the mines and deportation. Penalties for slaves were even more ferocious and capricious: if a slave killed their master, for example, then there was an assumption that every slave in the household was an accomplice. They could be questioned under torture and put to death. As Bauman (1996: 163) writes, 'the bottom line is that there were very few bleeding hearts in Ancient Rome.'

As regards Ancient Greece, it does indeed seem that private citizens were encouraged to settle disputes out of court – indeed, there was no official public prosecution. At the same time levels of informal social control, in relation to which gossip and rumour played a significant part, were extensive features in controlling deviance which certainly Braithwaite (1989) has argued should have an important role to play in the development of RJ today. We can thus find undeniable resonances between these particular pre-modern justice arrangements and RJ. However, there was no guarantee that something approximate to RJ would be the only product; instead, these arrangements could lead to activities that were far from RJ's ideal. Under these possibilities of public participation in the administration of justice and punishment, something rather more like vigilantism was often the result. Instances of self-help included:

> The arrest of common criminals and other designated offenders, intervention to rescue a free person from being seized as a slave, the confinement – sometimes even the killing – of an adulterer, distraint upon goods, and the expulsion from one's property of an interloper claiming to possess it. In embarking on any of these potentially violent acts, one normally sought the assistance of kin, friends, or neighbours. (Hunter 1994: 48)

At the same time, many penalties were administered in public in the presence of crowds of onlookers whose approval (or otherwise) was part of the proceedings. These included the whipping and torture of slaves, the execution of common criminals and the ignominious exposure of certain offenders in the stocks.

Again, historical reality seems rather more complex than the claims made by RJ scholars when we examine the justice practices of indigenous societies such as Canadian Aboriginals. For some tribes, penalties were usually decided upon before a 'council of the villagers':

> Minor offences were punishable in the same way as murder, but for refractory individuals who continually disturbed the tranquillity of the community there loomed in the background outlawry, which deprived them of all legal protection and permitted any one to kill them at sight. On the whole, public opinion and the

> knowledge that the entire village would be held responsible for wrong-doing seem to have proved adequate safeguards.

So wrote Diamond Jenness (1932: 138), the renowned New Zealand anthropologist. Again, then, we find undeniable resonances between justice in the pre-modern world and contemporary RJ: public opinion, local knowledge, gossip, decentred proceedings in the form of a village council and so on. Having said this, though, there was no *necessity* that such forms of dispute resolution would emerge in pre-modern indigenous societies (*cf.* Johnstone 2002): these were only one of a range of possibilities that evolved. Thus Jenness (1932: 125) also wrote of the justice practices of migratory tribes such as the Eskimos. Here:

> Law and order depended solely on the strength of public opinion [...] persuasion and physical force were the only methods of arbitrating disputes, social outlawry or physical violence the only means of punishing infractions of the moral code or offences against the welfare of the band or tribe. The band took cognizance of crimes that were believed to endanger the whole community [...] it left the individual families, with the help perhaps of near kinsfolk, to find their own redress for all other offences, from theft even to murder.

At the same time, it was a system of justice that only addressed the particular social relationships of the tribe and the way in which these ordered behaviour within it; outside of its parameters, 'strangers, even people of a neighbouring tribe might be robbed or killed with impunity; they had no rights, unless they married into a band or placed themselves under the protection of some powerful family.' Such fragile communities might thus ignore disputes occurring *within* them to avoid any further disturbance to what social coherence there was; at the same time, it was permitted to settle disputes *external* to them by violence, since any stranger was a potential threat to the precarious security they had.

What can we learn from these brief glimpses of justice and punishment in the pre-modern world? They certainly show that the claims about RJ having its roots there are at best tenuous – and are frequently quite mistaken. As Tony Bottoms (2003: 88) has written, such claims are both 'overstated and decontextualized'; they seem to be based on either highly selective readings of criminal justice history or, alternatively, an uncritical acceptance of historical claims made by other RJ scholars. Perhaps it is the case, though, as Daly (2002: 57) has astutely noted, that rather than intending these claims to be authoritative histories of justice, their authors are in fact 'constructing origin myths' – which then lend themselves to the idealism and evangelicism that have come to be associated with the RJ social movement: without them, its status and purity would be put in jeopardy. We can thus learn more from these claims about what has sustained this latest round of evangelical criminology, than about the historical origins of RJ; however, what we also learn from an examination of historical scholarship is the relationship between state formation and decentred modalities of justice, whatever the form they take. Essentially, as in the above examples, we are likely to find these in conjunction with the presence of *weak or absent or non-functioning central states*.

Even so, there is no essentialized, natural quality to the particular forms of justice and punishment that then emerge under these circumstances. Aside from the retributive rather than restorative nature of the proceedings in Dark Ages Germany and the notion of collective responsibility on which they were based which would surely be an affront to most modern societies, it is clear that they were necessary to prevent private warfare taking place in the absence of any authority to this effect from a strong central state (Berman 1983). Such modes of dispute resolution also served the necessary purpose of setting the boundaries for acceptable standards of behaviour within these communities when the state itself was unable to do this. The dispute resolution practices of Canadian Eskimo communities emerged because of fear of unending blood feuds and the capacity this would have to tear communities apart (Jenness 1932). And in relation to Greece, Hunter (1994: 187) writes that 'the Athenian state had no monopoly on the legitimate use of force nor for that matter was it solely responsible for the resolution of conflicts and disputes. Instead, individual and group self-regulation coexisted with order imposed by the central authority.' Overall, in these societies, the absence of a centralized state (or the presence of a weak, not fully developed one) and its monopolistic control of the administration of justice and the power to punish inevitably necessitated that such matters would reside to at least some degree with local citizens and community groups, who would then resolve them according to local cultural values, belief systems and power structures. The end products were very diverse, offering no guarantees that productive, reintegrative forms of justice similar to RJ would be the result.

Punishment and social structure in modern society

In the subsequent transition from the pre-modern to the modern world, such diversity faded away. During the course of the nineteenth and twentieth centuries in particular, as the central state grew in power, authority and influence, so the necessary conditions for the various forms of community justice, of notions of kinship responsibilities and other forms of public involvement in penal affairs that had marked justice and punishment in the pre-modern world declined. This took place in conjunction with the state assuming monopolistic control of dispute resolution procedures and penal arrangements: these came to be administered through its own bureaucracies rather than through local communities. Kinship responsibilities towards offenders and victims declined not simply with the fragmentation of the *gemeinschaft* communities in which this had been possible, but as a result of the state's new ownership of such problems: it prosecuted and punished individuals for the crimes they had committed against it. The pre-modern carnival of punishment that ranged from the bloody spectacle of public executions to local demonstrations of social disapproval such as the charivari[3] disappeared as punishment became centralized and standardized. During the course of the nineteenth century, the prison became the most important penal sanction, replacing these and at the same time creating a physical and administrative gulf between the bureaucratic authorities which now governed this realm and the general public.

It was the former who now began to dominate penal affairs, as we see in the following English examples. Overviewing this period, Rose (1961: 277) wrote:

> The influence of professional and technical advisers upon the departments of state is, of course, long standing. The prison system owes much to Sir Joshua Jebb, the engineer, and to a number of prison doctors and chaplains. Within the last thirty years the influence of psychiatrists has made itself felt, and recently the appointment of a Statistical Adviser and the setting up of the Home Office Research Unit has brought the statisticians' influence to bear.

These tendencies had reached their zenith in the post-1945 period in most modern societies and the commitment to state welfarism that then ensued. With the emphasis now on reform through treatment and rehabilitation, Mannheim (1946: 228) wrote that 'criminology will hail the day when science comes to its succour with all its methods for diagnosis and treatment of the socially unacceptable.' For Grunhut (1948: 471–2), the rehabilitative ethos would be put into effect by 'the rise of social services [...] the future of penal reform is linked with these wider efforts in the scientific field as well as in practical social work': in other words, the development of penal policy would be underpinned by the confluence of state bureaucracies and scientific expertise. Mannheim (1946: 228) was also aware, however, that 'it is no use denying that in its practical consequences, individualization of treatment, that dominating principle of modern penology, is bound to clash with the traditional requirements of justice as understood by the man in the street.'

However, by now, any input to penal affairs from the general public was looked upon disparagingly by the elites in control of criminal policy: Sir Lionel Fox (1952: 137), Head of the Prison Commission, wrote that 'one cannot be unaware that the body of assumptions underlying the common talk of common people and directing their praise and praise alone are not in these matters, the assumptions on which contemporary prison administration is based.' At a time of growing public concern about prison escapes, Sir John Simon, Under Secretary at the Home Office, stated:

> The public should accept something less than one hundred per cent security. Protection of this standard, or something like it, could no doubt be brought about by the strategic confinement of prisoners by loading them with fetters and manacles and irons and so on. No-one today would countenance such a thing. It would not only inflict injury on the prisoners, but would debase and brutalize the society which perpetrated such infamy. (Report of the Director of Penal Services 1957: 8)

One of the consequences of this arrangement of penal power that was concentrated around governments and their civil servants and other elite representatives was that it could (although it need not necessarily) lead to a penality that was largely anonymous and remote, and which the growing power of bureaucratic forces shaped, defined and made understandable: this had become a particular characteristic of the main English-speaking countries by the 1970s (Pratt 2002). It was an arrangement which ignored victims and which was capable of inflicting great brutalities and privations on the recipients of punishment – particularly prisoners. Such matters could then go largely unchecked or unheeded by a public whose formal detachment from penal affairs over the course of the previous two centuries had eventually led to a general indifference to such matters. This was only periodically shaken off by scandals that might emerge from time to time (prisoners being punished too much or too little, for example, in line with the general public expectations about how they should be treated in such institutions), only for it then to dissipate. It should also be remembered, however, that this arrangement of power also brought considerable reform to the penal system: usually well ahead of public opinion and frequently in spite of it. Probably the best example to illustrate this point relates to the abolition of the death penalty in most of the English-speaking countries during the 1960s and 1970s. As one contributor to the British parliamentary debate on these matters in 1965 explained:

> I doubt very much whether at the moment public opinion is in favour of the change but I doubt also whether at any time during the last one hundred years a plebiscite would have carried any of the great penal reforms that have been made [...] there are occasions when this House is right even if the public may not at that moment be of that opinion. (Hansard [536] 2083, 10 February 1965)

Furthermore, most governments during this postwar period were normatively committed to pursuing a well-known path towards reform and liberalization; those countries (particularly the Scandinavian ones) which punished the least and the most humanely were thought to be leading the way along this route. In these respects, the New Zealand Justice Minister wrote, after a visit by his Swedish counterpart, that 'although a comparison between what has been achieved in Sweden['s prisons] and in New Zealand gives us no cause for shame, there is much that we can still learn from that country both in measures and in spirit' (Report of the Department of Justice 1968: 4). At the same time, it was axiomatic that under these arrangements of penal power, policy development reflected the aims and aspirations of its elite advisers who were a long way removed from public understandings and aspirations of criminal justice and punishment. By the same token, there could be no approved community participation, and no public imprint left on penal affairs. In other words, then, the model of the Keynsian state that rose to prominence in the postwar period (Braithwaite 2000), and which revolved around public sector provision of services, precluded the development of RJ and the other forms of expressive, emotive punishment characteristic of today's penal environment.

Justice and punishment in the post-welfare period

What has since happened to bring about this transition? I think there are two decisive but contradictory factors at work here, which have the effect of pushing the possibilities of punishment into the diverse trajectories we can now find.

Demands for less government and more individual choice

These are the first factors, and they emerged out of a growing sense of dissatisfaction with the postwar welfare state and began to gather force during the 1970s. The great public bureaucracies that had become so powerful during this period were criticized for their remoteness, expense and inefficiency, and in particular their inability to solve the social problems and issues for which they had assumed responsibility. Indeed, one of the reasons for the success of neoliberal politics since the late 1970s is the way in which governments have acknowledged this and have been prepared to develop alternative modes of governance that are no longer privileged around the idea of a strong central state working at one with its own bureaucratic organizations: politicians such as Margaret Thatcher have been prepared to speak to the anxieties and aspirations of 'ordinary people', simultaneously bypassing government departments – procedures which have since come to be solidified in the form of accepted acknowledgements (through Citizen's Charters and the like) that these will now be addressed (rather than being deflected by bureaucrats). This has also been reflected in the willingness of the state to move to both private and voluntary sectors as providers of public services. At the same time, the emphasis has been on the empowerment of the public amid a much greater affinity between politicians and the public mood, with simultaneous attempts to make government bureaucracies more transparent and accountable. In relation to criminal justice, there has been a corresponding decline in the prominence of the elite expert of the welfare era (see Pratt and Clark 2005 in relation to New Zealand) and their replacement with other influential community-based pressure groups, pointing to new directions, setting new boundaries for punishment. As a result, many of the assumptions that had dominated modernist penal thought and which had acted as the audits and safeguards of penal development in that era have been challenged.

Thus, in the post-1970s period, we find the rising influence of new social movements, frequently coalescing around single-issue politics and demanding that their 'rights' (no longer their channels to welfare) be acknowledged and addressed: in particular, for our purposes here, victims' rights groups who were in the forefront of this shift in power and authority, and ethnic rights groups for whom, in post-colonial societies in particular, the existing criminal justice system seemed both culturally inappropriate and institutionally racist. In effect, the shift away from central state governance that neoliberal polity brought about then allowed these and other new sources of influence to gain momentum.

In these respects, as Braithwaite (2000: 227) has written, 'the state that has gone furthest in winding back Keynsianism, New Zealand, has been the state that has gone furthest with the new social movement for [RJ].' This is no coincidence – the two are directly related. The retreat from the Keynsian welfare state model of governance began in 1984 in that country (see Pratt and Clark 2005). What then allowed for the breakthrough for RJ was the way in which the existing welfare-oriented juvenile justice system was seen to be failing its indigenous Maori community (Department of Social Welfare 1985), particularly in the aftermath of the publication of one portentous research report (Jackson 1987), which situated criminal justice concerns within broader issues relating to Maori governance and autonomy. An initial proposal to introduce a 'justice model' design was rejected as being monocultural and insufficiently responsive to Maori needs and concerns. The subsequent paradigmatic legislation – the Children, Young Persons and their Families Act 1989 – attempted to rectify these matters: in particular, by decentring justice proceedings and by making some sort of reconciliation between offender and victim (usually with the payment of goods or services from the former to the latter with an apology[4]) the main focus of the justice 'event', with friends/supporters/ extended family of both parties in attendance. Importantly, then, New Zealand was no longer looking exclusively outwards for leadership in criminal justice reform, but was now prepared to turn to new sources of influence, such as the Maori community, for guidance. While this certainly did not herald a 'return' to Maori justice (apart from anything else, its traditional sanctions of death, banishment, shaming and plunder had disappeared), it certainly incorporated a significant injection of Maori ideas, sentiments and values in relation to the administration of (juvenile) justice and the dispensation of punishment.

Coinciding with the publication of Braithwaite's (1989) massively influential *Crime, Shame and Reintegration*, the New Zealand legislation helped to provide the momentum for new overtures in criminal justice in other post-colonial societies such as Australia and Canada in the early 1990s. As we know, these ideas have since spread remarkably in the international criminal justice arena. We thus see a variety of developments across jurisdictions at the level of the local state, as a result of governments being prepared to open up the delivery of services to different providers in attempts to be more responsive to the new influences on penal development. Overall, though, if in post-colonial societies much of the early momentum for RJ grew out of indigenous rights issues, in countries such as England it seems to have built onto already existing bureaucratic arrangements to streamline criminal justice and make it more efficient – particularly in relation to the development of elaborate pre-court cautioning practices (certainly for juveniles). Nonetheless, attempts to make victims and offenders central to these processes with offers of reparation and apology to resolve the harm done have been established in the form of youth offending panels. As Crawford and Newburn (2002: 479) write:

> There are several important 'restorative' and 'reintegrative' aspects to the new provisions. [The panels] adopt a conference-type approach to decision making that is intended to be both inclusive and party-centred [...] as such, they mark a significant shift away from a court-based judicial model in which the parties are represented rather than speak for themselves.

Demands for more government and tougher, authoritative punishments

Second, however, this retraction of central state governance coincided with a more general unravelling of deeply embedded structures of modern society which had previously provided a sense of solidity and identity: party political affiliations, union membership, family life, tenured employment, church membership and so on all began to fall apart (Beck 1992; Bauman 2001; Fukuyama 1995). The breaking up of previously secure, wide-ranging social interdependencies that had been developed through these institutions has since led to a preoccupation with new areas of danger, vulnerability and uncertainty. Risks increasingly seem incalculable and unpredictable – indeed, the very act of providing more personal choice at the expense of less central government direction adds to the sense of uncertainty and insecurity. In such ways, a large-scale insatiable sense of fear and anxiety has been created over this period, with a yearning for security and certainty, which always seems elusive as new risks and dangers reveal themselves.[5] Paradoxically, at a time when governmental authority has been contracting and it no longer claims to have the solution to all the difficulties we are likely to face, there have also been demands for a strong, central government that, by reaffirming its own authority, can provide tangible remedies to what seem to be our biggest dangers, particularly those which seem to be the most easily solvable – crime and punishment issues. This is particularly so when common-sense knowledge, frequently articulated through new social movements and pressure groups and based on anecdotes, memories and folklore, begins to displace scientific rationalities and more traditional expertise as the mode of knowledge through which such matters are formally addressed. Now, if interdependencies have become more diffuse and insubstantial as a result of the social changes of the last twenty years or so which have undermined security, they are also able to reconfigure and unify against common, easily identifiable enemies who seem to put us further at risk.

Thus, as officially reported crime escalated during the 1970s and 1980s, so it came to be represented as a problem out of control, beyond the existing modalities of governance and of increasing alarm to the general public. Again, as such matters were opened up to political debate and scrutiny rather than left to be quietly administered by the penal bureaucracies, so sentencing and parole practices and the efficiency of the judicial authorities began to be regularly challenged, revealing the gulf that existed between court-imposed sentences and the reality of prison terms after parole, remission etc. had been taken into account. This only gave further grounds for public suspicion and distrust of the bureaucratic organizations which had managed these developments. It was around such scepticism and disenchantment that popular movements such as 'Truth in Sentencing' began to emerge, rather slowly at first in the late 1970s, but later with gathering speed and momentum, until this slogan, with others, was turned into a populist rallying call against a supposedly out-of-touch liberal bureaucracy and judiciary.

Now, the formal language of punishment reflects the way in which expressive and emotive sentiments characteristic of the general public are able to influence policy development. Instead of a predominance of talk of reform and rehabilitation (which bore the stamp of the influence of liberal elites within the bureaucratic establishment), we become much more familiar with the emotive, unrestrained language of 'three strikes', 'zero tolerance', 'life means life' and so on, language deliberately designed to incorporate public anger and resentment – and particularly aimed at those criminals whose risks seem incalculable and who constitute the greatest dangers to us. Groups such as 'sexual predators' are no longer thought to be in need of scientific scrutiny and examination – instead, they become fantastic, irredeemable devils who have to be degraded and then excluded from the rest of us for as long as possible. Previous public indifference and diffidence to such matters thus gives way to demands for a much greater input to penal affairs.

In this way, we find the use of political mechanisms such as plebiscites and referenda which provide for more direct injections of public sentiment on policy development, sometimes to the exclusion of bureaucratic and expert opinion altogether (Zimring 1996; Pratt and Clark 2005). In the New Zealand general election of 1999, there was a 91.75 per cent vote in favour of the following Citizens Initiated Referendum: 'Should there be a reform of our justice system placing greater emphasis on the needs of victims, providing restitution and compensation for them and imposing minimum sentences and hard labour for all serious violent offences?' Notwithstanding its inherent contradictions and inconsistencies, and its implicit breaches of human rights conventions, the referendum was then heavily influential in the development of subsequent penal legislation in 2002 which, in particular, prescribed and encouraged the use of much longer prison terms for some groups of offenders. Indeed, immediately on the passing of this legislation, the Justice Minister telephoned the organizer of the referendum to congratulate him on its success (Pratt and Clark 2005). Thus, as an example of the volatile and contradictory nature of the penal changes that are likely to emanate from this post-1970s reconfiguration of penal power (O'Malley 1999), Braithwaite might also have added that the state that has gone furthest in winding back Keynsianism, New Zealand, in addition to going furthest with the social movement for RJ, now also has the second highest rate of imprisonment in the OECD – 179 per 100,000 of population, with the actual number of prisoners nearly trebling since 1985.

Nonetheless, the security offered by such growth in prison numbers may not be sufficient to contain the human sentiments that have been unleashed. As a weak and fragmented state loses its monopolistic hold on the power to punish, or where the state's authority was particularly underdeveloped, then we are likely to find the resurgence of a more expressive, emotive penality, readily facilitated by the shifts in governance towards greater public involvement in penal affairs and enhanced community participation. This can lead to the reactivation of readily available local cultural heritages, and the subsequent shaping of new penal sanctions by them: if this allows for the development of RJ on the one hand, on the other it also allows for the return of public shaming punishments in parts of the USA and Australia, and the distribution of naming and shaming posters around neighbourhoods in New Zealand, which alert the community to troublemakers, ex-prisoners and so on. Where there are no formal penal outlets available to soak up and assuage community sentiments, then extra legal penal activity may be the product. This was vividly demonstrated in the summer of 2000 in Britain when anti-paedophile vigilante activities spontaneously erupted across that country. It is surely significant that they took place there because of the presence of a strong, unified central penal bureaucracy in that country; and because, as well, the British government had refused to extend provision for community notification registers to the general public. With no legitimate outlet for their punitive sentiments, they found expression in vigilantism. Clearly, vigilantism is not the same thing as RJ, as Morris (2002) above assured us. The problem is, though, that vigilantism, along with similar forms of 'community justice', shares the same penal DNA as RJ.

Prospects for RJ?

Where, then, does this leave the prospects for RJ? As noted, evangelical criminal justice reform movements in the past have since been found to have a range of undesirable, unintended consequences. RJ may have as well, as some scholars have begun to demonstrate.[6] In addition, there is little consideration given to the price that has to be paid for RJ. Indeed, it has been so rapturously received that there appears to be no cost at all to it, only benefit. Essentially, however, its presence means an end to the penal configuration characteristic of much of the modern period which had precluded its existence. Is this a high or a low price to pay? Whatever the answer to this question, it is undeniable that some of the most significant and humane penal reforms of that period would never have been passed if there had been the level of community input to policy development that there is in some jurisdictions today.

Then there is a further issue: how will RJ flourish in the void that has been left by the redrawn state boundaries? This political process created the opportunity for RJ to emerge but the problem is that the whole space that has been left is open for contestation. In these respects, Braithwaite (2000: 233) is incorrect when he writes that '[RJ] founders when the welfare state is not there to support it.' On the contrary, it owes its existence to *the decline* of the welfare state, and the decline of the particular arrangements of penal power characteristic of much of the modern period, which denied it, as well as the excesses of contemporary penality, an existence. In an era when so much importance is attached to the emblem of RJ – the apology between victim and offender – this in itself is indicative of the way in which crime conflicts are no longer the exclusive property of the state: there is a form of private justice going on as well, between the two central players to the crime committed, as they try to reach some satisfactory resolution between themselves. Even so, such developments take place in the vortex that now exists beyond the restricted regions of state bureaucracies. As it is, beyond more narrowly drawn demarcation lines of state authority, it is possible to see penal arrangements bearing the imprint of a range of competing social movements and sets of ideas, reflecting shifting positionings for power in local jurisdictions and the impact of differing cultural traditions. However, the empowerment of the public at a time when the sense of threat and insecurity are heightened as a result of law and order concerns seems likely to balance the scales in favour of the new punitive trends, in a penal realm that has lost its sense of stability, permanence and direction.

In these respects, there is surely the danger of 'capture'. As Crawford and Newburn (2002) have remarked in relation to England, there is the danger that RJ might simply become one element of a much stronger, coercive body designed to more efficiently control deviant youth. The very imprecise nature of what RJ actually is lends itself to such possibilities. In New Zealand, the Labour government in 2004 introduced the Prisoners and Victims Claims Bill. This had been prompted (amid much public outrage) after a group of prisoners had successfully sued the Department of Corrections for human rights abuses they had experienced while subjected to prison conditions equivalent to those in a US 'supermax'. The legislation allows victims of crime and their families to sue ex-prisoners for financial compensation for up to ten years after their release should they come by any windfall (for example, a winning lottery ticket or even the assets built up by pursuing a successful career after prison[7]). The Justice Minister declared that this was restorative justice: making offenders recompense their victims.

This is no prediction of catastrophe, however (O'Malley 2000). Very many RJ strategies are indeed making important inroads in transforming both formal and informal local justice practices, avoiding both the unresponsive bureaucratic detachment associated with the former and the repressive brutality that can emerge from the latter as, for example, McEvoy and Mika (2002: 556) have demonstrated in relation to Northern Ireland where RJ has mitigated against the punishment violence of sectarian authorities. Equally, Clifford Shearing (2001) has shown with regard to South Africa that it is possible to develop models of interaction between the state and its poorest communities which maximize people's ability to take control over the direction of their own lives without the original programmes then being swallowed by the state infrastructure. Does this mean that it might be possible to have, after all, a strong, modern democratic state where RJ flourishes? My answer to this question is to suggest that RJ flourishes in these two examples because in the former, the modern democratic state had effectively failed or at least had no legitimacy in a good part of the sectarian communities; in the latter, the post-apartheid state was being newly constructed and could accommodate this and other new initiatives, in the absence of already existing bureaucratic impediments elsewhere. What we can learn from these developments, what we can learn from pre-modern forms of justice and from the reconstituted New Zealand state, is that the opportunity for RJ to become institutionalized itself occurs when the central state is weak. And in such societies today it flourishes only as one segment of a much broader reconfiguration of penal responses to crime.

Notes

1   See particularly Blagg (1997), Daly (2002).
2   Borstal (named after a prison of that name) was introduced to the English penal system in 1900 as a special form of prison treatment for young offenders between the ages of 16 and 21.
3   A form of highly theatrical local community action against particular individuals that involved shaming or humiliating them (often for adultery or some other breach of public morals). See Pratt (2002: 16–17).
4   Once the issue to be resolved is between the offender and victim, rather than the state, the apology becomes a particularly appropriate way to resolve the matter, since once given and accepted it can convey the important message to the offender that they still belong to the local community: 'apologies are intimately related to the problematics of membership status of one kind or another, whatever else is at stake' (Tavuchis 1991: 40).
5   Even the presence of RJ can add to the sense of risk, insecurity and disillusionment: 'Youth justice system failing [...] two thirds of young criminals dealt with by family group conferences reoffend, and one in five end up behind bars within three years, research shows [...] about one quarter of victims who attended a family group conference did not even get an apology from the offender [...] the father of a victim said the family group conference he attended was 'a complete waste of bloody time''' (*The Dominion*, 4 October 2002: 3).
6   See, for example, Ashworth (2002) in relation to human rights issues and Levrant et al. (1999) in relation to the lack of effect on recidivism.
7   At the time of writing (January 2005), the bill is likely to become law in April 2005.

References

Ashworth, A. (2002) 'Responsibilities, rights and restorative justice', *British Journal of Criminology*, 42: 578–95.

Bauman, R. (1996) *Crime and Punishment in Ancient Rome*. London: Routledge.

Bauman, Z. (2001) *Liquid Modernity*. Cambridge: Polity Press.

Beck, U. (1992) *Risk Society*. Oxford: Basil Blackwell.

Behan, B. (1959) *Borstal Boy*. London: Hutchinson.

Berman, H. (1983) *Law and Revolution*. Cambridge, MA: Harvard University Press.

Blagg, H. (1997) 'A just measure of shame', *British Journal of Criminology*, 37: 481–501.

Bottoms, A. E. (2003) 'Some sociological reflections on restorative justice', in A. von Hirsch, J. Roberts, A. E. Bottoms, and M. Schiff (eds), *Restorative Justice and Criminal Justice: Competing or Reconcilable Paradigms?* Oxford: Hart Publishing, pp. 79–114.

Bottoms, A. E. and McClintock, F. (1974) *Criminals Coming of Age*. London: Heinemann.

Braithwaite, J. (1989) *Crime, Shame and Reintegration*. Cambridge: Cambridge University Press.

Braithwaite, J. (1996) 'Restorative justice and a better future', in J. Braithwaite (ed.), *Regulation, Crime, Freedom*. Aldershot: Dartmouth, pp. 317–39.

Braithwaite, J. (1999) 'Restorative justice: assessing optimistic and pessimistic accounts', in M. Tonry (ed.), *Crime and Justice: A Review of Research*, 25: 1–127.

Braithwaite, J. (2000) 'The new regulatory state and the transformation of criminology', *British Journal of Criminology*, 40: 222–38.

Christie, N. (2000) *Crime Control as Industry*. Oxford: Martin Robertson.

Cohen, S. (1985) *Visions of Social Control*. Cambridge: Polity Press.

Consedine, J. (1995) *Restorative Justice: Healing the Effects of Crime*. Christchurch: Ploughshares Publications.

Crawford, A. and Newburn, T. (2002) 'Recent developments in restorative justice for young people in England and Wales', *British Journal of Criminology*, 42: 476–95.

Daly, K. (2002) 'Restorative justice: the real story', *Punishment and Society*, 4: 55–79.

Department of Social Welfare (1985) *Daybreak*. Wellington: Department of Social Welfare.

Fox, L. (1952) *The English Prison and Borstal Systems*. London: Routledge & Kegan Paul.

Fukuyama, F. (1995) *Trust: The Social Virtues and the Creation of Prosperity*. New York: Free Press.

Garland, D. (1996) 'The limits of the sovereign state', *British Journal of Criminology*, 36: 445–71.

Garland, D. (2001) *The Culture of Control*. Oxford: Oxford University Press.

Grunhut, M. (1948) *Penal Reform*. Oxford: Clarendon Press.

Hood, R. (1965) *Borstal Re-Assessed*. London: Heinemann.

Hunter, V. (1994) *Policing Athens*. Princeton, NJ: Princeton University Press.

Jackson, M. (1987) *The Maori and the Criminal Justice System*. Wellington: Law Commission.

Jenness, D. (1932) *Indians of Canada*. Toronto: Toronto University Press.

Johnstone, G. (2002) *Restorative Justice*. Cullompton: Willan.

Levrant, S., Cullen, F., Fulton, B. and Wozniak, J. (1999) 'Reconsidering restorative justice: the corruption of benevolence revisited?', *Crime and Delinquency*, 45: 1–27.

McEvoy, K. and Mika, H. (2002) 'Restorative justice and the critique of informalism in Northern Ireland', *British Journal of Criminology*, 42: 534–62.

Mannheim, H. (1946) *Criminal Justice and Social Reconstruction*. London: Routledge & Kegan Paul.

Miers, D. (2001) *An International Review of Restorative Justice*. London: Home Office.

Mika, H. and Zehr, H. (2003) 'A restorative framework for community justice practice', in K. McEvoy and T. Newburn (eds), *Crime, Conflict Resolution and Restorative Justice*. London: Palgrave, pp. 135–52.

Morris, A. (2002) 'Critiquing the critics: a brief response to critics of restorative justice', *British Journal of Criminology*, 42: 596–615.

O'Malley, P. (1999) 'Volatile and contradictory punishment', *Theoretical Criminology*, 3: 175–96.

O'Malley, P. (2000) 'Criminologies of catastrophe: understanding criminal justice on the edge of the new millenium', *Australian and New Zealand Journal of Criminology*, 33: 153–67.

Paterson, A. (1932) *The Principles of the Borstal System*. London: HMSO.

Platt, A. (1969) *The Child Savers*. Chicago, IL: University of Chicago Press.

Pratt, J. (1987) 'Dilemmas of the alternative to custody concept', *Australian and New Zealand Journal of Criminology*, 20: 148–62.

Pratt, J. (2002) *Punishment and Civilization*. London: Sage.

Pratt, J. and Clark, M. (2005) 'Penal populism in New Zealand', *Punishment and Society* (in press).

Pratt, J., Brown, D., Brown, M., Hallsworth, S. and Morrison, W. (eds) (2005) *The New Punitiveness*. Cullompton: Willan.

Report of the Department of Justice (1968) Wellington: Government Printer.

Report of the Director of Penal Services (1957) Melbourne: Victoria V and P (1958–9) 2.

Rose, G. (1961) *The Struggle for Penal Reform*. London: Stevens & Sons.

Rusche, G. and Kirchheimer, O. (1939/1968) *Punishment and Social Structure*. New York: Russell & Russell.

Shearing, C. (2001) 'Transforming security: a South African experiment', in H. Strang and J. Braithwaite (eds), *Restorative Justice and Civil Society*. Cambridge: Cambridge University Press, pp. 14–34.

Tavuchis, N. (1991) *Mea Culpa: A Sociology of Apology and Reconciliation*. Stanford, CA: Stanford University Press.

Weitekamp, E. (1999) 'The history of restorative justice', in G. Bazemore and L. Walgrave (eds), *Restorative Juvenile Justice: Repairing the Harm of Youth Crime*. Monsey, NJ: Criminal Justice Press, pp. 75–102.

Zimring, F. (1996) 'Populism, democratic government and the decline of expert authority', *Pacific Law Journal*, 28: 243–56.

Chapter 4

The intermediate position of restorative justice: the case of Belgium

Ivo Aertsen

In Belgium, restorative justice has been developed in a progressive and pronounced way. Numerous initiatives have been taken since the late 1980s, in the sphere of both practice and policy development, often in cooperation with representatives of the academic world. Restorative justice in its various forms in Belgium is being institutionalized to a large extent, after important new steps in the sphere of legislation have been undertaken in 2005. This chapter deals with the institutionalization of restorative justice in this country within the broader perspective of theoretical analysis and exploration.

In the first section, an overview of restorative justice developments and models in Belgium and their most important features will be briefly presented. The second section will focus on the theme of institutionalization, and more precisely on different theoretical approaches which subsequently will be applied to the Belgian case. Thirdly, an attempt is made to discuss the institutionalization of restorative justice against the background of some ambivalent influences from crime policies and societal developments in general. Fourthly, a theoretical reflection is set up in order to find ways of dealing with some of these tensions and to explore a further positioning of restorative justice. In this final section, the emphasis will be on the specificity of both restorative justice processes and organizational models, for which again reference will be made to the Belgian situation.

The Belgian landscape

Belgium is a small but – when looking at its state structure – complicated country, and this helps us to understand from the outset a paradox: how it is possible, on the one hand, to develop restorative justice practices in a more or less generalized and well coordinated way, and, on the other hand, how implementation can suffer from a halt to growth at the same time.[1] Both tendencies are present in the process of institutionalizing restorative justice in the country. But first, let us draw the Belgian picture more precisely, be it in broad brush strokes – detailed overviews can be found in other publications (Aertsen 2000; Willemsens 2004). It should be mentioned in advance that, as is the case in most European countries, restorative justice in Belgium predominantly takes the form of victim–offender mediation.

Origins and development

Juvenile assistance

An outspoken pedagogical approach was at the forefront when the first mediation initiatives with juveniles started in the late 1980s. Small-scale initiatives have multiplied and are operating even today within the framework of the Belgian Juvenile Justice Act of 1965. This law is clearly based on a rehabilitative philosophy (the so-called 'protection model') and does not refer explicitly to mediation. It is against this pedagogical background that juvenile assistance services, in both the Flemish and French Communities, became interested in setting up mediation schemes. For many years, however, the number and practice of mediation programmes for juveniles developed slowly. Several reasons can be mentioned for this rather hesitant development: the strong identification with a strict educational role by many social workers, the mixing up of mediation with community service and other educational measures, a lack of a clear legal framework promoting mediation, and – related to the latter – the absence of unambiguous federal and Community policies and funding provisions for local programmes. The always-imminent presence of conflicts of competence between the different policy levels in the federalized state, and more in particular the unclear allocation of authority between the Communities and the national state in respect to juvenile delinquency policies, has impeded a breakthrough of victim–offender mediation programmes for many years. This ambiguous situation also hindered conceptually the growth of a culture of and specific strategies oriented towards restorative justice for juveniles (Buonatesta 1998).

These ambiguities were not removed when in 1999 the Flemish government, after a resolution by the Flemish Parliament on the further development of the juvenile assistance sector, decided to implement in each judicial district 'restorative justice programmes'. Under this general notion, three models were promoted: victim–offender mediation, community service and training programmes. Local NGOs receive subsidies to realize these three types of practices, which are most frequently carried out by one and the same organization. More or less the same policy was followed by the French Community and the Walloon Region. In four locations in Flanders, on the initiative of the Catholic University of Leuven, a conferencing pilot project started in 2000, oriented to more serious offences and based on the New Zealand model (Vanfraechem and Walgrave 2004; Vanfraechem 2005). Finally, several legislative initiatives at the federal level have been launched during the first years of 2000 to amend the 1965 Juvenile Justice Act. In these proposals, mediation and conferencing are given a clear and central position. However, differences in vision on the future of juvenile justice between the Southern and the Northern part of the country seem to hamper the reaching of a political consensus again. The Walloon part of the country strongly defends a youth protection model whereas the Flemish part is more in favour of a legal rights and/or restorative justice approach.

Adult criminal law
The description above might explain, at least partly, why Belgium – contrary to developments in other countries – has witnessed a more sustained development of restorative justice in the field of adult criminal law. From 1991 onwards, different (nationwide) programmes of victim–offender mediation emerged: 'penal mediation', 'mediation for redress', 'mediation at the police level' and 'mediation in the prison'.

Penal mediation
After a short experimental period without any proper evaluation, 'penal mediation' was enacted by the law of 10 February 1994, which introduced the new article 216 *ter* in the code of criminal procedure. The ease by which this legislation took place must be seen in the political context of the early 1990s: confronted with the success of the extreme right party 'Vlaams Blok' during the parliamentary elections of 1991, the federal government felt a strong need to develop multifaceted policies in order to tackle insecurity problems and to regain public trust. Penal mediation, a diversionary measure at the level of the public prosecutor, was part of the governmental programme. This legislative

initiative had at least a double official aim: on the one hand, providing a quick social reaction to common 'city crime' and, on the other hand, paying more attention to the victim. In minor criminal cases, for which a penalty of over two years' imprisonment is not deemed necessary by the public prosecutor, the law offers the possibility of proposing to the suspect one or more of the following conditions or measures which, when complied with, result in a discharge ('extinction of the public action'): reparation to the victim, treatment for crime-related personal problems, training or community service. As may be seen, mediation (to support reparation) is only one of four possible applications of this law. Therefore the term 'penal mediation' as a generic title for this legal procedure – following the French example of 'médiation pénale' – was clearly mistaken.

Penal mediation is applied in each judicial district from within the public prosecutor's office. Mediation as well as the preparatory work and the follow-up of the other measures is done by 'mediation assistants'. These are civil servants who, since the reform of the probation system in 1999, have been called 'justice assistants' and are part of the newly created 'Houses of Justice'. Quantitatively, the legal system of penal mediation has developed quite fast and until now the justice assistants have carried out the majority of mediation cases in Belgium on an annual basis.

Mediation for redress
The origins of 'mediation for redress' (Dutch name: 'herstelbemiddeling'; French name: 'médiation après poursuite') go back to a 1993 initiative of the Catholic University of Leuven, in partnership with the public prosecutor of Leuven and a local NGO working with victims and offenders (Peters and Aertsen 1995). The pilot project aimed at developing a concept and a method for mediation in cases of more serious crime which do not qualify for a conditional dismissal or for 'penal mediation'. As this was not a diversionary measure, the object of scientific approach was the impact of this type of mediation on the decision-making processes by the public prosecutor and the judge, and more generally on the rationale within the criminal justice system. After an experimental period of three years, the project adopted a more definitive status. It received recognition and funding from the ministry of Justice, and gradually the model – as a national programme – was transferred to other judicial districts. Two umbrella organizations, the Flemish NGO Suggnomè and the Walloon NGO Médiante, became responsible for the implementation of the model throughout the country. Apart from the seriousness of the crimes dealt with, another

characteristic of 'mediation for redress' is the establishment of local partnerships which direct the programme. These partnerships are composed of representatives of the municipality, the House of Justice, victim support, the local police, the public prosecutor, the court, the bar of lawyers, the prison and, if available, a research or academic institution. In some districts, the juvenile mediation scheme is also covered by this partnership, as well as the mediation programme at police level and mediation in prison (see below). This multi-agency model is founded on a written 'protocol' of cooperation, signed by all partners, in which the general aim and objectives of the partnership and the respective responsibilities are stipulated.

In June 2005, the national parliament voted in a law on mediation for redress, in order to establish legally the model in each judicial district. The law is based on a clear restorative justice philosophy, defining mediation as a communicative process and guaranteeing the principles of confidentiality and voluntariness. Mediation is conceived as an offer of service to victims and offenders, not merely as a judicial measure. The criminal justice system has to inform parties and to make the offer available at all stages of the criminal justice process, including after sentence. Only with the explicit consent of both victim and offender can information on the mediation process and outcome be communicated to the prosecutor or the judge. In the latter case, the judge must mention this in his sentence.

Mediation at the police stage

Since 1996, mediation programmes at the level of the police have been set up in some Flemish cities and in different municipalities of the Brussels Region. The total number of programmes in the beginning of 2005 was 11. This model takes place within, or in a close cooperation with, local police departments. Common features of these programmes are their main focus on minor property (and violent) offences with clearly specified financial or material damages for which a (rapid) settlement can be reached. The mediator is a civil servant, not a policeman. The programmes are supported by federal government funding related to security and employment policies. The local mediation programmes are based on divergent ideologies, ranging from civil dispute resolution over community policing to zero tolerance (Lemonne and Aertsen 2003).

Restorative justice in prisons

(a) Victim–offender mediation

Financed by the Flemish Community, an experimental victim–offender mediation programme with prisoners was set up in 2001 by the umbrella organization Suggnomè. The project operates mainly in three prisons. Two independent mediators, based in the local 'mediation for redress' service, carry out mediation on the request of the inmate, the victim or the victim's family. The programme focuses on serious crimes, including cases of rape, armed robbery and murder.

(b) Restorative detention

The option to integrate restorative approaches in the criminal justice system as a whole, which inspired the initial 'mediation for redress' programme in 1993, resulted in 1998 in a pilot project and action research by the universities of Leuven and Liège in order to conceive a restorative justice model to be applied during the administration of the prison sentence (Vanacker 2002; Robert and Peters 2003; Aertsen 2005). On the basis of the outcomes of the project, the Minister of Justice decided in 2000 to implement this restorative justice model in each prison in the country. The most important tool for this has been the appointment of a 'restorative justice advisor' in each prison, operating at the level of the prison management. The full-time task of this advisor is not to work personally on a case-by-case basis with inmates and victims, but to support within the prison system the development of a culture, skills and programmes which give room to the victims' needs and restorative answers. Therefore the restorative justice advisor informs, trains and supports prison officers and staff and is starting cooperation and specific programmes with external agencies such as victim support and mediation services. The national programme is coordinated by two staff members within the Ministry of Justice.

Moreover within the prison context, the Flemish Community is funding a victim-awareness programme 'Victim in Perspective' which is carried out by victim support. This programme is also being applied as an alternative sanction in cooperation with the Houses of Justice. Finally, an experimental compensation fund for prisoners was established in 2000, managed by Suggnomè and sponsored by a charity. This fund operates in accordance with principles which also apply to a similar compensation fund for juvenile delinquents: through a process of communication with the injured party, an insolvent offender can ask for support by the fund in order to reimburse the victim, on the condition that he carry out volunteer work in the community in consultation with the victim.

Some features of the Belgian development

Belgium is on its way to applying restorative justice in a generalized manner, both in the field of juvenile delinquency and adult criminal law. The service of victim–offender mediation will be available from the beginning of 2006 onwards over the whole territory, and this for different types of crime, varying degrees of seriousness and at all stages of the criminal justice process. This perspective positions restorative justice not just in a diversionary context, but makes it an integral part of criminal justice. Stated this way, the aim appears ambitious: to reorient criminal justice processes in a restorative direction. Whether this can be done without giving up some of the core values and principles of restorative justice remains an open question and an enormous challenge.

Also for Belgium, the role of legislation has proven to be crucial in order to make an effective general implementation possible and in order to preserve the legal principle of equality (Lauwaert 2003). A further and even more fundamental attempt to integrate restorative justice principles in the legal system has been undertaken by the Belgian Commission 'Holsters' (an official advisory commission on the administration of sanctions, the legal status of prisoners and sentencing). The sub-commission dealing with sentencing reform proposed in its final report (2003) to include as one of the four possible sentencing goals in the penal code 'problem solving and restoration', and to inscribe in the code of penal procedure 'principles of a communicative and participatory criminal justice system' (Aertsen and Beyens 2005).

Another decisive factor has been the role of NGOs. In Belgium, as in many other countries, NGOs have been the driving force in restorative justice developments. Clear differences are perceivable between the state-directed 'penal mediation' and the voluntary sector-initiated 'mediation for redress' with respect to the underlying ideology, policy development and modus operandi. The distinction once made for the UK between a social work or probation model of mediation on the one hand and an independent mediation model on the other is still highly relevant (Marshall 1996). The relationship of restorative justice programmes to criminal justice will be analysed more extensively later in this chapter. Notwithstanding the eminent role of NGOs, the community orientation of restorative justice programmes has been stressed and discussed in Belgium to a much lesser degree than its relationship to criminal justice.

The role of academics in developing restorative justice is an important feature of the Belgian situation. The Catholic University of Leuven has taken the lead, by conceiving and even initiating various pilot projects accompanied by action research ('mediation for redress', 'family group conferences', 'restorative detention'). During the implementation process, a close cooperation between academics and practitioners has continued. The same academic support from within Belgium has been influential at the international level, including the foundation of the European Forum for Restorative Justice.

The voluntary sector and the academic world together have been successful in convincing or supporting governmental bodies both at the federal and the Community level. Important has been the personal role of the consecutive federal Ministers of Justice (remarkably, from the three traditional political families: Christian democrats, liberals and social democrats), who since 1996 have supported restorative justice practices and policies. Significant in this regard has been the proposal, by the Belgian government, of a European Council Decision to set up a European Network of National Contact Points for Restorative Justice, in the meantime dealt with by the European Parliament (*Official Journal* C 242 of 8.10.2002, p. 20).

Institutionalization

In this section we will first present different approaches to insti-tutionalization and then apply these conceptualizations to restorative justice developments in Belgium.

Different notions of 'institutionalization'

According to the classic sociological interpretation, institutionalization refers to the process of how institutions in society emerge. Insti-tutionalization occurs when certain behavioural patterns among several people become current and usual. Therefore the notion refers to a process wherein human activity becomes 'habitualized'. Berger and Luckmann (1966) consider that institutionalization happens 'whenever there is a reciprocal typification of habitualized actions by types of actors'. The institution itself typifies individual actors and individual actions, by positing that 'actions of type X will be performed by actors of type X'. Institutionalization – as a form of social construction of reality – takes place through a common, dialectic process consisting of different stages: (1) externalization of human activity, both physically and mentally, making it a human product; (2) objectivation, when typification forms social behaviour as a reality as such, independently from particular persons; and (3) internalization, where the objectivated social world is retrojected into consciousness in the course of socialization. Thus an institution represents a definite, collective pattern of behaviour or a coherent entity of social acts. This entity is more than the sum of individual acts and shapes individual and collective behaviour. Stated this way, an institution is a regulating body and by its mere existence is exercising a form of primary social control. Institutions control human behaviour by setting up predefined patterns of conduct.

Institutionalization, according to Berger and Luckmann (1966: 57), presupposes a continuing social situation 'in which the habitualized actions of different individuals interlock'. If we consider practices of conflict-handling in a social group as a possible focus of typification, then it is questionable whether the practice of victim–offender mediation as it has developed in Belgium and other countries, even after a process of practical implementation and legislation, corresponds sufficiently to the above given definition of institutionalization. It can hardly be argued that mediation in criminal matters (already) functions as a socially infused institution, since it is missing a collective basis, continuity and historicity. However, a particular mode of conflict-handling can evolve alongside the lines of institutionalization, as the Belgian practice of mediation in collective labour disputes since the 1960s demonstrates.

A particular approach to the issue of institutionalization is offered by Baskin (1988), who analyses the development and current practices of 'community mediation'. Community mediation, she confirms, does not reflect an independent, self-determining system, but is emerging in the context of new regulatory modes which are reconstructing the relationship between state and society and by which new mediating structures are shaped. These structures are designed to re-establish trust in public authorities and the justice system. Moreover, mediation – according to Baskin – constitutes a new market for service industries, which requires little investment of capital and assists unemployment policies (the latter is at least recognizable in Belgium, where some mediation programmes at the level of the municipality have benefited since 1994 from the so-called 'Global Plan', a governmental employment programme). These new types of community regulation have a highly ambivalent character. On the one hand, through individualizing and depoliticizing processes they take part in 'the institutionalization of private life':

> Within community mediation programs, coercion is indeed relaxed. Parties reach programs through 'referrals' even in the case of arrest. (...) Penalties become 'agreements' or 'contracts' and tend to include promises for behaviorial change or transfers of money or property. Since coercion is less extreme and less visible, regulation does not depend necessarily on a legal violation. As a

result, regulation moves in the direction of the entire population, expanding existing categories of those who are in 'need' of control. (Baskin 1988: 103)

On the other hand, Baskin argues, by reallocating responsibilities and self-governance, mediation has a strong liberating and transformative potential, including a direct link to social action. This line of thinking has been further elaborated by others putting the practice of community mediation in a postmodern conceptual framework of governmentality: 'Community mediation sessions extend the points at which lives become accessible to authority figures and could – if successful – expand "normality" to greater numbers in the population' (Pavlich 1996: 123).

The impending dependent position of mediation becomes more visible and observable when looking at its concrete organization. Legal pluralism – as will be seen more extensively in a following section – offers a further, critical approach in this respect, by studying new forms of informal justice in their relationship to existing institutions. In this sense, mediation (in civil law disputes) has been analysed from its degree of incorporation in existing public or private social structures. According to Merry (1989), 'institutionalization' of a new method of conflict resolution occurs when an existing social structure controls three essential components of the new programme: funding, case referrals and staff. This definition offers a clear criterion for evaluating the 'risk' of institutionalization. Underlying this is a concern for safeguarding the alternative and pure character of the new model. Therefore the topic of 'institutionalization' in the context of restorative justice implementation is often given this (negative) connotation. It leaves us with the option whether to consider the phenomenon of institutionalization as a dynamic process with a constructive social meaning and potential, or to see it from a restrictive and dependent perspective when new practices are developing under the roof of existing judicial or social structures.

Institutionalization in the Belgian context

Looking at the *organization* of restorative justice programmes in Belgium and applying Merry's criterion, we must definitely conclude that at least 'penal mediation' and 'mediation at the police level' are strongly 'institutionalized'. Funding, referrals and staff are completely controlled by sections of the criminal justice system or – although not always completely – the police. 'Restorative detention' is in a formal way totally integrated in the prison department. 'Mediation for redress' and 'mediation with juveniles' remain more autonomous, respectively by making use of a buffer organization responsible for staff or by clearly disconnecting funding and staff (controlled by the Communities) from referral decisions (by judicial authorities).

By analysing mediation *practices*, a trend towards 'instrumentalization' has been discerned. Both 'mediation at the police level' and 'penal mediation' are functioning under particular police and public prosecutor's policies, clearly oriented to offering quick, strict and visible offender-focused answers to minor crime. 'Mediation with juveniles' has proven to be useful as an educational tool. All in all, the impact of the organizational framework on restorative justice practices in Belgium cannot be denied. Mediation methods and principles are highly influenced by the type of organizational context. This is most clear for 'penal mediation', whose methods are less focused on communication processes; for 'mediation with juveniles', which is located in the sector of juvenile assistance and thus determined to a high degree by its educational logic; and for 'restorative detention', where the new function of restorative justice advisor is situated within the prison administration, more precisely within the prison governor's staff. A common – and logical – characteristic of these three restorative justice models is the subordinate orientation to victims' needs. For each of these practices, alternative ways of organizing and positioning were available when started up.

The high degree of professionalization of restorative justice practices in Belgium reinforces a tendency towards institutionalization as defined by Merry. No volunteers or community representatives are directly active in mediation or conferencing practices. Some professional interest groups, for example in the field of juvenile assistance, claim their own restorative justice structures separately from other local programmes.

Finally, a typical phenomenon related to institutionalization could be observed repeatedly. In the first years of their existence, both 'penal mediation' and 'mediation with juveniles' were supported by their own supervisory staff. Once mediation practice was established within the mother organization, this support was withdrawn or reduced, officially because of ongoing reorganization. When restorative justice is being implemented within a bigger organization, it can be expected that it (also) will serve the legitimization and strengthening of the existing institution. This also could apply to the national programme of 'restorative detention', since the prison system is permanently confronted with crises and urgent needs and priorities other than restorative justice.

Institutionalization within an ambivalent societal context

A following step towards understanding the institutionalization of restorative justice is to confront it with related but ambivalent developments in society and crime policies. First we will deal with some reflections on the idea of participation, then our focus will be on the theme of security.

Restorative justice and participation

The growth of restorative justice practices fits with the shift, during the last decades, from the societal model of the welfare state to the neoliberal participatory state. The welfare state has been criticized because of its one-sided orientation on service delivery to the citizens–consumers, assuming that all types of services by definition can be delivered by public authorities. This welfare state was considered to be making citizens dependent and negligent in their responsibilities towards the state and the community. In the 'active welfare state', as introduced in the Netherlands and Belgium in the 1990s, unemployment, poverty, migration and social policies and regulations in general drew more and more on the presumption of an active and responsible role by the recipient of the service. A combination of citizens' self-care and governmental responsibility became the leading principle in the organization of different sectors of society (Schuyt 1994). Social work in Flanders, for example, evolved from the dominance of a welfare paradigm to the eminence of a participatory paradigm: problematic situations were redefined as participation problems, and making participation possible became an objective on its own.

Also criminal procedure in European continental law has shown a growing impact of participatory elements, together with aspects of negotiation and consensus which had existed already for some time (Tulkens and van de Kerchove 1996). In this context, mediation initiatives more recently have found their legitimacy in an overall programme of social activation and responsibilization, pushed forward by victim policies and penal reform. The launching of mediation programmes took place within the politics of shared responsibility between government and citizens. This evolution is characterized by several ambiguities, which also affect and orient the further development of restorative justice.

Firstly, the activation of the individual citizen – at the micro level – is not usually accompanied by the activation of relevant organizational and structural frameworks at a meso or macro level. Applied to restorative justice, the quasi-absence of intermediate structures has as a consequence that conflict-handling at the individual level is not linked up with the detection of underlying social needs and has no effect on policy-making at a local or central level. Restorative justice does not go hand in hand with 'restorative governance' (Benzvy Miller and Schacter 2000).

Secondly, the principle of participation in criminal law and criminal law reform is highly individualised. This also refers to a more global evolution of the individualization of social solidarity. This makes 'community involvement' not at all self-evident for restorative justice practitioners. Lay people involved in mediation and conferencing practices do not necessarily reflect and activate local communities as such (this might be more the case in the model of sentencing circles). As mentioned already, much more attention is being paid to discussions on the relationship of restorative justice to criminal justice than to its relationship to and place in society. The sociological themes of informal justice and de-institutionalization have disappeared completely in restorative justice discussions.

Thirdly, the participatory principle – also in the administration of criminal justice – is subject to particular types of normalization and instrumentalization in respect of social integration and control. Participation is no longer seen as an intrinsic goal or a societal value to be realized for its own sake or for its emancipatory potential, but rather as a condition for receiving a service or for justice to be administered. Participation, in this restricted meaning, for those directly involved – victims, offenders and their surroundings – does not refer to a practical and manageable normative perspective which surmounts a rule-conforming approach of morality. So stated, restorative justice practices are losing their potential to restore or revalorize the law as a cultural and communicative phenomenon with its potential for 'de-reification' of dominant meanings around criminality through the active involvement of those seeking justice (Peters 1976).

To conclude, by putting the institutionalization of restorative justice within the context of broader developments in society, it becomes clear that its participatory principle is being applied in a severely restricted way. Participation in criminal law reform is reduced to the individual level without touching informal communities and public policies. Restorative justice is part of a 'satisfaction story' much more than of a 'social justice story' (Bush and Folger 1994).

Restorative justice and security

Whereas the emergence of the participatory principle still can be seen as – at least partially – supportive for restorative justice developments, the growing emphasis on security and security policies in most Western countries gives much less room for such conclusions. Many will argue that the successor to the welfare state is not so much the participatory state but the 'security state'. During the 1980s and 1990s, the notion of security in society has broadened and adopted an 'integral' character. It concerns 'a political-cultural development referring to a new moral order based on an omnipresent desire for safety and risk reduction' (Boutellier and van Stokkom 1995). Again, public authorities are considered to be responsible for providing safety. Under this pressure, crime policies are expanding to all kinds of risk situations and are moulded in a more regulating, non-normative form with less democratic control (Takala 1995).

For Braithwaite (2000), the 'new regulatory state', based on the centrality and globalizing logic of risk thinking, has emerged from the simultaneous development of privatizing tendencies and the rise of new, non-state regulatory institutions and techniques. In this way, the state makes use of a multitude of 'arenas of governance', without decreasing official initiative. Restorative justice can be part of this strategy and should not necessarily be seen in contradiction to the goals of an actuarial security model (Fattah 1998). Moreover, restorative justice programmes in certain contexts can give a new content and form to security and prevention policies: 'Peacemaking or restorative justice conferences often become occasions that supply the motivation to plan locally to prevent a recurrent threat to citizen safety' (Braithwaite 2000: 232). In order to prevent the dominance of an indirect state control over the diverse forms of self-regulation in society, in an ideal-typical concept according to Braithwaite, mutual control should be established between the state, the international community, private enterprises and non-governmental organizations.

Others are less optimistic with respect to the viability of counteracting unilateral state-driven security logics and policies. In the case of Belgium, for example, 'security contracts' between the federal state and local municipalities – which have also provided funding for mediation programmes – have been characterized as manifestations of a 'douce violence' ('soft violence'), binding citizens to authorities and putting the voluntary sector in a subordinated relationship. These new provisions have been seen as the affirmation of a 'défense sociale' approach focused on control and exclusion (Cartuyvels and Van Campenhoudt 1995). The same ambiguity can be recognized in the Belgian concept of Houses of Justice – in the framework of which the official job description of the 'justice assistants' has been defined at least partly in terms of restorative justice. The finality of the Houses of Justice, set up in 1996, relates to a mixture of objectives, such as a better coordinated and more efficient justice system, and also a higher involvement of the local community. Penal mediation in Belgium and France – with its diversity of forms of application – has been situated in a field of tension between a 'socialisation du pénal' and a 'pénalisation du social' (Cario 1997; Mary 1997).

Towards a theoretical position

Restorative justice practices, in the form in which they have been expanding since the late 1990s, have been discussed above as functioning in the broader context of a control–release dialectic. How can these practices be conceived (and possibly organized) in a more clear direction which combats a further externalization of conflict vis-à-vis those involved and which encourages citizens and the justice system to take responsibility for each other in an emancipatory way? The notion of 'emancipation' means that a unilateral top-down institutional perspective of crime control is discarded for a bottom-up perspective of justice-seeking at various levels: the individual, the relational, the informal community, the societal–structural and the cultural. In the last part of this chapter, we will explore some (not so new) theoretical frameworks which, starting from this question, can offer new avenues for the further conceptualization and organization of restorative justice practices. Where appropriate, we will refer mainly to the underlying philosophy and practical organization of one of the restorative justice practices in Belgium, namely 'mediation for redress'.

The process of mediation

The participatory principle in restorative justice practices invites the emphasis of elements of procedural justice, as initially developed by social-psychological theory and later applied to practices of victim support and victim–offender mediation (Peachy 1986; Lind and Tyler 1988; Wemmers 1996). Procedural justice has taught us that the personally experienced treatment and the perceived control of the process of conflict-handling, more than the control of the final decision or the outcome, determines feelings of justice and fairness. From a criminal justice point of view, procedural law rather than substantive law provides a framework for participatory practices. Observations and case studies of restorative justice processes – be it mediation or conferencing – which are not predominantly settlement or outcome driven, give evidence of the outspoken (inter)personal dynamics which occur during and in between sessions. One of the key elements in the dialogue is the discussion of 'what happened': facts and meanings are repeatedly redefined, as well as possible solutions. The subjectivity of the stories often results in different, more complex or more nuanced meanings than the objectivity of the police report and the legal qualification of the facts can provide. These interpersonal dynamics, with their ongoing redefinition of meanings around the crime, are easier to observe in cases with a strong personal impact. Case studies in the Belgian 'mediation for redress' programme, which is focusing on more serious crimes, do illustrate this potential.

Besides the horizontal dialogue between victim and offender, 'mediation for redress' shows the perspective of a vertical communication between victim and offender on the one hand and the sentencing judge on the other. The latter is, in practice, not (yet) realized, but ideas are growing on how the mediation (or conferencing) process could be extended by a direct (face-to-face) session or an indirect communication with the judge. The need to do so has been revealed in cases of more serious crime, where victim and offender discuss among themselves the sentence to be expected or desired. After exchange between victim and offender, the topic should also be discussed with the judge. If courts could provide a forum for an in-depth and non-adversarial communication, both the parties directly involved and the justice system could inform each other on the meaning and consequences of the crime and on how to reach individual redress and social pacification.

Conceiving restorative justice practices as part of procedural criminal law releases them conceptually from their direct instrumentalization. The new Belgian law of 22 June 2005 on 'mediation for redress' confirms this option, where it considers mediation as an offer (not a measure) to be used by those involved (see above). Moreover, during the discussions at various stages, the context of procedural law with its emphasis on participation and communication gives room to arguments and (sentencing) goals of a very different or even contradictory nature. Restorative justice thus conceived recognizes and revalorizes the multi-functionality of criminal law and supports its expressive function.

The organizational model

From the preceding analysis follows the option for an organizational model of restorative justice services which offers room for an ongoing exchange and interaction between the mediation or conferencing dynamics on the one hand and the formal criminal justice system on the other. Such a model requires an autonomous or independent institutional position of the restorative justice programme. It needs an organizational structure in between but related to the respective institutional partners which guarantees and protects the neutral space where arguments and influences among these partners and from the wider community can interact on an equal footing and by which the neutrality of the mediation or conferencing process is preserved. In Belgian practice, such a balanced intermediate position of the restorative justice programme could be achieved by a careful and patient building of local partnerships which at a certain moment are structured in the form of steering committees. This model (and process) of constituting local partnerships according to certain principles will probably be confirmed and generalized over the whole country as a consequence of the new law of June 2005.

It is not our intention here to describe in detail the way of functioning of these local partnerships – this is at least partially done elsewhere (Aertsen 2004: 373–415) and particular research on this subject is on-going – or to compare this formula with similar models in other countries. What we try to do in what follows, is to initiate a theoretical underpinning of the intermediate position by making use of various legal-sociological and criminological frameworks.

'Semi-autonomous social fields'

Quite logically – but rarely found in restorative justice literature – reference can be made to the school of 'legal pluralism', a legal-sociological movement which in the 1970s and 1980s opposed the view and attitude of legal centralism that considered justice only as a product of the state and in practice impeded all endeavours to improve access to the law (Galanter 1981). Legal pluralism discerned multiple systems of norms in society with formalized law being only one of many. Law in society appeared to be more pluralistic than monolithic, both private and public in character, and the ordering role of the official legal system more secondary than primary. The large number of self-regulating social fields and lower normative orders and their functional relationships with the official legal system are lost from sight because the official system has become portrayed as 'universal, uniform, exclusive and actually in control'.

This approach partially dates back to the ideas of anthropologist Sally Moore, who in her study of the so-called 'semi-autonomous social fields' demonstrated how certain forms of private regulation take place and how conflicts are settled based upon private and public rules. These fields did not so much concern separate well-defined groups but rather overlapping and mutually penetrating networks or 'partial communities' structuring daily life in various contexts (family, work, leisure activities, religion, politics, ...). A semi-autonomous social field was defined by Moore as 'an area of social life that can generate rules and customs and systems internally, but that (...) is also vulnerable to rules and decisions and other forces emanating from the larger world by which it is surrounded. The semi-autonomous social field has rule-making capacities, and the means to induce compliance (...)' (quoted in Galanter 1981: 20).

How are restorative justice programmes and their organization related to the concept of semi-autonomous social fields? May these programmes be understood as more or less self-regulating normative orders in constant interaction with the formal system? That a mediation service internally generates its own rules, customs and systems seems plausible. Enforcing compliance with rules is less obvious. To the extent that semi-autonomous social fields constitute relatively permanent structures for their members, restorative justice services appear to be different. However, this theoretical approach opens the perspective of a restorative justice organizational model where a number of relationships and interactions are continued as permanent arrangements. In practice, some arrangements are going in this direction, for example where ex-clients of mediation are linked up with the mediation service on a more permanent basis, lay mediators form an ongoing group, affiliations are established with related organizations in the fields of education and social-political action and – of course – the mediation programme is directly governed by a partnership of organizations.

In reality, the perspective of transforming and extending restorative justice programmes in this way remains a challenge. More fundamentally, for many restorative justice programmes one could question the extent to which they really leave behind the paradigm of legal centralism, as many of these programmes are developed against the background of, and are continuously referring to, formal criminal law. This remark applies to restorative justice programmes in Belgium as well, including 'mediation for redress' whose procedures are mainly shaped on the basis of legal categories.

'New informalism'

Later versions of 'legal pluralism' have clarified the interrelation and mutual influence between informal regulatory systems and the official system of justice ('inter-legality'). Based upon an interest for the dynamics of change, the object of study became more specifically the dialectic, mutually constitutive relationship between the informal and the formal (Merry 1988). The concept of 'integral plurality' (Fitzpatrick 1988) refers to the thesis that state law is integrally constituted in

85

connection with a plurality of social norms. According to Fitzpatrick, semi-autonomous fields have their own discrete legal order that in the end need not be subordinated to the coordinating order of state law. Here he reacts against the known attitude of 'leftist-oriented academics' that dismisses informal legal forms as a mere manifestation or a reinforcement of existing state or social control ('mediation as a confirmation of patriarchal and middle-class values'). Law must not only be examined for its dominating characteristics, but also for its formative potential with respect to social life. The concept of 'facilitating law' (Sugerman, quoted by Merry 1988: 885) might be useful in this context: justice functions, not by imposing obligations, but by extending facilities to persons with a view toward the realization of their projects. This is done, among other ways, by granting legal competencies for engaging in certain legal acts. In this way, private regulation is expanded, but a possibility is also formally created to criticize government policies through legal participation.

This approach then is highly relevant to our study, as we might find here new insights into the possible mutually constitutive relationship between a restorative justice practice (mediation, conferencing) on the one hand, and the formal criminal justice system, more specifically the procedural moment of sentencing, on the other. Fitzpatrick's analysis (1988) is of relevance, in his exploration of attitudes that grant informal locations an independent identity, and in addition attitudes that place the informal under one large, coordinating identity. He undertakes this study by reinterpreting the phenomena concerned based upon the dynamics of modern forms of power. Power, in its positive and productive form and inhabiting social relations in a pervasive and constitutive way, expresses itself in a multiplicity of power relations. These power relations each have their own form of organization and operate through strategies that can be recognized in an institutionally crystallized way in various social forms of hegemony, including the formulation of law. At first sight there appears to be no place for 'resistance' in this all-inclusive view of power. But there are areas, Fitzpatrick points out following Foucault, where power also adopts a certain degree of exteriority and where resistance can outmanoeuvre power in an autonomous way. Reference is made to Foucault's historical study of penal and psychiatric settings where the presence of 'subjugated knowledges' promotes critique and struggle against power.

From here, the step to restorative justice practices might seem quite big. But the question should be raised whether mediation or conferencing from its informal context could be seen as 'modes accommodating the oppositions between the various power dimensions of justice'? In other words, to what extent can restorative justice mobilize informal elements of power and processes as a test of the power of justice? Effective resistance, Fitzpatrick argues, cannot be ensured by the law itself, but must come from outside. This 'positive politics of the informal' can turn to identifying countervailing powers in the domain of the informal that are otherwise neglected or hidden. This comes down to finding locations where socio-legal practices for resistance take place, where conflicts are settled not only extra-judicially but where the focus also lies upon the elaboration of a general alternative ordering. Mediation, based in authentic experience, manifests itself as counter-power in justice, on condition that the restorative justice forum can be organized in such a way that it can generate actual, independent resistance.

'Interactive settings'

Another theoretical approach concerning the interaction between official and non-official law has been developed by Henry, starting from research on conflict-handling, disciplinary bodies and mechanisms in industrial and commercial organizations, professional associations and unions, and the voluntary sector of self-help and mutual aid groups (Henry 1983, 1987). These forms of 'private justice', according to Henry, do not exist independently, but interrelate continuously with the formal system of state ordering. Private justice often reflects aspects of the legal order, but moments of opposition also occur. For Henry, a genuinely legal pluralism consists of abandoning the mythic, positivistic distinction between justice and other forms of social control. In his view, justice is a continuum rather than a series of separate, ideal typical models. He criticizes traditional approaches to the informal where informalism is seen either as a condition of existence for positive law or as an autonomous strategy. Both approaches now have to be integrated, says Henry. Hence, '(...) the informal is an integral part of the totality of law and not an alternative to it. If participation in the administration of law simply leads to the separation of those who administer and those who receive, then there will have been no transformation in conception, merely a change of personnel' (Henry 1983: 46). Thus the informal is not the object of future developments in law but the subject of the continuous 'creation' of law. It can be observed how people, in their contacts with each other, construct and reconstruct 'the manifest appearances of law'. For this, 'typical settings of social interaction' are examined where informal forms of settlement interfere with official forms of justice. The workplace forms such a typical situation for Henry, in which he studied different models of discipline in their (implicit) interaction with state law and where it was demonstrated how both dimensions of law penetrate each other by influencing each other's definitions and concepts. An example of these mutually influencing processes is offered by the way in which enterprises deal internally with crimes such as theft among employees, and more precisely how opinions are formed about the nature and the seriousness of the event.

Internal restorative justice processes – the interaction between victim, offender and their surroundings – are clearly influenced by judicial definitions and approaches, for example when participants and mediator, but also the referral agent, anticipate how the criminal justice system would or will react. The other way round is less obviously observable in practice, and in this respect Henry states that conceptually state law nevertheless remains the dominant frame of reference. Therefore he too is searching for possibilities of liberation from the existing structures of compulsion, which he does by interpreting expressions of justice and social control as discursive productions. In order to obtain a real deconstruction, not an oppositional discourse but a 'replacement discourse' should be deployed. This can come about, for example, by seeing control in the context of everyday contact referring to practical talks and initiative on the basis of responsibility. The cooperative is one type of organizational model where this form of social control exists, but Henry observes this potential also in some community-oriented mediation schemes (Henry 1985, 1989). In later theoretical work on a 'constitutive criminology', the view on criminality as a discursive co-production by various actors (offenders, victims, law enforcement representatives, academics, ...) and on possible strategies of how to reach 'harm reduction through replacement discourse' is much further elaborated, albeit in a quite abstract way (Henry and Milovanovic 1996).

Conclusion

In the preceding paragraphs we have been searching for theoretical responses to the ambivalent tendencies in crime policies and societal developments which affect the implementation of restorative justice programmes as they are evolving in western countries. Different approaches to 'institutionalization' were sketched against the background of the application of mediation programmes in Belgium. Throughout that overview, a concern for an autonomous, non-coopted and emancipatory practice and organizational framework for restorative justice programmes emerged. It was not our intention to find theoretical answers for all issues and contradictions dealt with, only to explore avenues which can lead to further theoretical insight in confrontation with practice.

In the last section, we first defended a conceptualization of restorative justice practices as part of procedural criminal law in order to support participatory practices in their full and autonomous understanding and in order to cope with tensions from the security and regulatory debate. Then, the conceptualization of an independent organizational model for restorative justice programmes formed the central focus of our reflection. We were looking for a theoretical foundation to assign a semi-autonomous position to restorative justice programmes: a space in between the positions of, on the one hand, the formal criminal justice system and, on the other hand, the informal and community-oriented ways of conflict-handling. This neutral space should allow and even promote at its crossroads the development of its own rationale for dealing with crime.

In order to feed these intertwining processes, restorative justice practice should be brought into interaction with criminal justice procedures in a more explicit way. Some practices with more serious crime, such as the Belgian 'mediation for redress' programme, reveal the possibility of positive confrontation at the level of sentencing by the court. However, the same vertical dialogue can be envisaged at the level of prosecution and diversion – which contains, in theory, a potential for the Belgian practice of 'penal mediation'. A pre-requisite for preserving these autonomous forms of interaction is the availability of support and guidance by an independent organizational structure which is not dominated by the logics of one of the concerned actors. In this respect, the Belgian experience of constituting local partnerships is promising. It has been shown in practice how steering committees during regular meetings create at that level a mediating structure where crime approaches, definitions and reactions are discussed fundamentally. This cannot be realized merely from a top-down approach. As in all types of mediation, a climate of confidence between the partners has to be established. Developing such an organizational model in the form of a partnership might finally underpin the institutionalization of restorative justice as a 'definite collective pattern of behaviour'.

Note

1   Under the Belgian Constitution there are three cultural Communities (the Flemish, the French and the German) and three economic Regions (the Flemish, the Walloon and the Brussels Region). Brussels conurbation has a bilingual status.

References

Aertsen, I. (2000) 'Victim–offender mediation in Belgium', in European Forum for Victim–offender Mediation and Restorative Justice (ed.), *Victim–offender Mediation in Europe. Making Restorative Justice Work*. Leuven: Leuven University Press, pp. 153–92.

Aertsen, I. (2004) *Slachtoffer-daderbemiddeling: een onderzoek naar de ontwikkeling van een herstelgerichte strafrechtsbedeling*. Leuven: Leuven University Press.

Aertsen, I. (2005) 'Restorative prisons: a contradiction in terms?', in C. Emsley (ed.), *The Persistent Prison. Problems, Images and Alternatives*. London: Francis Boutle Publishers, pp. 196–213.

Aertsen, I. and Beyens, K. (2005) 'Restorative justice and the morality of law – a reply to Serge Brochu', in E. Claes, R. Foqué and T. Peters (eds), *Punishment, Restorative Justice and the Morality of Law*. Antwerpen: Intersentia, pp. 101–17.

Baskin, D. (1988) 'Community mediation and the public/private problem', *Social Justice*, 15(1): 98–115.

Benzvy Miller, S. and Schacter, M. (2003) 'From restorative justice to restorative governance', *Canadian Journal of Criminology*, 3: 405–11.

Berger, P.L. and Luckmann, Th. (1966) *The Social Construction of Reality: A Treatise in the Sociology of Knowledge*. Garden City, NY: Anchor Books.

Boutellier, J. C. J. and van Stokkom, B. A. M. (1995) 'Consumptie van veiligheid', *Justitiële Verkenningen*, 5: 96–111.

Braithwaite, J. (2000) 'The new regulatory state and the transformation of criminology', *British Journal of Criminology*, 40: 222–38.

Buonatesta, A. (1998) 'Mediation and community service within the Belgian law on juvenile protection. A paradoxal approach to a restorative model', in L. Walgrave (ed.), *Restorative Justice for Juveniles. Potentialities, Risks and Problems*. Leuven: Leuven University Press, pp. 219–28.

Bush, R. A. B. and Folger, J. P. (1994) *The Promise of Mediation. Responding to Conflict Through Empowerment and Recognition*. San Francisco, CA: Jossey-Bass.

Cario, R. (ed.) (1997) *La médiation pénale. Entre répression et réparation*. Paris: L'Harmattan.

Cartuyvels, Y. and Van Campenhoudt, L. (1995) 'La douce violence des contrats de sécurité', *La Revue Nouvelle*, 3: 49–56.

Fattah, E. (1998) 'Some reflections on the paradigm of restorative justice and its viability for juvenile justice', in L. Walgrave (ed.), *Restorative Justice for*

Juveniles. Potentialities, Risks and Problems. Leuven: Leuven University Press, pp. 389–401.

Fitzpatrick, P. (1988) 'The rise and rise of informalism', in R. Matthews (ed.), *Informal Justice?* London: Sage, pp. 178–98.

Galanter, M. (1981) 'Justice in many rooms: courts, private ordering and indigenous law', *Journal of Legal Pluralism*, 19: 1–47.

Henry, S. (1983) *Private Justice. Towards Integrated Theorising in the Sociology of Law.* London: Routledge & Kegan Paul.

Henry, S. (1985) 'Community justice, capitalist society, and human agency: the dialectics of collective law in the cooperative', *Law & Society Review*, 2: 303–27.

Henry, S. (1987) 'The construction and deconstruction of social control: thoughts on the discursive production of state law and private justice', in J. Lowman, R. J. Menzies and T. S. Palys (eds), *Transcarceration: Essays in the Sociology of Social Control.* Aldershot: Gower, pp. 89–108.

Henry, S. (1989) 'Justice on the margin: can alternative justice be different?', *The Howard Journal*, 4: 255–71.

Henry, S. and Milovanovic, D. (1996) *Constitutive Criminology. Beyond Postmodernism.* London: Sage.

Lauwaert, K. (2003) 'Le cadre légal de la médiation victime-auteur en Europe continentale', *The International Journal of Victimology*, 1: 4 (http://www.JIDV.COM).

Lemonne, A. and Aertsen, I. (2003) *La médiation locale comme 'mesure alternative pour les délits de faible importance en Belgique'. Rapport final.* Leuven/Bruxelles: Katholieke Universiteit Leuven/Université Libre de Bruxelles.

Lind, E. A. and Tyler, T. R. (1988) *The Social Psychology of Procedural Justice.* New York: Plenum Press.

Marshall, T. (1996) 'The evolution of restorative justice in Britain', *European Journal on Criminal Policy and Research*, 4(4): 21–43.

Mary, Ph. (1997) 'Le travail d'intérêt général et la médiation pénale face à la crise de l'état social: dépolitisation de la question criminelle et pénalisation du social', in Ph. Mary (ed.), *Travail d'intérêt général et médiation pénale. Socialisation du pénal ou pénalisation du social?'*, Brussels: Bruylant, pp. 325–47.

Merry, S. E. (1988) 'Legal pluralism', *Law & Society Review*, 5: 869–96.

Merry, S. E. (1989) 'Myth and practice in the mediation process', in M. Wright and B. Galaway (eds), *Mediation and Criminal Justice. Victims, Offenders and Community.* London: Sage, pp. 239–50.

Pavlich, G. C. (1996) *Justice Fragmented. Mediating community disputes under postmodern conditions.* London: Routledge.

Peachy, D. E. (1986) *Restorative Justice in Criminal Conflict: Victims' and Observers' Perspectives.* Waterloo: University of Waterloo, Department of Psychology.

Peters, A. A. G. (1976) 'Recht als vals bewustzijn', in C. Kelk, M. Moerings, N. Jörg and P. Moedikdo (eds), *Recht, macht en manipulatie.* Utrecht/Antwerpen: Uitgeverij Het Spectrum, pp. 189–220.

Peters, T. and Aertsen, I. (1995) 'Restorative justice. In search of new avenues in judicial dealing with crime. The presentation of a project of mediation for reparation', in C. Fijnaut, J. Goethals, T. Peters and L. Walgrave (eds), *Changes in Society, Crime and Criminal Justice in Europe*, Vol. I. Antwerpen: Kluwer Rechtswetenschappen België, pp. 311–42.

Robert, L. and Peters, T. (2003) 'How restorative justice is able to transcend the prison walls: a discussion of the 'restorative detention' project', in E. Weitekamp and H.-J. Kerner (eds), *Restorative Justice in Context*. Cullompton: Willan, pp. 93–122.

Schuyt, C. J. M. (1994) 'Moraal en sociaal-economische ontwikkelingen in de verzorgingsstaat', *Justitiële Verkenningen*, 6: 74–84.

Takala, H. (1995) 'On risks and criminal law', in A. Snare (ed.), *Beware of Punishment. On the Utility and Futility of Criminal Law*. Oslo: Pax Forlag, pp. 51–67.

Tulkens, F. and van de Kerchove, M. (1996) 'La justice pénale: justice imposée, justice participative, justice consensuelle ou justice négociée?', in Ph. Gérard, F. Ost et M. van de Kerchove (eds), *Droit négocié, droit imposé?* Brussels: Publications des Facultés Universitaires Saint-Louis, pp. 529–79.

Vanacker, J. (ed.) (2002) *Herstel en detentie. Hommage aan Prof. Dr. Tony Peters*. Brussel: Politeia.

Vanfraechem, I. (2005) 'Evaluating conferencing for serious juvenile delinquency', in E. Elliott and R. Gordon (eds), *Restorative Justice: Emerging Issues in Practice and Evaluation*. Cullompton: Willan, pp. 278–95.

Vanfraechem, I. and Walgrave, L. (2004) 'Herstelgericht groepsoverleg voor jonge delinquenten in Vlaanderen. Verslag van een actieonderzoek', *Panopticon*, 6: 27–46.

Wemmers, J. M. (1996) *Victims in the Criminal Justice System. A Study into the Treatment of Victims and its Effects on their Attitudes and Behaviour*. Amsterdam: Kugler Publications.

Willemsens, J. (2004) 'Belgium', in D. Miers and J. Willemsens (eds), *Mapping Restorative Justice. Developments in 25 European Countries*. Leuven: European Forum for Victim–offender Mediation and Restorative Justice, pp. 23–36.

Chapter 5

Institutionalizing restorative justice? Transforming criminal justice? A critical view on the Netherlands

John Blad

Dutch scholars and practitioners in the criminal justice field have become aware of international discourses and practices of restorative justice in the past decade. Moreover, there are even several experiments going on with mediation and conferencing in the Netherlands. In this contribution I will analyse to what extent the present experimentation with restorative practices represents an incipient institutionalization of restorative justice. In order to do this it is necessary to have a theoretical understanding of the process of institutionalization. In the first two sections I therefore discuss institutionalization from a fundamental sociological angle, making use of my experiences in studying and discussing penal abolitionism. Restorative justice differs in a number of important respects from abolitionism. It is not a movement of de-institutionalization, but much more clearly a movement aiming at criminal justice reform.

Next, restorative practices as they exist today in the Netherlands will be described and analysed with respect to their (actual and potential) meanings for the criminal justice system. In this presentation I use a distinction between (informal) restorative practices (section three) that are not understood to be related to criminal justice and restorative practices that are intended to be somehow related to the criminal process (section four). Sections five and six deal with two questions: to what extent is restorative justice becoming institutionalized and to what extent is there the transformation of criminal justice that one might expect to see as a result? In view of the conclusions I arrive at some strategic considerations will be given in the last section on how to reduce the use of punishment to the mimimum and to maximize the use of restorative procedures and sanctions.

Institutionalization

Having read a certain amount of sociological literature, though not being a sociologist myself, the most convincing theory of institutionalization I came across was the one developed by Berger and Luckmann (Berger and Luckmann 1966) – convincing because it is so easily recognizable in everyday life and because it offers us many explanations for the phenomena of unease and even panic when confronted with proposals for social change, let alone fundamental social change.

Berger and Luckmann's theory begins with a fundamental assumption about mankind. It is different from all other species because it 'has no species-specific environment, no environment firmly structured by his own, instinctual organization' (Berger and Luckmann 1966: 65). Man's 'world-openness' leads to the necessity to create order in what would otherwise be chaos. Mankind's social order is created by the process of institutionalization that comprises a number of dynamic components: externalization, habitualization, legitimation and internalization. It begins with activity: the expression of intentions, needs and meanings through action and interaction. 'Human being must ongoingly externalize itself in activity. [...] The inherent instability of the human organism makes it imperative that man himself provide a stable environment for his conduct' (Berger and Luckmann 1966: 70).

One of the implications of this theory is that initial action is expressive of needs which man tries to satisfy: it is basically problem-solving by trial and error. But when any action appears to be successful it will be repeated and that is where habitualization starts: 'Any action that is repeated frequently becomes cast in a pattern, which can then be reproduced with an economy of effort and which, *ipso facto*, is apprehended by its performer *as* that pattern' (Berger and Luckmann 1966: 71).

Since man is inconceivable on his own and always acts in a social context habitualized actions are coordinated within interaction patterns which make up the next step:

Institutionalization occurs whenever there is a reciprocal typification of habitualized actions by types of actors. [...] The typifications of habitualized actions that constitute institutions are always shared ones. They are available to all members of the particular social group in question, and the institution itself typifies individual actors as well as individual actions. The institution posits that actions of type X will be performed by actors of type X. (Berger and Luckmann 1966: 72)

As a result of this process subjective action acquires intersubjective, shared meaning, contributing to the 'objectivation' of social action: this means that 'types of action' become available to all. This objectivation becomes perfected by legitimation practices that become necessary when new generations have to be socialized in the habits and customs of the social group. Socializing requires justification, because 'the original meaning [...] is inaccesible in terms of memory. It [...] becomes necessary to interpret this meaning to them in various legitimating formulas' (Berger and Luckmann 1966: 79).

In the process of legitimation the routines of the older generation are acquiring a normative character: the ways thing have always been done are the ways they ought to be done, for the reasons given.

Legitimation practices are discursive and they are perceivable on at least four levels of everyday life. Firstly, it is incipient in the way people talk about everyday experiences using the concepts deemed appropriate in everyday language. On a second level, they are present in many 'rudimentary theoretical propositions' expressed in proverbs, sayings and moral maxims. Thirdly, there are explicit theories legitimating institutions in terms of a differentiated body of knowledge (in our case: criminal law, criminology, forensic sciences, etc.). And last but not least, there are 'symbolic universes'. This most abstract level of legitimation allows for an intersubjective integration of all existing (cognitive, affective, performative) experiences into something 'symbolic', perhaps also to be indicated as something narrative, as stories. Symbolic universes 'are bodies of theoretical tradition that integrate different provinces of meaning and encompass the institutional order in a symbolic totality' (Berger and Luckmann 1966: 113).

In our case, the relevant symbolic universe is obviously 'justice'. Justice, while inherently contested and undefinable, always has an undeniable desirability and great motivational and organizational power.

One can criticize actual practices sold as 'justice' but one can never legitimately choose against it. And indeed, restorative justice presents itself as a form of justice.

The final crucial element of institutionalization is internalization. It is 'the immediate apprehension of an objective event as expressing meaning, that is a manifestation of another's subjective processes which thereby becomes subjectively meaningful to myself' (Berger and Luckmann 1966: 149).

Besides *non-discursive* (exemplary) action *discursive* activity – speaking – is the way in which an adequate internalization of institutions is achievable.

> With language, and by means of it, various motivational and interpretative projects are internalized as institutionally defined [...]. These projects provide the child with institutionalized programs for everyday life, some immediately applicable to him, others anticipating conduct socially defined for later biographical stages. (Berger and Luckmann 1966: 155)

Institutions always imply social control by establishing predefined patterns of conduct:

> [...] the primary social control is given in the very existence of an institution as such. To say that a segment of human activity has been institutionalized is already to say that this [...] activity has been subsumed under social control. Additional control mechanisms are required only in so far as the processes of institutionalization are less than completely successful. (Berger and Luckmann 1966: 73)

Although Berger and Luckmann do not explicitly put it in these terms I would like to use the term 'secondary institutions' for the additional control mechanisms and the term 'primary institutions' for the stabilized action and interaction patterns that we have been looking at. It is important to be aware of the fact that socialization does not only concern the primary institutions but also the secondary: the various types of additional control mechanisms (remedies and interventions) and the typical actions and actors in these intervention or remedial activities become, by learning, part of the common stock of knowledge of well socialized and competent social actors. Clearly, in this theoretical framework, restorative practices are patterns of interaction, potentially routines, of a secondary nature, to be applied when things go wrong in everyday social interaction.

This conclusion implies that any discourse about institutionalizing restorative justice is not concerned with primary institutions. Restorative justice is not about whether citizens should be allowed to use hard drugs, to marry as homosexuals or to kill their beloved ones at their request when they suffer severely and hopelessly from a fatal disease. In terms of social normativity it only conveys certain values such as solidarity and equal respect, which are elaborated in a specific set of practices designed to react to breaches of stipulated social and legal norms.

Some observations about institutionalization

It is important to see how, if the basic premise of mankind as prone to chaos and therefore obliged to permanently impose order upon his world is right, we all live through institutions and how these institutions live through us.

Our collectivities produce and reproduce institutions: these may be *expressed* in formal agencies – often also called institutions – but *they have no location there*. The location of institutions is in our everyday life: our learned, self-evident actions and interactions, understood in an unproblematic way. Even the secondary institutions, which are often formally organized and gain a certain autonomy that can sometimes lead to feelings of estrangement,[1] are deeply intertwined with our primary institutions. I would like to illustrate that fact a bit more by focusing on criminal justice.

If we agree that social norms are indices of legitimate social – reciprocal – expectations within a common social frame of reference we can recognize these social norms as indicating our primary institutions. Important legal norms in the substantive criminal law ought to, and most often do, relate to important social norms. The prohibition of rape has to do with our institutions with regard to sexual conduct. The prohibition of theft refers to the institution of property and to the appropriate ways of dealing with property. In terms of institutionalization theory it is relevant to note that we all know this – it is a common stock of knowledge – and furthermore, it seems to me that most important social norms, and also their legal reflections, are widely accepted also by the proponents of restorative justice. Being socialized in contemporary modern societies[2] implies that most of us would also agree that the appropriate reaction to crime would be to prosecute, try and convict offenders in the ways indicated in our criminal procedural law books. The criminal justice system, in other words, is not located in the agencies of criminal justice, but is located in a shared social system of expectancy and interaction patterns. I think this fact is expressed in the general unease and indeed panic that is often generated by the radical discourse of penal abolitionism. The experience of a crime is itself a more or less intense 'border experience', shaking all that has been taken for granted. To question the way in which the collectivity will deal with this (anti-institutional) experience is something many cannot bear: in any case even an abolitionist will tend to call the police after a rape or a burglary. My conclusion from the many intensive discussions I have had about penal abolitionism is that people would rather hang on to (secondary) institutions that they recognize as being imperfect than do away with them. In fact, institutions cannot be abolished by decision.[3] They can only under certain conditions be reformed.

I am not suggesting that we should be pessimistic about man's ability to reform imperfect institutions. But if we want to institutionalize restorative justice we must consider where it is best to start. To what social contexts should most of our energy and efforts go? Is it in the criminal justice system or in other social systems that we can most effectively build up the foundations for maximizing the (secondary) institution of restorative justice?

If mankind lives under an 'institutional imperative'[4] we can assume that even in this era, where (postmodern) sociological analysis and dominant political discourse alike presume or suggest a social world that is falling apart, more and more lacking social cohesion and social integration, most people are most of the time living up to reciprocal behavioural expectations. This implies that it is a feasible strategy to develop a participatory style of justice and that we can trust most of our fellow citizens to play an adequate role in maintaining social and legal norms. Moreover, should the abovementioned postmodern analysis of our social condition have a certain adequacy, our fundamental human need to institutionalize indicates or even prescribes that people should become included in rebuilding new forms of cohesion and integration. By shaping the form of participation in a different (inclusive) way, restorative justice offers a fundamental (and necessary) alternative to existing exclusionary ways of formal social control that are to a certain degree undermining the integrative capacity of (primary) institutions.

Informal restorative practices

In the Netherlands, like in other western societies, we see signs that might be interpreted as the beginning of the process of institutionalizing restorative justice. Restorative practices (predominantly mediation, but also conferencing) are used in different social contexts, justifying theories are available and are being further developed, practices are being improved and training sessions are spreading the skills and values that characterize restorative procedures. At the moment there is little conceptual debate about the question whether restorative practices outside the formal (criminal) justice system amount to what might be called informal restorative justice. One of the conceptual problems is that the translation into Dutch of restorative justice ('herstelrecht') literally refers to either law or rights, inducing connotations to formal legal systems. Although academics such as myself are inclined to reserve the concept 'herstelrecht' to the use of restorative practices in the domain of criminal law – if only for the sake of some clarity – we should not overlook the fact that restorative justice conveys a number of radically different cultural notions with regard to conflict resolution which translate themselves into distinct restorative practices (which are the structural component of restorative justice).

It seems to me that to the extent that these radically different cultural notions – such as the focus on face-to-face encounters between those directly involved, the importance of dialogue and the aim of consensual resolutions redressing the (wrong and) harm, the cooperation between lay people and professionals, both in their capacity as active citizens, the integration of control and support, etc.[5] – are present in practices outside the formal domains of law, these practices may be taken to represent an informal kind of restorative justice.

What we can see clearly in the Netherlands is that the application of restorative practices is most rapidly growing in *informal* social contexts characterized by two conditions. The first condition is that the social conflicts that are the substance of the restorative practices concern actions which are outside the (formal or functional) reach of state agencies that may intervene on the grounds of exclusive legal competence. The social actors involved are free from state interference in what they try to achieve. The second condition is that there are social actors that promote restorative practices and offer these to people in conflict, who recognize the constructive potential of committing themselves to a restorative interaction. In other words, the social actors are and feel free to use restorative practices for dealing with their social problems and see reasons for engaging in restorative practices.

The three most prominent contexts that I can refer to here are neighbourhoods, schools and the workplace.

Neighbourhood (or community) conflict mediation has rapidly expanded from 4 projects in 1996 to 51 in 2004. The conflicts dealt with involve breaches of social expectations between neighbours, e.g. with regard to noise, the use of collective spaces such as galleries and halls, and the conduct of children and pets. Sometimes there are minor offences involved which remain outside the criminal process for various reasons connected to the reporting behaviour of citizens and the functional ideas of police (Blad 2003a). In particular the projects run at neighbourhood level appear to be highly effective, more effective than projects run at city level (Spierings and Peper 2002).

Peer mediation seems to be rapidly growing in schools, some of which use the conferencing model. The social conflicts here predominantly concern matters such as bullying, disobedience, fighting among pupils, etc. Mediation is also sometimes used in conflicts between teaching staff and parents. Thus far no research has been conducted with respect to peer mediation in schools so there are no data available.

In the workplace there seems to be a growing awareness of the importance of mediation in matters of (individual) labour conflict[6]. However, here we also lack data about the number of cases in which mediation is used (De Roo 2001).

Civil law and family problems

There are two other contexts outside the sphere of criminal justice in which we can expect restorative practices to be increasingly used in the near future. Both contexts are not informal like the ones discussed above. The first context concerns a situation in which there is a civil law claim brought before a civil court. Here, in principle, there is party control but a third party, the court, has been addressed. Since April 2004 the Dutch Ministry of Justice is officially promoting the use of mediation in these *civil law matters*, in the wake of some successful experiments which ran from 2000 until 2003. The experiments dealt with among others divorce matters, civil liability for damages and labour conflicts. Mediation in civil law matters is recognized as an important new form of access to the law and of relieving the civil courts of their case-loads.

In a letter to parliament about his policy with regard to mediation the Minister of Justice stated that government has an exemplary role to play in how Dutch society wishes to deal with conflicts and therefore mediation is also stimulated in *administrative law matters*. This concerns conflicts between citizens and administrations about the use of administrative competences and aims at avoiding expensive and dissatisfactory administrative appeal procedures (Ministerie van Justitie 2004).

More important for us is the second context: youth protection law. Here the initiative has been taken recently (1999–2001) to experiment with *family group conferencing*[7] as a model to deal with problematic situations in families regarding parents and children. One of the main aims is to let the wider family develop safe and sound plans to provide security for children and to avoid their outplacement, which almost always implies some form of placement in an institution.

This initiative has been very successful and gained a lot of professional and political support, to such an extent that family group conferencing will almost certainly become part of the legal arrangements in the sphere of youth welfare. In 2003 50 family group conferences were evaluated which resulted in 48 plans. Rob van Pagee summarizes the results in the following way:

> Almost all conferences have a plan, made and supported by the family, as a result. Referents accept the plans the families make and rate these with an average of 7.8. Also the participants' appreciation of the conference is high. Families rate the conference with an average of 7.4 and the plan receives an average of 7.9. This is a very important conclusion because everyone with some experience in the field of youth care knows how difficult it is for families and care professionals – given the painful situation and the sometimes long history and the distrust towards help – to develop a good plan and to achieve a consensus with everyone who has an important role to play.[8] (Van Pagee 2003: 47–8).

The design of the family plans was generally appreciated and, in addition, these plans were well implemented.

Since placement of juveniles in a closed institution is known to be an important criminogenic factor, the avoidance of such placement has a high relevance for the prevention of crime and the avoidance of criminalization of juveniles.

Restorative practices in criminal justice

It is clear that the restorative practices mentioned above do not directly touch upon the criminal justice system as such, in the sense that they do not imply any fundamental change in the penal process. Indirectly though, they have an important potential function for the criminal justice system because they can be recognized as ways of implementing the subsidiarity principle of penal law. To some extent they may prevent the use of criminal procedure by preventing the escalation of social conflicts to a criminal level or by dealing with offences which could have been dealt with by the criminal justice system if they had remained unaddressed.[9]

Now we will focus on restorative practices which are directly linked to the criminal justice system because they address events, situations or actions that have become known to the police and have become defined as criminal offences in police reports, constituting the basic condition for further criminal justice intervention. In all cases the offence has also been cleared up. In a recent book chapter Lauwaert (2004) has described these Dutch restorative practices in great detail so I will refrain from repeating her account and limit myself to a typification and discussion of them in view of our thematic interest: the institutionalization of restorative justice.

HALT

It is not unusual nor incorrect to mention the HALT programme[10] for juveniles as one of the first projects with a potentially high degree of restorativeness. Initiated in 1981 as a project to address problems of graffiti and vandalism in general in the city of Rotterdam (Hauber 2001: 332), by obliging juvenile perpetrators to clean and/or repair the damaged objects, it indeed has a restorative core idea. The HALT project was well received and acquired a legal status and national applicability for juvenile offenders between 12 and 18 years old. Interestingly, the participation of the juvenile in the HALT programme is *voluntary* and when he fulfils his obligations he can in principle no longer be prosecuted.[11] With a total number of around 17,000 applications per year the HALT project is in quantitative terms the most important restorative programme, although qualitatively it is only *partially* restorative. HALT offices only rarely organize victim–offender mediations and are predominantly offender-oriented. The development from 1997 onwards of an explicit restorative discourse in the public realm and the fact that more and more HALT functionaries are trained in mediation and conferencing may imply that the HALT project will become more fully restorative in the future.[12]

Restorative mediation and family group conferencing

In the second half of the 1990s a number of pioneers began to think and speak about reacting to crime in a restorative way, inspired by the developing restorative literature and experiments abroad. The first restorative programme was probably the project called Restorative Mediation ('herstelbemiddeling'), initiated in 1997 by Victim Support and the Probation Service in The Hague.

The explicit aim of this project was to offer an opportunity to victims and offenders to deal with their trauma and feelings of guilt. It only aimed at non-material or symbolic reparation at the request of victim or offender and explicitly did not want to influence penal procedure nor sentencing. Although mediation was possible at any stage of the penal process, in many cases it took place *after* sentence. Although the project dealt with 314 requests from 1997 till the end of 2002 (of which 15 per cent were considered to be inappropriate in terms of the selection criteria of the project) and evaluation research indicated a potential 'market' of 4100 cases per year,[13] the restorative mediation project was abandoned in 2003. It was not because clients were dissatisfied,[14] but because the founding organizations (Victim Support and Probation Service) felt that the project was not satisfactorily embedded in their organization and that the administration of the project had been suboptimal. Budget cuts imposed by government decisions, necessitating hard choices with regard to what is to be 'core business', figured in the background.

The next project was initiated in the city of Tilburg in 1999, inspired by experiments done by the Thames Valley Police and by the 'real justice' model[15], imported in the Netherlands by the organization Echt Recht in 1998. The project organizes family group conferences primarily for juveniles, including cases of severe crime, which are prepared by mediators but chaired by senior police officers in uniform (trained in the 'real justice' model). The project is operational in the initial stage of the criminal procedure before prosecutorial decision-making. It is left to the discretion of the Public Prosecutor to decide if and how he will take the results of the conference into account in his final decision. The project is a product of inter-agency co-operation, a characteristic shared by comparable projects that were initiated later in time, between legal and para-legal organizations such as the police, the Council for Youth Protection, the Public Prosecution Service and HALT offices.

The Tilburg project was one of seven projects that were evaluated (in terms of process and product) over a period of 15 months in 2001/2002 and which all used some (locally developed) variant of family group conferencing. Hokwerda (2004) investigated 50 conferences (of the 52 organized by all projects together) in great detail by means of participant observation and questionnaires.

What is important to note is that five of these projects had no formal relation to the criminal procedure. In view of the fact that in these projects the focus has mainly been on offering an occasion to the offender to apologize and to the victim to come to a better understanding of offence and offender, this seems to reveal that there has *not* been an *intention* to develop a restorative *justice* programme. This impression is confirmed by the fact that the agreements reached through conferences remained oral in 42 per cent of the cases and that provisions on monitoring the agreement were virtually absent. The latter can be explained by the fact that most of the agreements contained – besides apologies – mere promises about future behaviour (Lauwaert, 2004: 94). Hokwerda (2004: 186) concludes correctly that in most cases the agreements were 'without sanctionable engagement'.

In one of the projects conferencing formed part of the HALT procedure, which implies that it functioned in a diversionary way. In only one of the projects – in Utrecht – the conference and its result were treated as the formal substitute for a caution by the Public Prosecutor. Unfortunately it is precisely this project that was discontinued for reasons that I will discuss later.

Prison

Victim–offender mediation has already been introduced into the prison context by the restorative mediation programme discussed above and now conferencing also takes place in a small number of cases, involving (mostly but not only juvenile) detainees, their families and their victims. An informal platform has been established to promote restorative practices in the prison context and the development of a more comprehensive restorative detention, inspired by among others the Restorative Prison Project.[16]

Claims mediation

Lauwaert also discusses the legal practice called 'claims mediation' ('schadebemiddeling') in her overview of restorative justice in the Netherlands. Although there is some justification for this – it is a practice that invites the offender to pay a sum of money to compensate for damages and in this sense it is victim-oriented – it must be noted that this is not a mediation practice: a police officer or a functionary of the Public Prosecution Service (PPS), acting as caretakers (mandated by a directive) of the financial interests of the victim, addresses the suspect and proposes that he compensate for the victim's damages, if the victim has expressed a wish to receive such compensation. No actual contact between victim and offender is intended. In 2002 the financial damages of 6,000 victims[17] were effectively compensated through this administrative procedure. A financial compensation by the suspect often leads the PPS to dismiss the case or to offer a transaction.[18]

In six of the 26 existing neigbourhood offices of the PPS (so-called JIBs[19]) there occasionally are practices that go further than simply arranging financial compensation for the victim's damages. The general aim of these offices is to provide a more visible and more effective form of (criminal) justice on the basis of (physical, geographical) proximity to people in urban problem areas. Sometimes functionaries of the JIB become aware of conflicts that might lead to criminal offences and offer a kind of preventive mediation, in which there really is a face-to-face encounter and a possibility for a negotiated resolution.

Moreover, the mediation with regard to the financial damages described above is sometimes extended to deal also with emotional and psychological damages in a facilitated meeting between victim and offender. In circles of the PPS this tends to be termed *claims mediation plus*. In 2003 the number of cases in which this has happened was close to 100 (Slump 2003).

Institutionalizing restorative justice?

What I have demonstrated so far is that restorative practices are present both in informal and formal social contexts in Dutch society. But do they amount to the institutionalization of a new form of justice? My impression is that the informal restorative practices discussed above are not consciously experienced as a form of justice – despite the fact that they can analytically be depicted as such – let alone as a new form of justice. In general they will be seen as contributions to the resolution of social conflicts that might otherwise remain unsolved or escalate. In both cases these conflicts constitute a heavy burden upon personal and social life (Blad 2003a). As such, practices like neighbourhood conflict mediation or peer mediation in schools represent a new – or only newly discovered – secondary institution, situated between the repressive options of ignoring or even denying conflicts on the one hand and punishing criminalizable actions on the other.

In order to conclude that we are really institutionalizing restorative justice – both in a formal and informal sense – it will be crucial to see restorative practices being passed on to new generations, consolidated with a clear ideological, cultural identity as a new or at least distinct social interaction pattern, suitable to deal adequately with specified social problems. In the end, the use of restorative practices should become a self-evident resort to redress (certain) harms and wrongs. [20]

But despite the fact that the use of restorative practices is most rapidly growing in contexts outside the criminal justice domain, there are no strong indications that people engaged in these practices do recognize the general applicability of the foundational ideas of restorative practices. What I consider to be of crucial importance is whether these informal restorative practices will become and remain recognized by people as a general form of justice, as an exemplary model for how all justice ought to be: participatory, dialogic, narrative, consensual in principle and redressing recognized damages and wrongs.

Indeed, analytically the discourse of restorative justice does inscribe itself in the more general theoretical discourse on justice. According to Broekman (1978) the symbolic universe of *justice* – from a legal-anthropological viewpoint – is characterized by (a) the organization of speech and action in terms of 'subject' and 'subjectivity', (b) the design (or 'projection') of causality sequences of conflict and/or disturbed balances and (c) the orientation of speech strategies on 'restoring balance'.

On this abstract level justice comprises all known disciplines of (procedural) law and what we would want to see happening is a further differentiation of this symbolic universe of justice by the inclusion of restorative justice as a separate legal discipline with its own restorative integrity.

Therefore, in order to institutionalize restorative justice successfully, next to the mere use of restorative practices we need the development and public communication of a *restorative culture* to guide and accompany the use of restorative interaction patterns so that we do not only have – collectively available – 'different practices' but that we also collectively understand these practices differently, e.g. in their difference from both civil and penal law.

In this endeavour we will ultimately also have to deal with *punitive culture*, but to the extent that social interactions are now free from punitive claims and interventions by penal agencies, we could achieve a lot by spreading such a restorative culture.

Transforming the criminal justice system?

Whether institutionalizing restorative justice – which implies the development and consolidation of restorative practices understood as expressions of restorative culture in general – will be able to bring about a *transformation* of criminal justice is quite another question with very complex dimensions.

My suggestion is that transforming the criminal justice system can only be achieved if the general culture in our societies has moved in the direction of a restorative and away from a punitive culture. In this sense the development of informal restorative justice seems to be a pre-condition for a (cultural and procedural) transformation of criminal justice systems.

Criminal justice is shaped by the core idea that it makes sense for various reasons to threaten with punishment and to punish criminal offences. Criminal justice *is* punitive justice and, indeed, punishment is defended in the retributive tradition as the necessary and inevitable means to restore the balance disturbed by crime. In the other powerful justifying tradition(s) of consequentialism punishment is portrayed as an effective instrument to manage, contain and control crime and criminals.

Our theoretical view on institutionalization implies that we – or at least most of our contemporaries – are carriers of this punitive justice model, which is most visible in the criminal justice system, but which has 'functional equivalents' in most other social contexts, such as family life and school. We become socialized in the punitive model, including its justifications, and this has been so for at least the last eight centuries.[21]

Criminal punishment is characterized as the authoritative imposition of intended pain (hard treatment) based on a penal law, effectuating the initial threat of punishment. Because this is a practice of exerting the power of the collectivity against an individual, and because it has to be an authorized and legitimate exertion of power, the criminal procedure is thoroughly structured as a judicial procedure, checking the validity of the penal claim of the state, thereby protecting the legal rights of the defendant.

Penal culture has translated itself into patterns of interaction which are structured by the finality of the foreseen imposition of pain. It is punitive culture and structure and their flaws that have initiated the development of restorative justice (McElrea 2005). We are looking at two fundamentally different cultures which exclude each other at a fundamental level.[22]

It is not unimportant to note that at present, in democratic nations which embrace the rule of law, penal laws are the product of democratic decision-making. It means that our fellow citizens, who represent us in parliaments, should be addressed as crucial allies for restorative justice. Until now, at least in the Netherlands, most of them would be inclined to opt for the punitive approach to important social conflicts caused by identified harmful or wrongful behaviour.

Looking at the context of criminal justice, Lauwaert correctly concludes that restorative practices – in view of the small numbers of cases – remain a marginal phenomenon in the Netherlands (Lauwaert 2004: 96). I agree with her and I would even go further. It is my impression that most of the Dutch initiatives connected to criminal justice are not at all intended to develop a restorative *justice* model.[23] A crucial indicator for the meaning of most of the initiatives is that there is no deliberate programmatic attempt to achieve justice by repairing the harm (and/or wrong) caused by an offence. In most initiatives there are humanitarian considerations with regard to both the victim and the (most often juvenile) offender which motivate the initiators to develop a project as an add-on to the criminal justice procedure which in itself is not challenged. The aim of restoration is in most initiatives limited to the social-psychological sphere: it is argued that the victim might benefit from facing the culprit and might come to a deeper and richer understanding of the background of the criminal offence and of the offender. It is argued that the juvenile offender should be offered an opportunity to show that he is not *all bad* and that he feels sorry for what he has done. It might work to his advantage when he agrees to take part in a mediation process or in conferencing but this is not made explicit for reasons of protecting the victim from offenders with impure, opportunistic motivations (e.g. to get a better deal from the public prosecutor). The additional and mainly social-psychological meaning of most initiatives is also expressed by the fact that the main outcome sought after is only some form of apology by the offender. Serious obligations, laid down in a written agreement and followed up, are rarely intended and produced.

Obviously, the initiatives now taken to expand victim–offender mediation and conferencing in prisons are only likely to mediate the negative consequences of punitive justice, not to challenge and change it.

The restorative practices as they exist today in the domain of criminal justice in the Netherlands do not as yet represent a clear and integral restorative *justice* model but are only fragmentary resonances of it and risk misrepresenting restorative justice because they are adapted to the punitive rationality of the criminal justice system.

Obstacles

There are several important factors that may explain this state of affairs. Probably the most important and all-pervasive factor is the high level of institutionalization, division of labour and bureaucracy within the criminal justice system itself. The model of restorative justice – which in its integrality represents a fundamentally different organization of the justice procedure, different process personnel, etc. – and its core rationality ('restoration') is being received and perceived by highly developed agencies with strongly instititutionalized other rationalities, such as the rationality of punishment, rehabilitation and probation of offenders, therapeutic intervention, support and care for victims, and the state provision of security and safety.[24] These fragmented organizational rationalities – coordinated within the symbolic universe of criminal justice – are decisive for these organizations when considering engaging in a restorative initiative. As a consequence, the core idea of restorative justice is suppressed in the shaping of restorative practices and cannot come to a full realization.

In this respect it is important to note that the initiatives for restorative practices are all[25] taken by collaborators of criminal justice agencies or para-legal organizations, such as the police, the Council for Youth Protection, the Probation Service and the HALT offices. Moreover, these pioneers are perceived by their own organization as marginal experimenters who can be relieved of their 'core business' for the time being to prove that their initiatives may contribute to that core business which in itself does not become redefined. This explains how it could be that a potentially innovative and successful project such as the restorative mediation programme was abandoned (see the section on restorative practices above). Divided and dividing organizational interests were also the cause for the malfunctioning of the restorative (conferencing) project in Utrecht. This project was so carefully attuned to these interests that it became so complex and time-consuming that a sufficient number of referrals to the project could not be produced within a reasonable time-span after the criminal offence.[26]

Secondly, with the exception of the Utrecht project which *did* design the restorative procedure (conferencing) as a substitute for the formal caution, there has been virtually *no consultation* of academics involved in the restorative justice movement. This implies that in most initiatives there is only a fragmentary and superficial conception of restorative justice. A truly restorative culture has as yet not come into being as a common frame of reference. Hokwerda (2004: 187) mentions that in most of the seven initiatives she researched there seemed to be no awareness of the *inherent* sanctioning character of restorative practices, – a sanctioning character which they possess, I would argue, even when they are *only* about apologies.

Furthermore, a high level of institutionalization also exists in the domain of care and support for victims of crime. Support for victims is considered to be of a comparatively high standard (Brienen and Hoegen 2000). There is a strong national organization that not only organizes practical and emotional support for victims but also claims to express authoritative views on what would be in the victims' interests in general. Legal and para-legal arrangements oblige the police and the PPS to take notice and care of the expressed needs of victims in the criminal procedure. In so far as there are therapeutic needs or needs concerning general assistance – e.g. in acting as a civil party in the criminal procedure – Victim Support has local offices to which the victim will be referred for assistance. Professional and volunteer victim assistance workers regularly contribute to a generally displayed reluctant or hesitant attitude of criminal justice personnel towards restorative initiatives. They do so, for example, by stressing a supposed need to protect victims from risks in participating in a restorative procedure or even to protect certain victims from being approached with a request to participate.

In other words, supposed victim interests are strongly and separately voiced, sometimes as opposed to the interests of others, such as offenders. While support and care for victims are high on the political agenda at the moment, the offenders' interests seem more and more to be equated with the interest of society in general that they should refrain or be withheld from criminal activity. This expresses itself in a culture of *instrumentalism* in those founding organizations of restorative initiatives which have core tasks in relation to offenders: reducing recidivism of (juvenile) offenders is their prime criterion (Blad 2003b). My impression is that a number of initiatives only see the light of day because organizations are willing to try anything to cope better with the problem of crime or, to be more precise, the problem of recidivism (Leest 2002). Following the evaluative research by Hokwerda (2004) the Ministry of Justice has sponsored a partially new set of restorative experiments for 2005, imposing the condition that independent research be done to show results in terms of reduced recidivism. This research started at the end of 2004 and has to demonstrate these results in a time-span of one year. In my frequent contacts with field workers involved in restorative initiatives I seldom meet anyone who recognizes the absurdity of this demand.[27]

The general culture reigning in the criminal justice archipelago remains one of separating and opposing the interests of victim, offender and society as contradictory interests, in terms of the traditional criminal justice ideology.

Finally, it is important to note the general decline of a long tradition of theoretical and social critique of punishment and the managerial approach in general to problems such as crime. The 'bleak house' perspective on punishment which dominated criminal justice in the Netherlands for ages was swept away with the punitive turn in the 1980s, creating 'great expectations' of an increased use and level of punishment (Rutherford 1986, 1996). As a consequence of the political programme to make criminal justice credible again all legal and para-legal agencies have become disciplined in a managerial, output-oriented culture that has driven out all relevance of theoretical debate. It is quantity that counts, not quality (Van Swaaningen and Blad 1992, 1993).

From restorative practices to restorative justice

Most probably restorative practices will become *defined in* (Mathiesen 1974: 13–28) by criminal justice agencies, politicians and scholars as yet another punitive method. In the process they will lose all competitive potency and end up expanding and reinforcing punitive culture. This also happened with so many alternatives to the penal system that were proposed and produced by abolitionist thinkers (Mathiesen 1974).

Personally, in discussing and reflecting upon penal abolitionism, I came to the conclusion that the penal system will always be there and, indeed, that we should want it to be there. Because if we can imagine that there *could* be only one crime per year so horrible and committed under such circumstances that we could accept the state's right to punish,[28] we should want it to be punished in a framework that guarantees due process. The problematic place of punishment in contemporary society, in my view,[29] is therefore not so much related to the right to punish in principle but to the widespread instrumentalist abuse of punishment and the notorious disregard of the foundational and limiting principles of penality itself (Packer 1968; Christie 1981).

The *functional* reasons for a restorative culture to develop are all related to the socially destructive, dysfunctional and often even counterproductive consequences of over-criminalization and over-penalization. So there are good reasons for expanding restorative practices.

But if we want to continue and maximize the application of restorative practices in the field of criminal justice and still keep their restorative integrity, the process of defining restorative practices into the punitive – cultural and structural – framework can only be counteracted by developing, communicating and safeguarding a very clear identity of restorative justice, differentiated from the identity of punitive justice. We should strive for an integration of restorative practices within the criminal justice system *understood* as restorative practices and *not* as punitive practices. In view of the dominance of punitive culture this is not an easy task.

Unlike penal abolitionism (e.g. Hulsman 1986) restorative justice in principle accepts criminal law definitions of undesirable or 'problematic' social conduct and deliberately wants to deal with *criminal cases* as produced by criminal justice agencies. In so far as restorative practitioners are willing to do this, they have to develop working relations with the exponents of the criminal justice system and become, by definition, integrated into it. One of the main *conceptual* problems (with great impact on what this integration will mean also in practical terms) is that actions defined as crime have institutionally become – almost inextricably – connected to reactions defined as punishment (De Haan 1990).

Hence the efforts of some scholars in criminal law and legal theory to argue for a conception of the restorative agreement as a *punishment* (Hildebrandt 2003; Dignan 2003; von Hirsch *et al.* 2003).

The argument basically is that restorative agreements do create – often painful – obligations for the offender and may limit the exercise of certain civil rights, deprive him of time and money, etc. The conceptual flaw in this line of reasoning is the (implicit or explicit) syncretism of 'punishment' and 'sanction'.[30]

I do agree with Dignan (2003: 139) who argues that it is not very convincing when restorativists reply that these pains are *not intended* because, indeed, professionals who are involved in restorative practices know and hope that the offender, willing to face up to his responsibility, will agree to certain obligations in order to compensate for the harm and/or restore the moral wrongs, expressing his remorse in serious restorative activities. For me, the issue here is not the intention or knowledge that conferences and their results are usually painful for the offender. Crucial is the consensual and negotiated character of these obligations. Through its procedures of inviting to dialogue and invoking consensus and agreement about a harmful and wrong act restorative justice is indeed a *sanction system*, but it is not of a punitive kind. It does not seek to impose punishment but to avoid its imposition: this fundamentally different finality explains and justifies the fundamentally different character of restorative procedures compared to the penal procedure. Restorative justice does not want to deliver a threatened pain, but invites the offender to experience the pains of his own responsibility (guilt) and those of his victim(s). Criminal courts which approve of a restorative agreement are not punishing but ratifying and establishing the legal implications and consequences of the agreement, in particular the public recognition of the wrong done and the (legal) obligations the offender has accepted.

My cultural portrayal of restorative justice has many implications which cannot all be discussed in this chapter. But it indicates how restorative justice can be integrated as an institutional part of the criminal justice system while maintaining its integrity. Restorative justice offers a programmatic way to seriously implement and operationalize the fundamental principle of *subsidiarity* of punishment. By expanding the use and scope of restorative justice we can push back punishment as far as we dare to (Christie 1981), hopefully to the position of an *ultimate remedy* (which is the only acceptable place of punishment).

The fact that restorative justice wants to address criminal cases as defined by public law and with the participation and assistance of the existing criminal justice agencies, implies that it is not a movement towards privatization of conflict or towards informalism. Rather its institutionalization implies a reorganization of the formal sphere of public law, a restructuring of formality (Blad 2003a).

This restructured formality must facilitate the cooperation of citizens (involved in criminal events) and professionals in developing constructive sanctioning proposals, addressing needs, interests and causal factors in each individual case. Especially for legal professionals, socialized into the continental inquisitorial traditions, this implies a major challenge.

Ultimately, this institutionalization depends upon legislative decisions which demand political courage, such as the clear-cut and sound decision of the New Zealand legislator to install family group conferencing in 1989 as the prioritized way to deal with almost all types of juvenile offences. Only these kinds of systemic decisions can guarantee a reasonable expansion and consolidation of the restorative model.

Criminal justice interventions, it seems to me, can and must be liberated from a purported obligation to *impose punishment*: they must only be aiming at this imposition of punishment if this *appears* to be – in the concrete case and in view of its circumstances – inevitable.

A recognition of the inherent *sanctioning* character of restorative practices may provide sufficient and legitimate reason to replace, in as many cases as feasible, imposed punishment through ratified restorative agreements. The core normative function of criminal justice – re-establishing the broken norm – remains unaffected but, because of the active participation of the culprit and the constructive implications of the restorative agreement, the disadvantages of imposed punishments are avoided.

Roberts and Roach (2003) refer to a statement of the Canadian Parliamentary Justice Committee[31] of 1988 with regard to the purposes of sentencing that is very interesting because of the order in which the purposes of sanctioning are mentioned, reflecting the *ultima ratio* character of punishment (a concept that is even totally absent in the statement):

The purpose of sentencing is to contribute to the maintenance of a just, peaceful and safe society by holding offenders accountable for their criminal conduct through the imposition of just sanctions which:

(a) require, or encourage when it is not possible to require, offenders to acknowledge the harm they have done to victims and community, and to take responsibility for the consequences of their behaviour;

(b) take account of the steps offenders have taken, or propose to take, to make reparations to the victim and/or to the community for the harm done or to otherwise demonstrate acceptance of responsibility;

(c) facilitate victim–offender reconciliation where victims so request, or are willing to participate in such programmes;

(d) if necessary, provide offenders with opportunities which are likely to facilitate their rehabilitation [...][32] as productive and law-abiding members of society; and

(e) if necessary, denounce the behaviour and/or incapacitate the offender.

(Roberts and Roach, 2003: 245)

It is this kind of reframing of the purposes of interventions that can help us in re-orientating criminal justice in general and in creating a structural space for institutionalized restorative justice.

Notes

1 I suggest that 'agencies' are always reflections of 'secondary institutions' and that the estrangement derives from the fact that primary institutions are more flexible and become more quickly adapted to changes in the modes of production induced by technological inventions.

2 This competency means that most of us only possess general ideas about specific provinces of meaning, which allow us to orient our behavioural choices. These general ideas can be in contradiction to the expert knowledge that is gained by those who function in a specific province, such as justice.

3 Although sometimes public decisions seem to abolish institutions, they are only the consolidation of the result of a long process of transformation leading to the 'fading away' of certain (symbolic) interaction patterns (slavery, communism and the Berlin Wall, etc.).

4 Concept used by the Dutch cultural sociologist Zijderveld (2003). It means that mankind cannot survive without building and maintaining institutions that provide order and meaning.

5　Of course I give here my interpretation of core cultural notions in restorative justice.

6　In the Dutch 'poldermodel'-society, an institutionalized form of mediation has always been common practice in *collective* labour disputes.

7　This model is to a large degree a copy of the New Zealand family group conferencing model in family matters, run by the Child, Youth and Family Service as the equivalent of the family group model in criminal matters.

8　My translation of the original Dutch text (van Pagee 2003). Satisfaction and appreciation were measured on a scale from 1 to 10.

9　The latter is not a certainty because many offences remain unaddressed *and* unknown to the police or are *known* to the police but defined as not important enough for policy – and various other organizational – reasons to be addressed as penal matters.

10　The name and concept 'HALT' has an intended double meaning: 'Het ALTernatief' = the alternative to formal punishment and 'stop this conduct' (Hauber 2001: 333).

11　So the programme has a restorative and a diversionary character (section 77e, Dutch Criminal Code).

12　Lauwaert (2004: 94) reports that HALT Nederland (the national office of HALT) has announced this as a policy objective.

13　For the two jurisdictional districts in which the project has functioned.

14　The satisfaction of participating victims and offenders has not even been measured.

15　The most important characteristic of this model is that the conferencing procedure is thoroughly scripted and that the coordinator is obliged to strictly enact this script. The 'real justice' model is developed by the International Institute for Restorative Practices (see: www.restorativepractices.org).

16　This English project stopped in June 2004 but was continued by the North East Restorative Community Partnership. See: www.prisonstudies.org and www.prisonsne.com

17　Of a total of 92,000 victims known to and registered by the PPS in that year (Openbaar Ministerie 2003).

18　A 'transaction' is a procedural decision by the Public Prosecutor to drop charges if the suspect complies with some proposed condition(s), mostly the payment of a sum of money (art. 74 DCC). Although formally not designed as such, it functions as a negative sanction imposed by the Public Prosecutor. A transaction can only be imposed by the Public Prosecutor if the evidence for the offence is clear and sufficient for a conviction by the court and when the offender agrees with this imposition to avoid standing trial.

19　Lauwaert (2004: 88) describes these JIBs excellently. JIBs are small offices of the PPS, located in urban problem areas, having as their main goal the provision of swift and visible criminal justice interventions in local crime problems. 'JIB' is shorthand for 'Justitie In de Buurt' (Justice In the Neighbourhood).

20 This self-evident character is typical for all institutions: they do not need a special justification on each occasion. They are justified in the general culture.

21 Forms of mediation, compensation and reconciliation were dominant until around 1200. Thereafter they became gradually replaced by punishment by or in the name of the sovereign.

22 See Hoebel (1954). He emphasizes how fundamental cultural preferences must always exclude other choices that might have been made. In our case, the notion of restorative obligations, voluntarily taken up by the citizen responsible for a harm or a wrong, excludes imposed punishment and vice versa.

23 Restorative *justice* has been defined by Bazemore and Walgrave (1999: 48) as 'every action that is primarily oriented toward doing justice by repairing the harm that has been done by a crime'. This expresses the ambition to have the disturbed balance(s) restored by either having the offender 'repairing' or 'compensating' for the damages or, when the offender is not found, orienting the justice system's activities toward restoration. Recognizing the inherent sanctioning character of this obligation to do justice in this way implies a very subsidiary role – if any – for imposing other sanctions on the offender.

24 Berger and Luckmann (1966: 97–109) predicted the development of more and more competing professional organizations – representing more and more differentiated and segmentary disciplinary domains – and discussed the general implications under the heading 'scope and modes of institutionalization'.

25 With the exception of the initiative to import the real justice model into the Netherlands, which was taken by a citizen, not related to the criminal justice system.

26 Important is that the Council for Youth Protection has the authority to conduct an inquiry into the background of the juvenile offender and the offence and to advise the public prosecutor on how to deal with the case. The selection for the conferencing scheme was linked to this inquiry. This implied that in fact the Council decided which young offenders would be suitable for conferencing and which not. Even though this might be defensible from the dominant punitive logic, it implies that the whole procedure is from the beginning dominated by professionals deciding for those directly involved. Of course it would be perfectly possible to conduct inquiries after or in the context of organizing a conference, using the (preparation of the) conference also as a diagnostic instrument.

27 This absurdity lies in the instrumentalist illusion that there could be a type of unilateral action ('intervention') that is guaranteed to produce exactly and exclusively the kind of social behaviour that is expected from a social actor (and the related illusion that one could scientifically isolate the determining factor in producing the desired conduct). The alternative that restorative justice offers is to build constructive interaction patterns, from the outset on a participatory basis, which offers perspectives but no guarantees.

28 Of course this is an understatement for theoretical and rhetorical reasons.
29 In my view society suffers from many negative and even counter-productive effects of over-penalization and over-criminalization which is not the subject of this paper. I addressed some of them in my paper on instrumentalism (Blad 2003b).
30 As a consequence of this syncretism also, already formalized and institutionalized alternatives to punishment, such as our Dutch (diversionary) HALT scheme, would be punishments. My impression is that this syncretism is an expression of and vehicle for over-penalization.
31 In full: House of Commons Standing Committee on Justice and Solicitor General (Roberts and Roach, 2003: 255).
32 The quotation of Roberts and Roach (2003: 245) seems to have a minor flaw here because rehabilitation is mentioned twice.

References

Bazemore, G. and Walgrave, L. (1999) 'Restorative juvenile justice: in search of fundamentals and an outline for systemic reform', in G. Bazemore and L. Walgrave (eds), *Restorative Juvenile Justice: Repairing the Harm of Youth Crime.* Monsey, NY: Criminal Justice Press, pp. 45–74.

Berger, P. L. and Luckmann, T. (1966) *The Social Construction of Reality. A Treatise in the Sociology of Knowledge.* London: Penguin Books.

Blad, J. R. (2003a) 'Community mediation, criminal justice and restorative justice', in L. Walgrave (ed.), *Repositioning Restorative Justice.* Collumpton: Willan, pp. 191–207.

Blad, J. R. (2003b) 'Against penal instrumentalism', in *Building a Global Alliance, Fourth International Conference on Conferencing, Circles and other Restorative Practices.* International Institute for Restorative Practices, pp. 130–41. Also available on video through the website of the International Institute for Restorative Practices (www.restorativepractices.org).

Brienen, E. and Hoegen, E. (2000) *Victims of Crime in 22 European Criminal Justice Systems.* Nijmegen: Wolf Legal Productions.

Broekman, J. M. (1978) *Recht en antropologie.* Antwerpen: Standaard Wetenschappelijke Uitgeverij.

Christie, N. (1981) *Limits to Pain.* Oxford: Martin Robertson.

De Haan, W. (1990) *The Politics of Redress. Crime, Punishment and Penal Abolition* London: Unwin Hyman.

De Roo, A. (2001) 'Mediation in arbeidsgeschillen', *Tijdschrift voor Herstelrecht,* 1: 52–8.

Dignan, J. (2003) 'Towards a systemic model of restorative justice', in A. von Hirsch, J. Roberts, A. E. Bottoms, K. Roach and M. Schiff (eds), *Restorative Justice and Criminal Justice. Competing or Reconcilable Paradigms?* Oxford: Hart Publishing, pp. 135–56.

Hauber, A. (2001) 'Situationele en individuele preventie', in E. Lissenberg, S. van Ruller and R. van Swaaningen (eds), *Tegen de regels IV.* Nijmegen: Ars Aequi Libri, 325–41.

Hildebrandt, M. (2003) 'Mediation in strafzaken. Afdoening buiten recht?', *Delikt en Delinkwent*, 33: 353–74.

Hoebel, E. A. (1954) *The Law of Primitive Man*. Cambridge, MA: Harvard University Press.

Hokwerda, Y. M. (2004) *Herstelrecht in Jeugdstrafzaken*. The Hague: Boom Juridische Uitgevers.

Hulsman, L. (1986) 'Critical criminology and the concept of crime', *Contemporary Crises*, 10: 63–80.

Lauwaert, K. (2004) 'Netherlands', in D. Miers and J. Willemsens (eds), *Mapping Restorative Justice. Developments in 25 European Countries*. Leuven: European Forum for Victim–Offender Mediation and Restorative Justice, pp. 87–97.

Leest, J. (2002) 'We moeten alles proberen', *Tijdschrift voor Herstelrecht*, 1: 7–18.

McElrea, F. W. M. (2005) 'Restorative justice: a New Zealand perspective', in D. J. Cornwell (ed.), *Criminology and Criminal Punishment: Past, Present and Future Perspectives*. Winchester: Waterside Press, forthcoming.

Mathiesen, T. (1974) *The Politics of Abolition*. Oxford: Martin Robertson.

Ministerie van Justitie (2004) *Brief d.d. 19 april 2004 (kenmerk 5280305) inzake Mediation en het rechtsbestel*. The Hague: Ministerie van Justitie.

Openbaar Ministerie (2003) *Jaarverslag 2002*. The Hague: SDU.

Packer, H. L. (1968) *The Limits of the Criminal Sanction*. Stanford, CA: Stanford University Press.

Roberts, J. V. and Roach, K. (2003) 'Restorative justice in Canada', in A. von Hirsch, J. Roberts, A. E. Bottoms, K. Roach and M. Schiff (eds), *Restorative Justice and Criminal Justice. Competing or Reconcilable Paradigms?* Oxford: Hart Publishing, pp. 237–56.

Rutherford, A. (1986) *Prisons and the Process of Justice*. Oxford: Oxford University Press.

Rutherford, A. (1996) *Transforming Criminal Policy*. Winchester: Waterside Press.

Slump, G. J. (2003) *Bemiddelingsmodaliteiten bij Justitie in de Buurt*. Amsterdam: DSP-Groep BV.

Spierings, F. and Peper, B. (2002) 'Effects of voluntary mediation in the neighbourhood: the Dutch practice', *Employee Assistance Quarterly*, 18(2): 1–28.

Van Beek, F. (2003) *Eigen Kracht. Volgens plan?* Voorhout: WESP Onderzoek.

Van Beek, F. and Gramberg, P. (2003) *Is dit de toekomst van de jeugdzorg?* Voorhout: WESP Onderzoek.

Van Pagee, R. (ed.) (2003) *Eigen Kracht. Family Group Conferences in Nederland. Van model naar invoering*. Amsterdam: SWP.

Van Swaaningen, R. and Blad, J. R. (1992) *A Decade of Criminological Research and Penal Policy in the Netherlands. The 1980s: The Era of Business-Management Ideology*. Rotterdam: Centre for Integrated Penal Sciences, Erasmus University Rotterdam, Working Document No. 4.

Van Swaaningen, R. and Blad, J. R. (1993) 'Une décennie de recherche sur la production normative et le contrôle pénal aux Pays-Bas', in P. Robert and L. Van Outrive (eds), *Crime et Justice en Europe*. Paris: L'Harmattan, pp. 265–327.

Von Hirsch, A., Ashworth, A. and Shearing, C. (2003) 'Specifying aims and limits for restorative justice: a "making-amends" model?', in A. von Hirsch, J. Roberts, A. E. Bottoms, K. Roach and M. Schiff (eds), *Restorative Justice and Criminal Justice. Competing or Reconcilable Paradigms?* Oxford: Hart Publishing, pp. 21–42.

Zijderveld, A. C. (2003) 'De wisselende aandacht voor het slachtoffer. Enkele cultuursociologische beschouwingen', in Handelingen Nederlandse Juristen Vereniging (ed.), *Het opstandige slachtoffer. Genoegdoening in strafrecht en burgerlijk recht.* Deventer: Kluwer, pp. 1–32.

Chapter 6

Institutionalizing restorative youth justice in a cold, punitive climate

Adam Crawford

The 'New Labour' government that swept to power in 1997 did so with the promise of transforming youth justice in England and Wales. Tackling youth crime and disorder was identified as a principal plank of public policy upon which the government's fortunes in office would hinge. After 18 years of opposition the Labour Party was keen to distance itself from earlier 'law and order' policies which had come to constitute an electoral Achilles heel. After the defeat in 1992, key figures in the Labour Party set about constructing an embryonic package of 'law and order' policies. This was promoted by Tony Blair, while Shadow Home Secretary, who in 1993 first used the slogan: 'Tough on crime; tough on the causes of crime'. This catchphrase evocatively suggested a break with a 'soft on crime' stance traditionally associated with Labour. It marked a watershed in so far as it broke with discourses associated with both the traditional Left, of societal responsibility for crime, and the Right, which emphasized individual responsibility for crime. Labour's subsequent election victory, therefore, was supposed to signal a new dawn in youth justice.

This chapter considers New Labour government attempts to institutionalize elements of restorative justice as part of major reforms to youth justice in England and Wales. The chapter has two essential parts. The first outlines the background to and central components in recent youth justice reforms, introduced primarily by the Crime and Disorder Act 1998 and the Youth Justice and Criminal Evidence Act

1999. The eclectic ideas informing the legislation are delineated. The second part focuses upon the implementation of the referral orders and youth offender panels at the heart of the youth justice system. I use this as a lens through which to consider fundamental questions about the institutionalization of restorative justice inspired interventions against a punitive political background, highlighting and critically assessing some of the ambivalent dynamics that infuse government policies and their potential implications. Specifically, the chapter explores tensions between a managerial emphasis of policy and restorative ideas, notably the role of lay participation and victim involvement in institutionalizing restorative justice principles.

Youth justice in England and Wales

Youth crime has long been an enduring focus of anxiety in England and Wales (Pearson 1983). The history of juvenile justice has revolved around a tension between a focus on 'care and welfare', on the one hand, and 'control and punishment', on the other. Compared to their European neighbours – and Scotland – England and Wales have traditionally adopted a more punitive and less welfare-oriented approach to youth justice. Nevertheless, the twentieth century was dominated by a welfare orientation that reached its high-water mark in the late 1960s. Despite the 'authoritarian populism' of the Thatcher years (Hall 1979), the 1980s actually saw a significant and sustained decline in the use of custody for juveniles. One element underpinning this change in juvenile justice was practices of multi-agency diversion that saw an expansion in the use of cautioning[1] and an increasingly bifurcated system that distinguished the serious and persistent offenders from the rest. According to Pratt (1989) the debate about justice and welfare became less relevant in this period and a new form of penological discourse and practice was emerging: namely 'corporatism'. Efficient and effective 'management' of the juvenile offending population increasingly became a defining logic.

In many senses, the juvenile cautioning policy of the 1980s was one of the criminal justice success stories of the period. Driven largely at the local level, cautioning of juvenile offenders increased dramatically over the decade without a subsequent increase in crime. This was encouraged by the Conservative government by way of circulars 14/1985 and 59/1990. While, in 1971 the number of persons cautioned was 77,300, by 1993 this figure had risen to 311,300, a more than fourfold increase and nearly double the number cautioned ten years earlier.

A punitive shift

In 1993 there was a dramatic punitive swing in political and popular responses to youth crime. This was particularly marked in the aftermath of the murder of two-year-old James Bulger by two ten-year-old boys and the media frenzy generated by the event and the subsequent trial. This led to a renewed emphasis upon individual responsibility, early intervention and the use of custody. The government's mood shifted away from a managerialist informed pragmatic politics to one of 'populist punitiveness' (Bottoms 1995) with an emphasis upon a rhetoric of 'prison works'.

However, contrary to political and media portrayal of ever-rising youth lawlessness, juvenile crime generally was declining and, in particular, offences by children. The number of boys aged 10–14 found guilty or cautioned per 100,000 of the population was 2,926 in 1983 and 1,686 in 1993; the corresponding figures for girls were 941 and 621 (Home Office 1994: 122). As a consequence, each year about 180,000 young people aged 10–17 were being convicted or cautioned for offending: over 80 per cent being young men. Moreover, comparative research suggested that English youths did not commit more offences than their counterparts in other Western European countries (Junger-Tas et al. 1994).

Nevertheless, in the new punitive context, repeat cautioning of young people came to be seen as promoting 'lawlessness'. Circular 18/1994 signalled a significant retrenchment as it sought to reverse the use of repeat cautions. The circular declared that the use of multiple cautions 'brings cautioning into disrepute'. It suggested that 'it is only in exceptional circumstances that more than one caution should be considered'. Consequently, by 1996 the number of offenders cautioned for all offences fell by 2 per cent to 286,000 whereas the numbers cautioned had increased by an average of 6 per cent per annum between 1985 and 1992. In this more punitive climate, the number of young people in young offender institutions increased by more than 74 per cent in the nine years between 1993 and 2002 (see Figure 6.1).

Background to the youth justice reforms

It was against this increasingly punitive background that the Labour Party sought to articulate a 'new vision' for youth justice. Their proposals were heavily influenced by two publications: the findings of a Home Office research study into young people and crime (Graham and Bowling 1995) and the recommendations of the Audit Commission's Report *Misspent Youth* (1996). Both helped to set a

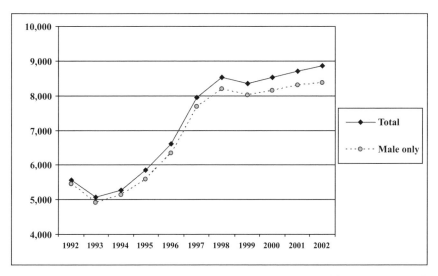

Figure 6.1 Young people in prison 1992–2002 (15–20 year olds at 30 June each year).
Source: Home Office (2003b: 66).

particular agenda premised on certain assumptions about youth crime and the appropriateness of given responses to it (Newburn 1998).

Graham and Bowling's research, based upon a self-report study of 14–25 year-olds, revealed that one in two males and one in three females admitted that they had committed an offence at some time. Most young people committed only one or two minor offences, but one in four males admitted to committing an offence in the previous 12 months and a quarter of these offenders said they committed more than five offences in the year. According to the research, about 3 per cent of young offenders accounted for a quarter of all offences committed by juveniles. Moreover, the research suggested that young people (particularly young men) were not 'growing out of crime' in the way that it had previously been thought (Rutherford 1986). Despite a small sample and the fact that it appeared to contradict other research findings (Hagell and Newburn 1994), it helped to affirm the view that a small but distinct group of young offenders exists who are responsible for much crime. It reinforced the belief that non-intervention from the courts and other criminal justice agencies would not result in young people merely 'growing out of crime'. The research suggested the need for intervention to encourage 'desistence' from crime by identifying risk, and protective, factors in child development in order to change behaviour when young people first start offending.

The timing of the Audit Commission's report was significant in that it was published in late 1996, just before the general election campaign in early 1997. The report concluded that about £1billion a year was being spent on a youth justice system which was both inefficient and ineffective. It found that youth justice was preoccupied with processing and administering young offenders rather than working to address offending behaviour. The report argued that:

- prosecution through the courts was too slow;
- cautioning became less and less effective the more often it was used with a particular offender;
- little money was being spent on addressing and changing offending behaviour;
- traditional criminal justice agencies involved with young people often worked in an uncoordinated way, with different priorities and performance targets; and
- little was being done to prevent young people from offending in the first place.

The report read as a damning indictment of the youth justice system. As such, it played into the hands of the Labour opposition, which seized upon the report to present itself as the party of 'law and order' with radical proposals to address the concerns raised.

Once in office, the Labour government set about a hasty consultation process over the summer of 1997 (Home Office 1997a). The subsequent White Paper that informed and set the tone of the youth justice elements of both the Crime and Disorder Act 1998 and the Youth Justice and Criminal Evidence Act 1999 was provocatively entitled *No More Excuses*. The two Acts claim to 'build on principles underlying the concept of restorative justice', defined as the '3Rs of restorative justice':

> *restoration*: young offenders apologising to their victims and making amends for the harm they have done;
> *reintegration*: young offenders paying their debt to society, putting their crime behind them and rejoining the law abiding community; and
> *responsibility*: young offenders – and their parents – facing the consequences of their offending behaviour and taking responsibility for preventing further offending.
>
> (Home Office 1997b: para. 9.21)

The government presented its reforms as fundamentally changing the underlying values of the system 'away from an exclusionary punitive justice and towards an inclusionary restorative justice' (Muncie 2000: 14).

More recently, the government has published a consultation document on restorative justice (Home Office 2003a), in which it identifies restorative interventions as a key means through which to deliver government commitments to 'placing victims' need at the centre of the criminal justice system'. It declared that restorative justice

> gives rights to victims and challenges offenders, communities and victims to take part in building a better future. And, by helping citizens resolve conflicts between themselves, it forms a key part of this Government's emphasis on civil renewal, empowering ordinary people to tackle problems at a local level. Restorative justice recognizes that crime is not just an offence against the state, but a breaking of trust between people. This recognition can transform how we approach crime and justice. (Home Office 2003a: 9, para 1.4)

The new youth justice reforms

The 1998 Act paid considerable attention to reforming the youth justice infrastructure by introducing the Youth Justice Board (YJB) to oversee the changes at the national level. The youth justice system was given an overarching aim: 'to prevent offending by young people' and a duty on all youth justice agencies to have regard to it. At the local level the legislation established multi-disciplinary Youth Offending Teams (YOTs) to implement and deliver the 'new' youth justice.[2] Since April 2000 every local municipal authority was required to have a YOT in place. There are now 155 YOTs composed of about 2,500 staff from the different agencies across England and Wales.[3]

Significantly, the Act abolished the principle of *doli incapax* thus lowering the age of criminal responsibility from 14 to 10.[4] The Act also introduced the 'anti-social behaviour order' (ASBO), providing a civil remedy to restrain anti-social behaviour by individuals or a group, supported by criminal sanctions if breached. It also gave a power for local authorities in consultation with the police to introduce a 'local child curfew' (not exceeding 90 days) for all children under the age of 10 in a specified area between the hours of 9 p.m. and 6 a.m. unless accompanied by a parent or responsible adult.

As a central element of the changes, cautions were replaced by a system of reprimands and final warnings. The latter trigger interventions whereas reprimands stand alone as a formal police caution. Together, they act as two sequential levels of response prior to court appearance. Following one reprimand a further offence will lead to a final warning or a charge. Any further offending following a final warning will normally result in a charge being brought. Once an offender has received either a reprimand or a final warning he or she must not be given a second, except in the limited circumstances where the latest offence is not serious and more than two years have passed since the first reprimand or final warning was given. Police forces and YOTs administer final warnings which, according to the government, are 'designed to end repeat cautioning and provide a progressive and meaningful response to offending behaviour' and ensure that juveniles who reoffend after a 'warning' are dealt with quickly through the courts (Home Office 2000: para. 1).

The principal restorative work of YOTs under the Act was through the final warning scheme, reparation orders and action plan orders (Dignan 1999). Reparation orders are sentences of the court that involve supervised and directed reparation to victims. The Act states that the consent of victim(s) is required before a reparation order can be made. Finally, 'action plan orders' involve an intensive three-month programme of supervised and directed activities for young offenders, which may involve restorative elements, including victim reparation.

The YJB subsequently funded some 46 restorative justice projects[5] which were subsequently evaluated. Most of these were either at final warning or reparation order stage and took the form of family group conferencing, mediation (direct and indirect), reparation (direct and to the community) and victim awareness. Over half of the projects experienced lower than expected referrals and a lower than expected proportion of cases progressing to the intervention (Wilcox with Hoyle 2004: 7). The national research also highlighted inadequate victim contact procedures and poor communication between YOTs and projects (where subcontracted), resulting in 'insufficient or inappropriate referrals' (*ibid.*). They also found that pressures to reduce delays in the criminal process through 'fast-tracking' had adverse implications for the quality of assessment and work with victims. The research concluded that in implementation there was an over-reliance upon community reparation and that the extent to which different projects facilitated dialogue between the offender, victim and community (hence their restorativeness) was variable.

Referral orders

While the youth justice provisions in the 1998 Act reworked earlier initiatives, albeit with a new emphasis upon partnerships, by contrast the 1999 Act 'belongs unambiguously to New Labour' (Ball 2000: 211). It goes much further down the restorative justice path than did the 1998 Act. It introduces a new order which requires the automatic referral of most young offenders convicted by the court for the first time to a youth offender panel. As such, the referral order is *the* primary sentence for first-time young offenders under the age of 18. A referral order should not be made where the court considers custody or a hospital order appropriate, nor should it be given where an absolute discharge is the appropriate disposal. In all other cases where the juvenile is convicted for the first time and pleads guilty, a referral order will be the compulsory sentence.[6] The court retains the power to determine the length of the referral order, which can last from 3 to 12 months, depending on the seriousness of the crime.

The court refers the young person to a youth offender panel and into the charge of the YOT. Panels consist of one YOT member and two lay panel members (one of whom chairs the meeting). YOTs have responsibility for the recruitment and training of community panel members, administering panel meetings and implementing referral orders. Youth offender panels are designed to provide a less formal context than court for the offender, the victim, their supporters and members of the community to discuss the crime and its consequences. A parent of a young offender aged under 16 is expected to attend all panel meetings.[7] It is not intended that legal representatives acting in a professional capacity be invited to panel meetings either directly or as an offender's supporter. The purpose of the panel is 'to provide a constructive forum for the young offender to confront the consequences of the crime and agree a programme of meaningful activity to prevent any further offending'. To encourage the restorative nature of the process a variety of other people may be invited to attend given panel meetings (albeit any participation is strictly voluntary). Where there is no direct victim the panel may wish to invite 'someone who can bring a victim perspective' to the meeting, 'for example a local business person or an individual who has suffered a similar offence' (Home Office 2002).

Panels draw eclectically from a variety of sources. They borrow explicitly from the experience of the Scottish Children's Hearings system, in operation since 1971 (Waterhouse *et al.* 1999). Panels also draw from the experience of family group conferencing in New Zealand (Morris and Maxwell 2000). Finally, they draw upon the history of victim–offender mediation in England and Wales (Marshall 1999) and the practice of 'restorative cautioning' by the Thames Valley Police (Hoyle *et al.* 2002). The aim of the initial panel meeting is to devise a 'youth offender contract' and, where the victim chooses to attend, for them to meet and talk about the offence with the offender. Negotiations between the panel and offender about the content of the contract should be led by the community panel members. The YOT member's role is to advise on potential activities and to ensure proportionality. The resulting youth offender contract should always include both reparation to the victim or wider community and a programme of activity designed primarily to prevent further offending. According to the national *guidance*, 'contracts should be negotiated with offenders, not imposed on them' (Home Office 2002). If no agreement can be reached or the offender refuses to sign the contract, then he or she will be referred back to court for re-sentencing.

The YOT is responsible for monitoring the contract and is expected to keep a record of the offender's compliance. The panel is expected to hold progress meetings with the offender at least once every three months. The number of progress meetings required will depend on the length of the contract and the level of supervision considered necessary in each case. Once the period of the referral order is successfully completed the offender is no longer considered to have a criminal record under the Rehabilitation of Offenders Act 1974.

Referral orders and youth offender panels were initially introduced as pilots in eleven areas across England and Wales in 2000, which were the subject of national evaluation (Newburn *et al.* 2001, 2002). National implementation began in April 2002. As a consequence of the mandatory nature of the new order it swiftly became a central court disposition. In the first year of national implementation (April 2002–3), referral orders accounted for nearly one-third (29 per cent) of all youth court orders. As such, the referral order constitutes a third step in a new 'sanctions escalator' by which young people now move through the reformed youth justice system (see Figure 6.2). In practice, however, many young people often miss out the first two steps, arriving directly at the court and a referral order. According to research, the referral order is often the first response to the young person's offending behaviour, rather than a pre-court diversion; some 54 per cent of referral orders were made in cases where the young person had received no previous reprimand or final warning by the police (YJB 2003).

The pilot evaluation suggested that the YOTs in the eleven areas responded well to the considerable new challenges set by implementation. Possibly the most encouraging result was the fact that within a year panels appeared to have established themselves as deliberative and participatory forums in which to address a young person's offending behaviour. The informal setting of panels seems to allow young people, their parents or carers, community panel members and YOT advisers

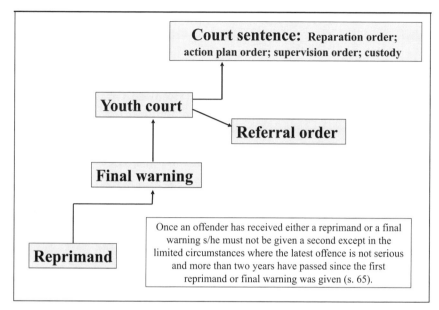

Figure 6.2   The youth justice sanctions escalator.

opportunities to discuss the nature and consequences of a young person's offending, as well as how to respond to this in ways which seek to repair the harm done and to address the causes of the young person's offending behaviour (Newburn *et al.* 2001: 89). Panels are not only forums for deliberation about the harm and its consequences, but also act as a means of monitoring contract compliance and championing reintegration. In this regard, referral orders accord a more central role to the panel beyond the initial meeting at which the contract is agreed than do other restorative interventions.

However, the research raised concerns about the number of relatively minor cases being dealt with by way of a referral order, notably where it replaced the conditional discharge as a sentence. One of the major disappointments of implementation was found to be the low level of victim involvement. It was estimated that victims only attended in 13 per cent of relevant cases,[8] which contrasts poorly with victim involvement in restorative justice interventions in New Zealand and Australia.[9] This would suggest that in England and Wales attempts to locate restorative justice processes at the heart of a 'reluctant' criminal justice system (Shapland 2000) raise important cultural and organizational challenges (Crawford and Newburn 2003: 213). The referral order represents both a particular and a rather peculiar hybrid attempt to integrate restorative justice ideas and values into youth justice practice. It does so in a clearly coercive, penal context that offends cherished restorative ideals of voluntariness. Despite the consensual imagery some young people may feel they have little choice, in a room full of adults, but to comply with what they are told to do. As such referral orders have received mixed reactions from commentators (Crawford 2002b). While Dignan has argued that the changes should ensure restorative justice is 'no longer a marginal, irregular and highly localized activity' (1999: 53), this optimistic view is not shared by other commentators (Morris and Gelsthorpe 2000).

Yet, by establishing an almost mandatory sentence of the court (for young offenders appearing in court for the first time), the referral order delivers a steady supply of cases to youth offender panels. In so doing, the referral order circumvents the frequent stumbling block for many restorative justice initiatives, namely small, self-selective caseloads and a lack of referrals (as noted in the experience of the YJB restorative justice projects mentioned earlier (Wilcox with Hoyle 2004)). Unlike most initiatives that deal with very small caseloads and remain peripheral to the coercive system, the referral order moved centre stage almost overnight. Moreover, voluntariness in most restorative justice interventions is circumscribed, often surrounded by various 'coercive sticks' and inducements. Moreover, the research evidence shows that panels received high levels of satisfaction from young people and parents on measures of procedural justice, including being treated fairly and with respect, as well as being able to have their say and given a voice in the process (Crawford and Newburn 2003).

In the case of referral orders, coercion provides the capacity to move certain restorative justice values to the very heart of the youth justice system. The loss of voluntariness, it would appear, is the price paid for this. While the coercive nature of the referral order undoubtedly constrains the restorative work of youth offender panels, nevertheless they offer a process through which to engage young people and their parents in a different, and more positive, process of communication and reasoning than that found generally in the criminal courts. Thus one of the positive lessons for restorative justice may be that, despite the coercive context, and possibly partly as a consequence of it, change in the direction of delivering a more deliberative process can be realized.

Data on one-year reconviction rates from the national 2003 cohort (Home Office 2005c) show that referral orders compare favourably with all other court disposals.[10] The 12-month reconviction rate among the 5,895 young people given a referral order in 2003 was 37.1 per cent, significantly lower that the rates for other first-tier penalties, including a discharge (51.9 per cent), a fine (57.7 per cent) and a reparation order (62.3 per cent), and considerably lower than rates for community penalties (average 67.7 per cent)[11] and custody (69.4 per cent). The 2003 cohort also showed statistically significant reductions as compared to previous years for offenders given a referral order (down 6.5 per cent on the 2002 cohort). Inevitably, variations in reconviction rates across different disposals are largely explained by differences in the characteristics of the young offenders given each disposal. Those young offenders given a referral order, on first appearance in court, are likely to have lower intrinsic risk of offending as compared to those given a custodial sentence, for example. Consequently, reconviction rates for pre-court disposals are even lower than for a court-ordered disposal such as a referral order. According to the 2003 cohort, reconviction for final warnings and reprimands stood at 19.7 per cent.

Institutionalizing restorative justice

As I have argued elsewhere, the restorative justice literature all too often evades a detailed exploration or analysis of the organizational, legal, political and cultural contexts in which different interventions are implanted and the social practices that influence the manner in which they are received and implemented (Crawford 2002a). In what follows, I want to use the referral order as a specific lens through which to expose the wider policy dynamics and tensions, as well as the prevailing political and social forces that have shaped the institutionalization of this particular restorative justice inspired initiative in an English context.

Managerialism and restorative justice

There is an inherent tension between, on the one hand, the managerialist pre-occupation with speed, cost reductions, performance measurement and efficiency gains and, on the other hand, a desire for a greater relational dynamic and community involvement in local responses to crime. One of New Labour's five key pledges in the 1997 election was to 'fast-track punishment for persistent young offenders by halving the time from arrest to sentencing'. The introduction of statutory time limits has been central to realizing this aim. Thus, according to national standards, the initial panel meeting should be held within 20 working days of a referral order being made in court where a victim is involved and 15 working days where there is no identifiable victim. However, this managerialist impulse allows little space for the expressive and emotive aspects of restorative justice, particularly with regard to victim input.

Victim consultation and input often takes a considerable investment in time if victims are not to be unduly pressurized and their needs addressed sensitively. Research findings suggest that the emphasis upon speed may be a significant impediment to victim input (Newburn *et al.* 2001: 52; Crawford and Burden 2005). This is supported by research into the reparative work of YOTs which concluded that: 'fast-tracking is best regarded as a means of achieving the aims of increasing the accountability of offenders, reducing the risks of re-offending and meeting the needs of victims rather than as an unyielding end in its own right' (Dignan 2000: 3).

Organizing youth offender panels presents considerable administrative hurdles that challenge traditional ways of working. Holding panels in the evening and at weekends requires different working patterns; facilitating the attendance of the diverse stakeholders presents difficulties of organization and timing; and finding appropriate venues challenges the extent to which panels are rooted in local community infrastructures. Moreover, administering panels creatively and flexibly often sits awkwardly within a risk-averse professional culture. Rotas of community volunteers, for example, are not ideal ways of constituting youth offender panels, but present a rational means of managing them. So too does the strategy of scheduling numerous back-to-back panels in one sitting. Nevertheless, these all serve to limit the restorative potential of panels. In practice, balancing the demands of rational management and accommodating the emotional, expressive and human dimensions of restorative justice constitute a fundamental but precarious dynamic in implementing youth offender panels.

Local justice versus centralized control

Similarly, there is a tension between the devolution of authority to local institutions of criminal justice, such as local magistrates' courts and YOTs, and the greater centralization of control exerted through standard-setting and performance monitoring, backed by regimes of audits and inspections. The managerialist concern with efficiency gains has often led to a move away from 'local justice' and encouraged greater centralization, in which government departments and related agencies closely govern local practices. This tension is particularly apparent in the implementation of referral orders where the philosophy of youth offender panels evokes the importance of local knowledge, local people contributing to the handling of cases in their own local area, and hence the importance of local normative orders, and local service provision. In many ways, youth offender panels appeal to a form of 'legal pluralism' (Merry 1988), which is sensitive to local conditions and needs but is at odds with the close central steering of initiatives by government departments.

Understandable concerns over proportionality and the monitoring of discrimination – notably sexist and racist practices – have often served or been used as a cipher to promote central standard setting. In relation to referral orders, not only do national standards and targets exist (against which an individual YOT's performance is judged) in relation to the percentage of victims contacted,[12] the number of working days within which young people and victims are to be first contacted and the number of meetings to be held (YJB 2004a), but there also is central *guidance* on the amount of reparation in hours that should be agreed in the youth offender contract, dependent upon the length of the order.[13] As such, rather than the panel process and outcome according to the needs and desires of the parties, in large part they are determined by the dictates of central guidance and standards. On a personal note, as someone who has been intimately involved in researching and observing the implementation of youth offender panels (having been part of the initial pilot evaluation team and more recently conducted further evaluation research), what has struck me most has been the manner in which youth offender panels, under bureaucratic and managerial pressures, have become routinized, normalized and standardized, losing much of their party-centred creativity and flexibility in the process. Standardized hours of community reparation, packaged activities drawn from a pre-determined list (like coats off a peg) and standard-term contracts, all leave less scope for the deliberative qualities of panels.

At one level, this may be an explicable response to the complexities of the referral order as an intervention, but it is also symptomatic of a broader ambiguity within government of governing 'at arm's length but hands on' (Crawford 2001: 63). As Rhodes notes, for government '"hands off" is the hardest lesson of all to learn' (2000: 361). On the one hand, there is the centralist desire to control, to issue guidance, to ensure minimum standards, and to authorize, license and inspect the doings of others. On the other hand, there is the fluid and creative potential of party empowerment that informs the principles of restorative justice and which demand flexibility, deliberation and adaptation to circumstances.

Lay involvement and the professionalization of justice

The idea of justice as entailing participation and deliberation by citizens, as the referral order suggests through its involvement of lay panel members and deliberative process, has deep normative and historic roots in England and Wales. This is most notable in the institutions of the jury and the lay magistracy, both of which share the notion of 'judgement by one's peers'. However, both of these institutions have become increasingly circumscribed in recent years under managerialist pressures. In the name of modernization there has been a reduction in the role of lay people in court processes. The right to trial by jury has been increasingly eroded by successive legislation. So, too, there has been an increased reliance upon professional stipendiary magistrates,[14] in part at the expense of the lay magistracy. To an extent, this is due to a perception in government circles that the lay magistracy 'as a symbol of the unmodernized court' is 'now under pressure as never before' (Raine 2001).

Against this background, the centrality of lay volunteers within the institutionalization of youth offender panels might come as some surprise. And yet the involvement of lay panel members has served to resist some of the excesses of recent managerialist pressures on youth justice. As volunteers are not driven by the same organizational imperatives as YOT staff, they have been able to safeguard some of the key restorative ideals. Where volunteers are embedded in their local communities, they have been able to facilitate localized practices which, because they are fostered, determined and owned by volunteers rather than professionals, are relatively resistant to the demands of bureaucratic managerialism. In this manner, panels potentially open a space for a different type of dialogue to occur in response to incidences of crime. For example, panel members were likely to allow greater time over meetings than practitioners might otherwise have preferred given organizational and work constraints upon them, time to allow the expression of emotions and feelings, for deliberation and discussion. YOT panel members in the pilots invariably told us that they could have run the meeting more speedily, but to have done so might well have diminished their restorative potential (Crawford and Newburn 2003).

Nevertheless, the involvement of community panel members, albeit a significant feature of youth offender panels, is not unproblematic. According to national guidance, community panel members should be people who are properly representative of the community they intend to serve and who have the appropriate personal characteristics for the task of dealing effectively with young offenders, and their victims, in a restorative justice context. As such, volunteer involvement raises acute questions of legitimacy regarding the representativeness of those involved (see Crawford and Newburn 2002). If lay involvement is intended to reflect the parties' 'peers' or the general citizenry, then this accords a significant import to their representative composition. Critical questions of representation can also be levelled at professionals who may be unrepresentative in more significant ways than volunteers. However, representation has a slightly different order of importance for lay people, whose primary justification for involvement may be their representativeness, as against professionals whose primary justification lies in their accountability and expertise: an amalgam of their specialization, training, education and professionalization which, to a degree, sets them apart from the general citizenry.

Research conducted eight months after the national implementation of referral orders suggests that by the end of December 2002 there were some 5,130 panel volunteers across England and Wales who had completed training and were sitting on panels, with a further 2,009 people awaiting training (Biermann and Moulton 2003). The research also found that, despite an over-representation of women (65 per cent of all volunteers), panel members broadly reflected the general population as against recent census data (see Table 6.1). Certainly, panel volunteers are more representative of the population than lay magistrates, particularly with regard to age and ethnic origin.

If the role of community panel members is to reflect the profile and composition of the wider community, then YOTs appear to have done well to attract a diverse group of volunteers. Naturally, there are important local variations.[15] However, the research also highlighted the fact that YOT managers remained keen to attract a greater number of people from ethnic minority backgrounds and younger people, notably young men. There are good reasons to suggest that an *over-representation* of volunteers from these groups is consistent with the idea that volunteers should reflect those young people referred to panels.

Table 6.1 Panel volunteers and lay magistrates as against census data

	Census 2001	Youth offender panel volunteers 2002	Lay magistrates 2001
Female	52%	65%	49%
Under 40	35%	37%	4%
60–75	19%	12%	32%
Black	2%	7%	2%
Asian	4%	3%	3%
Other none-white	2%	1%	2%
Unemployed	3%	3%	N/A

Source: Adapted from Biermann and Moulton (2003).

Nevertheless, working with volunteers as equal partners in an inclusive process presents real challenges to the way in which professional YOT staff work. In the pilot sites, though making significant progress, panels only uncovered a small part of the potential contribution of volunteers. There is much more that could be done in relation to their involvement as a broader resource in delivering a form of justice that links panels to wider communities in which they are located and the latent forms of social control that reside therein. In this, panels in England and Wales potentially suffer the same dichotomy identified by Karp and Drakulich in relation to volunteer Reparative Board members in Vermont, that 'competency building is one of the most theoretically exciting but practically disappointing parts of the program' (2004: 682).

Nevertheless, despite implicit (or sometimes explicit) desires of government to use lay people as a cheaper alternative to established and costly professionals, lay involvement may not amount to a cost saving. Volunteers often introduce new costs and perceived 'inefficiencies' into practices, as well as frequently generating new workloads. Even though a system may be based on unpaid volunteers (such as boards and panels), of itself, this does not mean that it is necessarily cheap. There are significant costs associated with training, advice and information provision for volunteers, as well as with other supporting infrastructures that are required simply because volunteers are involved. There is also a growing recognition that lay volunteers tend to work at a slower pace than do professional counterparts. This may itself be a positive outcome of lay involvement, in that they allow greater time and space for the human and deliberative aspects of restorative justice. However, for governments keen to speed up justice and remove inefficiencies, such consequences of lay involvement may jar with wider managerialist goals.

There are concerns that lay involvement may affront cherished notions of 'non-partisanship', key criteria in the legitimate exercise of power, particularly in criminal justice, both at a normative level and in terms of how justice is experienced by individuals (Tyler 1990). There is an ambiguity in that the more attached to the community lay panel members are, the less likely they are to hold the required 'detached stance' which constitutes a central value in establishing facilitator neutrality and legitimacy. While the intention is for the social distance between panel members and participants to be reduced, it is undesirable for justice to be compromised by prior personal relations. Experience suggests the volunteers themselves prefer not to work in areas where they live or know people too well (particularly if these are high crime areas). As well as concerns for personal safety and reprisals, this is often explained in terms of the inappropriateness of exerting power and authority over those with whom they have close social relationships. Both psychologically and normatively to do so would conflict with justice.

Ironically, it is exactly this pressure to provide neutral and detached facilitators that increases the likelihood of professionalization of lay panel members and the formalization of otherwise fluid and open restorative processes. Experience suggests that over time many schemes come to rely upon a group of 'core' staff who increasingly are seen as semi-professionals by virtue of their work turnover, their training and experience. The early evidence suggests that a core group of panel members are increasingly relied upon by YOTs for much of the work. As a result, panel members may begin to look and behave more like 'quasi-professionals' than ordinary lay people. In this context, lay volunteers raise questions about the appropriate competencies and skills that particular personnel should have in delivering a given service, and hence about the nature and quality of the service to be delivered, as well as the accountability of volunteers and panel outcomes.

Victim involvement and community participation

The low level of victim involvement in the implementation of referral orders (Newburn *et al.* 2002) and final warnings and reparation orders (Dignan 2000) suggests that in practice the reforms may not yet be delivering victims' needs nor according with the ultimate principles of restorative justice. More fundamentally, there are dangers that victims' interests may be subverted either 'in the service of offenders' – their rehabilitation or management – or in the service of the youth justice system more generally (Crawford 2000: 292). This can serve to reinforce the secondary status of victims within criminal justice processes. For example, victims in some of the pilots attended a panel only to be asked to leave once the panel had dealt with issues of reparation and were keen to focus on discussions about the programme of activities for the young person – not deemed appropriate for victims to participate in. In this context, victims may see themselves as a 'prop' in an offender-focused drama.

Under such pressures, one potential consequence may be that reparation becomes 'tokenistic' or mechanical and may 'appear to both victims and offenders as ritualistic and formulaic' (Dignan 2000: 17). The heavy reliance upon 'community reparation' (often vaguely conceived) rather than direct victim reparation in youth offender contracts[16] and as outcomes of restorative justice projects elsewhere in youth justice

(Wilcox with Hoyle 2004) suggests that the community can be, and often is, appropriated as a surrogate victim. This expanded notion of victim feeds into restorative justice models of harm (Young 2000) but may serve to dilute direct victim engagement and reparation.

One broad lesson for restorative justice from the experience of both youth offender panels in England and Reparative Boards in the US may be that in practice there can be a tension between community participation and victim involvement. As Karp and Drakulich note, their research into Reparative Boards in Vermont found 'substantial *community involvement* and limited *victim involvement*' (2004: 678, emphasis in original). The concern is that involvement of community representatives can serve to sideline or operate at the expense of direct victim input. The community may be felt to be capable of bringing a victim perspective through its own role as an indirect or secondary victim of the crime. This expanded understanding of victimization may limit the involvement of actual victims. This is not to suggest that community involvement will always function in this way, but rather that in a system that is unwilling or reluctant to accord to victims a central stake, community participation can be used as an excuse for victim non-attendance. The low level of victim participation at English panels and Vermont Reparative Boards raises important questions about the cultural and organizational challenges presented by attempts to integrate victims into the heart of criminal justice processes.

The role of practitioners in implementation

Despite the centralized steering of implementation and the heavy weight of national standards, one of the enduring lessons of the pilot experience was the capacity of practitioners working with lay panel members to ensure that programmes, as far as possible, sought to accord with restorative principles and were not over-intensive or overly interventionist. Here, the institutionalization of restorative justice is not merely a series of discrete stages but a more interactive and constitutive process. As Anderson notes, 'policy is made as it is being administered and administered as it is being made' (1975: 79). In this sense, youth justice practitioners constituted the 'street-level bureaucrats', in Lipsky's (1980) terms, who had a significant impact on the ways in which the referral orders were implemented. In diverse ways they acted to transform, subvert or redirect the intentions of policy: sometimes inadvertently, sometimes due to administrative necessity and sometimes for ideological reasons. Practitioners did much to limit the nature of the referral order as a sentence, particularly in less serious cases where the administrative demands, personnel commitment and intervention in the lives of those affected often appeared out of proportion to the nature of the offending. YOT staff worked hard with panel members to keep the contractual terms to a minimum so that they could realistically be achieved. In training and in practice YOT staff sought to keep in check any benevolent, yet overly intrusive, desires on behalf of community panel members to intervene in the lives of the young people and their parents. Practitioners were often flexible in interpreting national guidance and standards, particularly with regard to the number of review meetings as well as how to interpret a breach of conditions. In some respects, such activities helped realize the more restorative and inclusive aspects of the referral orders process.

Earlier and more intensive intervention?

Nevertheless, the changes to the cautioning system introduced by the 1998 Act through reprimands and final warnings have created a much more rigid structure of incremental steps encircling and limiting the discretion of practitioners (see Figure 6.2). There is a danger, first, that police and prosecution services usher young people into court at an earlier stage because of the availability of the referral order as a mandatory sentence for most youths. This may be reflected in the evidence that young people not previously having been given a reprimand or final warning are nevertheless being given referral orders, which national research has shown to be the case for more than half of young people (YJB 2003). There is also the real likelihood of increased intensiveness of response as the conditional discharge – which previously represented 28 per cent of disposals – is replaced by referral orders, despite being a valued and useful sentence with relatively low reconviction rates. There is a second danger that youth courts view referral orders as a 'third and final' or 'last chance' and hence, adopt an increasingly punitive approach to those who breach them or who are considered to have squandered their opportunity by appearing subsequently in court. There is a distinct possibility of significant 'net-widening' and 'mesh-thinning' (Cohen 1985), as young people are drawn into and through the youth justice system more rapidly. The fact that the use of youth custody has continued to rise since the implementation of referral orders reinforces this concern (see Figure 6.1). Furthermore, these possible unintended consequences of the reforms also have implications for costs; the more intensive the greater the financial burden.

More intensive intervention is also to be found in the growth of non-criminal orders and the government's anti-social behaviour agenda. Within the 1998 Act particularly, there is a significant criminalization of previously sub-criminal or non-criminal activities. This has been extended by the more recent Anti-Social Behaviour Act 2003.[17] Concern has been expressed that the ASBO is indiscriminate and sweeping, containing no requirement that the behaviour that triggers it should be serious or persistent or that it requires an actual victim. Initially little used, was nearly an eightfold increase in the number of ASBOs issued in the third quarter of 2004 as compared to two years earlier (Home Office 2004). In total some 2,186 ASBOs were taken out in the year to September 2004, and this figure is set to continue to rise (see Figure 6.3).

Approximately half of ASBOs are issued against young people. The lower evidentiary burdens that accompany a civil order supported by criminal sanctions (if breached) and the much broader range of restrictions that ASBOs afford in relation to behaviour, activities, places and people make ASBOs attractive to police and councils as a means of governing youthful conduct. In addition, the absence of press reporting restrictions enables the use of local media to promote deterrence through the public shaming of individuals and as a means of encouraging ordinary citizens and businesses to police any exclusions and restrictions granted under an order. Local newspapers often assist these endeavours by publishing names and photographs in prominent places. Recent Home Office guidance explicitly encourages councils to use publicity to help enforce individual ASBOs (Home Office 2005b).

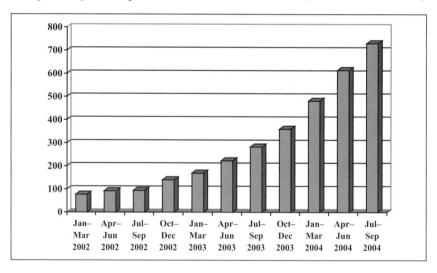

Figure 6.3 The number of ASBOs issued at all courts in England & Wales (2002–2004, persons all ages and unknown).
Source: Home Office (2005a).

In announcing the new guidance,[18] the Home Secretary Charles Clarke made it clear that offenders can expect to have their personal details publicized to protect the community:

> Many offenders think that they are untouchable and above the law. If they thought that there would be a news blackout on their actions they must now think again. Publicising ASBOs has been tested in the courts and today we are making the position crystal clear – your photo could be all over the local media, your local community will know who you are, and breaching an ASBO could land you in prison.[19]

The shaming elements of this approach would seem to approximate more closely to what Braithwaite (1989) describes as disintegrative or stigmatizing, rather than the reintegrative shaming associated with forms of restorative justice. The YJB in its Annual Review of 2003/4 has raised critical concerns about the extent to which breaches of ASBOs may be a factor in fuelling the numbers of young people entering custody (YJB 2004b: 7). Home Office data show that of those youths who breached their ASBO on one or more occasions, 46 per cent received immediate custody.

More recently, Part 4 of the Anti-Social Behaviour Act 2003 creates a power to disperse groups of two or more people (s. 30). With local authority agreement, a senior police officer can designate an area where there is believed to be persistent anti-social behaviour and a problem with groups causing intimidation. Once a senior police officer and the local authority have agreed to designate an area, they must publish that fact in a local newspaper or through notices in the area, and it can then be designated for up to six months. In these areas police will have a power to disperse groups where their presence or behaviour has resulted, or is likely to result, in a member of the public being harassed, intimidated, alarmed or distressed. The individuals can then be excluded from a specified area for up to 24 hours.[20]

While ASBOs require some evidence of past individual conduct upon which the exclusion is based, the dispersal order only requires that anti-social behaviour has been a 'significant and persistent problem' in the area and the individuals' behaviour or *presence* is likely to offend a member of the public. Unlike the ASBO, the length of the exclusion is much shorter. The dispersal power is likely to be used against young people and may be broad enough to prevent youths from gathering simply because some youths have behaved in a persistently anti-social manner and some members of the community find the mere presence of even a small group of youths makes them fearful.[21]

In popular discourse and public consciousness the referral order with its restorative justice inspired logic has had to compete for attention with the more media-friendly attraction of ASBOs with their punitive and exclusionary logic. As a consequence, there has been very little public debate about referral orders, youth offender panels or restorative youth justice, while popular debate remains dominated by dispersal, exclusion and incarceration.

Rights and responsibilities

It is ironic perhaps that in the same year that the Crime and Disorder Act was given royal assent, with its communitarian and responsibilizing logic (Crawford 2001), the New Labour government also incorporated the European Convention of Human Rights into domestic law via the Human Rights Act 1998. It has been argued that the human rights agenda initiated by the latter development poses a number of direct challenges to the institutionalization of restorative justice ideas. These challenges may take the form both of substance and principle. At one level, the informality of the youth offender panel would appear to conflict with the emphasis upon formal legal rights and due process to be found in the Human Rights Act. Pressures to formalize panels, which may have their origins in administrative and managerial imperatives (as suggested earlier), may be further stimulated by (potential) challenges under the human rights legislation. Consequently, interest-based and party-centred negotiations might be undermined by rights-based and lawyer-centred proceedings. This would run counter to the initial intentions of referral orders.

However, while there are tensions between an agenda that advances individual and collective responsibilities to the wider community and a liberal rights-based programme, it would be wrong to suggest that the 'rights versus responsibilities' debate is a simple zero sum game whereby more responsibilities inevitably equals less rights and vice versa. Formal legal rights and due process can act as important bounding mechanisms that empower and constitutionalize informal processes. As such, they can foster responsibilities within a context of checks upon the arbitrary exercise of power.

Nevertheless, there is a distinct responsibilization agenda in New Labour's youth justice reforms, some of which feed off notions of responsibility embedded within restorative justice. The abolition of *doli incapax*, together with many of the new orders, notably the ASBO, draws upon the 'no more excuses' theme of responsibilizing children and parents. As Gelsthorpe and Morris have argued, the 'importance of the presumption lay in its *symbolism*: it was a statement about the nature of childhood, the vulnerability of children and the appropriateness of *criminal justice sanctions* for children' (1999: 213, emphasis in original). So too, its abolition was heavily symbolic with regard to its implications for the manner in which children are viewed and are to be treated through penal means by the state (Bandalli 1998).

There are also strong responsibilizing elements to the referral order and youth offender panels. First, the process seeks to enlist and evoke responsibility on the part of those individual participants at a panel meeting – most notably young people and their parents. This is what Braithwaite refers to as *active*, rather than passive, responsibility; 'the virtue of taking responsibility for putting things right', rather than passively holding someone to account by allocating blame, which is both after the event and backward-looking (Braithwaite 2002: 129). This notion of individual active responsibility is forward-looking, engendering an instrumental approach to 'governing the future'. While passive responsibility is a necessary element in all forms of justice, the significant potential of deliberative forms of restorative justice is to be found in its stimulation of active responsibility.

In this, not only are parents (and other supporters) enlisted into the process of arriving at (and to a degree enforcing) a youth offender contract, but young people are themselves constructed as 'enterprising offenders' with choices. Through the availability of incentives and disincentives, they become an 'entrepreneur' of their own personal development. This is reflected in the centrality of the 'contract' within the referral order process and of 'agreements' within other restorative aspects of the legislation. However, there is a lingering concern that 'failed entrepreneurs', those individuals who are unable or unwilling to fulfil commitments they have agreed to keep, are double failures: not only have they failed the community (and their victims) but also themselves. Thus the inclusionary logic of 'contractual governance' (Crawford 2003) may sit comfortably alongside the exclusionary logic of mass incarceration.

Behind the consensual imagery of the contract lies the reality of coercion (Wonnacott 1999). Here, there is a central paradox in *imposing responsibility through coercion*. This echoes throughout the reforms, notably in the use of various curfews and court-based orders behind which stand criminal sanctions. Yet research suggests that strategies such as victim–offender mediation and work with parents are most effective where they are voluntary rather than compulsory. There are concerns as to the efficacy and effectiveness of such compulsory orders.

Secondly, the reforms evoke a responsibility to the wider community, not merely those with whom individuals share intimate and familial relations, but also people who share some broader collective affinity often defined in terms of space. The presence of community panel members and the centrality of 'Community Payback' schemes for reparation foreground this within the panel process and outcomes. However, there are consequentialist implications of evoking responsibilities to the wider 'community' that should warn against allowing individual rights to be trampled in the stampede to assert a specific 'moral order'. 'In the name of the community' can become an instrumental totem for illiberal policies on the back of which the exclusion of undesirable young people is legitimized.

Conclusions

In this chapter, I have sought to excavate some of the ambiguities present in attempts to institutionalize restorative justice in England and Wales, and the manner in which restorative practices are shaped by the prevailing political and social forces. What I hope this shows is the need to ground understandings of restorative justice practices firmly within the institutional and political frameworks that sustain them and the social and cultural contexts that give them meaning. As Muncie (2005) usefully notes, in the attempt to understand the manner in which global shifts in youth justice, through policy transfer and convergence, impact upon specific practices, we must not lose sight of the important moulding effects of local contingencies, policy ambiguities, cultural practices and institutional resistances. I have sought to highlight some of the ways in which certain restorative ideals have been shaped through implementation by not only the actors themselves but also the wider environment that both nourishes and distorts them.

In England and Wales dominant factors in the institutionalization of restorative justice have been an emphasis upon a particular managerial culture and the punitive climate and culture of severity that has accompanied the introduction of referral orders and youth offender panels. There remains a cultural fascination with the demonization of youth, whereby contemporary insecurities are channelled into the construction of young people as varied forms of folk devils around which moral panics coalesce (Cohen 2002). As Downes (1998: 13) notes, there has been a danger that the strategy of being 'tough on crime' (which helped to win elections) may prove counter-productive with regard to the more radical elements of the youth justice reforms, most notably those restorative justice-influenced legislative changes. More surprisingly, the punitive edge to government rhetoric remains firmly in place despite the recent reversal in the historic rise of crime since the 1960s which has dominated criminological thinking. Rather than using the opportunity presented by declining overall crime rates to temper punitive instincts, New Labour has competed with Conservatives in promoting the image of 'disorderly Britain', particularly in recent election campaigns.[22]

The eclectic origins and penal philosophies of the recent youth justice reforms have further confused the institutionalization of restorative justice in England and Wales. At their most radical, they challenge traditional state paternalism and monopoly by seeking to empower diverse stakeholders in the resolution of conflicts, encourage forms of deliberative justice and the engagement with victims – all-too-often the impassive bystander – in responses to crime, and foster active responsibility and civic values. However, the reforms may also promote a logic of punitiveness and exclusion, as well as facilitate greater and earlier intervention in the lives of young people and hence extend the reach of state control. The extent to which the reforms will tackle the causes of youth crime and assist the reintegration of young offenders as well as provide adequate responses for victims of crime remains to be seen, as does whether the reforms signify the dawning of a new restorative era or merely constitute muddled eclecticism.

Notes

1 Prior to the introduction of the Crime and Disorder Act, a caution was given if it was deemed appropriate by the police to a person who admitted committing an offence as an alternative to prosecution. This largely took the form of a verbal warning but also included developments known as 'caution-plus' whereby conditions were attached to a caution.

2 Each YOT must include a probation officer, a social worker, a police officer, a representative of the local health authority and a person nominated by the chief education officer.

3 Now referred to as Youth Offending Services (YOS) rather than teams, as most services comprise a number of teams.

4 *Doli incapax* was the legal presumption that children under 14 and over 10 years of age are incapable of knowing the difference between right and wrong which required the prosecution to establish that the child knew that what he or she had done was 'seriously wrong' and not merely naughty or mischievous.

5 At a cost of £13.3 million (over half of which was provided by the YJB).

6 In the light of the pilot evaluation research some amendments were made with regard to the imposition of a referral order in relation to minor

offences by way of the Referral Order (Amendment of Referral Conditions) Regulations 2003 (SI 2003 No. 1605) (Home Office 2003c). In addition, the timescale stipulated in national standards for the initial panel meeting to be held was increased from 15 to 20 working days for cases involving a victim.

7   The failure of parents or guardians to attend without reasonable excuse may result in contempt proceedings under the Magistrates' Court Act 1980.

8   More recent research suggests that this low level of direct victim involvement remains a problem. In a study of Leeds Youth Offending Service (with one of the largest caseloads in England) victims only attended in 9 per cent of relevant cases (Crawford and Burden 2005). More generally, low levels of victim involvement have been noted by other English research into the reparative aspects of the Crime and Disorder Act pilots (Holdaway *et al.* 2001) and the Thames Valley restorative cautioning evaluation, where only 16 per cent of victims attended (Hoyle *et al.* 2002).

9   Morris and colleagues (1993) found that in the early years of the introduction of family group conferences in New Zealand victims attended in 51 per cent of cases in which there was an identifiable victim. In Queensland evaluators found that 77 per cent of conferences took place with victims in attendance (Hayes *et al.* 1998) and the RISE initiative in Canberra saw victims attend in 73 per cent for offences against personal property and 90 per cent for violent incidences (Strang *et al.* 1999). Evaluation of youth justice conferencing in New South Wales in 1998 reported a 73 per cent victim participation rate (Trimboli 2000).

10   Reconviction, here, is defined as all reoffending that ends with either a conviction at court or a formal pre-court disposal.

11   Community penalties include a variety of orders in which YOTs manage and supervise young offenders outside of a custodial institution, including an action plan order, supervision order, attendance centre order, curfew order, community punishment order and community rehabilitation order.

12   The Youth Justice Board has set a target for YOTs that 80 per cent of victims of youth crime should be offered participation in restorative justice interventions (by 2004) and that 75 per cent of those who participate should say they are satisfied.

13   The *Guidance* suggests the following length of order and amount of reparation as a yardstick (Home Office 2002):

Length of order	*Hours of reparation*
3–4 months	3–9 hours
5–7 months	10–19 hours
8–9 months	20–29 hours

14   Now referred to as district judges.

15   For example, the percentage of black people sitting as panel members ranged from 0 to 62% across different YOTs.

16 See Crawford and Newburn (2003: Chapter 8) and Crawford and Burden (2005: chapter 6).

17 The 2003 Act extends powers to issue fixed penalty notices (provided by the Criminal Justice and Police Act 2001) with regard to anti-social behaviour to community support officers, wardens and accredited persons. It also enables fixed penalty notices for disorder to be issued to 16 to 17 year olds.

18 In the light of the judgment by Lord Justice Kennedy in the case of *Stanley v. Brent* [2004] EWHC 2229 (Admin) QBD.

19 http://www.homeoffice.gov.uk/n_story.asp?item_id=1247

20 The group does not commit an offence because an officer has chosen to use this power. However, if individuals refuse to follow the officer's directions to disperse they will be committing an offence.

21 According to Home Office records, some 418 dispersal orders were made between January and September 2004.

22 The number of young people under 21 who were found guilty of, or cautioned for, an indictable offence in 1999 was 35 per cent less than the figure in 1985 and 13 per cent less than in 1992. Nevertheless, by May 2000 young offenders accounted for 17 per cent of the full prison population.

References

Anderson, J. E. (1975) *Public Policy-Making*. New York: Praeger.

Audit Commission (1996) *Misspent Youth*. London: Audit Commission.

Ball, C. (2000) 'The Youth Justice and Criminal Evidence Act 1999, Part I', *Criminal Law Review*, pp. 211–22.

Bandalli, S. (1998) 'Abolition of the presumption of doli incapax and the criminalisation of children', *Howard Journal*, 37: 114–23.

Biermann, F. and Moulton, A. (2003) *Youth Offender Panel Volunteers in England and Wales, December 2003*, Online Report 34/03. London: Home Office.

Bottoms, A. E. (1995) 'The philosophy and politics of punishment and sentencing', in C. Clarkson and R. Morgan (eds), *The Politics of Sentencing Reform*. Oxford: Clarendon, pp. 17–49.

Braithwaite, J. (1989) *Crime, Shame and Reintegration*. Cambridge: Cambridge University Press.

Braithwaite, J. (2002) *Restorative Justice and Responsive Regulation*. Oxford: Oxford University Press.

Cohen, S. (1985) *Visions of Social Control*. Cambridge: Polity Press.

Cohen, S. (2002) *Folk Devils and Moral Panics* 3rd edn. London: Routledge.

Crawford, A. (2000) 'Salient themes towards a victim perspective and the limitations of restorative justice', in A. Crawford and J. Goodey (eds), *Integrating a Victim Perspective within Criminal Justice*. Aldershot: Ashgate, pp. 285–310.

Crawford, A. (2001) 'Joined-up but fragmented: contradiction, ambiguity and ambivalence at the heart of New Labour's "Third Way"', in R. Matthews and J. Pitts (eds), *Crime, Disorder and Community Safety: A New Agenda?* London: Routledge, pp. 54–80.

Crawford, A. (2002a) 'The state, community and restorative justice', in L. Walgrave (ed.), *Restorative Justice and the Law.* Cullompton: Willan, pp. 101–29.

Crawford, A. (2002b) 'The prospects for restorative youth justice in England and Wales: a tale of two Acts', in K. McEvoy and T. Newburn (eds), *Criminology and Conflict Resolution.* Basingstoke: Palgrave, pp. 171–207.

Crawford, A. (2003) 'Contractual governance of deviant behaviour', *Journal of Law and Society*, 30(4): 479–505.

Crawford, A. and Burden, T. (2005) *Integrative Victims in Restorative Youth Justice.* Bristol: Policy Press.

Crawford, A. and Newburn T. (2002) 'Recent developments in restorative justice for young people in England and Wales: community participation and representation', *British Journal of Criminology*, 42(3): 476–95.

Crawford, A. and Newburn, T. (2003) *Youth Offending and Restorative Justice.* Cullompton: Willan.

Dignan, J. (1999) 'The Crime and Disorder Act and the prospects for restorative justice', *Criminal Law Review*, 48–60.

Dignan, J. (2000) *Youth Justice Pilots Evaluation: Interim Report on Reparative Work and Youth Offending Teams.* London: Home Office.

Downes, D. (1998) 'Toughing it out: from Labour opposition to Labour government', *Policy Studies*, 19(3/4): 191–8.

Gelsthorpe, L. and Morris, A. (1999) 'Much ado about nothing – a critical comment of key provisions relating to children in the Crime and Disorder Act 1998', *Child and Family Law Quarterly*, 11(1): 209–21.

Graham, J. and Bowling, B. (1995) *Young People and Crime.* London: Home Office.

Hagell, A. and Newburn, T. (1994) *Persistent Young Offenders.* London: Policy Study Institute.

Hall, S. (1979) *Drifting Into a Law and Order Society.* London: Cobden Trust.

Hayes, H., Prenzler, T. and Wortley, R. (1998) *Making Amends: Final Evaluation of the Queensland Community Conferencing Pilot.* Brisbane: Griffith University.

Holdaway, S., Davidson, N., Dignan, J., Hammersley, R., Hine, J. and Marsh, P. (2001) *New Strategies to Address Youth Offending: The National Evaluation of the Pilot Youth Offending Teams.* London: Home Office.

Home Office (1994) *Criminal Statistics England and Wales 1993.* London: HMSO.

Home Office (1997a) *Tackling Youth Crime.* London: Home Office.

Home Office (1997b) *No More Excuses.* London: Home Office.

Home Office (2000) *Final Warning Scheme: Guidance for Youth Offending Teams.* London: Home Office.

Home Office (2002) *Referral Orders and Youth Offender Panels.* London: Home Office/Lord Chancellor's Department/Youth Justice Board.

Home Office (2003a) *Restorative Justice: The Government's Strategy.* London: Home Office.

Home Office (2003b) *Prison Statistics for England and Wales, 2002*, Cm 5996. London: Home Office.

Home Office (2003c) *Important Changes to Referral Orders from 18 August 2003*. London: Home Office/Dept for Constitutional Affairs/Youth Justice Board.

Home Office (2004) *Confident Communities in a Secure Britain: The Home Office Strategic Plan 2004–08*, Cm 6287. London: Home Office.

Home Office (2005a) *Anti Social Behaviour Order Statistics, Quarterly to September 2004*. See: http://www.crimereduction.gov.uk/asbos2.htm

Home Office (2005b) *Guidance on Publicising Anti-Social Behaviour Orders*. London: Home Office.

Home Office (2005c) *Juvenile Reconviction: Results from the 2003 Cohort*, Online Report 08/05. London: Home Office.

Hoyle, C., Young, R. and Hill, R. (2002) *Proceed with Caution: An Evaluation of the Thames Valley Police Initiative in Restorative Cautioning*. York: JRF.

Junger-Tas, J., Terlouw, G.-J. and Klein, M. W. (1994) *Delinquent Behaviour Among Young People in the Western World*. Amsterdam: Kugler.

Karp, D. and Drakulich, K. (2004) 'Minor crimes in quaint settings: practices, outcomes and limits of Vermont Reparative Probation Boards', *Criminology and Public Policy*, 3(4): 655–86.

Lipsky, M. (1980) *Street-Level Bureaucracy: The Dilemmas of the Individual in Public Services*. New York: Russell Sage Foundation.

Marshall, T. F. (1999) *Restorative Justice: An Overview*. London: Home Office.

Merry, S. E. (1988) 'Legal pluralism', *Law and Society Review*, 22(5): 869–96.

Morris, A. and Gelsthorpe, L. (2000) 'A comment on the prospects for restorative justice under the Crime and Disorder Act 1998', *Criminal Law Review*, 18–30.

Morris, A. and Maxwell, G. (2000) 'The practice of family group conferences in New Zealand', in A. Crawford and J. Goodey (eds), *Integrating a Victim Perspective Within Criminal Justice*. Aldershot: Ashgate, pp. 207–25.

Morris, A., Maxwell, G. and Robertson, J. P. (1993) 'Giving victims a voice: a New Zealand experiment', *Howard Journal*, 32(4): 304–21.

Muncie, J. (2000) 'Pragmatic realism? Searching for criminology in the new youth justice', in B. Goldson (ed.), *The New Youth Justice*. Lyme Regis: Russell House, pp. 14–34.

Muncie, J. (2005) 'The globalisation of crime control – the case of youth and juvenile justice', *Theoretical Criminology*, 9(1): 35–64.

Newburn, T. (1998) 'Tackling youth crime and reforming youth justice', *Policy Studies*, 19(3/4): 199–212.

Newburn, T., Crawford, A., Earle, R., Goldie, S., Hale, C., Masters, G., Netten, A., Saunders, R., Sharpe, K., Uglow, S. and Campbell, A. (2001) *The Introduction of Referral Orders into the Youth Justice System: Second Interim Report*. London: Home Office.

Newburn, T., Crawford, A., Earle, R., Goldie, S., Hale, C., Masters, G., Netten, A., Saunders, R., Hallam, A., Sharpe, K. and Uglow, S. (2002) *The Introduction of Referral Orders into the Youth Justice System*, HORS 242. London: Home Office.

Pearson, G. (1983) *Hooligans: A History of Respectable Fears*. Basingstoke: Macmillan.

Pratt, J. (1989) 'Corporatism: the third model of juvenile justice', *British Journal of Criminology*, 29: 236–54.

Raine, J. W. (2001) 'Modernizing courts or courting modernization?', *Criminal Justice*, 1(1): 105–28.

Rhodes, R. A. W. (2000) 'The governance narrative', *Public Administration*, 78(2): 345–63.

Rutherford, A. (1986) *Growing Out of Crime*. London: Penguin.

Shapland, J. (2000) 'Victims and criminal justice: creating responsible criminal justice agencies', in A. Crawford and J. Goodey (eds), *Integrating a Victim Perspective within Criminal Justice*. Aldershot: Ashgate, pp. 147–64.

Strang, H., Barnes, G., Braithwaite, J. and Sherman, L. (1999) *Experiments in Restorative Policing: A Progress Report on the Canberra Reintegrative Shaming Experiments (RISE)*. Canberra: ANU.

Trimboli, L. (2000) *An Evaluation of the NSW Youth Justice Conferencing Scheme*. New South Wales: Bureau of Crime Statistics and Research.

Tyler, T. (1990) *Why People Obey the Law*. New Haven, CT: Yale University Press.

Waterhouse, L., McGhee, J., Loucks, N., Whyte, B. and Kay, H. (1999) *The Evaluation of Children's Hearings in Scotland: Children in Focus*. Edinburgh: The Scottish Office Central Research Unit.

Wilcox, A. with Hoyle, C. (2004) *Restorative Justice Projects: The National Evaluation of the Youth Justice Board's Restorative Justice Projects*. London: Youth Justice Board.

Wonnacott, C. (1999) 'The counterfeit contract – reform, pretence and muddled principles in the new referral order', *Child and Family Law Quarterly*, 11(3): 271–87.

Young, R. (2000) 'Integrating a multi-victim perspective into criminal justice through restorative justice conferences', in A. Crawford and J. Goodey (eds), *Integrating a Victim Perspective within Criminal Justice*. Aldershot: Ashgate, pp. 227–51.

Youth Justice Board (2003) *Referral Orders: Research into the Issues Raised in The Introduction of Referral Orders into the Youth Justice System*. London: YJB.

Youth Justice Board (2004a) *National Standards for Youth Justice Services 2004*. London: YJB.

Youth Justice Board (2004b) *Annual Review 2003/4: Building in Confidence*. London: YJB.

Chapter 7

The French phantoms of restorative justice: the institutionalization of 'penal mediation'

Jacques Faget

The concept of restorative justice is relatively unknown in France, by academics and practitioners alike. There are many reasons for this, the first of which is linguistic. The concept has been formed in English-speaking countries and there is no work specifically devoted to this subject in French. The few studies or review articles that have approached this subject have only done so incidentally (Cario and Salas 2001; Faget 1997). The second reason is historical and political. Restorative justice was born in countries significantly marked by colonization (Australia, New Zealand, the United States, Canada) in which the post-colonial state was incapable of finding any solution other than repressing the problem of adapting its indigenous peoples. Faced with this impasse the revalorizing of normative community traditions was a way of acceding to the identity claims of these people (Jaccoud 2003). But the French colonial context, for political and economic reasons that are too long to address here, is entirely different. The third reason is institutional. The French model of 'social justice', constructed after 1945, was at the forefront of western systems (Faget 1992) and, even if it has been exhausted, the practitioners (juvenile judges, social workers, etc.) still believe that they possess a sufficient range of educative measures and do not express the desire to research new modes of action. The fourth reason for this ignorance is conceptual. Seen from France or French-speaking countries the concept of restorative justice seems, to those who are familiar with it, too ambiguous to be diffused. Originally devised in opposition to the punitive system (Zehr 1990), then to the educative and therapeutic model (Walgrave 1994), it is unclear if it is inspired by a reformist will to humanize the judicial approach (according to the term restorative justice), if it is a strategy of conflict against the expiatory foundation of the criminal law system or whether it pursues the ambition to disseminate restorative practices in all domains of social life.

These arguments explain the phantomlike existence of restorative justice in French-speaking countries and particularly in France. In Quebec they prefer to speak of a *justice réparatrice*, that is to say a form of justice that gives priority to the reparation of the harm caused by an infraction and invites the complainant and the offender to negotiate solutions to the conflict with the support of the community (Jaccoud 2003). In Walloon Belgium some refute the utility of the concept of restorative justice seeing it as too specifically penal and prefer mediation, of which the heuristic value is much greater for it is 'the emblem of a new model of negotiated justice' resulting in 'a mutation of our relationship to norms and authority' (Cartuyvels 2003). In France Bonafé-Schmitt has proposed the term 'comprehensive justice' to designate a mode of managing conflicts founded on a communicational rationality (Bonafé-Schmitt 2003). But in the end neither the concepts of restorative or comprehensive justice nor 'justice réparatrice' have had success. So one generally speaks of mediation and here specifically of penal mediation.

My reflection on the institutionalization of restorative justice could stop at this point. However I would prefer to speak of its invisibility and its phantomlike presence rather than its inexistence. Even though the words to designate them are different, there exist, at least in western countries, social practices that share the same philosophy. Arriving at the same stage of their institutional and social history these countries feel the same need to invent new ways of 'making society' (Donzelot *et al.* 2003), to have recourse to fluid and flexible modes of managing the complexity of social issues (Faget 2005).

The French analysis of restorative justice runs into difficulties when defining its object. Choosing a broad conception appears at first sight to be appropriate because one cannot separate the rapid development of 'penal mediation' from other forms of mediation. France has experienced since the mid-1980s but above all in the 1990s a sudden increase of mediation practices (family, intercultural, school, community-oriented, business and work-related, in consumerism, healthcare, etc.). They have often developed without a conceptual framework or are based on disparate foundations but their development attests to a global transformation in the modes of governing society (Faget 2005). But this broad conception strays too far from the object of this study. We might then prefer a restrictive conception of restorative justice and centre it on the criminal field. However, here again nothing is clear. French 'social justice' (Faget 1992) since 1945 has created numerous pedagogical innovations that break with the repressive logic of the legal institution. Some of them like the *travail d'intérêt général* (Faget 1994) or reparation for minors (Milburn 2002a) are not so far removed from a restorative perspective in so far as they pay attention to the victims and to reparation. But a careful analysis shows that they are simply pursuing, in another way, the same restitutive or educative objectives as old fashioned penal measures. Table 7.1 enables us to understand the different but also complementary principles between the different penal logics. And it becomes clear that the restorative model presents particularities that demand a specific approach to its implementation.

In France, only mediation relating to criminal law corresponds to the criteria of the restorative model. We will see later that the diversity of modalities of its implementation leads us to moderate this affirmation. Community conferencing and sentencing circles are non-existent. The political system, inherited from the French Revolution, condemns all forms of communitarianism and forces individuals to renounce their cultural particularities. This 'society of individuals' is not particularly favourable to community mobilizations. The effects of the urban crisis have weakened traditional forms of solidarity and have made them even more unlikely.

Before taking on the cultural conflict that traverses the implementation of 'penal mediation' I will distinguish the different sequences of the process of its institutionalization. As we will see this scenario is not specific to mediation. It concerns all innovative social practices that attempt to impose their difference.

Table 7.1 Models of treatment of penal conflicts

	Retributive	*Therapeutic*	*Restitutive*	*Restorative*
Object	Culpability	Need	Harm	Conflict
Focus	Offender	Offender	Victim	Relation
Process	Imposed	Imposed/ accepted	Imposed/ accepted	Negotiated
Solution	Punishment	Help	Reparation	Agreement/ resolution

An unachieved institutionalization

The explosion of mediation practices is not the fruit of a particular conjecture. It inscribes itself in the context of a profound transformation of the world, an abrupt change beginning in the 1970s from modernity to postmodernity (one also speaks of advanced, reflexive, acute or hyper modernity etc.). The avalanche of mutations that result from it necessitates investigations of other ways of regulating the articulation between worlds of multiple and heterogeneous meaning. Mediation constitutes one of the methods to assure the smooth functioning of this complex society which, given its instability, accommodates better adaptable processes than permanent institutions and rigid norms. The metaphor of a penal rhizome (Faget 1992), used to designate public action characterized more and more by the dispersion of the centres of decision, the blurring of the frontiers between the public and private sector, the redefinition of its territorial limits, the juxtaposition of multiple rationalities, illustrates the evolution of a penal field less and less autonomous, crossed with economic and social logics which transform its modes of action.

The lost dream of autonomy

In such a context the debate about the autonomy of mediation practices appears to relate to a romantic vision of the social game. The 'believers' of mediation have condemned its instrumentalization by a criminal justice system disrespectful of its philosophy. This process of institutionalization lies in the belief of the existence of non-institutionalized and autonomous practices. This postulate can be found in writings that present mediation as a natural activity free of any institutional constraint (Six 1995) or in certain anthropological visions which argue that mediation is 'as old as the hills'.

But the autonomy of mediation is probably imaginary in the absence of a culture of mediation that would see citizens spontaneously seek out mediation or themselves play the role of mediator in the conflicts that concern them. Institutionalization is not only, as it is generally conceived, a process of normalization of social practices in which we try to submit them to a regularizing social control. This definition that presupposes the existence of autonomous social practices and a political will to subject them to a process of legitimation and normalization does not take into consideration zones of play and uncertainty that exist in all social practices. I have evoked this indetermination in a text showing that if mediation led a double life, a community life on one side and a legal life on the other, the first was much more organized than it appears and the second much more flexible than we believe it to be, so much that the line dividing the two was not as clear as previously thought (Faget 1995).

This process of institutionalization only concerns certain isolated researchers or practitioners. It is not in the French republican tradition and mostly appears in Anglo-Saxon countries which have the tendency to oppose 'the good community' to 'the bad institution' and demonize all practices forming an alliance with the state or its apparatuses. But this perspective wrongly assimilates community participation and the autonomy of practices. In reality it consecrates a restrictive conception of institutionalization because the idea of non-institutionalized mediation practices does not resist a sociological approach. It is advisable to distinguish between an autonomous institutionalization when somewhat disorderly practices take form and develop stable modes of action, and a dependent institutionalization when institutions themselves create programmes of mediation. These two processes can combine when the only chance for the innovation to last is to return to the repertoire of institutional practices (Noreau 2003). The analysis of the institutionalization of 'penal mediation' shows that it is situated in a bottom-up framework in so far as the first experiments were developed outside of the criminal courts at the initiative of innovators, the majority of whom did not belong to the legal system. In some way we can even say that 'penal mediation' has been constructed 'against' the criminal justice system. For most of the initial programmes had been conceived to transform the repressive logic considered to be too bureaucratic, inattentive to the human dimension of situations, ignorant of the victims and degrading to offenders.

The sequence of institutionalization

The way autonomous institutionalization is achieved can be broken down into six phases which can follow, overlap and sometimes reverse. The French context confirms this general model.

1 Everything begins with the initiative of a handful of people inspired by a collective reflection or experiments from abroad. They strive to create by trial and error a practical model that attempts to reconcile the initial 'utopia' with the surrounding social context. It is during this phase that new methods develop. This has been happening since 1983 in Paris, 1984 in Strasbourg, 1985 in Valence, Besançon, Marseille, Tulle, 1986 in Bordeaux, Grenoble, Saint Etienne... Social activists backed by pioneering magistrates inspired by American

experiments of the *victim–offender reconciliation program* or Quebec's 'community conciliation' created the first mediation programmes within the criminal justice system (Faget 1997).

2 The establishment of the practical rules of the art brings about a codification and a normalization of procedures at the same time as a ritualization of the activity. A doctrine or orthodoxy is elaborated by leaders in the field under construction (social workers, magistrates, left-oriented academics). They organize meetings and write ethical and deontological principles that will guide the practice. This phase is generally accompanied by the production of a public (via newspapers, interviews, conferences) and/or a scientific (through articles and books) discourse that serve to legitimize the activity. The rhetoric usually consists of criticizing earlier methods of regulating conflicts to differentiate it from other professions and to offer another way to proceed.

3 This phase is generally concomitant with a request for private or public funding which guarantees the perpetuation of the experiment but gives it at the same time an institutional legitimacy in which the actors take much pride. In this way the French Minister of Justice, concerned with developing a genuine policy in favour of victims, but equally confronted with the overload of cases due to the considerable increase in the number of charges, was quick to finance the first initiatives. But the short-term mode of financing NGOs (contractual or annual subsidies) combined with the power given to prosecutors to direct cases of mediation to NGOs of their choice created a situation of reinforced economic dependence.

4 A phase of identity construction then imposes itself through the creation of more structured professional organizations. Thus the INAVEM (*Institut d'aide aux victimes et de la médiation*), which represents the combat for victims, and the CLCJ (*Comité de liaison des associations de contrôle judiciaire*), representing the neo-realist tendency of social work (which agrees to collaborate with the judicial institution), developed a federative national strategy. Since 1986, the Ministry accorded a quasi-monopoly to these two organizations to initiate experiments on penal mediation. They exercised from then on a control over the field by developing programmes of specialized training. Having had a privileged status conferred on them, these movements lose a part of their autonomy. From then on, in order to conserve their position, they must conform to ministerial injunctions. The relations between state and private organizations, in the French political structure, no longer belong to the model of consultation

but of cooperation. Consequently this logic of identity construction will partially fail, as a result of subordination to the state but also because of the competition, cleverly maintained by the Ministry of Justice, between two organizations, the INAVEM and the CLCJ, who are driven by different values and interests.

5 The next phase of institutionalization is the legalization of practices. In a democracy this is the outcome of an interaction between various types of actors, representatives of the state, the elect, technocrats, legal academics, interest groups (big national associations of mediators, social workers, lawyers, etc.) and the media (Faget 1997). The nature of the interaction between these different scenes varies according to the political circumstances, the issues of the reform, the distribution of power between the actors and the visibility of the problem concerned. In France the promulgation of the law of 1993 creating 'penal mediation' has gone relatively unnoticed. The lobbies concerned (INAVEM, CLCJ), relying on at least ten years of experiments, were pursuing the objective of spreading mediation practices throughout the country. The Ministry of Justice shared the same intention but with the concern of organizing this diffusion around a unique model (*note d'orientation de 1992*). Despite the fear of lawyers who saw the jurisdictional powers of the prosecutor increase, the legalization of 'penal mediation' was neither the object of a debate in parliament nor in the media. It was integrated in sweeping reforms which overshadowed its visibility.

6 The outcome of the process of institutionalization is generally the professionalization of the activity. For French 'penal mediation' this last sequence has not always been achieved although the practice of family mediation has since 2004 been restricted to those possessing a diploma from the state. There are many reasons for this. On the one hand the magistrates who have the power to authorize penal mediators according to criteria of competence (Milburn 2002b) which they alone have established (in order to avoid role confusion and promote neutrality, judicial and legal practitioners are prohibited from practising penal mediation) are not inclined to renounce their prerogatives. On the other hand the lobbies concerned do not have the same position on this point. The INAVEM always consists of a significant number of volunteers (about 40 per cent) while Citizens and Justice (*Citoyens et Justice*, formerly CLCJ) is a totally professionalized movement. Finally it is possible to become a mediator without belonging to either of these two organizations. The legitimacy of the mediator doesn't necessarily depend on specific training but on the authorization given by the courts.

In this way one can say that the process of institutionalization of 'penal mediation' is in progress but remains unachieved, as is demonstrated by a cultural conflict between two opposing conceptions of its implementation.

A conflicting institutionalization

It is surprising that the criminal justice system has been the first institution to integrate mediation. Paradoxically it is in this particularly constraining system that one assigns the subject a bigger role and creates places of dialogue and negotiation. Table 7.2 presents some lines of opposition between judicial logic and the logic of mediation which renders their marriage necessarily problematic.

One cannot understand this juxtaposition without making reference to the unprecedented crisis confronting the criminal justice system as a result of the increasing juridification of social conflicts. Faced with the irrational need for law and justice due to the propensity of citizens to place the regulation of their conflicts in the setting of the criminal law, the system finds itself forced to search for methods to manage this flood of complaints. Mediation can, in this perspective, constitute a way of treating more delicately sensitive disputes (e.g. one thinks of conflicts between people who are close and in particular family conflicts) and a way of responding institutionally to charges that previously had no follow-up. In the French system, the 'principle of opportunity' gives to prosecutors the possibility of abandoning certain cases.

'Penal mediation' is a form of diversion and is aimed at adults (18 years and over). By virtue of the power to choose the most appropriate course of action to deal with a criminal case, the public prosecutor can suggest mediation for the complainant and the offender. They are referred to a mediator or to an information session about the mediation

Table 7.2 Justice v. mediation

Justice	Mediation
Vertical logic	Horizontal logic
Search for truth	Search for balance
Public order	Private needs
Reference to the law	Reference to equity
Principle of rupture	Principle of bond

process, which they are then free to refuse or accept. If mediation is opted for, one or more sessions are organized by the mediator (or mediators if co-mediation is practised) to take place within three months. This period can be extended if necessary. On the basis of the report provided by the mediator at the conclusion of these sessions, the public prosecutor makes a decision to proceed or not to proceed with prosecution.

A spectacular and confused rise to prominence

Although 'penal mediation' initially faced opposition from a number of lawyers, it rapidly attained a fairly significant level of development due to the combined effects of strategic militancy and institutional necessity. This rise of penal mediation was reinforced at the same time by its codification in 1993 and the increased generalization of a rapid procedure called *traitement en temps réel*, rather than several months or years after the crime. According to the annual statistics compiled by the Ministry of Justice, 11,552 victim–offender mediations were carried out in 1992 and the number continued to increase to the point where a record of 48,145 mediations were carried out in 1997.

However, this apparent success should not hide the extreme confusion which prevails in the implementation. The reality is that a considerable number of so-called mediations usurp the title, being more in the nature of a caution whose aim is to lecture or frighten the offender rather than to carry out a genuine mediation. According to mediation theory the particular nature of criminal law should not affect the ethical principles which form the basis of the mediation process. It should always be a consensual process in the course of which an impartial, independent third person, without decision-making power, strives to establish the conditions in which communication can occur between opposing parties so that they themselves can find a solution to the problem that divides them.

The progressive recognition, reinforced by the law of 23 June 1999,[1] of the distinction between a caution and mediation had the effect of deflating the total number of penal mediations which dropped to 25,972 in 1998 to climb steadily back to 40,000 in 2003. However, magistrates do not always clearly distinguish between the two and there is still considerable overlap between the two measures (Faget 1999a).

Two models of practice

A national evaluation (quantitative and qualitative research on a representative sample of 24 French tribunals and 1,200 cases) presents a fairly precise picture of the use made by tribunals of penal mediation (Faget 1999b). Despite disparities between the jurisdictions, some general tendencies can be observed.

A significant portion of disputes treated by means of mediation are related to physical (36 per cent) or psychological (11 per cent) violence. The percentage is even higher in the resort of the Court of Appeal of Paris (44 per cent for offences involving physical violence only) (Catala 2003). Next are the offences related to the family, such as the custody of children and family desertion (15 per cent) and vandalism (14 per cent). The cumulative total of all offences against property (thefts, fraud and so on) only represents 13 per cent of the volume treated.

It is important to underline that a mere 28 per cent of disputes treated in mediation are concerned with people who do not know each other. In all other cases, they involve affective relations (39 per cent), relationships of propinquity (friends, neighbours, 26 per cent) or social relationships (professional or contractual, 7 per cent). These figures demonstrate that 'penal mediation' has become a method of preference in the treatment of all disputes of proximity.

When mediation is offered, in 42 per cent of the cases mediation does not take place (due to non-response, refusal either initially or subsequently, or withdrawal of the complaint). Most often, complainants rather than offenders are the cause of this situation.

When mediation is accepted, the success rate is 76 per cent and varies according to the type of offences.[2] However, in examining this figure, one should take into account that certain agreements are not actually carried out while some mediations where no agreement has been reached nevertheless result in a lessening of the conflict and a better understanding of its nature. Research demonstrates that the success rate also depends on the mediator. Thus the percentage of 'success' seems to be inversely related to the level of competence (see Milburn 2002b).[3] Observation of mediations allows this paradox to be explained. Procedures used by mediators who are less well trained are often very directive; on the other hand, as the level of training and competence rises, so does the respect for the ethical principles of mediation.

The analysis shows that there are two models of practice (see Table 7.3):

- The first model, which one could call legal, is used in the majority of cases (two-thirds of the organizations observed). It is more often located in the courts or in a centre for justice and law (*maison de justice et du droit*) where 'penal mediation' is carried out by practising or retired lawyers who have not been specifically trained in mediation. The time available for the sessions is very short and the success rates are spectacular. Research on the Paris Court of Appeal confirmed that delegates[4] appointed by the public prosecutor (who have been mandated to mediate!) practising in the courts obtain the best results. Judicial logic is very evident: those who are designated as offenders and victims are 'summonsed', and the evidence is relied on to guide communication between the parties.

- The second model (one-third of the organizations observed), which one could call restorative, is carried out within the framework of associations by mediators who have received specific training in mediation. Judicial logic hardly impinges, people designated as complainants and accused are invited to meet the mediator who does not rely on the evidence but on his or her subjective impressions of the disputants and their needs. The time available for these sessions is longer, several meetings between the parties can be conducted and the 'success rates' are much lower than for the preceding model.

'Penalization' of the social or a new model of justice?

'Penal mediation' represents an excellent indication of the cultural conflict which opposes the defenders of two antagonistic ideas of justice,

Table 7.3 Comparison between judicial and restorative models of practice

	Judicial model	*Restorative model*
Place	• Centres for justice and law • Courts	• Local associations
Mediators	• Individuals or associations • Men • Sessional employees • Legally trained • No specific training in mediation	• Associations • Gender balance • Professionals or volunteers • Trained in the social sciences • Specific training in mediation • No supervision • Analysis of practice
Process	• Offender/victim • Short period of time • One meeting • Significant % of agreements (between 70 and 90)	• Accused/complainant • Intermediate or long period of time available • One or more meetings • Moderate % of agreements (between 40 and 60)

one based on a very vertical and symbolic idea about the regulation of conflict, the other oriented towards a more democratic and instrumental view. The question arises then how these two forms of logic are to meet. If mediation is reinterpreted by legal logic, does it then become a little like a false nose stuck onto the face of legal institutions or does it actually result in the production of a new model of justice?

Some analysts (and it is a view that enjoys a certain success) see the strategy of diversifying legal responses as a 'penalization of the social'. It is true that mediation allows situations to be treated legally – and by the public prosecutor, a position identified with repression – that formerly were not. It is true that the power of legal ideology is considerable. The confrontation of magistrates with a less professionalized, less structured and less prestigious body than their own usually highlights a relationship of domination, and all social practices institutionalized by the judicial apparatus run the risk of becoming predominantly instrumentalized and of losing their soul. Two recent legislative changes illustrate this scenario, the first intensifying the weight of the 'imaginary law' of mediation by requiring the mediator, if agreement is reached, to make a record of proceedings to be signed by him or herself and the two parties (Law of 9 March 2004), the second sanctioning a relationship of dependency by qualifying the mediator with the title of 'Mediator of the Public Prosecutor of the Republic' (Decree of 27 September 2004).

We can give a few precise illustrations of the way in which judicial logic and therefore the effects of its institutionalization threatens the autonomy of the practice of mediation. Some of these threats are objective:

- the choice of mediator or of the organization employing him or her is made by the prosecutor;
- the mediator receives his or her payment from the criminal justice system;
- the mediator is accountable to the prosecutor who raises questions about the confidentiality of the mediation;
- the final approval of the agreement by the prosecutor can constitute an obstacle to its consensual character.

Other threats have a more qualitative character and depend on the modalities of the organization of the activity. These threats surface above all in the 'judicial' model while they give rise to an ethical reflection in the 'restorative' model:

- The consent of the people involved is not entirely freely given; it is said to be under 'judicial pressure'.

- The reading of the criminal report by the mediator is done to the detriment of the human dimension of the conflict for it transmits a pre-constructed reality derived from the professional ideology of the police.

- The juridical logic of designating one party the offender and another the victim is not objective. (Particularly in conflicts of proximity where rights and wrongs are often blurred it would be better to employ the terms complainant and defendant.)

- The presence of lawyers, in order to protect the rights of persons, can weaken and distort the process of communication between the opposing parties and creates the conditions for an inferior form of justice (*sous-justice*) without a judge.

- The time-frame of mediation is dependent on the necessities of the judicial time-frame.

- The implicit demand for productivity from magistrates drives mediators to adopt a more directive attitude or even propose solutions themselves.

Moreover, the spectacular progress of mediation has aroused a certain amount of trepidation, mainly in lawyers, sometimes based on commercial considerations and sometimes on democratic imperatives. The flexibility that mediation brings to the regulation of disputes in comparison with the legal process is not without danger for the fundamental rights of the person and has the potential to create the conditions for the development of an inferior form of justice (*sous-justice*). The devolution of numerous penal disputes to mediators may have the effect of shutting the door of the courthouse to the underprivileged and of privatizing situations which should be debated on the public stage. This is the case, for example, with domestic violence where the search for consensus risks hiding the social warfare that leads women to challenge their domestic oppression (Faget 2004).

On the other hand, others have remarked on the potential of mediation when compared with legal intervention. They present mediation as a process in which 'an act of communication' may be kinder and more reparative for the victims and makes offenders more responsible for what they have done. Mediation could therefore constitute one of the ways of importing restorative justice where the conflict is not appropriated by the state but given back to the community and to the interested parties, where priority is given to the construction of the future, to a commitment to do good to compensate for the harm done rather than to the expiation of the past. From this perspective, it would be wise to apply it to the regulation of more serious disputes and to all stages of the penal chain.

However, while recognizing the educational benefits of mediation, it is appropriate not to minimize the dangers of uncontrolled deregulation in the management of disputes of a penal nature. It therefore appears useful to envisage the judicialization of mediation, not by confining its procedures into a logic which would turn it into an additional battleground for litigation, but by adopting a preventive strategy based on the need to provide specific training in mediation for mediators and more sustained information for court mandated mediators (Faget 2003). In this way, increasing understanding and respect for the ethical principles of mediation will avoid the perils of mixing different forms of logic which could end either in a deformalization of the law or a subordination of mediation to legal reasoning. By identifying its zones of relevance and irrelevance, one would more wisely choose the circumstances in which to use mediation and more readily accept the complementary nature of the different modes of handling disputes.

Conclusion

Mediation associations and mediators themselves, in pursuit of legitimacy and financial security, have sought the institutionalization of their practice and built compromises between institutional demands and ethical principles. The state strategy was to leave this institutionalization unfinished. The economic precariousness of mediation associations and the absence of a constructed identity and of a genuine professionalization of penal mediators maintains a condition of dependency. The pre-eminence of a judicial conception of mediation in practice demonstrates that this strategy has succeeded. However, like the inhabitants of a Gallic village resisting the Roman occupation some 'restorative' experiments have not been normalized. It symbolizes the secretive way phantoms of the restorative idea float through the legal world. They experience difficulties appearing in daylight because the restorative project collides with the foundations of a legal system dominated by the cult of the law and structured in a vertical manner. Because mediation is antagonistic to the dominant trends of French legal culture, it is a very 'unfrench legal response' (Crawford 2000). More than a 'homeopathic' reform, introducing timidly restorative justice in the criminal justice system it is better to provoke shock rather than to make slight adjustments.

Notes

1   Notably, the Law of 23 June 1999, in Article 41-1 of the Code of Penal Procedure, lists the possibility, among other alternatives to prosecution, of informing the offender of his or her rights under this law and the possibility of 'proceeding, with the agreement of the parties, to a session of mediation between the offender and the victim'.
2   Although contested by many mediators, magistrates take the number of agreements reached as the criterion for success.
3   Here the level of competence is based on indicators such as the quality and length of specific training, participation in sessions analysing techniques, etc.
4   The delegate of the public prosecutor is a non-professional agent appointed by him (especially among former police officers or magistrates), who, under his supervision, implements (in the case of minor offences) measures such as the 'rappel à la loi' which, in order to responsibilize the offender, consists in confronting him personally with the content of the law.

References

Bonafé-Schmitt, J. P. (1998) *La médiation pénale en France et aux Etats-Unis*. Paris: LGDJ, Droit et société.
Bonafe-Schmitt, J. P. (2003) 'Justice réparatrice et médiation pénale: vers de nouveaux modèles de régulation sociale ?', in M. Jaccoud (ed.), *Justice réparatrice et médiation pénale. Convergences ou divergences?* Paris: L'Harmattan, pp. 17–49.
Cario, R. and Salas, D. (2001) *Œuvre de justice et victimes*. Paris: L'Harmattan.
Cartuyvels, Y. (2003) 'Comment articuler médiation et justice réparatrice', in M. Jaccoud (ed.), *Justice réparatrice et médiation pénale. Convergences ou divergences?* Paris: L'Harmattan, pp. 51–74.
Catala, P. (2003) La médiation pénale dans le ressort de la cour d'appel de Paris', in J. Faget (ed.), *Les modes alternatifs de règlement des litiges*. Paris: La documentation française, pp. 127–37.
Crawford, A. (2000) 'Justice de proximité – the growth of "Houses of Justice" and victim/offender mediation in France: a very unfrench legal response?', *Social and legal studies*, 9(1): 29–53.
Donzelot, J., Wyvekens, A. and Mevel, C. (2003) *Faire société. La politique de la ville en France et aux Etats-Unis*. Paris: Le Seuil.

Faget, J. (1992) *Justice et travail social. Le rhizome pénal.* Toulouse: Erès.
Faget, J. (1994) 'L'enfance modèle du travail d'intérêt général', in J. Faget (ed.), *Le travail d'intérêt général a dix ans: le résultat en vaut la peine.* Paris: Ministère de la Justice, Etudes et recherches, pp. 101–22.
Faget, J. (1995) 'La double vie de la médiation', *Droit et société*, 29: 25–38.
Faget, J. (1997) *La médiation. Essai de politique pénale.* Toulouse: Erès.
Faget, J. (1999a) *Les représentations de la médiation pénale dans la Cour d'appel de Bordeaux*, Ministère de la Justice, GERICO no. 9.
Faget, J. (1999b) *La médiation pénale. Evaluation nationale*, Fonds national de la vie associative/CLCJ, GERICO, no. 11.
Faget, J. (2003) 'La juridicisation de la médiation', in J. Faget (ed.), *Les modes alternatifs de règlement des litiges.* Paris: La documentation française, pp. 75–88.
Faget, J. (2004) 'Mediation and domestic violence', *Champ pénal/penal field*, Vol. 1, http://champpenal.revues.org/document50.html
Faget, J. (ed.) (2005) *Médiation et action publique. La dynamique du fluide.* Bordeaux: Presses universitaires de Bordeaux.
Jaccoud, M. (ed.) (2003) *Justice réparatrice et médiation pénale. Convergences ou divergences?* Paris : L'Harmattan, pp. 7–14.
Milburn, P. (2002a) *La réparation pénale à l'égard des mineurs.* Paris: Mission de recherche Droit et Justice.
Milburn, P. (2002b) *La médiation: expériences et compétences.* Paris: La Découverte.
Noreau, P. (2003) 'L'institutionnalisation de la justice réparatrice', in M. Jaccoud (ed.), *Justice réparatrice et médiation pénale. Convergences ou divergences?* Paris: L'Harmattan, pp. 209–26.
Six, J. F. (1995) *Dynamique de la médiation.* Paris: Desclée de Brouwer.
Walgrave, L. (1994) 'Au-delà de la rétribution et de la réhabilitation: la réparation comme paradigme dominant dans l'intervention judiciaire contre les délinquants?', in J. F. Gazeau and V. Peyre (eds), *La justice réparatrice et les jeunes. Paris:* Mission recherche droit et justice, Etudes et documents, p. 11.
Zehr, H. (1990) *Changing lenses: a new focus for crime and justice.* Scottsdale: Herald Press.

Chapter 8

The institutionalization of restorative justice in Canada: effective reform or limited and limiting add-on?

Kent Roach[1]

Introduction

Over the last decade, there has been extensive political and legal deployment of restorative justice as a concept intended to reform and even transform Canadian criminal justice. Restorative justice has been advocated by Canadian law reform commissions, by parliamentary committees and by the courts as an effective way to reform criminal justice. Canada has probably gone further than any other country in developing a 'restorative jurisprudence' (Braithwaite 2003: 16) reflected in its laws and legal cases. Although Canada was a pioneer in developing one of the first restorative justice programmes and many individual projects continue, it remains a country where there has been more top-down political and legal mobilization and institutionalization of restorative justice than measurable bottom-up actualization of restorative justice.

Restorative justice has multiple faces. Some definitions of restorative justice focus on processes in which offenders, victims and their supporters meet face to face and attempt to reach some agreement about what should be done in the aftermath of an offence. A strict requirement for such procedures, however, would exclude most activity in the criminal justice system and limit restorative justice to attempts to deal with crime outside the criminal justice system. Within the criminal justice system, the focus is more often on restorative outcomes which in turn are used to describe a great variety of outcomes that different people may view as positive. For example, some understandings of restorative justice stress an almost retributive form of accountability to both the community and the offender while others stress the rehabilitative healing of the offender. Still other readings of restorative justice present it as an effective form of crime prevention that responds to the failure of the conventional criminal justice system to deter crime. One of the reasons why restorative justice has become so popular is because it means different things to different people (Roach 2000).

There are also ambiguities in restorative justice about what is being restored. Sometimes, restoration of the offender is sought through rehabilitation. At other times, restoration of the victim is sought through reparation. Other approaches seek to restore the relationship between the offender and the victim. The affected community may also be restored by being able to deal with its own disputes and pathologies. Not everyone even agrees that restoration should be the goal especially with regard to disordered communities, disordered offenders and victims who may want privacy and fear re-victimization. In short, there are a large number of different approaches to restorative justice and some fear that the concept is being used as a 'catch-all' (Hughes and Mossman 2002: 130).

Although the many faces of restorative justice can make it a popular reform discourse and perhaps even a replacement discourse for more punitive discourses based on retribution or deterrence (Dignan 2003), the contradictory nature of restorative justice also means that it will inevitably disappoint some of those who have been sympathetic to some of its aims. Indeed, various attempts to institutionalize restorative justice in Canada are generating a wide and growing range of critical commentary from many commentators who are by no means defenders of the conventional criminal justice system (Hughes and Mossman 2002; White 2002; Llewelyn 2003; Acorn 2004; Rudin 2005; Laprairie and Dickinson 2005). As such, a Canadian case study raises in stark relief both the benefits and pitfalls of institutionalizing restorative justice.

In this chapter, I will focus more on the pursuit of restorative outcomes in the criminal justice system than on restorative processes that bring together offenders, victims and their supporters, most often outside of the criminal justice system. Canadian efforts to institutionalize restorative justice have so far focused at the national level on attempts to achieve restorative outcomes such as rehabilitation of offenders and reparation for victims as part of sentencing reforms. Restorative justice can be added to sentencing without concerns about protecting the innocent. At the same time, the focus on institutionalizing restorative justice at sentencing has some constraining effects. There is considerable reluctance to bring victims into the sentencing process or even to order sentences that seek restorative outcomes for victims (Roberts and Roach 2005). Even when judges are prepared to include restitution or reparation as part of the sentencing process, many offenders may be unable to make meaningful repayment to the victim. Sentencing also has a limited capacity to rehabilitate offenders or improve communities. The idea that restorative justice can be institutionalized through sentencing reforms raises the question whether such institutionalization may amount to a limited add-on to the justice system.

It is not clear, however, that the answer is to go back to process-based definitions of restorative justice that require victims, offenders and other affected parties to be brought together in a less coercive and more open-ended forum than a sentencing hearing. The concern with a demand for such restorative processes is that they may limit the range of legitimate responses to crime. As will be seen, Canada's new Youth Criminal Justice Act (YCJA) 2002 has avoided imposing a restorative model for pre-sentencing interventions such as cautions and conferences, even though it is possible that such interventions could be conducted in a restorative manner or seek restorative outcomes. In other contexts, however, restorative approaches have had more of a constraining effect. For example, there have been difficulties in Canada in convincing courts that a restorative approach to sentencing is as appropriate for disadvantaged groups such as African-Canadians as for Aboriginal people. Even with respect to Aboriginal people, some Aboriginal justice initiatives do not easily fit into definitions of restorative programmes that require offenders and victims to meet with facilitators. In other words, there is a danger that restorative justice may not only be a limited add-on to criminal justice, but also a limiting one.

The first part of this chapter will examine how the rhetoric of restorative justice has been employed in Canadian sentencing law with an emphasis on the ability of sentences to achieve outcomes such as offender rehabilitation and victim reparation through the 'restorative purposes' of sentencing. One of the major problems of Canadian criminal justice, indeed one that has widely been recognized as a crisis, is the dramatic overrepresentation of Aboriginal people in Canadian prisons. The second part of the chapter will examine how restorative justice has been institutionalized with respect to the sentencing of Aboriginal offenders. The difficulties of fitting some Aboriginal justice programmes into definitions of restorative justice which require facilitated meetings between offenders and victims will also be examined. The third part of the chapter will consider recent and unsuccessful attempts to extend the emphasis placed on restorative outcomes in the sentencing of Aboriginal offenders to the sentencing of other disadvantaged offenders, most notably African-Canadian offenders. The fourth part of this chapter will examine Canada's new YCJA with a view to how it continues to institutionalize reparation as a purpose of sentencing while also providing a flexible framework for the use of cautions and conferences that allows but does not require restorative justice. A conclusion will then offer a preliminary evaluation of the effectiveness of Canada's attempts to institutionalize restorative justice.

The 'restorative purposes' of sentencing

Despite claims that restorative justice harkens back to older ways of responding to crime in pre-modern and Aboriginal societies, the institutionalization of restorative justice must be examined in a more contemporary historical context. Specifically, restorative justice should be understood as a response to crime that gained momentum in many western countries in the 1990s at a time when crime was declining but prison populations continued to rise. In Canada, there was a particular focus on the overrepresentation of Aboriginal people in jail and interest in Aboriginal justice as an alternative to the frequent incarceration of Aboriginal people. It was also a time during which victims played a greater role in public discourse about crime (Roach 1999a) and there was a diminishing faith in the ability of professionals to prevent crime or to rehabilitate offenders (Garland 2001).

In Canada, restorative justice really only took off in the last half of the 1990s. For example, the widely respected 1987 report of the Canadian Sentencing Commission did not include any discussion of restorative justice as a concept or an alternative to retribution, deterrence or rehabilitation. A year later, however, a Parliamentary Committee placed greater emphasis on encouraging offenders to acknowledge and repair harm done to victims and the community (Daubney 1988). In 1996, Parliament finally responded to both these proposals by codifying the purposes of sentencing for the first time. The retributive principle that the sentence must be proportionate to the gravity of the offence and the offender's degree of responsibility was recognized as the fundamental principle of sentencing. Parliament rejected a pure just deserts model by also endorsing the traditional denunciatory, deterrent and rehabilitative purposes of sentencing. A new sanction, the conditional sentence of imprisonment, was created to encourage judges to allow offenders to serve sentences of imprisonment in the community when consistent with the multiple purposes of sentencing. Most importantly for our purposes, Parliament endorsed in sections 718(e) and (f) of the Criminal Code the provision 'of reparations done to victims or the community' and the promotion of a 'sense of responsibility in offenders, and acknowledgment of the harm done to victims and the community' as new purposes of sentencing. Restorative justice was added onto more traditional concerns about deterrence, incapacitation and retribution in the 1996 sentencing reforms.

Restorative justice, an idea that had to that point existed as an alternative to the criminal justice system, was brought into the system through the 1996 sentencing reforms. This institutionalization of restorative justice was based on the implicit premise that restorative outcomes such as offender rehabilitation and victim reparation could be achieved without restorative processes based on voluntary, free and facilitated interaction between offenders, victims and others affected by the crime. Did acknowledgment of harm at sentencing really refer to the often emotional face-to-face acknowledgment that can occur at some restorative conferences? Or did it only add a restorative veneer to routine guilty pleas, invariably accompanied by perfunctory claims that the community and the victim have been saved the expense of a trial? Reparation could be directed towards the victim in terms of restitution or it could be directed toward the community through more conventional and state-centred punishments such as fines, probation and imprisonment. Would Parliament's new restorative purposes of sentencing languish as rhetorical add-ons and poorer second cousins to the more traditional multiple purposes of sentencing?

The Supreme Court of Canada surprised many when in two landmark cases decided in 1999 and 2000 it reclassified the purposes of sentencing into two new categories: 'restorative' and 'punitive' (*Gladue* 1999; *Proulx* 2000). The new restorative purposes of sentencing were defined to include the new references to reparation and acknowledgment of harm coupled with rehabilitation of the offender. The Supreme Court stated that the restorative purposes of sentencing 'focus upon the restorative goals of repairing the harms suffered by individual victims and by the community as a whole, promoting a sense of responsibility and an acknowledgment of the harm caused on the part of the offender, and attempting to rehabilitate or heal the offender' (*Gladue* 1999: para. 43). The Supreme Court's approach to restorative justice focused on restorative goals or outcomes rather than restorative processes. The Court rebranded rehabilitation as an attempt to 'heal the offender'. Such rebranding may have been necessary after rehabilitation and accompanying claims to expert knowledge and success were discredited by conclusions that 'nothing works' and growing punitiveness towards offenders (Garland 2001). To be sure, the renewed emphasis on rehabilitation raised concerns about net-widening (Roach and Rudin 2000) and the difficulty of healing (Acorn 2004: 70). Nevertheless, it fits well into the 1996 sentencing reforms which introduced a new conditional sentence of imprisonment that allowed offenders to serve some sentences of imprisonment in the community.

The Supreme Court stressed that the new restorative purposes of sentencing, including rehabilitation, were intended by Parliament to 'expand the parameters of the sentencing analysis of all offenders' and to respond to what it described as 'the problem of overincarceration in Canada' and the failure of prison to deter crime or rehabilitate offenders. The Court explained that 'restorative sentencing goals do not usually correlate with the use of prison as a sanction' and that they usually involve 'some form of restitution and reintegration with the community' (*Gladue* 1999: para. 43). With reference to literature on Aboriginal justice including 'healing and sentencing circles and aboriginal community council projects' (*Gladue* 1999: para. 74), the Court stated:

> Restorative justice may be described as an approach to remedying crime in which it is understood that all things are interrelated and that crime disrupts the harmony which existed prior to its occurrence, or at least which it is felt should exist. The appropriateness of a particular sanction is largely determined by the needs of the victims, and the community, as well as the offender. The focus is on the human beings most closely affected by the crime. (*Gladue* 1999: para. 71)

The Court also responded to criticisms that restorative approaches to sentencing might not result in a meaningful sanction. It argued that 'the existing overemphasis on incarceration in Canada may be partly due to the perception that a restorative approach is a more lenient approach to crime and that imprisonment constitutes the ultimate punishment. Yet in our view a sentence focussed on restorative justice is not necessarily a "lighter" punishment' (*Gladue* 1999: para. 72). The Court noted that 'facing victim and the community is for some more frightening than the possibility of a term of imprisonment and yields a more beneficial result in that the offender may become a healed and functional member of the community rather than a bitter offender returning after a term of imprisonment' (*Gladue* 1999: para. 72). One of the appeals of restorative justice was its ability to include all of the traditional retributive, rehabilitative and deterrent goals of sentencing.

A year later in the *Proulx* case dealing with conditional sentences and non-Aboriginal offenders, the Supreme Court returned to the same theme of the new restorative purposes of sentencing. It stated that 'by placing a new emphasis on restorative principles, Parliament expects both to reduce the rate of incarceration and improve the effectiveness of sentencing' (*Proulx* 2000: para. 20). This was consistent with the new mantra that was being heard throughout government: improve effectiveness while reducing costs. At the same time, the Court indicated that the need to deter, denounce and punish serious crimes would place some limits on the use of community sanctions and by implication the relevance of restorative justice. There were subtle but potentially important differences between the two landmark cases. The 1999 *Gladue* case leant more in the direction of seeing restorative approaches as a possible response to almost all offending (Dignan 2002) while the 2000 *Proulx* case contemplated a more dichotomous approach in which the punitive purposes of sentencing, including deterrence and denunciation, would take over when restorative approaches were insufficient or inappropriate (Braithwaite 2002).

In *Proulx*, the Supreme Court more starkly contrasted the restorative and punitive purposes of sentencing by stressing that punitive conditions such as house arrest were necessary to distinguish the new conditional sentence from probation orders. Thus conditions such as house arrest and strict curfews were justified not in terms of restorative justice, but as punitive measures that were intended to make conditional sentences a harsher response to crime than the use of probation orders. Although punitive aspects could be added to community sanctions, the Court conceded that incarceration would generally be the preferable sanction 'where objectives such as denunciation and deterrence are particularly pressing' (*Proulx* 2000: para. 127).

The bottom line in both landmark cases suggests that the Court was certainly not moving to a prison abolitionist version of restorative justice. The 1999 *Gladue* case involved a manslaughter described as a near murder and the Court did not interfere with a three-year imprisonment sentence. The Court, however, noted that Ms Gladue had already by the time the appeal was heard been granted parole after six months' imprisonment subject to electronic monitoring and conditions that she live with her father and take alcohol and substance abuse counselling. The *Proulx* case involved a drinking driver who pleaded guilty to dangerous driving causing death and bodily harm. The Court affirmed the trial judge's sentence of 18 months' imprisonment as necessary for deterrence and denunciation. Although restorative sanctions have been used in some serious cases in Canada, the idea that restorative approaches are not appropriate for serious crimes still lingers and it could help legitimate a retributive approach for serious crimes and support concerns that restorative justice is only a small add-on (White 2002).

Jennifer Llewellyn (2003: 307–8) has criticized the Supreme Court for embracing a 'limited and misguided understanding of restorative justice' in the above decisions. To be sure, the Court did not provide a detailed discussion of theories of restorative justice and drew on a limited amount of literature surrounding Aboriginal justice initiatives. In addition, Professor Llewellyn is also right to argue it is a serious mistake to assume that restorative outcomes will occur simply from the use of alternatives to imprisonment (Llewellyn 2003: 316). In its laudable desire to give meaning to the new purposes of sentencing and to the new conditional sentence of imprisonment, the Supreme Court may have oversold what sentencing could deliver, especially in terms of reparation to the victims but also in terms of rehabilitation of offenders.

The shortcomings of the restorative purposes of sentencing run much deeper than a failure of the Supreme Court to consider various theories of restorative justice. To the limited extent that the Court addressed the goals of restorative justice, its statement that a restorative approach responds to the actual needs of offenders, victims and the community does not seem any more flawed or ambiguous than other definitions of restorative justice. The Supreme Court's theory of restorative justice was no less sophisticated than that which some years later emerged in the United Nations Basic Principles which define restorative outcomes as any agreement reached by a restorative process in which victims, offenders and others affected by crime participate together to resolve matters arising from crime (United Nations 2002). One difference, however, is that the United Nations' principles focus on restorative processes whereas the Supreme Court of Canada, perhaps in recognition of the more coercive and more limited nature of sentencing, focuses on attempts to achieve restorative outcomes for offenders, victims and the community.

The problems with restorative purposes of sentencing stem more from the procedures of sentencing than the failure of the Supreme Court to offer a fuller theory of restorative outcomes. Sentencing is a bi-polar, adversarial and inherently coercive process that does not engage restorative processes and may only reach restorative outcomes occasionally. The attendance of the offender is mandatory, but offenders generally only speak in certain limited ways at sentencing hearings. The attendance of the victim at sentencing hearings is very infrequent. Most victims play no role in sentencing and the victims that do participate can only do so in limited ways through the submission of victim impact statements which in Canada cannot speak to what the victim believes is an appropriate disposition. The community is represented by a prosecutor operating within the confines of a bureaucracy and agreements between prosecutors and defence lawyers about the appropriate sentence generally bind the judge. Parliament and subsequently the Supreme Court introduced the concept of restorative justice into a criminal justice system that only grudgingly gives victims of crime a very limited role to play in sentencing. Although the 1996 Canadian sentencing reforms proudly proclaimed reparation of harm to victims as a new purpose of sentencing, they also restricted the ability of judges to require offenders to make reparations to victims as a condition of a community sanction (Roach 1999b). In 1999, Parliament responded to low usage of victim impact statements by requiring judges to inquire about their availability and allowing them to be delivered orally. Nevertheless, research since that time suggests that victim-oriented conditions in Canadian conditional sentences are relatively rare and that victims are often left without accurate information about an offender's community sanction (Roberts and Roach 2005).

The problems of the restorative purposes of sentencing are more structural than theoretical. Better theory from the judges cannot cure fundamental structural impediments to the use of restorative processes and the achievement of restorative outcomes at sentencing. Canadian courts remain reluctant to order restitution especially in cases where the financial damages cannot be easily ascertained. They are worried about criminal courts being turned into civil courts (Roach 1999a: 296–8) while restorative processes deliberately blur the legal categories of public and private law and criminal and civil law. Guilty pleas are strategic and routinized and do not resemble the face-to-face acknowledgments of responsibility and apologies that are encouraged in restorative processes. The offender may only speak a few rote and coached words at a guilty plea and the victim will most often not be present and when present will be constrained by legal rules as to what can be said. Sentencing, even when it results in an alternative to imprisonment and comes after a guilty plea, is a much more coercive and involuntary process than restorative proceedings. Even if the focus is on restorative outcomes, as opposed to restoration processes, it may be difficult to achieve genuine healing, acceptance of responsibility and acknowledgment of harm and reparation in an involuntary and coercive process. The point here is not to suggest that the new restorative purposes of sentencing have had a harmful effect on sentencing practices. They may well have rehabilitated rehabilitation as a purpose of sentencing and contributed to the success of the new conditional sentence of imprisonment as a community sanction (Roberts 2005). At the same time, however, sentencing may not be the optimal process through which to institutionalize restorative justice.

Restorative justice and Aboriginal people

An important motivating force behind the recognition of restorative justice in the 1996 sentencing reforms were prior sentencing innovations with respect to Aboriginal people such as the use of sentencing circles and concerns about the dramatic overrepresentation of Aboriginal people in Canadian prisons.

Sentencing circles

One of the most cited and celebrated uses of sentencing circles in Canada in the early 1990s came from a fly-in court in Canada's northern Yukon territory and involved a 26-year-old Aboriginal man, Philip Moses. Mr Moses had already received 43 prior convictions and combined jail sentences of eight years of imprisonment when he came to be sentenced for using a baseball bat to threaten a police officer. The existing system had failed to prevent his reoffending which was in part related to substance abuse. After setting an upper limit on possible punishment and adjourning to allow time for work to be done in the community, the trial judge convened a circle of about 30 people including members of the offender's family, his First Nation and police officers. In lengthy and eloquent reasons for judgment, Judge Barry Stuart commented about the importance of reconfiguring the court into a circle. 'The circle significantly breaks down the dominance that traditional courtrooms accord lawyers and judges: All persons within the circle must be addressed. [...] The circle denies the comfort of evading difficult issues through the use of obtuse, complex technical language' (*Moses* 1992: 356–7). Following the circle's recommendation, Mr Moses was placed on probation and required to live and reintegrate with his family on a remote trap line and later to attend an alcohol treatment programme for Aboriginal men.

Moses was a creative and courageous decision, but it focused almost entirely on attempting to rehabilitate the offender. Despite noting the support of the local police for the sentence, Judge Stuart does not mention if the police officer who had been threatened by Mr Moses attended the circle or agreed with the sentence. Judge Stuart stressed that: 'The leaders of the community where Philip will live out his life are willing to risk their safety in a rehabilitative program. His family and First Nation are willing to invest in Philip' (*Moses* 1992: 381). As with the more formal restorative purposes of sentencing that were to be implemented later in the 1990s, sentencing circles were a means to rehabilitate rehabilitation as a sentencing purpose. The difference was that rehabilitation was no longer a matter solely for expert health care providers and probation workers whose claims to expertise had been undermined by visible failures of the criminal justice system (Garland 2001). Rather, rehabilitation was a matter in which elders, communities and families could assist.

Sentencing circles are not without controversy. There are neither systemic studies nor clear protocols concerning the functioning or effectiveness of sentencing circles in Canada. Although they allow more community participation, sentencing circles ultimately depend on the sentencing discretion of the trial judge and some of the outcomes from sentencing circles have been reversed on appeal. Sentencing circles take much more time than conventional sentences and cannot be used in most cases. Although sometimes conflated with Aboriginal justice, sentencing circles are not a form of Aboriginal justice that applies Aboriginal law. Patricia Monture, a prominent Aboriginal commentator, criticized sentencing circles as 'small add-ons to the existing system, which stands ready with the full force of its adversarial and punishment-oriented values if the "nice" solution does not work' (Monture 1994: 226). One Métis probation officer who participated in a sentencing circle that recommended 18 months of imprisonment (and was overturned by the courts as too lenient) commented that she thought it was 'a misuse of this Sentencing Circle, which is a healing process [...] we're talking periods of time here' (*Morin* 1995: 142). Although sentencing circles were too harsh for these commentators, others criticized them as too lenient. Teressa Nahanee (1993: 360, 373) argued that Aboriginal women opposed the leniency of approaches 'which allow Aboriginal male sex offenders to roam free of punishment after conviction for violent offences against Aboriginal women and children'. She emphasized the need for 'punishment and deterrence of the "guilty" victimizer'. The focus on institutionalizing restorative justice at sentencing meant that the issue of the appropriate treatment of serious crimes of violence loomed large in debates about the restorative purposes of sentencing.

Gladue

As part of the 1996 sentencing reforms, section 718.2(e) of the Criminal Code was amended to require the trial judge to consider all reasonable alternatives to prison 'with particular attention to the circumstances of aboriginal offenders'. The Supreme Court first considered this new provision in the 1999 case of Jamie Tanis Gladue, a woman who was convicted of manslaughter in the stabbing death of her male partner. The Court examined statistics concerning Aboriginal overrepresentation in prison and concluded that they represented a 'sad and pressing social problem' that could 'reasonably be termed a crisis in the Canadian criminal justice'. The Court recognized that the overrepresentation was related to many problems that it could not address 'including poverty, substance abuse, lack of education and lack of employment opportunities', but it also stressed that trial judges had some role to play in addressing overrepresentation. The Court indicated that factors such as 'poor social and economic conditions' and 'the legacy of dislocation' could in an appropriate case be relevant to whether a sentence of imprisonment would actually deter or denounce crime (*Gladue* 1999). The Court made clear that the section was intended to remedy both overincarceration in general and Aboriginal overrepresentation in particular. To its credit, the Court recognized that many Aboriginal people live in Canadian cities and held that the trial judge had erred in dismissing the relevance of section 718.2(e) to the accused who came from an urban environment. Nevertheless, the Court did not alter the three-year manslaughter sentence received by Ms Gladue for the 'near murder' of her partner. In a subsequent sexual assault case, the Court also upheld a sentence of 20 months' imprisonment, stressing that the more serious and violent the crime, the more likely it was that the appropriate sentence would be the same for an Aboriginal and non-Aboriginal offender (*Wells* 2000).

Despite the actual results in these cases, the idea that Aboriginal offenders should be singled out for particular attention was controversial. The media were often hostile to the provision which was widely perceived as a race-based discount for sentencing even though the Supreme Court had stressed the continuing obligation to determine an appropriate sentence for the individual offender (Roach and Rudin 2000: 380). Philip Stenning and Julian Roberts published a controversial article arguing that Aboriginal overrepresentation was not a national problem; that Aboriginal persons actually received shorter sentences for similar crimes and that all social disadvantages that played a causal role in the commission of a crime should be considered at sentencing (Stenning and Roberts 2001). Some of their arguments were contested

(Rudin and Roach 2002), but there was widespread agreement that *Gladue* would not provide a quick or simple solution to Aboriginal overrepresentation in prison.

The statutory direction to trial judges to pay particular attention to the circumstances of Aboriginal offenders has so far not reduced Aboriginal overrepresentation. In the post *Gladue* years of 1999–2000 and 2000–01, Aboriginal admissions have constituted 18 and 19 per cent of all provincial admissions, compared to a 17 per cent average between 1978 and 2001. The picture is even more bleak in the period following the 1996 sentencing reforms as non-Aboriginal admissions have declined by 22 per cent while Aboriginal admissions have increased by 3 per cent. In the western province of Saskatchewan, absolute numbers of Aboriginal admissions to custody have declined by over 500 in the post-*Gladue* era, but because of declines in non-Aboriginal admissions, the percentage of Aboriginal admissions has actually increased to an astounding 75 per cent of all admissions (Roberts and Melchers 2003: 220, 226, 229). Although some of the declines in sentenced admissions are related to the use of conditional sentences and other alternatives to imprisonment, some simply represent the fact that offenders have already served their sentence before trial because they were denied bail. In addition even alternatives to imprisonment may generate breaches that may result in incarceration. The failure of *Gladue* so far to reduce Aboriginal overrepresentation may point in the direction of the need for front-end reforms to keep Aboriginal people out of the system including social and economic strategies (Roach and Rudin 2000: 376; Roberts and Melchers 2003: 239). In addition, adequate resources in the community are necessary to make alternatives to imprisonment an appropriate sanction, particularly for more serious crimes, and these resources are often lacking. *Gladue* places new and onerous obligations on trial judges to inquire into the circumstances and background of Aboriginal offenders (Turpel-LaFond 1999), but it is not clear that judges will always be in a position to demand such information let alone community support for offenders or victims.

In Toronto, a special *Gladue* court was created with dedicated court-workers, probation officers and trial judges for Aboriginal offenders who wish to be sentenced in such an environment. One of the prime features of this court is the preparation of extensive *Gladue* pre-sentence reports prepared by specially trained people working for an Aboriginal agency, Aboriginal Legal Services of Toronto, to inform lawyers and judges about the resources available in Toronto's Aboriginal community. In many other jurisdictions, however, special resources have not been dedicated to implementing *Gladue*. The Supreme Court anticipated this problem and ruled that 'the absence of alternative sentencing programs specific to an aboriginal community does not eliminate the ability of a sentencing judge to impose a sanction that takes into account principles of restorative justice and the needs of the parties involved' (*Gladue*: para 93). Nevertheless restorative outcomes cannot be mandated by top-down direction from the bench. They require ongoing community support.

In *Gladue*, the Supreme Court stated that 'most traditional conceptions of sentencing place a *primary* emphasis upon the ideals of restorative justice' (*Gladue* 1999: para. 70 emphasis in original). The Court did not identify the precise nature of these traditions, but it mentioned the experience of 'healing and sentencing circles, and aboriginal community council projects' as examples of innovations that indicated that 'community-based sanctions coincide with the aboriginal concept of sentencing and the needs of aboriginal people and communities' (*Gladue* 1999: para. 74). At the same time, most sentencing circles, and in particular the famous Moses sentencing circle discussed above, focused on attempting to rehabilitate the offender. As will be seen, one of Canada's most important community council projects also had a similar focus. Restorative justice with its focus on acknowledgment and repair of the harm to the victim may not always fit well with Aboriginal justice initiatives that may focus on the healing of the offender and his or her integration into the community.

Restorative justice principles and guidelines and Aboriginal justice

Drawing on his extensive experience with Aboriginal justice programmes, Jonathan Rudin has recently warned that principles of restorative justice inspired by the UN Basic Principles can threaten Aboriginal justice programmes. Although UN principles and related Canadian principles and guidelines for restorative justice[2] 'explicitly credit the development of restorative justice programmes to Aboriginal justice concepts, the guidelines do not recognize that Aboriginal justice initiatives are not historic relics from which lessons can be drawn but rather vital contemporary projects which have their own needs that must be acknowledged and addressed' (Rudin 2005: 109).

Aboriginal Legal Services of Toronto's long running Community Council programme involves diversion from the criminal process and meetings of those diverted with volunteers from Toronto's Aboriginal community. Evaluations of this programme found high levels of compliance with the terms proposed by the elders of the Community Council. This may suggest that the process used by the Council is restorative for the offender. Nevertheless, the progamme may score less well on evaluations that demand restorative outcomes for victims and restorative encounters between offenders and victims. One evaluation suggests that only 12.5 per cent of cases heard by the Council result in letters of apology and only 7.1 per cent of cases result in restitution to victims. These results may indicate a greater concern for victim restoration than the low percentages suggest given that many of the cases diverted from the system may not have individual victims. In any event, the most frequent disposition of cases in Community Council are offender centred and involve continued contact with Aboriginal Legal Services of Toronto in 41.8 per cent of cases and referrals of the offender to other Aboriginal agencies in 39.3 per cent of cases (Proulx 2003: 199). In addition, crime victims do not generally attend Community Council meetings with offenders and the programme might not easily fit within federal Department of Justice guidelines for restorative justice programmes that, while recognizing diversity among programmes, still require that offenders and victims participate in any restorative justice programme with the assistance of facilitators and provide follow-up for victims as well as offenders. In short, the Community Council does not satisfy procedural definitions of restorative justice which require face-to-face meetings between offenders and victims and it only produces restorative outcomes such as letters of apology and restitution in a minority of its cases. Toronto's successful and durable Community Council programme might not score well on formal measures of restorative justice.

Rudin also warns that restorative justice-based Aboriginal justice programmes offered by police and non-Aboriginal groups may, despite good intentions, only import approaches that do 'not build community capacity and challenge colonial assumptions' (Rudin 2005: 110–11). Another example of how restorative programmes can become professionalized and get away from the community is found in the Law Commission of Canada's disappointing final report culminating in over five years' work of often creative and path-breaking endeavours on restorative justice. The final report discusses a variety of restorative justice initiatives both inside and outside of the criminal justice system along with very different developments such as the use of court-annexed mandatory mediation and commercial arbitration designed to reduce court backlog in civil cases. It asserts that 'participatory processes are appropriate for all types of conflict' and 'have potential values for all types of Canadian communities, Aboriginal and non-Aboriginal' (Law Commission 2003: 208). Among its uninspired recommendations are that lawyers receive the same type of legal aid payments for their mediation and conference work as they do for litigation and that law students, lawyers and judges receive increased training 'in alternative conflict resolution processes' (Law Commission 2003: 216). Although the Commission entitled its report 'Transforming Relationships Through Participatory Justice', it is difficult to believe that transformation can be achieved through the report's professionalized and acontextual vision of lawyer-driven alternative dispute resolution. Once restorative justice is institutionalized in legal processes, lawyers will play a more important role. Restorative justice may also be wrongly equated with initiatives such as mandatory mediation of civil cases that are designed to make the justice system less costly and more efficient.

The institutionalization of restorative justice may have unintended consequences. In the case of Aboriginal justice initiatives, it may pressure programmes that for good reasons focus on the rehabilitation of the offender to take on victim issues in order to qualify as restorative justice programmes that are eligible for funding or diversion. It may also involve the use of professional mediators trained in alternative dispute resolution or therapeutic jurisprudence. Restorative justice, no less than formal adjudication, may involve police, social workers, mediators, lawyers and other professionals stealing conflicts from the community (Christie 1977). A procedural definition of restorative justice that requires facilitated meetings between offenders and victims may also inhibit the ability of Aboriginal communities to decide for themselves the most appropriate means to deal with crime and could frustrate initiatives that could achieve positive outcomes for offenders and perhaps for victims and communities.

Restorative justice and disadvantaged groups

As discussed above, the Supreme Court associated the restorative purposes of sentencing with Aboriginal justice even though some of the initiatives may not fit easily into definitions of restorative justice based on restorative procedures. In this section, attempts to expand restorative approaches to sentencing to other disadvantaged offenders will be examined.

In 2003, the Ontario Court of Appeal observed that African-Canadians suffered from some of the same social disadvantages as Aboriginal people and that such disadvantages could be considered as mitigating factors at sentencing when appropriate in individual cases. The Court reduced from five to four years' imprisonment a sentence for aggravated assault with a loaded gun by a young African-Canadian man who had an absentee father, a mother who suffered from mental health problems and a history of substance abuse (*Borde* 2003). This case fell into a pattern similar to that observed above with respect to *Gladue* and *Proulx* in that the court opened the door to the use of alternatives to imprisonment while at the same time being reluctant to employ such alternatives given the seriousness of the offence. To the extent that the one-year reduction in sentence could be seen as based on offender disadvantage and the social context of the offence, it was used in mitigation. A more robust approach would see a desire to achieve restorative objectives not as a factor in mitigation, but as a more effective way of making a person responsible for his offence.

In response to the Court of Appeal's decision in *Borde*, a respected trial judge in suburban Toronto asked counsel to consider the relevance of data that he had collected relating to the overrepresentation of black women in prison in a case in which two black women pled guilty to importing cocaine from Jamaica to Canada. The active role of the judge in this case was controversial. The Crown appealed arguing that the trial judge had erred by departing from the tariff and injecting the issue of race into the sentencing proceedings. The Court of Appeal concluded that the trial judge had erred by raising issues of race and gender at sentencing. The Court of Appeal was not impressed by the trial judge's reliance on the figure that 6 per cent of the female penitentiary population was black as opposed to 2 per cent of the total Canadian population. Such small numbers meant that '.007 per cent of the female black population in Canada is in the penitentiary' (*Hamilton* 2004: para. 78). The court feared that black women with connections to Jamaica would only be increasingly used as drug couriers if they were given non-custodial sentences and that such a sentence would cause harm to the black community in Ontario (*Hamilton* 2004: para. 148). In this way, the Court of Appeal relied on the problematic assumption that incarceration would deter crime.

The Court of Appeal stressed race neutrality when it stated that 'the fact that an offender is a member of a group that has historically been subject to systemic racial and gender bias does not in itself justify any mitigation of sentence. Lower sentences predicated on nothing more than membership in a disadvantaged group further neither the principles of sentencing, nor the goals of equality' (*Hamilton* 2004: para. 133). Although this may not preclude the use of individual specific mitigating factors (Ives 2004), this decision suggests that African-Canadians may have more difficulties than Aboriginal people in having systemic discrimination considered at sentencing or in persuading judges that alternatives to imprisonment may be an appropriate response to their background.

The Court of Appeal in *Hamilton* concluded that a restorative approach was not appropriate in part because there was no evidence that 'poor black women share a cultural perspective with respect to punishment that is akin to the aboriginal perspective' (*Hamilton* 2004: para. 98). There are a number of problems with the use of ascribed cultural essences of Aboriginal people being used to dismiss the appropriateness of restorative approaches for other groups. One problem is that the court overestimates the cultural homogeneity of Aboriginal people, many of whom live off reserves and in urban environments. The Supreme Court in *Gladue* was alive to this risk and held that the trial judge had erred when he suggested that reference to the circumstances of Aboriginal people did not apply because the offender was living off reserve in a city (*Gladue* 1999: paras 73, 94). A related problem is that the Court of Appeal in *Hamilton* in searching for evidence of the perspective of 'poor black women' may have ignored the socio-cultural and economic diversity of Canada's black population. In short, the Court of Appeal assumed an unrealistic unity of culture among both Aboriginal people and poor black women. It would be unfortunate if the connections that many have drawn between Aboriginal justice and restorative justice was used to exclude other groups from restorative approaches. Such exclusion would undermine Parliament's deliberate decision in the 1996 sentencing reforms to codify restorative purposes of sentencing for all offenders and not just Aboriginal offenders. In my view, the question should not have been whether the offenders in *Hamilton* share the same perspective on punishment as Aboriginal people (this in itself would be difficult if not impossible given the diversity of both populations) but whether there are community resources and circumstances in the case that may have made a community-based sanction appropriate in the circumstances and whether such an approach could have achieved restorative outcomes for offenders, victims and the larger community. The *Hamilton* case suggests that one unfortunate consequence of the institutionalization of restorative justice around Aboriginal issues may be the exclusion of non-Aboriginal people from the potential benefits of restorative approaches.

The impact of restorative justice on other disadvantaged groups is also a matter of concern. Patricia Hughes and Mary Jane Mossman have warned that 'there has been inadequate consideration of the gender implications of restorative justice practice' and that they 'have concern about the use of restorative justice practices in connection with crimes such as sexual assault and domestic abuse' (Hughes and Mossman 2002: 130). Some Aboriginal commentators in Canada have also raised concerns that alternatives to imprisonment may discount the seriousness of violence against women (Nahanee 1993).

Hughes and Mossman also warn that restorative justice may privatize justice initiatives and have an adverse impact on the economically disadvantaged. Requiring impoverished offenders to make financial restitution to victims could have retrogressive impacts. It may encourage neoliberal states to retrench from the provision of state-funded compensation to crime victims (Roach 1999a). The ability of well-off offenders to make financial payments to victims may only aggravate class-based disadvantages in the criminal justice system. The Supreme Court has indicated that a $10,000 payment made by a 'successful entrepreneur' convicted of assaulting and sexually assaulting an employee 'weighed in favour of restorative objectives' (R. (A.) 2000). Although the court held that the need to deter and denounce serious crimes justified a sentence of one year imprisonment in that case, the case indicates the advantage that offenders who can make payments to victims may experience under restorative approaches to sentencing. One Canadian study of an Aboriginal specific victim–offender reconciliation programme found no actual reparation in part because all of the offenders did not have a job (Longclaws 1996). As discussed above, 7.1 per cent of cases referred to the Aboriginal Legal Service of Toronto's Community Council resulted in monetary restitution. Thought should be given to a broader and more creative approach to restoration that would not simply draw on the existing and unequal distribution of financial resources among offenders. If restitution is equated with the ability to pay and does not involve state support for both offenders and victims, the institutionalization of restorative justice may advance neoliberal and punitive strategies that place the responsibility of providing compensation for crime on offenders as opposed to the state.

Restorative justice and the Youth Criminal Justice Act

Much experience with restorative justice throughout the world has focused on youth justice. In Canada, however, the institutionalization of restorative justice discussed in the above sections has focused on the sentencing of adult offenders. Restorative justice only played a more visible role with respect to youth with the enactment of the Youth Criminal Justice Act (YCJA) in 2002.

The YCJA built on the experience of sentencing reforms in the adult system by recognizing the acknowledgment of the harm done to the victim and the community as purposes of sentencing. In addition it instructs the judge to consider any reparation made by the young person to the victim or the community in determining an appropriate sentence. Although this provision is designed to encourage voluntary reparation by offenders, it may also give offenders whose parents are able and willing to contribute to reparations an advantage over young offenders without access to such financial resources.

Section 42(2)(h) of the YCJA is a more innovative approach to reparation because it allows the sentencing judge to 'order the young person to compensate any person in kind or by way of personal service' for pecuniary damages. The order cannot exceed 240 hours of community services or 12 months and the victim must consent to the personal service order (YCJA, s. 54). Although the requirement for the victim's consent appropriately follows the UN Basic Principles, refusals by victims to consent may limit the utility of this restorative sentencing option. Programmes that enable young offenders to work may be necessary so that all offenders, including the most disadvantaged, have an equal opportunity to make reparation to victims (Roach 1999b). Such programmes might resemble community service orders except that the victim would benefit from the offender's work as opposed to the community at large. A failure to devise such programmes may mean that the new emphasis on reparation at sentencing may be something of a false promise for victims not fortunate enough to have offenders who come from advantaged backgrounds. It will also mean that offenders from disadvantaged backgrounds will be further disadvantaged by not being able to satisfy the reparative purposes of sentences. This could aggravate the over-incarceration of Aboriginal youth and youth from other disadvantaged backgrounds.

In addition to the recognition of various restorative purposes of sentencing, the YCJA encourages the use of extra-judicial measures and conferences at various stages of the prosecution process. Victim–offender reconciliation programmes, mediation and restitution programmes are all mentioned as possible extra-judicial measures, but the Act itself does not mandate that the conferences be conducted or that they be conducted on the basis of restorative principles. Victims have a right to be informed of the disposition of the offence through extra-judicial measures, but no right actually to participate in such measures (YCJA, s.12). In this way, the YCJA does not mandate restorative processes which bring offenders together with victims. As with restorative sentencing, the focus in many extra-judicial measures may be more on rehabilitation of offenders than acknowledgment of harm and reparation to victims. There may be nothing wrong with such an offender-based approach, especially with respect to young offenders, but it may be misleading to sell such extra-judicial measures as restorative either in terms of their process or their outcomes.

Section 19 of the YCJA empowers a wide range of justice system participants to convene conferences for the purposes of making various decisions under the Act. Some conferences could be genuine family conferences or victim–offender reconciliation programmes that follow restorative procedures and seek restorative outcomes. Some conferences, however, will simply be consultations between criminal justice professionals about whether a young offender should be released on bail or about the duration of his or her sentence. The latter perhaps more frequent type of conference cannot be described as restorative because it does not follow restorative procedures or attempt to achieve restorative outcomes.

The YCJA does not go as far as New Zealand legislation in endorsing a restorative justice and conference-based approach to youth crime with substantial investment in full-time youth justice coordinators. Much will depend on how the provinces, which in Canada have jurisdiction over the administration of criminal justice, structure and use conferences. The YCJA allows for a diversity of provincial and even local approaches to the use of conferences. Although a case can be made that Canada should have followed the more structured New Zealand approach, there is something to be said for a more flexible approach in a large and diverse country such as Canada. A mandated restorative approach in Canada would have to be accompanied by sufficient funds to hire the necessary coordinators of family conferences and to ensure that the conferences were properly run and evaluated. Without such a national commitment, it is probably best that the YCJA has taken a flexible approach that allows restorative procedures to be used, but does not mandate them or promise restorative outcomes. One of the dangers of the institutionalization of restorative justice in Canada is the danger of overselling measures as restorative when they do not include restorative processes and when they may not be optimally designed to achieve restorative outcomes, especially for victims.

Some provinces in Canada may take a more restorative approach to the implementation of the YCJA. Even before the new Act took force, Nova Scotia had established a comprehensive youth restorative justice process that provides support for restorative family conferences at the police, prosecutorial, trial and correctional stages (Archibald 2001). Some judges on their own initiative have conducted family conferences and have been able to implement the recommendations of these conferences through the vast range of non-custodial sanctions available under YCJA (Harris *et al.* 2004: 380–6). The YCJA may provide a flexible and non-binding framework for the institutionalization of restorative approaches to youth offending. It may provide an accommodating framework for more community-based developments while not attempting to impose restorative procedures or principles from above. Experimentation in youth courts, such as the use of therapeutic jurisprudence or other interventions centred on the offender, may not be constrained by a restorative template that demands facilitated meetings between offenders and victims.

The YCJA also introduces police and Crown cautions as extra-judicial measures. The United Kingdom has much more experience with police cautions and some interesting experiments have attempted to administer these cautions in a more restorative manner. The available research suggests, however, substantial difficulties in having the cautions administered by the police in a truly restorative manner (Young and Hoyle 2003). This raises the general theme of whether restorative justice will be corrupted and made more punitive as it is integrated into mainstream criminal justice processing. Restorative cautions, like restorative sentences, may strike some restorative justice purists as a contradiction in terms. Cautioning is not easily seen as a voluntary process that brings together those affected by crimes to achieve some agreement about appropriate responses. Nevertheless, there may be something to be said for attempting to use cautions and other alternatives to imprisonment to achieve restorative outcomes that are more positive for offenders, victims and the community. At the same time, however, there may not be agreement about what constitutes a positive or a restorative outcome.

Conclusion

Since the 1996 sentencing reforms, Canada has been quite active in institutionalizing restorative justice, mainly at sentencing. The restorative movement in sentencing has to some extent been an effective reform that has rehabilitated rehabilitation as a purpose of sentencing and has helped the conditional sentence emerge as an important alternative to actual incarceration (Roberts 2005). At the same time, there is less evidence that restorative purposes of the sentence have provided tangible benefits for crime victims despite the formal recognition of reparation and acknowledgment of the harm done to victims as purposes of sentencing (Roberts and Roach 2005). Victims are excluded more because of the structural constraints of a sentencing process that does not easily include victims than any failure to theorize or recognize the possibilities of restorative justice as an alternative approach to crime.

Concerns about the overrepresentation of Aboriginal people in Canadian prisons has been a prime motivator in attempts to institutionalize restorative justice in Canada. The Supreme Court first recognized restorative justice as a legitimate and important purpose of sentencing in a case involving the sentencing of an Aboriginal offender (*Gladue* 1999). Unfortunately, as noted earlier in the chapter, the available evidence suggests that the restorative turn in Canadian sentencing has not reduced Aboriginal overrepresentation (Roberts and Melchers 2003). In addition, attempts to squeeze Aboriginal community justice initiatives into the mould of restorative procedures may also threaten such initiatives (Rudin 2005), including their ability to achieve restorative or positive outcomes such as the healing and reintegration of offenders. The dangers here are not only that restorative justice may turn out to be a limited add-on, but also a limiting add-on that constrains some positive Aboriginal justice initiatives. Simplified perceptions about a distinctive Aboriginal perspective on punishment have been used to justify not extending restorative approaches to sentencing to other disadvantaged individuals such as African-Canadians (*Hamilton* 2004). Some courts have at times been reluctant to use alternatives to imprisonment in serious cases (*Wells* 2000) and there is a possibility that the use of restorative approaches in less serious cases will help legitimate the need for punishment and deterrence in more serious cases (*Proulx* 2000). There are limits to what restorative approaches can achieve at the sentencing stage and there is a need for restorative interventions earlier in the criminal process if the institutionalization of restorative justice in Canada is not to amount to a limited add-on.

Canada's new YCJA should be carefully monitored because it may turn out to be the country's most ambitious attempt to institutionalize restorative justice. Consistent with the adult regime, it recognizes restorative purposes of sentencing. It remains to be seen whether this approach will, as in the adult system, primarily allow rehabilitation to be rejuvenated and rebranded as a sentencing purpose or whether it will result in a new emphasis on offender reparation to the victim. The latter could promote restorative outcomes such as reparation for crime victims, but may result in discrimination against disadvantaged offenders, including those from Aboriginal and other disadvantaged groups, who cannot afford to purchase a restorative outcome such as reparation.

The YCJA provides a flexible structure for conferences. Conferences can be conducted on the basis of restorative procedures and they can seek restorative outcomes should the participants desire, but at the same time, conferences can also be run in different ways that focus either on the offender or the needs of professionals for the efficient processing of cases. In this way, the institutionalization of restorative justice in the YCJA will not be a limiting or constraining feature. At the same time, the use of restorative processes and/or the achievement of restorative outcomes for offenders, victims and communities are by no means guaranteed and will require careful monitoring and evaluation to determine whether restorative justice is an effective reform or a limited add-on to youth criminal justice.

Notes

1   I thank Julian Roberts and Jonathan Rudin, both good colleagues, friends and co-authors on related articles, for helpful comments on an earlier draft. I also thank Megan Stephens who provided valuable and insightful comments on an earlier draft. The author represented Aboriginal Legal Services of Toronto in its interventions in three of the cases discussed in this chapter, *Gladue*, 1999, *Wells*, 2000 and *Hamilton*, 2004, but his views do not necessarily represent those of that organization.
2   In the wake of Canada's support for the United Nations Basic Principles on the use of restorative justice programmes in criminal matters, Canada's federal Department of Justice has issued 'Values and Principles of Restorative Justice in Criminal Matters' at http://fp.enter.net/ restorativepractices/RJValues-DOJCan.pdf and 'Restorative Justice Program Guidelines' at http://fp.enter.net/restorativepractices/RJGuide-DOJCan.pdf The Canadian principles include voluntary participation by offenders and victims, acceptance of responsibility by the offender, access to legal advice for each party, concern for power imbalances, a presumption of confidentiality, non-use of a failure to reach agreement against the offender and regular evaluation. The Canadian guidelines call for meetings between offenders and victims with respected facilitators. They also call for follow-ups with both offenders and victims.

References

Acorn, A. (2004) *Compulsory Compassion: A Critique of Restorative Justice.* Vancouver: University of British Columbia Press.

Archibald, B. (2001) 'Citizenship participation in Canadian criminal justice: the emergence of "inclusionary adversarial" and "restorative" Models', in S. Coughlan and D. Russell (eds), *Citizenship and Citizen Participation in the Administration of Justice.* Montreal: Themis, pp. 149–92.

Braithwaite, J. (2002) 'In search of restorative jurisprudence', in L. Walgrave (ed.), *Restorative Justice and the Law.* Cullompton: Willan, pp. 150–67.

Braithwaite, J. (2003) 'Principles of restorative justice', in A. von Hirsch, J. Roberts, A. E. Bottoms, K. Roach and M. Schiff (eds), *Restorative Justice and Criminal Justice: Competing or Reconcilable Paradigms?* Oxford: Hart Publishing, pp. 1–20.

Canada, Department of Justice (n.d.) 'Restorative Justice Program Guidelines', at http://fp.enter.net/restorativepractices/RJGuide-DOJCan.pdf

Canada, Department of Justice (n.d.) 'Values and Principles of Restorative Justice in Criminal Matters', at http://fp.enter.net/restorativepractices/RJValues-DOJCan.pdf

Christie, N. (1977) 'Conflicts as property', *British Journal of Criminology*, 17(1): 1–15.

Daubney, D. (1988) *Taking Responsibility: The Report of the Standing Committee on Justice and Solicitor General on Its Review of Sentencing, Conditional Release and Related Aspects of Corrections.* Ottawa: Queen's Printer.

Dignan, J. (2002) 'Restorative justice and the law: the case for an integrated, systemic approach', in L. Walgrave (ed.), *Restorative Justice and the Law.* Cullompton: Willan, pp. 168–90.

Dignan, J. (2003) 'Towards a systemic model of restorative justice', in A. von Hirsch, J. Roberts, A.E. Bottoms, K. Roach and M. Schiff (eds), *Restorative Justice and Criminal Justice: Competing or Reconcilable Paradigms?* Oxford: Hart Publishing, pp. 135–56.

Garland, D. (2001) *The Culture of Control.* Chicago, IL: University of Chicago Press.

Harris, P., Weagant, B., Cole, D. and Weinper, F. (2004) 'Working "in the Trenches" with the YCJA', *Canadian Journal of Criminology and Criminal Justice*, 46: 367–421.

Hughes, P. and Mossman, M. J. (2002) 'Re-thinking access to criminal justice in Canada: a critical review of needs and responses', *Windsor Review of Legal and Social Issues*, XII: 1–131.

Ives, D. (2004) 'Inequality, Crime and Sentencing', *Queens Law Journal*, 30: 114–55.

Kaiser, A. (2003) '*Borde* and *Hamilton*: facing the uncomfortable truth about inequality, discrimination and general deterrence', *Criminal Reports* (6th Series), 8: 289–98.

Laprairie, C. and Dickinson, J. (2005) *The Circle Must Not be Broken.* Toronto: University of Toronto Press.

Law Commission of Canada (2003) *Transforming Relationships Through Participatory Justice.* Ottawa: Law Commission of Canada.

Llewellyn, J. (2003) 'Restorative justice in *Borde* and *Hamilton* – a systemic problem?', *Criminal Reports* (6th Series), 8: 308–16.

Longclaws, L. (1996) 'Piloting family group conferences for young offenders in Winnipeg', in J. Hudson and B. Galaway (eds), *Family Group Conferences. Perspectives on Policy and Practices.* Annadale: Federation Press.

Monture, P. (1994) 'Thinking about aboriginal justice: myths and revolution', in R. Gosse (ed.), *Continuing Poundmaker's and Riel's Quest.* Saskatoon, Sask.: Purich Publishing, pp. 222–32.

Nahanee, T. (1993) 'Dancing with a gorilla: Aboriginal justice, women and the charter', in Royal Commission on Aboriginal Peoples (ed.), *Aboriginal Peoples and the Justice System*. Ottawa: Supply and Services.

Proulx, C. (2003) *Reclaiming Aboriginal Justice: Identity and Community*. Saskatoon: Purich Publishing.

Roach, K. (1999a) *Due Process and Victims' Rights: The New Law and Politics of Criminal Justice*. Toronto: University of Toronto Press.

Roach, K. (1999b) 'Crime victims and sentencing', in D. Stuart *et al.* (eds), *Towards a Clear and Just Criminal Law*. Toronto: Carswell, pp. 513–19.

Roach, K. (2000) 'Changing punishment at the turn of the century: restorative justice on the rise', *Canadian Journal of Criminology*, 42(3): 249–80.

Roach, K. and Rudin, J. (2000) '*Gladue*: the judicial and political reception of a promising decision', *Canadian Journal of Criminology*, 42(3): 355–88.

Roberts, J. V. (2005) *The Virtual Prison*. Oxford: Oxford University Press.

Roberts, J. V. and Melchers, R. (2003) 'The incarceration of Aboriginal offenders: an analysis of trends, 1978–2001', *Canadian Journal of Criminology and Criminal Justice*, 45(2): 211–42.

Roberts, J. V. and Roach, K. (2003) 'Restorative justice in Canada: from sentencing circles to sentencing principles', in A. von Hirsch, J. Roberts, A. E. Bottoms, K. Roach and M. Schiff (eds), *Restorative Justice and Criminal Justice: Competing or Reconcilable Paradigms?* Oxford: Hart Publishing, pp. 237–56.

Roberts, J. V. and Roach, K. (2005) 'Conditional sentencing and the perspectives of crime victims', *Queens Law Journal*, 31: 560–600.

Rudin, J. (2005) 'Aboriginal justice and restorative justice' in L. Elliott and R. Gordon (eds), *Restorative Justice*. Cullumpton: Willan, pp. 89–114.

Rudin J. and Roach, K. (2002) 'Broken promises: a response to Stenning and Roberts' "Empty promises"', *Saskatchewan Law Review*, 65: 3–46.

Stenning, P. and Roberts, J.V. (2001) 'Empty promises: Parliament, the Supreme Court and the sentencing of Aboriginal offenders', *Saskatchewan Law Review*, 64: 137–68.

Turpel-Lafond, M. (1999) 'Sentencing within a restorative paradigm: procedural implications of *R. v. Gladue*', *Criminal Law Quarterly*, 43: 34–50.

United Nations (2002) *Basic Principles on the Use of Restorative Justice Programmes in Criminal Matters*. UN Economic and Social Council.

White, R. (2002) 'Restorative justice and social inequality', in B. Schissel and C. Brooks (eds), *Marginality and Condemnation. An Introduction to Critical Criminology*. Halifax: Fernwood Publishing, pp. 381–96.

Young, R. and Hoyle, C. (2003) 'New, improved police-led restorative justice: action research and the Thames Valley Police Initiative', in A. von Hirsch, J. Roberts, A. E. Bottoms, K. Roach and M. Schiff (eds), *Restorative justice and criminal justice: competing or reconcilable paradigms?* Oxford: Hart Publishing, pp. 273–92.

Cases

Borde (2003) 63 Ontario Reports (3d) 417 (OntCA).
Gladue [1999] 1 Supreme Court Reports 688.
Hamilton (2004) 72 Ontario Reports (3d) 1 (OntCA).
Moses (1992) 71 Canadian Criminal Cases (3d) 347 (YTC).
Proulx [2000] 1 Supreme Court Reports 61.
R. (A.) (2000) 1 Supreme Court Reports 163.
Wells [2000] 1 Supreme Court Reports 207.

Chapter 9

The institutionalization of principles in restorative justice – a case study from the UK

Robert E. Mackay

Introduction

This chapter projects into relief the issues that arise when a policy community attempts to develop a set of principles for restorative justice. It draws upon the account of a review in 2002 of the UK Restorative Justice Consortium's (RJC) then current statement of 'Standards for Restorative Justice' (Restorative Justice Consortium 1999). This review led to the publication of a *Statement of Principles* (Restorative Justice Consortium 2002). The exercise reported here was presented at a workshop of the International Conference on Restorative Justice 'Effective Restorative Justice' in Leicester that year. Since that time the RJC has undertaken a further review of the Statement of Principles. This has radically emended the 2002 document, and has given rise to the 'Principles of Restorative Processes' (Restorative Justice Consortium 2004). In addition, there has been an exercise in Scotland to set up principles for restorative justice in the Children's Hearings system. This chapter concentrates on the 2002 exercise, but makes brief reference to the subsequent revision and to the Scottish development (Scottish Executive 2005).

The method adopted is rather unusual in contemporary academic papers, although it has some resonances with narrative theory (Gehm 1998). The sources of data are a set of exchanges, mostly by e-mail, between the contributors to the exercise, together with minutes of meetings. The writer was a protagonist in the process and therefore is not an unbiased observer. He had written the paper which was used as a basis for the consultation; he acted as an interlocutor with the other members of the group who produced comments on his original draft. He also held the role of chair of the organization conducting the exercise, although the process was led and organized by the organization's policy officer. In this paper he has attempted to draw out the most significant exchanges to illustrate the range of the debate. The effect is sometimes that of a dialogue in which the author is reported as a regular protagonist. This is deliberate, because it aims to expose the dynamic of the argument as well as the outcomes. The method was directly inspired by the Melian Dialogue in *The Peloponnesian War* (Thucydides 1977: 400–8). It also follows in some respects the method adopted by Wright of a fictional symposium of representative figures in the criminal justice–penal archipelago, with the distinction that this dialogue really happened (Wright 1999). The chapter provides an account of the process, followed by further reflections occasioned by the two subsequent developments already mentioned. The account reflects all the significant areas of debate that arose during the exercise. The writer has not reported points raised by participants in the first round of comments on the initial document (the *Outline* – see below) on which there was immediate agreement. Furthermore, in this account, the writer has refrained from all but the most minimal comment.

The paper has six sections after this introduction. Section one describes the background and the reasons for the exercise. Section two deals with the question of the need for a recognized code of ethics and principles for restorative justice practice. Section three contains an account of the review and revision of *Standards in Restorative Justice*. Section four provides some reflections on the exercise. Section five relates two sequels in the quest to develop restorative justice principles in the UK. Section six contains the conclusion.

This chapter provides an account of a particular facet of institutionalization. It captures the point at which restorative justice values are translated into public statements about the way in which restorative justice practitioners will provide services in a principled way. At this point the different value perspectives of those who are advocates of restorative justice are brought together in a debating arena. The outcome of this debate is of critical importance to its protagonists, because it will shape the way in which restorative justice is perceived by the wider community, and in particular by the agencies of the state.

The setting

The impetus for the 2002 review was the wish of the RJC to revise the well recognized *Standards for Restorative Justice* which were developed by an *ad hoc* group known as SINRJ (pronounced 'synergy' and standing for 'Standards in Restorative Justice') (SINRJ 1999). The RJC published the original *Standards*.

For some time it had been thought that the SINRJ document required to be revised. In 2000 Mackay published a number of criticisms of the document. He was concerned that it tended to avoid dealing comprehensively with the relationship between formal criminal justice agencies and 'Restorative Justice Agencies'. The emphasis on society's responsibility to effect the rehabilitation of offenders suggested an offender-orientated account of restorative justice (Mackay 2000).

Restorative justice had acquired much greater prominence in England and Wales with the advent of Referral Orders and the development of Family Group Conferencing. In that spirit, the RJC established a mechanism for reviewing the *Standards* in late autumn 2001. The mechanism we adopted was to use the paper by Robert Mackay which contained an outline for a *Statement of Principles* (referred to as the *Outline* in this paper) (Mackay 2000). The RJC set up a review group to examine how these could be adapted for a new *Statement of Principles*. It was intended that the *Principles* would provide the basis for a series of standards in particular loci of practice, namely adult criminal justice, juvenile criminal justice, schools, workplaces and neighbourhoods (community mediation).

The process of developing the *Principles* exposed a number of issues about the nature of restorative justice and the values that inform it. Indeed it has exposed some fault lines. The main aims of this paper are to illustrate these issues and fault lines and bring them to the arena of critical reflection.

The need for a recognized code of ethics and principles for restorative justice

The rapid growth of restorative justice practice, and what passes for restorative justice, has led to concern about whether what is being done in the name of restorative justice is consistent with its values. There is strong need for guidance at a time when the urge to experiment is strong. However, the provision of guidelines or standards or principles is not a simple matter. There are debates about what restorative justice is, as well as about its value base.

There are particular difficulties in establishing principles and codes of ethics across jurisdictions, and within jurisdictions where traditional forms of dispute resolution exist in parallel with state systems of justice. However, it is important to acknowledge that the European Union has endorsed restorative justice as an approach in its Council Framework Decision of 15 March 2001 (2001/220/JHA) on the standing of victims in criminal proceedings, and has set requirements for the promotion of mediation and the taking into account of agreements between victims and offenders in criminal cases. Legal and administrative measures must be in place in European Union member states by 22 March 2006. It is therefore imperative that those who wish to promote restorative justice practice are in a position to inform governments about how practice should be developed in their jurisdictions.

A further reason for developing statements of principle and standards is that they provide evaluative benchmarks. An important but often forgotten element of evaluation of practice is that of system integrity: has a scheme followed a defined set of principles in the development and implementation of practice?

The development of restorative justice alongside the criminal justice system also raises a number of critical legal and ethical issues. The criminal justice systems of the world, for all their faults, have developed in the ways they have in order to deal with particular problems and issues. It is not without good reasons that legal systems have developed rules and rights that are designed to protect accused persons, or that the judiciary has developed principles of proportionality in sentencing. When any attempt is made to change or reform, there is a danger in altering the balances of the existing system in such a way that it is damaged. It would be easy in the enthusiasm for encouraging victim–offender agreements to permit the ignoring of traditional legal safeguards. What prevents a family group conference degenerating into a kangaroo court, or victims dictating sentence when victim representation is permitted in criminal proceedings?

The development of principles to guide the development of restorative justice must in turn be guided by a clear set of legal and ethical theory justifications or accounts. These serve to influence those who hold power in the legal system (mainly lawyers, who may also be politicians). They also provide a clear basis for articulating a value base. In the current climate of law and international opinion, any theoretical justification of restorative justice that did not take into account and attempt to exemplify the discourse of fundamental human rights would be incongruent.

Finally, an important reason for developing principles and codes is to ensure that assumptions about the meaning and purpose of restorative justice are brought out into the open and acknowledged not only by those who support the concept, but also by those who have to work with it, like police officers and judges.

An account of the review and revision of *Standards in Restorative Justice*

This section draws upon the exchange of comments about the principles in the *Outline* between participants and Robert Mackay before the second meeting of the review group. This exchange is cited as 'Revision Text'. The representation of the debate may appear somewhat stilted. However, this method of presentation is justified because it is a true and verifiable record, and, because one of the authors is a key protagonist in the debates, for the sake of objectivity, he needs to specify his own contributions to the debate within the historical account.

The exercise was structured to take place over two working sessions involving the core group nominated by the RJC Forum and other invitees. The process was coordinated and chaired by Claire Phillips, the RJC's Policy Officer. Those who participated included individual members of the RJC, corporate members through their representatives and others associated with restorative justice. The participants represented practice, academic and policy sectors, and included a member engaged in victim support. In the event, three working sessions were required.

At the first session the review group decided that it would use Mackay's *Outline* (Mackay 2000; the *Outline* is also contained in the appendix), rather than go back to the original *Standards for Restorative Justice* (SINRJ 1999), or work from the draft UN *Basic Principles on the Use of Restorative Justice Programmes in Criminal Matters*. An important decision was taken at the outset that the terminology of the *Principles* should be couched in terms that are applicable to both civil and criminal jurisdictions because restorative justice theory and practice dealt with the civil aspects of a crime and they straddled both jurisdictions.

The exercise started with requests for responses to the structure and contents in the *Outline*. After these responses were received and collated by Claire Phillips, Robert Mackay made a number of detailed replies to the points made. Further responses and verbal comments were contributed at the second meeting. Claire Phillips provided a provisional draft with a more accessible textual framework and wordings, as well as some proposed substantive emendments based on the responses received. At the second meeting some elements of the

Principles were agreed, either in text or in principle. A number of areas remained outstanding for further debate.

The *Outline* was based upon the following premises:

1   We should use, wherever possible, terminology that could be applicable in both civil and criminal cases.
2   The principles operating in restorative practice should be compatible with the principles governing other forms of Alternative Dispute Resolution.
3   Restorative justice is bound up with the criminal justice system and is not a separate sphere (consistent with UN and EU regulation).
4   Restorative justice derives its justification as a model or theory from the core insight that much of the law derives its legitimation from social requirements to respond to harm done by members of the community to each other.
5   Those who cause harm to others, generally speaking and subject to social definition, are morally and sometimes legally bound to make reparation.
6   Restorative justice must work within the parameters of (4), and must not trade off the implications of this in favour of the principle of voluntariness.
7   Restorative practice sits alongside the criminal justice system, it is not a diversion.
8   Restorative justice can operate at all levels of the criminal justice system.
9   Where a case does not need to be prosecuted, it should not be.

It will be seen that some of these premises are themselves debatable within the restorative justice movement. In looking at the issues that arose in reviewing the *Outline*, it has been necessary to be selective. The main issues that caused debate were:

- the connection between restorative justice practice and the legal system;
- the relevance of rights as an underpinning concept to principles;
- the extent to which voluntariness should be an overarching principle;
- proportionality in restorative/reparative agreements;
- restorative justice as process or outcome;
- the extent to which remorse or effective conclusion of a restorative/ reparative agreement should affect the outcome of a criminal process;

- neutrality/impartiality;
- whether a document about principles is a regulatory document or a declaration of policy.

The connection between restorative justice practice and the legal system

The position of the *Outline* was that restorative justice derives its justification from the fact that a harm has been inflicted by one person on another, and that this gives rise to a moral and legal obligation. However, one participant suggested that the subordination of restorative justice to the legal system is only one model for restorative justice.

Mackay's reply to this was:

> There is a sense in which restorative justice will always be subject to the legal system, in the sense that Law will only permit what is lawful in any given country. Insofar as restorative justice practice intersects with the legal system, we face a choice: if we wish to see a restorative justice compliant legal system, that is, a system of justice that is wholly imbued with restorative justice principles, then we have to deal with the system as it is, with its positive values as well as the negative ones. Restorative justice is not, for instance, incompatible with due process. Rather, it will be discredited if it isn't. The alternative is for restorative justice to be a set of activities on the margin of the criminal justice system, that do not profoundly affect it. There is a place for courts where harm is significant, where there is a public policy issue at stake, or where the parties do not agree, crucially on guilt or facts of the case. (Revision Text: 4)

However, there is clearly a major difference of approach here. There is a strong view that restorative justice should not be subordinated to other policy objectives within criminal justice, such as diversion or punitive retribution. There is also widespread agreement that there is a danger of co-option by the criminal justice system. Some clearly go further, and wish to see restorative justice operating as a separate system, which is not organically accountable to prosecutors and courts. This view is associated with a sense that the conflict between the victim and the offender is for them primarily to resolve and that it is not for society through its courts to interfere. The restorative justice movement will need to do much more work on this issue if it is to present a coherent view to policy-makers. However, it is clear from the Council of the European Union Framework Decision 2001/220/JHA on the Standing of Victims in Criminal Proceedings and from the UN Basic Principles that international governmental organizations see the development of restorative justice in alignment with mainstream criminal justice systems and as part of the agenda for their reform.

The relevance of rights as an underpinning concept to principles

In the *Outline* reference to the responsibilies of offenders, which had been present in the *Standards*, was removed for the sake of symmetry. However, the removal of this reference to responsibility was balanced by principle 1.2(c). This stated that the right of those who have sustained loss to claim recompense should be vindicated.

The suggestion that victims of crime had rights to be vindicated raised some concerns. Mackay's response to this was that 'vindication' resonates with the emotional basis of the moral and legal claim of the victim. Victims have a right to feel angry, and their feelings must be given a place. The outcome of discussion was to downgrade the statement about a right to compensation in favour of 'a recognition of their claim for amends' (Revision Text: 4–5). However, there is a danger that the fundamental right of redress is not now being seen as a fundamental principle of restorative justice. If so, the logical foundation of the model may be compromised (*cf.* Johnstone 2002). It was also suggested that the removal of responsibilities looked strange in the face of the premise that rights implied responsibilities. However, it was suggested that human rights do not imply responsibilities on the part of the right holder and that the issue was dealt with under the principle relating to 'vindication'.

There is further pressure on the underpinning concept of rights with the suggestion that reference to 'rights-based practice' should be replaced by 'needs-based practice, subject to safeguarding of human rights', on the grounds that 'restorative justice is more concerned about human needs than about legal rights'. However, this lays bare a core concern that if restorative justice is not based in human rights then it will lose credibility and legitimacy. There is already a growing body of critical opinion suggesting that restorative justice does not uphold human rights. There is a heavy onus on restorative justice advocates to scotch this line of critique.

In the event, the consensus was to remove reference to 'rights' in the headings relating to the parties and to replace this with 'interests'. Although there is some merit in speaking of interests rather than rights (Waldron 1993), the weakening of the theoretical link to a human rights justification for restorative justice is a significant development. However, the review group agreed that restorative justice agencies should safeguard 'legal human rights' (Restorative Justice Consortium 2002).

The extent to which voluntariness should be an overarching principle

Two points arose under this head: participation and the imposition of agreements.

Participation

One participant questioned the extent to which participation was voluntary in the face of the imposition of referral orders in England and Wales. Another suggested that 'voluntary participation' needed to be defined more closely because of the variance in its meaning (*Outline* 1.1(a)). There was agreement about the need for closer definition, but there was debate about how far voluntariness went. Nobody agreed with coercion to participate. However, Mackay replied to the debate in the following terms:

> Forcing people to participate is counter-productive. On the other hand, offering an accused person an opportunity that may result in a lesser sanction if reparation is made is to present a free choice. (There is, I hold, no scenario of unfettered choice in conflict resolution. Even in commercial mediation in the free market, people choose mediation because of the fear that the alternative may be worse.) (Revision Text: 9)

Imposition of agreements

The principle 'Where a restorative requirement is possible and proportionate, it should be imposed regardless of the wishes of the parties in criminal cases. Where a victim refuses to participate, a surrogate should be found' (*Outline* 4(d)) caused considerable controversy. It was suggested that this sounded 'quite dire', contrary to the spirit of restorative justice, at odds with voluntary participation and informed consent, and a 'theft of the conflict'. In response Mackay suggested:

> I am speaking here of cases in which the authorities have already taken a decision about deferment of decision (prosecutor or court). The offender has an obligation, moral, and often legal, to make reparation. If the parties have consented to participate in a restorative process and have come to an agreement, it is only reasonable that the authorities make fulfilling this a formal requirement in consideration of their willingness to take a decision that is favourable to the accused. If an offender makes an offer of reparation, and the victim refuses, but the authorities think this is a fair offer and a reasonable way to deal with the case, then

it is entirely reasonable for them to require the offender to make reparation at a proportionate level to a surrogate. The victim forfeits her right. The accused is not placed at the mercy of the victim. [...] Finally, if an offender is capable of making reparation but declines to do so, he should be required to. Compensation Orders are far too meagre in scope. This idea in fact serves to the victim's benefit, in that he is not thereby required to pursue the offender in the civil courts. This is one of the implications of the suggested tendency to blur the civil–criminal distinction.

If restorative justice is to be taken seriously by courts and prosecutors and by the public we will need to recognise some of their concerns. Whilst it is quite right that nobody should be forced to participate in a restorative justice process, because the authorities have other sanctions, once an agreement is made it has the effective force of law (contract, order of the court, etc.). The analogy is with a probation order, which must be made with the consent of the accused. This is consistent with the UN document. (Revision Text: 20)

It is clear that this issue is a major area of debate for the implementation of restorative justice. In the final document the following principles were agreed:

- Where a restorative requirement is appropriate, but victims decline to participate, there should be opportunities for community reparation, or reparation to others who have suffered harm or loss.
- Where a restorative requirement is appropriate, but those who have caused harm or loss decline to participate, community reparation should be enforced.

> (Restorative Justice Consortium 2002: Principles 6c and 6d)

Proportionality in restorative/reparative agreements

This issue was broached in the *Outline* at 1.3(c): 'Reparative requirements, where imposed, should be proportionate, primarily to the capacity of the perpetrator to fulfil, and secondarily to the harm done. It also appeared in the *Outline* 4(d): 'Where a restorative requirement is possible and proportionate, it should be imposed regardless of the wishes of the parties in criminal cases. Where a victim refuses to participate, a surrogate should be found.'

References to proportionality drew a number of responses. One was that one 'should not bend over backwards to create a framework with goals (e.g. proportionality) that are from the "Just Deserts" punishment ethos' (Revision Text: 4). Many were happy that proportionality was referred to.

However, it should be noted that one participant suggested that a principle of proportionality

> ... could lead back towards something like a tariff, and away from the victim's and offender's agreement. I suggest that we should affirm their primacy – something like: 'Where the victim and offender are willing and able to reach an agreement about reparative requirements, these should be primarily a matter for them, subject only to the safeguard that they should not be disproportionate to the capacity of the offender to fulfil them, nor to the harm done.' (Revision Text: 13)

Others thought that '[...] reparative requirements should be primarily proportionate to the harm, not the offender (opposite as stated)' (Revision Text: 13). Some felt simply that, given its present wording, the statement seemed to cater to the offender in a way that might be offensive to victims, i.e. too heavily weighted on the capacity of the offender. Another simply objected to the stratification of words and thought there was no need for the use of primary and secondary proportionality (of proportionality to harm done or to the means or culpability of the perpetrator) (Revision Text: 13).

It was agreed by many that prioritization could be dispensed with. It was pointed out that proportionality, while appealed to by the 'just deserts' lobby, was also appealed to by those who criticized the open-ended and disproportionate sentencing (unlimited detention) that the rehabilitative model permitted (see Bottomley 1980). Finally, it was questioned whether it was sensible to permit an agreement that would beggar the perpetrator.

There is an important question as to whether restorative justice marches to a different drum to that of the rest of the legal system. It seems that some proponents of restorative justice believe that it does, which is a very strong claim. It is very different from the claims of those who have supported mediation and other forms of 'informal' justice, who have generally believed in the importance of working within a framework of legal values. Mackay responded that there was concern that some agreements could be disproportionate and simply could not be left to the parties to settle alone:

> If a criminal justice agency conditionally refers a case to mediation/

conferencing, it is going to retain an interest in the outcome. It is possible that an agreement is too onerous for the offender, or that it is derisory, either because the offender or the victim is intimidated. The victim and the offender may be in collusion of some type. In community settings a mediator may not know the true dynamics of a relationship. It therefore makes sense for the referrer (court or prosecutor) to have an eye to whether the agreement fulfils his-her expectation about meeting the ends of justice. They must retain confidence in the restorative justice model if it is to thrive. (Revision Text: 13)

In the event it was agreed that references to 'proportionality' would be substituted by 'appropriateness'. However, it was clear from the discussion that this was a compromise that was not comfortable for the majority of the participants on either side of the argument. In the final document the term 'appropriateness' was strengthened by reference to the capacity of the person making amends (Restorative Justice Consortium 2002: Principle 3b).

Restorative justice as process or outcome

Within the restorative justice movement there is considerable variety of opinion about the extent to whether process or outcome is given priority. In this review that expressed itself as a tension. There was a call to distinguish reparative outcomes from restorative processes. There was clear disagreement about whether an outcome could be seen as 'restorative' or reparative if the process had not been according to restorative procedures. However, that is to suggest (1) that formal procedures such as those of the courts cannot ever be restorative, and (2) that such outcomes are invalid from a restorative justice perspective. In some ways this tension reflects the tension about voluntariness explored earlier. In another sense it reflects a continuing strand in restorative justice thinking to prioritize the value of 'healing' in the process of mediation and conferencing. There is, however, considerable room for testing whether parties in dispute are more concerned about process or outcomes.

The extent to which remorse or effective conclusion of a restorative/reparative agreement should affect the outcome of a criminal process

This issue is closely connected with the previous one. There was not a great amount of debate or discussion, but two significant points were raised. One concerned whether and the extent to which one could verify that the perpetrator is remorseful. The other was, more generally, the question of whether remorse should play a part in the consideration of sentence.

Albrecht has posed the question in the following way:

> When inserting restitution in the line of criminal sanctions, it could be argued that the severity of the sanction should be reduced when the offender has 'surrendered' by offering compensation, and in doing so has accepted the social norm that he or she has transgressed, and has consented to the consequences of criminal liability. (Albrecht 2001: 300)

The European Union Framework Decision is clear that member states must make legal and administrative arrangements to enable agreements between victims and offenders to be taken into account in criminal proceedings (Article 10). In the final document it was agreed that Reparation should be appropriate to the harm done and within the capacity of the person causing the harm to undertake it (Restorative Justice Consortium 2002: Principle 3b).

Neutrality and impartiality

The inclusion of these terms led to considerable discussion. There was concern about whether these terms had been sufficiently distinguished, and also whether a mediator could be impartial in the face of an offence having been committed. It was suggested that the *Outline* 5e principle, 'Facilitating the participation of a weaker party in negotiation', dealt with the issue sufficiently. Another participant raised a more general point:

> Do we have anything to say to current YOT staff who mediate between their clients and victims? [Youth Offending Teams are interdisciplinary teams that deliver youth justice interventions in England and Wales. *Author*] The issue of impartiality is a thorny one – in most mediation situations in the Western world, impartiality and independence is highly prized. However, in many other countries, trustworthy local authorities (who may not be impartial) are more accepted: insider partials rather than outside impartials. May this be true in the world of some offenders and victims? (Revision Text: 8)

Mackay's response to these points was:

A neutral is somebody chosen to act in an umpiring role because they do not have a prior aligned relationship with one party rather than another. Thus there is an expectation that there is no prior partiality or bias. Neutrality is a status, how one is perceived. Impartiality means not taking sides on the basis of irrelevant criteria having acquired the role of mediator (like accepting the offer of a kick-back on a reparation settlement from one side, having exerted undue pressure on the other party). Thus certain people who might be very impartial could be excluded from acting as mediators because they were not perceived to be neutral.

It is questioned whether a mediator can be impartial in the face of an offence having been committed. However, following the requirement that mediators should uphold public morality (e.g. law-abiding behaviour) they could not be expected to condone crime. Therefore they are, to some extent, aligned with the claim of the victim (which the accused has accepted up to a point, by accepting guilt, or else there's no mediation). However, the mediator is impartial in this crucial way, that she shows equality of regard and respect towards each of the parties. Supporting the weaker party is not showing bias, rather the opposite. Not to support participation would be to favour the stronger party. Insofar as the purpose of mediation is participation, the mediator is only carrying out her contracted job by facilitating mediation [...].

On [X's] earlier general point [relating to trustworthy local officials in non-western settings], I think my definitions of neutrality and impartiality may help. The development of democratic processes has a certain universality about it. It certainly entails neutrality and impartiality of public officers and officials. Otherwise, corruption can and does thrive. The term 'trustworthy local officials' is too undefined for this debate. Does this mean a local official, a local politician, a local traditional chief, or even a paid member of a government-funded NGO? Some such may be known to both parties in dispute, and thus possibly neutral, and they may be impartial. Only the circumstances of individual cases will determine this. It is much safer to urge the place for an independent role. Perhaps that is a further principle. (Revision Text: 22)

The last point raises the issue of the standing of agencies which act as facilitators/mediators. Mackay proposed rephrasing *Outline* 5d in the following terms:

When an agency has both a regulatory or supportive role in respect of a party, and a role as mediator between the parties, it should ensure that its staff are not involved in both roles, and that there is no communication between staff in different roles of any matter that is confidential to their work in that role. (Revision Text: 22)

He added:

However, in the light of what I've written about neutrality, should agencies such as the Police or Probation or YOTs act at all in a mediatory capacity bearing in mind that they have roles that must be kept separate from mediation? If an individual cannot undertake such duality of role, because it offends against the principle of neutrality (see above), can agencies, which are, legally, corporate individuals? Perhaps there is a case for a principle of independence. (Revision Text: 22)

Johnstone goes further in critique of the position of agencies with different roles:

Where police officers or other criminal justice agents act as facilitators of restorative conferences, as they frequently do in restorative cautioning schemes, the idea that a facilitator is a neutral third party is clearly stretched to the limits of credibility. (Johnstone 2002: 159n)

In the event, the review group has kept references to both neutrality and impartiality. It has also agreed that 'Maintaining neutrality and impartiality, restorative justice practitioners should play no other role in the case' (Restorative Justice Consortium 2002: Principle 7e). It also agreed to two principles:

- Upholding respectful behaviour in restorative processes.
- Upholding equality of respect for all participants in restorative processes, separating this from the harm done.

(*Ibid.*: Principles 7i and 7j)

Is a document on principles a regulatory document or a declaration of policy?

It was suggested by some participants that:

[...] we believe measures should be introduced which are specifically designed to change popular attitudes. While clearly defined principles based on rigorous intellectual analysis as exemplified in the paper under review are important and necessary they will not, we suggest, of themselves lead to changes in popular cultural values. Our commitment to restorative justice, for example, grew out of our experience before we were aware of the term 'restorative justice' rather than as a result of rational analysis. On the basis of this experience and our involvement in a number of initiatives to promote restorative justice in our area we believe exposure to personal experience of restorative justice is essential for success in obtaining widespread community support. As most citizens perceive themselves as potential victims rather than offenders it is also essential to make it clear restorative justice is oriented to the victim no less than the offender. (Revision Text: 3)

Mackay responded:

[...] Practice needs principles that are derived from experience and reflection. Restorative justice, if it is to make inroads as a theory of justice which is accepted by those who broker ideas in policy debates, needs to be theoretically sound as well as practically applicable. The principles presented here for discussion are founded on personal practice experience, reflection on standards and on theoretical studies.

The purpose of a set of principles is not to provide a popular public relations document, but a basis of a code for practitioners. [...] The RJC has as part of its remit public education about the value of restorative justice, which we are pursuing in other appropriate ways. (Revision Text: 3)

This exchange of views represents a tension between those who see themselves as 'grass-roots' practitioners and those who are perceived as part of a 'professional elite'. It is not clear how this type of tension can be managed in an exercise of this nature.

It is perhaps relevant to notice that the 'Declaration of Leuven', in addressing the criminal justice policy community on the need for restorative justice, enunciated the need for principles for practice (INRRJJ 1997).

Reflections on the exercise

Since this records a process, it is worthwhile reflecting on the dynamics of an exercise of this nature. It is clear that the outcomes of this review depended on who was able to attend particular meetings. However, it is also the case that the group made every effort to accommodate the views of those who were unable to be present.

The exercise shows very clearly that there are major issues within the restorative justice movement which are unresolved. However, it is not unhealthy that this should be so. Long ago Nils Christie wrote that we should value our conflicts, that we do not have enough of them (Christie 1977). However, we must also be cautious about being too relaxed about continuing lack of agreement for three reasons.

First, practitioners need guidance. We cannot simply assume that what people say of restorative justice is automatically acceptable. Failure to provide clear guidance will in the long run affect our credibility in the eyes of the public.

Second, and related to the first point, there is a strong danger that restorative justice is subsumed under policy agendas which are not compatible with mainstream views about restorative justice values. There is much common ground within the movement about the goods of restorative justice, but there is also the danger of the Scylla of engulfment by the formal criminal justice–penal system, and the Charybdis of utopianism that fails to recognize the importance of a clear relationship between restorative practices and outcomes and the legal system. Failure to be clear about how restorative justice contributes to the policy agendas will lead to its marginalization at a political level.

Third, it is clear that although there is a common understanding of the emotive appeal of restorative justice, we are less clear within the restorative justice movement about the need for theoretically justified legitimations. Failure to provide these, and to accept the need for such an underpinning, will in the end undermine the credibility of restorative justice in the eyes of policy-makers and brokers, especially the judiciary.

Sequel

Since 2002, the RJC has revised the Principles once again (Restorative Justice Consortium 2004). This was in response to a suggestion by the Home Office which had set up a consultation on the use of restorative justice. The resulting emendments swept aside substantive reference to human rights, dealt with principles as process issues rather than substantive injunctions, and stripped out reference to the place of restorative justice within the legal system. Thus reference to human rights was relegated to a footnote relating to upholding the law. This move demonstrates a worrying level of political ingenuousness among restorative justice advocates in a country whose current government's adherence to the rule of law in both domestic and international matters is so highly contested among it citizens.

In another development, the Scottish Children's Reporter Administration (the office of a type of civil public procurator combined with tribunal clerk which services the Scottish Children's Hearings System) together with the Scottish Executive (devolved government) and SACRO (a Scottish voluntary organization that provides the bulk of restorative justice services in Scotland) have developed protocols for the use of restorative justice in the Scottish Children's Hearings System (Scottish Executive 2005). Unlike the exercises conducted by the RJC, this has been a closed process. What has emerged is that the resultant documentation has looked at restorative justice primarily from the point of system performance in respect of dealing with young offenders. There is little account of the position of victims. Although it is based on the UN Basic Principles, it departs from them at some points involving legal or practice principles. Thus the principle *non bis in idem* (i.e. avoidance of double jeopardy) is dropped, and there is no reference to the demands upon the performance of facilitators. The principle relating to standards of competence and ethical rules are substituted by reference to best practice.

Conclusion

From all this we see how many issues hung in the balance when the exercise in 2002 was carried out. While it was then just possible to hold out for a human rights focus, that has been largely lost. However, while proportionality was lost in 2002, and was not recovered in the subsequent RJC 2004 statement, it was included in the Scottish draft.

From the experience of involvement in this work, one would reiterate the view of Aertsen *et al.* (2004: 35) that in order to 'have an ethical framework for a system of justice, we must engage in a cycle of practical reasoning that [*inter alia*] identifies the ethical objective'. Thus, it is necessary to have an ethical theory of law that provides for a restorative theory of justice. Such a theory of restorative justice in turn provides an architecture for institutions and practices, including principles of practice. However, it may be suggested that in this review there were two dominant frames of reference within the 'practical reasoning' of the debate, represented as a legal–ethical approach and a social–political approach. The first was primarily concerned with the place of restorative justice as an expression of law, and the second was primarily concerned with the goods that restorative justice interventions provide within a socio-political programme of tackling offending, particularly by young people. These frames of reference can be reconciled, but only with rigorous theoretical application within the process of developing principles. What was apparent is that, generally, the debate was insufficiently rigorous, leading to a certain loss of focus on how relevant theoretical concerns bear upon principles of restorative justice, with the result that these different frames of reference were not integrated.

I also propose the following double hypothesis as a conclusion: to the extent that restorative justice becomes institutionalized within a socio-political agenda rather than a legal–ethical conceptual framework, the development of statements of principle and codes of practice will serve co-option of restorative justice by the state; their orientation will be a-theoretical; and their rhetoric will be dominated by an incontestable pragmatism. However, to the extent that a legal–ethical framework does not address the socio-political agenda, principles will be abstract and unrelated to the business of responding to harms perpetrated by citizens upon each other.

Documentary source

Revision Text: *Rob's [Robert Mackay] responses to first round of comments on draft principles.* Internal document of the RJC, 2002.

Appendix

The *Outline* took the following form (Mackay 2000):

1. Principles relating to interests of parties (needs and rights):
    1.1. Those relating to all parties:
        (a) Voluntary participation and informed consent
        (b) Non-discrimination, irrespective of the nature of the case
        (c) Accessibility to relevant helping agencies (including restorative practice agencies)

      (d) Protection of vulnerable parties in process

      (e) Maintaining accessibility to conventional methods of dispute/case resolution (including the courts)

      (f) Privilege should apply to information disclosed before trial (subject to public interest qualification)

      (g) Civil rights and dignity of individuals should be respected

      (h) Personal safety to be protected.

1.2. Those relating to parties who have sustained loss:

      (a) Their needs and feelings to be taken seriously

      (b) Their losses to be acknowledged

      (c) Their right to claim recompense to be vindicated.

1.3. Those relating to those liable for loss imposed on others (including those facing criminal sanctions):

      (a) Right to offer reparation before it is formally required

      (b) Right to due process in trial (including presumption of innocence in any subsequent legal proceedings)

      (c) Reparative requirements, where imposed, should be proportionate, primarily to the capacity of the perpetrator to fulfil, and secondarily to the harm done

      (d) Reparative requirements should be consistent with respect for the dignity of the person making amends.

2. Principles relating to the interests of local community and society:

      (a) Community safety should be promoted by measures to bring about crime prevention, harm reduction and social harmony

      (b) Social solidarity should be promoted by respect for cultural diversity

      (c) Social solidarity should be promoted by attitudes which promote public morality and respect for the law.

3. Principles relating to agencies working alongside the judicial system:

      (a) Consideration should be given to settlement of the case without prosecution except when the level of harm done, the risk of further harm, issues of public policy, disagreement about the facts or the appropriate outcome, requires open court action

      (b) The exercise of discretion either individually or systematically should not compromise rights under the law or lead to discrimination

      (c) Restorative justice measures should not be subordinated to other criminal justice objectives such as diversion or rehabilitation.

4. Principles relating to the judicial system:
    (a) Reintegration of the parties should be the primary aim of court proceedings
    (b) Repairing the harm should be key objective in disposal of the case
    (c) Restorative requirements should be proportionate to the case (see above)
    (d) Where a restorative requirement is possible and proportionate, it should be imposed regardless of the wishes of the parties in criminal cases. Where a victim refuses to participate, a surrogate should be found
    (e) Genuine willingness on the part of the perpetrator to repair harm should be taken into account in disposal
    (f) The content of mediation/conferences to be considered privileged, subject to public interest qualifications.
5. Principles relating to restorative justice practice agencies:
    (a) Commitment to rights-based practice, including a requirement that parties are advised of rights, and are encouraged to seek advice before commitment to mediated agreements
    (b) Impartiality of mediators
    (c) Neutrality of mediators
    (d) Confidentiality as between parties and with regard to other agencies, including 'Chinese walls' with another part of the same agency having a distinct function in respect of the case (this is to ensure that restorative practices are not undermined by drives towards system integration)
    (e) Facilitating the participation of a weaker party in negotiation
    (f) Upholding public moral standards of behaviour in the mediation/conferencing process and in proposed settlements
    (g) Mediators to have no other role in respect of the case
    (h) Adherence to best practice guidelines within the restorative justice movement
    (i) Commitment to initial and continuing accrediting training
    (j) Commitment to an ethos of constructive conflict resolution within the workplace (this is to ensure internal integrity)
    (k) Commitment to improving practice through monitoring, audit and participation in research
    (l) Commitment to improving practice through reflection upon practice and personal growth on the part of mediators.

References

Aertsen, I., Mackay, R., Pelikan, C., Willemsens, J., and Wright, M. (2004) *Rebuilding Community Connections – Mediation and Restorative Justice in Europe.* Strasburg: Council of Europe Publishing.

Albrecht, H.J. (2001) 'Restorative justice – answers to questions that nobody has put forward', in E. Fattah and S. Parmentier (eds), *Victim Policies and Criminal Justice on the Road to Restorative Justice – Essays in Honour of Tony Peters.* Leuven: Leuven University Press, pp. 295–314.

Bottomley, A.K. (1980) 'The "Justice model" in America and Britain', in A.E. Bottoms and R.H. Preston (eds), *The Coming Penal Crisis.* Edinburgh: Scottish Academic Press, pp. 25–52.

Christie, N. (1977) 'Conflicts as property', *British Journal of Criminology*, 17, 1: 1–15.

Gehm, J. (1998) 'Victim–offender mediation programs: an exploration of practice and theoretical frameworks', *Western Criminological Review*, at: www.wcr. sonoma.edu/v1n1/gehm.html

International Network for Research on Restorative Justice for Juveniles (INRRJJ) (1997) 'Declaration of Leuven on the Advisability of Promoting the Restorative Approach to Juvenile Crime, made on the occasion of the first International Conference on "Restorative Justice for Juveniles. Potentialities, Risks and Problems for Research", Leuven, May 12–14, 1997', *European Journal on Criminal Policy and Research*, 5, 4: 118–22.

Johnstone, G. (2002) *Restorative Justice – Ideas, Values, Debates.* Cullompton: Willan.

Mackay, R.E. (2000) 'Ethics and good practice in restorative justice', in European Forum for Victim–offender Mediation and Restorative Justice (ed.), *Victim–offender Mediation in Europe – Making Restorative Justice Work.* Leuven: Leuven University Press, pp. 49–68.

Restorative Justice Consortium (2002) *Principles of Restorative Justice.* London: Restorative Justice Consortium.

Restorative Justice Consortium (2004) *Principles of Restorative Processes.* London: Restorative Justice Consortium.

Scottish Executive (2005) *Restorative Justice in the Children's Hearing System.* Edinburgh: Scottish Executive.

SINRJ (Standards in Restorative Justice) (1999) *Standards in Restorative Justice.* London: Restorative Justice Consortium.

Thucydides (1977) *The Peloponnesian War.* London: Penguin.

Waldron, J. (1993) *Liberal Rights.* Cambridge: Cambridge University Press.

Wright, M. (1999) *Restoring Respect for Justice – A Symposium.* Winchester: Waterside Press.

Chapter 10

Risk and restorative justice: governing through the democratic minimization of harms

Pat O'Malley

Introduction: risk, uncertainty and justice

This chapter is concerned with two principal issues. How do the concepts of risk and governance, and the new configurations of knowledge and practice centred on them, relate to the ongoing institutionalization of restorative justice? And closely linked with this, how should we look at the possible new configurations of restoration, justice and risk which might surface? In addressing these questions, I wish to make two fairly abstract points about risk that are critical to considering its relationship with restorative justice. First, while we use the term 'risk' to refer to a wide array of ways of estimating the future, it is useful – perhaps important – for us to differentiate within everyday usage between risk and uncertainty. Along with others in the field (e.g. Beck 1992; Ericson and Haggerty 1997; Ewald 1991; Reddy 1996) I regard 'risk' as referring to probabilistic and usually statistical predictions. Usually, but not always, these predictions relate to possible harms that are to be avoided or mitigated. 'Uncertainty', on the other hand, refers to ways of estimating the future through various non-statistical techniques, primarily experience based. These would include a wide range of practices from professional judgment through rules of thumb to plain hunches. Those familiar with the literature on the 'risk society' promoted by Ulrich Beck (1992) and Anthony Giddens (1994) will be familiar with this distinction, although as will later be seen I do not share Beck's implied view that uncertainty is an inferior governmental technology (*cf.* Wynne 1996). My second point is that if risk is the probabilistic assessment of future harms, it is a very abstract technology and thus is capable of multiple and very divergent realizations in institutional or governmental forms. Even within such a narrow field as insurance, François Ewald (1991) has made clear that the way in which risk is deployed varies enormously, for the technique of statistical prediction and risk pooling is only one element of quite complex and distinct formations such as life insurance, marine insurance and social insurances. One of my central arguments, developed from these points, is that it is very difficult to assign any single political or moral evaluation to risk as such, and that we must always be quite specific about the particular configuration of risk to which we are referring when thinking about – and evaluating – possible convergences of risk and restorative justice.

This is an important point to make, for it is clear that risk has had a rather poor reception in social theory and critical criminology. For Ulrich Beck (1997) himself, of course, risk is a profoundly negative technology, for it 'tells us only what not to do, not what we should do'.[1] It freezes us into immobility and fear for it reveals only hazards and forecasts previously unanticipated harms. While ostensibly about security, it thereby generates insecurity. Many criminologists have followed down this rather pessimistic path, regarding risk as a negative technology in criminal justice, one that has displaced the integrative optimism of welfare sanctions and penal modernism aimed at reforming and reintegrating offenders with mass incapacitation and exclusion in the name of risk-reduction (Feeley and Simon 1994; Garland 2001; Rose 2000). We might therefore conclude that risk and restorative justice are diametrically opposed along many axes in the criminal justice arena. I will explore this argument in the first part of the paper.

Uncertainty, on the other hand, has been more variably received. Beck clearly regards it as an inferior technology to which we must resort in this new era of the risk society because risk can no longer reliably predict such catastrophic harms as global warming, terrorist attacks and nuclear disasters. These occur too infrequently to allow statistical prediction or are delivered to us through processes that only reveal themselves at the eleventh hour. In a sense, we *descend* into uncertainty. Yet other commentators have *embraced* uncertainty, for it is regarded as the technology of enterprise and invention. Risk can only 'work' for us if the past repeats itself, for its predictive power is founded on the assumption that what happened in the past will reoccur in much the same way and with much the same frequency in the future. It is in this sense conservative. Uncertainty on the other hand is associated with ways of forecasting that allow foresight to be combined with imagination to fabricate a *novel* future. In the words of Peter L. Bernstein (1998), in contrast to risk 'uncertainty makes us free'. In this statement he is representing not just an isolated vision but – clearly enough – one embraced by neoliberal governments everywhere, for these closely reflect the principles of free enterprise and the market economy. To borrow Tom Peters' (1987) phrase, rather than descending into uncertainty proponents of this vision 'thrive on chaos'. For such writers the mathematical predictions of experts, the implied technocratic domination and the calculative governmental plans that are based on these, are anathema.

In this light too, we might conclude that restorative justice will be incompatible with risk. With its deeply ambivalent orientation to expertise, its optimistic vision of the future, and the key role it gives to the participation of 'lay' publics, restorative justice appears aligned with government through uncertainty. Indeed, this is, by and large, consistent with the way in which the relationships between risk, uncertainty and restorative justice have been interpreted. For example, Chris Cunneen (2003: 183–6) argues that we should take care in developing restorative justice to the extent that it will take its place in a criminal justice system that is shaped by logics of risk. Like other writers (e.g. Rose 2000) Cunneen sees criminal justice becoming bifurcated along an axis of risk. Cunneen argues that high risk ofenders are identified and dealt with by actuarial (statistically predictive) judicial techniques such as 'three strikes and you're out' sentencing. In both the United States and Australia, such schemes consign large numbers of people – usually from visible minority groups – to lengthy prison sentences. This effectively excludes them from society on the basis of their previous convictions rather than the seriousness or circumstances of their last offence. Such 'actuarial justice', to be explored in detail shortly, thus works on principles diametrically opposed to restorative justice. Yet Cunneen warns that restorative justice has the capacity to form a key part of the total system of risk-based justice. On the one hand, restorative justice is likely to be infected or co-opted, for example through its emphasis on the potentially exclusionary notion of 'community'. In this environment Cunneen (2003: 185) argues, 'restorative justice can become what it opposes: a practice which closes, limits and excludes individuals rather than reintegrating them'. On the other hand, it focuses its own efforts on those deemed to be low risk rather than those perhaps in greatest need. Its concern is primarily with low risk offenders who accept their guilt, who have intact social networks into which they can be reintegrated, whose offending is not part of a long-term pattern of recalcitrance and recidivism.

As a description of the ways in which actuarial justice works, and of the potential place of restorative justice in this iniquitous arrangement, Cunneen's argument is not one with which I would take issue. The problem, rather, is the strong tendency to move from speaking specifically of actuarial justice to speaking of 'a risk-based criminal justice system'. In light of my earlier remarks, the two cannot be conflated. Risk may take many forms and actuarial justice is only one of these. As I will now argue, actuarial justice must be understood not as expressing or embodying the properties of risk *per se*, but rather as expressing the ways in which risk is deployed within a specific political environment.

Actuarial justice, neoliberalism and exclusion

That actuarial justice is an exclusionary technology is certainly very clear in the account of 'actuarial justice' provided by Feeley and Simon (1992, 1994), which has become definitive in the criminological literature. As is well known, in this outline, actuarial justice consists of four elements:

- the use of statistical probabilities to identify high-risk offenders;
- the connection of these probabilities to tables of sentencing so that risk (rather than the seriousness of the current offence) is the basis for calculating the severity of sentence;
- a sentence whose content is neither retributive nor rehabilitative, but is incapacitating – a sentence aimed only at risk reduction;
- a managerial emphasis on throughputs and numbers rather than 'outcomes', for when aggregated these figures indicate the total sum of risk reduction achieved.

Feeley and Simon regard this as a 'pre-political' system. That is, despite the view of many criminologists, they argue that it is not specifically a creation of politically conservative regimes. Partly this is because most conservative thinking would be more consistent with retributive justice rather than mere risk reduction. Moreover, they stress that actuarial justice programmes have often been put in place by liberal (i.e. Democrat) as well as conservative (Republican) governments. It is thus said to be pre-political because it does not reflect the 'pendulum swings' of right–left politics. However, their own analysis suggests that matters are more complicated, and that politics of a certain sort are central to understanding actuarial justice.

First, they perceptively argue that the advocates of incapacitation do not imagine offenders as rational choice subjects, the kinds of subject assumed by regimes of punishment and deterrence. A deterrent sentence assumes that offenders will perform the felicity calculus, and will judge the risk of harsh punishment greater than the rewards offered by crime. Rather, actuarial justice is said to envisage its offenders as 'inert': it is not interested in their mental calculations, only in their existence as risks. The role of incapacitation is simply to make it impossible for the risks to be realized. Feeley and Simon go on to suggest that this focus on incapacitation reflects a view that neither reform nor deterrence is appropriate to high-risk offenders. Why is this? Specifically they argue that the target population is regarded as having fallen below the threshold at which these technologies can operate. In practice, they suggest, this population is the 'underclass' – the largely Black and Hispanic people who have been rendered surplus to requirements by the impact of globalization. The heavy industrial 'dirty work' which was traditionally the role assigned to these people has been exported to the Third World, more specifically south and south-eastern Asia. For offenders drawn from this population sector, the hopes of reformation are discounted, for there is no place in the economy to which they can be rehabilitated. The reformist model of penal modernity, aimed at disciplining inmates to meet the labour demands of the economy and the routines of industrial time, thus has been rendered obsolescent by global changes. At the same time, this social transformation means that these people have nothing to lose: they have 'fallen below the threshold of deterrence'. They are thus abandoned and categorically excluded.

This is a brilliant and incisive argument. But surely what we can see here is that this form of criminal justice is precisely a political rather than merely economic creation and that thus actuarial justice is hardly 'pre-political'. Globalization, I would argue, is not merely an economic process, but something that is driven by a politics and formed in a political imaginary. It is advocated and enforced by organizations such as the United States treasury, the IMF and the World Bank. It is the creation of a neoliberal view that tariff barriers are 'artificial'; that the trades unions' defence of workers' jobs cannot be sustained and ultimately will be counterproductive; that 'careers for life' are a thing of the past; that these developments reflect an 'inescapable' globalizing process that must prevail regardless of our preferences; and so on. It is a form of politics that has abandoned and rejected a previously taken-for-granted strategy of government through 'the social' (Rose 1996). In this sense, the 'social' was the organic collectivity corresponding to the nation state. It was an imagined unity that gave to all citizens certain welfare securities – 'social securities'. It created a form of solidarity through risk-governing technologies such as social insurance, technologies that recognized that all members of the 'society' had a claim on it – and in this sense 'it' meant the state. This is a political vision shattered by the neoliberal politics of the late twentieth century in which security is no longer to be social. It is to be delivered by the market, by individuals, families, communities and other 'voluntary associations' such as the 'private sector'. The welfare state becomes anathema, imagined to be the creator of 'dependence' rather than 'solidarity'. The inclusive, organic whole that was 'the social' is abandoned and rejected.

We are now in a position to see more clearly that that 'underclass' is not simply the creation of an apolitical process of globalization so much as the effect of a neoliberal politics. It is a politics that can envision sectors of the population as 'dependent' and thus culpable rather than as 'victims' of global economics. In short, a welfare–social politics might well have regarded the 'underclass' as fellow members of society to whom we all owed some obligation rather than as something 'other', as risks to be excluded. In this sense, the issue that makes something 'political' is not the 'pendulum swings' between Democrat and Republican politics, but the political sea-change from a welfare to a neoliberal rationality of government. In this sense too, actuarial justice cannot be regarded as 'pre-political'. Rather it appears as a specific political configuration of technologies of risk: a shaping of risk that conforms with the assumptions and problematics of neoliberalism (a neoliberalism that both Democrats and Republicans as well as Conservatives and New Labour basically accept).

Restorative justice as 'inclusive' post-social justice

It takes comparatively little effort to see that restorative justice could be regarded as the inclusive side of a bifurcated neoliberal politics of crime control, for it reflects much that is valued in neoliberalism. To begin with, restorative justice focuses responsibility on the individual subjects of crime: the victims and offenders. It seeks to restore to the victims – as the consumers of justice – their personal losses. Its advocates reject the view that the state should govern these relationships, seeking instead to 'empower' the parties by handing over to them 'ownership' of the crime (Christie 1977). It privileges government by 'communities' that seek solutions to problems which *they* define as significant rather than are defined as such by professional experts. And it marginalizes expertise and expert solutions. Each of these characteristics echo parallel emphases in neoliberal governance more generally, as may be seen if we compare such features of restorative justice to Osborne and Gaebler's (1993: 66–73) outline of the virtues of community-based governance. In their bible of neoliberalism, *Reinventing Government*, they claim:

- Communities have more commitment to their members than service delivery systems have to their clients.

- Communities understand their problems better than service professionals.

- Professionals and bureaucracies deliver services; communities solve problems.

- Institutions and professionals offer 'service'; communities offer 'care'.

- Communities are more flexible and creative than large service bureaucracies.

- Communities are cheaper than service professionals.

- Communities enforce standards of behaviour more effectively than bureaucracies or service professionals.

- Communities focus on capacities; service systems focus on deficiencies (the latter having the effect of making families feel 'incompetent' rather than capable).

Restorative justice is also aligned with neoliberal governance because of the ways in which it deals with risk. Neoliberalism has promoted forms of risk that are characterized by community-based prevention (O'Malley 1992; O'Malley and Palmer 1996). A marked feature of restorative justice is that its exponents regard it as an effective means of securing order in the future, through community members seeking to ensure that the offence in question – or let us say the 'harm' in question – does not recur. It is thus relatively easy to see how restorative justice could appear as the favoured inclusive technique of crime control in a neoliberal polity where actuarial justice constitutes the exclusionary technique for dealing with the recalcitrant and the high risk. Perhaps too it is clear why so many post-social governments – no matter which side of the political spectrum they stand – regard restorative justice as attractive. In part, we must face the distinct possibility that this underlies such success as restorative justice has achieved.

Before moving further with this analysis, it is important to insert several caveats into the argument. In particular, it should not be assumed that restorative justice can be simply taken to be the creature of neoliberalism – especially if that claim is used to condemn it out of hand. First, as Nikolas Rose (1996) points out, it was not only 'neoliberals' who criticized the welfare state for its technocratic domination, its expense, and its lack of responsiveness to 'local' concerns. This was also the agenda of critics from the Left (e.g. Gough 1979). Restorative justice can thus appear attractive to diverse 'post-social' political positions. The fact that it is attractive to neoliberals may help explain its uptake in the present era, but does not mean that it can be accorded positive evaluations only from within a neoliberal politics. Second, actuarial justice, restorative justice's supposed counterpart, is neither the only, nor the most characteristic, risk-based response of neoliberal governments. As Simon and Feeley (1995) themselves have pointed out, actuarialism has not been widely adopted even in the United States. It has hardly at all developed in the United Kingdom (Kemshall and Maguire 2003), and Cunneen's (2003) own example of its application in Australia's Northern Territory was decisively rejected and abandoned once a conservative government was ousted at the polls soon after his paper was published. While all these states have neoliberal regimes, it can be argued that the application in the case of the United States (and, briefly, Australia) better illustrates neoconservative rather than neoliberal politics (O'Malley 1999). For this reason, I want to go further and stress that actuarial justice is only one way in which post-social governments have mobilized risk technologies, and is not to be taken as in any way typical even of neoliberalism.

If we are to consider the ways in which risk and restorative justice may be aligning with each other in contemporary criminal justice, we are not, therefore, restricted to the pessimistic and alarming scenarios suggested by Cunneen, Rose and others. Likewise, if we are to consider how to evaluate the promise and/or develop the potential of restorative justice and focus on what risk has to offer, we may turn to a consideration of different, more inclusive ways in which risk has been deployed in the governance of crime. In particular, one promising line of development is offered by policies of illicit drug harm minimization in Australia, New Zealand and to a lesser extent the United Kingdom. These policies are markedly risk-based and exhibit many of the hallmarks of neoliberal governance, yet their principal concern is with the reintegration of illicit drug users. As well, they offer styles of intervention and involvement that provide points of articulation with restorative justice, and provide some leads from which restorative justice advocates may learn some important, albeit challenging, lessons. Restorative justice's own concern with harm minimization (Braithwaite 2002) makes this alignment particularly clear.

Harm minimizing programmes for governing illicit drugs begin with the assumption that all harms are to be approached within a framework of risk, for harm minimization is assumed to have as its corollary a focus on systematic prevention.[2] Put another way, all harms are grasped as risks – as identifiable probabilistically, and as preventable or capable of being minimized – while all interventions optimally are directed at reducing risks. It is important here to stress that in these programmes risks are taken to include risks to drug-using individuals *and* risks to other individuals *and* risks more broadly to society. One consequence is that the array of risk/harms to which the policies attend is very wide, including health (drug overdose, Hepatitis C) and public health (needle stick injuries); crime (burglary committed to fund drug use, victimization of drug users, corruption of police); unemployment and loss of productivity resulting from drug consumption; family disruption and collateral harms to children; risks created for drug users themselves (social isolation, demonization and mental illness); and so on. As with restorative justice, therefore, criminal justice *per se* is decentred and harm is centred. Also, as I will later stress, there is therefore not an exclusive or principal focus on the risks that drug users represent to others. Risks are social in that they affect all including the users. Nor is there an assumption that all risks are generated only by drug users – some, indeed, are created by government policies as well as the actions of other individuals. These include prohibitionist and exclusionary responses that isolate and demonize users, and which carry risks to the user of mental illness, heightened health risks and so on. Yet other risks, such as the risks associated with a culture of drug consumption (licit and illicit) are located in much broader social processes. Accordingly, harms are not located as the effects of bad individuals nor even of the potent properties of drugs. More central are 'risky practices' and 'risk-creating situations' (*cf.* Garland 1996). These may include using unclean needles, polydrug consumption and using drugs in settings that expose others to risks. Some such examples render users individually responsible for harm and thus responsible for harm reduction. But they equally include such socially produced things as the absence of clean and safe sites for injection or of alternative sources of drugs that will minimize drug adulteration and make possible other means of drug administration (e.g. ingestion rather than injection).

What is immediately evident in harm minimizing policies is that drug users are, in a double sense, normalized in ways that are characteristically neoliberal. As noted, drug users are rendered *individually responsible* for harms created to others and to themselves. But this 'responsibilization' is not intended to render the user a target for social exclusion, punishment or coercive interventions. Quite the reverse, for their responsibility is to be *enlisted* in the process of harm reduction. Drug users are to be 'empowered' to deal with their problems responsibly, and to govern the collateral harms of their drug use. This empowerment includes advice on harm minimizing practices of drug administration and consumption; information on the effects of drugs and how to manage side effects; access to methadone programmes aimed at making users more able to manage and reduce their drug use; and the availability of services such as therapeutics and training programmes. Responsibilizing drug users is thus not tied to a responsibility for past actions, a process of shaming or blaming or making reparation, but to a responsibility for governing future consequences of their drug use. As a risk-based policy, harm minimization necessarily is forward looking and, to a considerable extent, invests little or no resources in moral evaluation of past behaviour. Indeed, explicitly moralizing interventions are avoided. Thus the category of the 'drug abuser' is rarely used in most of these programmes. Likewise, there is an avoidance of any discourse and practices that pathologize the drug user, especially with respect to the loss of their free will. The category of the 'responsible drug user', paralleling so much other neoliberal responsibilizing of individuals, assumes a rational choice actor – with the effect that the familiar subjectification of the enslaved 'drug addict' is also muted or erased altogether from harm minimizing discourses.[3] This discursive shift is related not only to responsibilization, but also and equally to a strong emphasis on social inclusion. The categories of 'drug addict' and 'drug abuser' are both morally charged in ways that render the drug consumer alien and pathological. These subjectifications are part of what David Garland (1996) would term a 'criminology of the other', where the offender is to be regarded as 'monstrous', unlike 'us', and thus a ready candidate for exclusion and coercion. The category of the 'drug user', however, creates a 'criminology of the self'. Drug users are like 'us', for they are (abstract) rational choice actors. More than this, harm minimization puts stress on the idea that 'consumers' – another neoliberal subjectification – of illicit drugs are not categorically distinct from the rest of us, for we all exist in a society in which drug problems are systemic. Alcohol and tobacco consumption, in particular, are invariably pointed to as the principal generators of drug-related harm in most societies. The generalized consumption of

225

pharmaceuticals is often located as at least as harmful as illicit drug consumption in socially aggregate terms. Illicit drug users are thus rendered 'normal' – if not unproblematic – for the 'problem' is not only one of individual responsibility, but a 'social problem' in societies said to be 'saturated with drugs'. Hence the drug user is not created as *the* problematic producer of risks, for this is a social problem in which we all share some responsibility, and from the resolution of which we would all benefit. This issue thus takes on a more collective and inclusive sense, infinitely more so than in neoconservative discourses of the 'war on drugs'. Finally, it will be noted that in this way the familiar 'demonization' of drug addicts and abusers is dispensed with. This is not simply a humane response, but an intensely utilitarian one, for harm minimization prioritizes the need to access drug users and to enlist them in the project of harm reduction. Demonization is the antithesis of harm minimization for it deters users from seeking help and drives them into more desperate and dangerous situations and increasingly risky practices.[4] Harm minimization exhibits a general aversion to coercive interventions for much the same reason.

Of course, the reality of such schemes is often rather less rosy than this programmatic image makes it appear to be. This is not my concern, for the same can be said of all programmes including restorative justice. And as I will make clear shortly, there are other reasons to regard harm minimization with circumspection. Rather, the importance of this schematic account is that it makes clear that we can abandon the assumption that risk-based interventions in the neoliberal governance of crime necessitate the kind of 'bifurcatory' and exclusionary model of criminal justice associated with actuarial justice. In consequence we may begin to explore the relationship between risk and restorative justice in a more positive light. In the last part of the paper I wish to pursue this in closer detail.

Articulating harm minimization and restorative justice

It is by no means the case that drug harm minimization policies exhaust what might be thought of as 'positive' or potentially positive neoliberal risk-based programmes for the governance of crime. For example, it is clear that many socially integrative approaches are being developed under such banners as 'developmental crime prevention'.[5] However, I have selected harm minimization for closer examination for several reasons. The first is that my own involvement in several drug commissions in Australia working within this framework has given me insights into 'on the ground' practices of harm minimization that resonate strongly with restorative justice.[6] But more generally, it is because harm minimization has some marked programmatic parallels with restorative justice, notably in that it:

- is strongly committed to socially inclusive solutions;
- is harm focused rather than rule focused;
- personally responsibilizes those who create or potentially create harms;
- is oriented toward the future and toward providing security for those affected by crime.

Having stressed these, perhaps obvious, parallels, we also need to focus on two major points of difference – even points of conflict – between the two approaches. First, unlike restorative justice, harm minimisation avoids the focus on victims and victimization. In particular, it eschews setting up a zero sum game in which one party (offenders) represent risks to the other party (victims). It also, and correspondingly, avoids focusing on the responsibility of the offender to make personal amends to the victim. As a part of this orientation, it largely dispenses with the discourse of community, focusing rather on 'stakeholders'. Second, while there is recognition that drug users and other stakeholders have their own experiences and wisdom, unlike restorative justice, it has tended to be dominated by expert knowledge that identifies risks and harms. That is, it is experts rather than 'lay' participants that are generally understood to develop and deliver the strategies and techniques for minimizing them. I will deal with each of these matters in turn, but should emphasize that I see these points not so much as problems but also as opportunities for fruitful synergies and constructive theoretical and practical consideration.

Avoidance of the victim focus

By identifying the locus of the drug problem in risks that can affect all parties including the users, by setting its goal as the reduction of future harms to users and to the rest of society, and by seeing drug use as a social problem with social foundations, harm minimization decentres the victim – at least in comparison with restorative justice. As noted, reparations to those harmed by users are almost never discussed, nor are issues such as the necessity for contrition or punishment. Of course, it can be argued that harm minimization can only adopt this stance because drug use is regarded as a 'victimless crime'. However, perhaps this is an effect rather than a cause of the policy, for there are many conservatives who would argue that drug use does harm to the moral order and should be punished. The 'War on Drugs', for example, has substantially contributed to the massive prison population in the United States. More to the point, of course, there are subjects who *could* be constituted – and who constitute themselves – as victims. For example, there are the small business owners whose businesses are adversely affected by drug users using their doorways to shoot up or whose presence deters customers. There are local residents outraged at used needles being dropped in their children's school playgrounds and parks, and who regard the resulting curtailment of their freedom as a form of victimhood. However, rather than suggesting users make amends (pointless in any case as the users frequently are without resources or supportive social networks on which to draw) the stress is on changing the future. Making one party the victim and the other the perpetrator is seen as providing a disincentive for users to participate, a key aim of the programmes. As well, the assumption is that staging the 'offence' as a moral issue tends to draw up 'sides' and thus gets in the way of resolving the problem of security or of reducing the risks. At the same time and in the same manoeuvre, *the future is privileged over the past.* Consequently there is also a move away from terms such as 'justice' as a righting of harms done to victims in the past. Or perhaps it is as important to note that when it is (occasionally) used, it is deployed in the same sense that Shearing (2001) uses it in his restorative justice projects in South Africa: justice becomes an assurance that harms will not happen again (or in the more realistic model of harm minimization, the stress is that harms will be minimized). This, as Shearing and his colleagues suggest, involves 'letting go of the past' *in order* that the future may be more secure, which a focus on victimhood makes difficult by setting up a zero sum game between the aggrieved and the perpetrator (Shearing *et al.* 2004). Individuals may be held responsible in harm minimization, but the emphasis on their responsibility is to ensure that harms do not recur.

Of course, this runs counter to much of what is dear to advocates of restorative justice, for giving voice to the victims is regarded as a key to ensuring their involvement in the process as well as having its own intrinsic importance. But as much research indicates (e.g. Daly 2002: 75–6), the victim's stake in the process, at least as measured in terms of their participation and thus the aggregate satisfaction, is one of the least successful aspects of restorative justice. Attention might thus be given to downplaying the place of victimhood and redress in restorative justice. If the focus is to a greater extent on harms and the prevention of their recurrence, then many of the strengths of restorative justice may be enhanced. Offenders are still rendered accountable, but in a positive and constructive way. Their enlistment in the broader issue of harm minimization (which as Braithwaite (2003) argues is at the heart of restorative justice) becomes the critical issue. Rather than interventions involving the restatement of the past and the opportunities this presents for generating resentment by offenders softly coerced into making amends (and for emphasizing a divide between offenders and their victims), the wider concerns of the programme are brought more into focus.[7]

Linked with this, the preferred discourse in harm minimization is that of 'stakeholders' rather than 'victims' and 'offenders'. This has two consequences: it allows *conflicts of interest* to be centred rather than an assumption that one party is necessarily in the right and the other to be blamed; and it allows 'victims', 'offenders', 'experts' and others to approach on equal terms. Recognition of the existence and even centrality of conflicts of interest is important because – contrary to the imagery of the 'community' as deployed in restorative justice – it allows for diversity of values and stakes within the network of those concerned. In this way, such an approach avoids the problem identified by George Pavlich (2001) that an assumption of communal consensus in restorative justice creates a potential for 'totalitarian' domination in which one set of values and experiences are to be the subject of condemnation, denial and apology. While no doubt this is sometimes defensible (for example with sexual assault), its ethical and political dangers are clear. It may ignore or suppress social diversity and sometimes social conflicts of a sort that is important for 'the community' to recognize, and itself come to terms with. They are themselves questions of justice, if not of individual justice. Restorative justice, I would suggest, is rather poorly equipped at present to deal with such matters precisely because it sets up a victim–offender binary, and by so doing prioritizes rectification of past wrongs by one party. With harm minimization strategies, on the other hand, we move from dispute *resolution* toward the possibility of dispute *management*. Thus the interests of drug users on the streets and of the shopkeepers who find the presence of users bad for business are not reduced to a scenario in which the shopkeepers are ultimately assumed to be in the right because they have suffered harms. This implicitly coerces users to conform or move to another area, but puts no obligation on shopkeepers (or anyone else) to do anything about the plight of users. All the more is this so where, as in most restorative programmes, the offender is required to acknowledge the offence as a condition of entering the programme. Harm minimization's stakeholder politics on the other hand sets up a process of negotiation. Rather than one of simply 'shifting the burden of risk' from one party to another, from victim to offender, the risk becomes the focus of attention. In the process, in such a negotiation over risk management, a value on *tolerance* comes to the fore: a recognition that perfect harmony may be an unrealistic – and even counterproductive or 'unjust' – goal. Again, this is not seemingly a question restorative justice seeks to address. While it may not be applicable to all scenarios which restorative justice may deal with, it would seem to indicate ways in which the approach could be reconstituted and thus diversified for certain purposes. It would seem especially to offer promise where offending is linked to situations in which 'community' responses may imply a potentially repressive consensus – such as racially or ethnically diverse settings, or culture clashes between generations or subcultures (such as drug subcultures).

Philosophically, this point draws on Foucault's (1982) notion of an *agonistic or agonic* politics: a process in which some working solution will be (must be) reached in order that harms can be minimized. But in order to minimize domination this remains under review, always subject to contestations and 'provocations'. Where problems are ongoing (as in the examples just mentioned), individual cases become sites in which the underlying issues and the adequacy and 'justice' of existing responses to them are constantly raised and reappraised. Risk, in such ways, becomes democratized – in spite of harm minimization's tendency to expert domination – but this is an issue to which I must now turn in more detail.

Expert domination and the democratization of risk

An ongoing problem in harm minimization – especially in its relationship to restorative justice – is a concern with technocratic domination. As an abstract form of knowledge, requiring statistical and related sophistication to manipulate and access to data to operationalize, risk very much appears as an expert system. Yet expert domination in this context is especially difficult to challenge, in part because risk takes on the appearance of being a technically neutral, 'objective' form of knowledge and practice (Simon 1988). In general terms, risk tends to trump the uncertainty of other ways of estimating the risks and of understanding what is best for the future. Lay people offering their 'uncertain' estimations are readily subjected to the more systematic and objective actuarial or risk-based data of expertise. Of course, this strikes a responsive chord among the concerns of restorative justice advocates, but by and large this issue has been resolved in favour of privileging 'lay' knowledges and participation. In the risk literature, however, this question of law and expert knowledge has been posed at a more theoretical – and I suspect more sophisticated – level.

As Brian Wynne (1996) has argued, in the field of risk it is critical to recognize that there is no essential opposition between lay and expert knowledge – there is no 'divide' corresponding to that between objective (risk) and subjective (uncertain) knowledge, or sophisticated and naive knowledge – as the academic literature often assumes. Rather we may regard 'expert' knowledge as abstracted and universal whereas 'lay' knowledge is local and particular, set in the social context in which the knowledge of particular risks is to 'apply'. (This does not imply that all lay knowledge is necessarily correct, but neither should it be assumed that the reverse is true or that expert knowledge is always right.) Epistemologically, we can regard 'lay' or 'local' knowledge as restoring to expert knowledge that which has been abstracted from it. That is, in the process of abstraction many of the issues taken for granted at the local level are removed as 'particular facts'. But Wynne (1996: 61) argues that there is more to it than this:

> The basis of lay public responses to expert knowledge is always potentially an epistemological conflict with science about the assumed underlying purposes of knowledge, or at least the scope of that epistemic remit, which is wrongly assumed to be just given in nature. This raises questions not only about the basis of the relationship between 'objective' scientific knowledge and 'subjective' lay knowledge, but also about the extent to which scientific knowledge is open to substantive criticism and improvement or correction by lay people. In other words, how far might lay people be involved in shaping scientific knowledge, and thus in providing the basis of alternative forms of public knowledge that reflect and sustain different dominant conceptions of the human, and of the social purposes of public knowledge?

This is not meant to imply that, in a Maoist or Stalinist sense, the truth should be subject to the opinion of the masses. Rather it is to stress that expert-abstract knowledge has been exhausted of content that is not in itself abstract-universal, and in this sense it has been 'dehumanized' (Wynne 1996: 57–60). Yet at the same time it remains shaped by social values, as must be all knowledge. Values have not in practice been deleted but merely repressed. In particular these relate to such matters as: the selection of those things that are to be considered as the risks to be reduced (and by implication which things – such as certain ways of living – that subjects are not willing to have altered); the prioritization and evaluation of risks (which risks 'matter' most); the specification of what shall be 'an acceptable level of risk'; the judgment about what constitutes 'security' or what is an adequate or desired 'reduction' of risk. Expert knowledges are, therefore, 'incipient social prescriptions, or vehicles of particular tacit forms of social order, relationships and identities', *as well as* formulations about how to get things done, based on abstract knowledge (Wynne 1996: 59). Perhaps most advocates of restorative justice do not need to be told this. Yet seen in this way, there is no need to exclude expert knowledge, as some advocates of restorative justice urge. Rather the key task is to subject expert solutions – which have technological sophistication in terms of how to get things done – to lay critique and evaluation. Again, the implication is not to prioritize one knowledge over the other, but to establish negotiations, if only because neither expert nor lay knowledges will themselves be of one voice. Thus in the harm minimization model of agonic relations, it is not simply the conflicts of interest between the disputants (the 'victims' and the 'offenders'). Also included are the conflicts that are layered upon and through the disputes between these parties, the experts and authorities, and the broader 'community' (including police, drug and youth workers, ambulance and paramedic staff, local government officials, etc.). Expertise appears neither as neutral and superior nor to be excluded, for almost inevitably these parties are *imbricated* in the disputes and inevitably *must* be imbricated in any solutions if these are to become institutionalized.

Concluding remarks: from risk and restoration to democratic harm minimisation

A key purpose of this paper has been to stress that risk should not be imagined as a fixed set of practices, and most especially should not be identified in the justice field with the negative and exclusionary example of actuarial justice. Alternative applications of risk techniques can be reintegrative, 'empowering' and constructive. The task of innovating new forms of justice may therefore include thinking through and experimenting with hybrids of risk and restorative justice. In this respect, it is important to make a last point – although it has been implicit in much of what I have argued throughout the chapter. Once it is recognized that risk can take many forms, it is a short step to seeing that risk itself is never a very large component of any technique, programme, or policy – even of those identified as 'instances' of risk. References above to the 'democratization' of risk, and to the relationships between risk and uncertainty, could be referred to as 'hybridizing' risk with other practices. But such an idea assumes that there is something that can be identified as 'pure' risk. At best, I would suggest that this is only the act of probabilistic calculation. Even the example of actuarial justice (referred to as 'pure risk' by Feeley and Simon) has been seen to be anything but this, for it incorporates all manner of political assumptions, specific constructions of social actors, theories of the global economy and so on, that are not in any way actuarial or probabilistic. Yet in our conception of actuarial justice as 'risk-based' we privilege the component that is risk. We accord it the determining role or executive function when this belongs elsewhere, in the political, economic and social values and assumptions that give it a specific institutional form. I suggest this is true of most of our current theorization and evaluation of the 'risk society'.

Perhaps, after all, we have made a fetish of risk, accorded it powers it does not have, and it is better to think of probabilistic prediction merely as one possible component of democratic government through harm minimization. In this way, no putative barrier can be imagined between risk and restorative justice. If we centre their respective roles as examples (or otherwise) of democratic harm minimization, then their commonalities, alignments and synergies, rather than their differences, are brought to the fore. At the same time, the *specific* character of the examples, rather than the abstract principle that subsumes them under the label 'risk' or 'restoration' and imagines this as their defining character, also comes to the fore. The presence or absence of a statistical or probabilistic element – that is, of risk – becomes a comparatively minor issue. As indeed, does the presumption of 'restoration' in restorative justice. Instead, the more critical and overtly moral and political matters are: what we should think of as 'harms'; and how they should be minimized by democratic means.

Notes

1   By 'technology' here I mean a broad family of ways of doing things related to each other by a single principle. The specific ways of doing things are referred to as 'techniques'. Thus if risk is considered to be united by the principle of using probabilities to predict harmful consequences associated with future events, it includes a variety of 'risk techniques' such as insurance, the use of risk factors in medical diagnosis and criminal profiling. The distinction is always relative. For example, insurance may in turn appear as a technology (i.e. risk that is linked with principles of financial compensation) where analysis focuses on a variety of specific techniques

of insurance such as individual life insurance or social insurances dealing with health or workplace injury.

2   The account here is drawn from more extensive analyses of harm minimization I have published elsewhere. See in particular O'Malley (2004 Chapter 8). For the sake of clarity and succinctness, I have not reproduced here the extensive referencing to policy and programmatic documents on which this account is based.

3   The nearest category is that of the 'dependent user'. But even here the user is not regarded as having lost their rational choice, but as being in a problematic relationship. Hence brochures promoting methadone use to such users are surprisingly frank in outlining the costs of enlistment (for example having to notify the supplier of even a few days' change of location), in order that the user can make an 'informed decision'.

4   For example, isolation and persecution of users is argued: to increase their re-use of needles with its attendant risks of HIV and Hepatitis C infection; to make users administer in secret situations where help is unlikely to reach them in the event of overdose or similar problems; to make users inject in unsanitary surroundings such as back alleys or public toilets; and so on.

5   In such programmes, intervention is planned in the lives of those young people exhibiting 'risk factors', with the aim of diverting them from careers in crime. There are some profoundly worrying aspects of such programmes (not least being the subjection of parents and children to the same kinds of expert and technocratic domination that concerned critics of the welfare state). Nevertheless, in effect these have redesignated as 'risk factors' many of the socially founded causes of crime that were familiar to the criminologies of the era of penal modernism. Social isolation, socio-economic disadvantage, cultural discrimination, poor socialization, blocked opportunities, educational deprivation, inadequate parenting and many others make their appearance here, to be matched with various programmes designed to ameliorate these conditions (O'Malley 2000). Whatever else is wrong with them, these are infinitely preferable to actuarial exclusion. They are basically inclusive programmes aiming to reintegrate young offenders and potential offenders and deliver some kinds of services, rather than simply responding by exclusion or coercion.

6   Namely, the Premier's Drug Advisory Council (PDAC 1996) and the Drug Policy Expert Committee (DPEC 2000), both of which recommended substantial further development of harm minimizing strategies in the state of Victoria, Australia; and the Crime Prevention Research Advisory Council (CPRAC 2002) which linked such developments to the need for ongoing criminological research strategies.

7   It cannot be denied that this may reduce the political attractiveness of restorative justice as a plausible alternative to criminal justice. However, it is more consistent with the abstract principles espoused by many advocates of restorative justice who regard the criminal justice system as a problem, the antithesis of restorative justice (e.g. Braithwaite 2002). The problem is thus one of whether to adopt a principled or a pragmatic approach.

References

Beck, U. (1992) *Risk Society: Toward a New Modernity*. New York: Sage.
Beck, U. (1997) *World Risk Society*. Cambridge: Polity Press.
Bernstein, P. (1998) *Against the Gods: The Remarkable Story of Risk*. New York: Wiley.
Braithwaite, J. (2002) 'Setting standards for restorative justice', *British Journal of Criminology*, 42: 563–77.
Braithwaite, J. (2003) 'Restorative justice and a better future', in E. McLaughlin, R. Fergusson, G. Hughes and L. Westmarland (eds), *Restorative Justice. Critical Issues*. London: Sage, pp. 54–65.
Christie, N. (1977) 'Conflicts as property', *British Journal of Criminology*, 1, 17: 1–15.
CPRAC (Crime Prevention Research Advisory Council) (2002) *Crime Prevention Research Advisory Council. Interim Report*. Melbourne: Department of Justice, Victoria.
Cunneen, C. (2003) 'Thinking critically about restorative justice', in E. McLaughlin, R. Fergusson, G. Hughes and L. Westmarland (eds), *Restorative Justice: Critical Issues*. London: Sage, pp. 182–94.
Daly, K. (2002) 'Restorative justice. The real story', *Punishment and Society*, 4: 55–79.
DPEC (Drug Policy Expert Committee) (2000) *Drugs: Meeting the Challenge*. Melbourne: Government Printer.
Ericson, R. and Haggerty, K. (1997) *Policing the Risk Society*. Toronto: University of Toronto Press.
Ewald, F. (1991) 'Insurance and risk', in G. Burchell, C. Gordon and P. Miller (eds), *The Foucault Effect: Studies in Governmentality*. London: Harvester/Wheatsheaf, pp. 197–210.
Feeley, M. and Simon, J. (1992) 'The new penology: notes on the emerging strategy of corrections and its implications', *Criminology*, 30: 449–74.
Feeley, M. and Simon, J. (1994) 'Actuarial justice: the emerging new criminal law', in D. Nelken (ed.), *The Futures of Criminology*. New York: Sage, pp. 173–201.
Foucault, M. (1982) 'The subject and power', in H. Dreyfus and P. Rabinow (eds) *Michel Foucault: Beyond Structuralism and Hermeneutics*. Chicago, IL: Chicago University Press, pp. 208–26.
Garland, D. (1996) 'The limits of the sovereign state: strategies of crime control in contemporary society', *British Journal of Criminology*, 36: 445–71.
Garland, D. (2001) *The Culture of Control*. Oxford: Oxford University Press.
Giddens, A. (1994) 'Living in a post-traditional society', in U. Beck, A. Giddens and S. Lash (eds), *Reflexive modernization*. Cambridge: Polity Press, pp. 56–109.
Gough, I. (1979) *The Political Economy of the Welfare State*. Basingstoke: Macmillan.
Kemshall, H. and Maguire, M. (2003) 'Public protection, "partnership" and risk penality', *Punishment and Society*, 3: 237–54.

O'Malley, P. (1992) 'Risk, power and crime prevention', *Economy and Society*, 21: 252–75.

O'Malley, P. (1999) 'Volatile and contradictory punishment', *Theoretical Criminology*, 3: 175–96.

O'Malley, P. (2000) 'Risk, crime and prudentialism revisited', in K. Stenson and R. Sullivan (eds), *Crime, Risk and Justice*. Cullompton: Willan, pp. 89–103.

O'Malley, P. (2004) *Risk, Uncertainty and Government*. London: Cavendish/Glasshouse.

O'Malley, P. and Palmer, D. (1996) 'Post-Keynesian policing', *Economy and Society*, 25: 137–55.

Osborne, T. and Gaebler, T. (1993) *Reinventing Government: How the Entrepreneurial Spirit is Transforming the Public Sector*. New York: Plume Books.

Pavlich, G. (2001) 'The force of community', in H. Strang and J. Braithwaite (eds), *Restorative Justice and Civil Society*. Cambridge: Cambridge University Press, pp. 56–68.

PDAC (Premier's Drug Advisory Council) (1996) *Drugs and Our Community: Report of the Premier's Drug Advisory Council*. Melbourne: Victorian Government.

Peters, T. (1987) *Thriving on Chaos: Handbook for a Management Revolution*. New York: Knopf.

Reddy, S. (1996) 'Claims to expert knowledge and the subversion of democracy. The triumph of risk over uncertainty', *Economy and Society*, 25: 222–54.

Rose, N. (1996) 'The death of the "social"? Refiguring the territory of government', *Economy and Society*, 25: 327–56.

Rose, N. (2000) 'Government and control', *British Journal of Criminology*, 40: 321–39.

Shearing, C. (2001) 'Transforming security: a South African experiment', in H. Strang and J. Braithwaite (eds), *Restorative Justice and Civil Society*. Cambridge: Cambridge University Press, pp. 15–34.

Shearing, C., Wood, J. and Font, E. (2004) 'Nodal governance and restorative justice'. Unpublished paper.

Simon, J. (1988) 'The ideological effects of actuarial practices', *Law and Society Review*, 22: 771–800.

Simon, J. and Feeley, M. (1995) 'True crime: the new penology and public discourse on crime', in T. Blomberg and S. Cohen (eds), *Punishment and Social Control: Essays in Honor of Sheldon Messinger*. New York: Aldine de Gruyter, pp. 147–80.

Wynne, B. (1996) 'May the sheep safely graze? A reflexive view of the expert-lay knowledge divide', in S. Lash and B. Wynne (eds), *Risk, Environment and Modernity*. New York: Sage, pp. 44–83.

Chapter 11

Reintegrative shaming and restorative justice: reconciliation or divorce?

Roger Matthews

Introduction

The honeymoon is over. The romantic illusion that the coupling of reintegrative shaming (the theory) and restorative justice (the practice) would be capable of producing a progressive transformation of the state-centred criminal justice system is wearing thin. Trouble and strife are arising from all quarters and even some gamekeepers are turning into poachers (Daly 2002; Roche 2003; Strang 2002). The gap between promise and performance is becoming increasingly evident and it is now becoming apparent that the hopes and aspirations of many well-meaning advocates are fading fast. A growing number of critiques have pointed to the chasm between the rhetoric and reality of restorative justice and its failure to realize its own claims and aspirations.

Significantly, some of the most powerful critiques have been directed towards the 'new generation' of restorative justice programmes that emerged in the 1990s. These include reviews of the Wagga Wagga conferences in New South Wales, family-based conferences in New Zealand and the police-led cautioning conferences that have been established in the USA and the UK.

The point of departure of these critiques is a rejection of the claim that contemporary forms of restorative justice are a continuation of ancient tribal ways of dealing with disputes (Daly 2002). The claim, for example, that the Wagga Wagga model of restorative justice constitutes a reworking of long-standing Aboriginal practices is to engage in what Harry Blagg (1997) calls 'epistemological violence' and involves a serious misreading of history and social relations. Restorative justice conferences, he argues, relegitimize new forms of domination and the extension of police powers. The overall effect of these conferences is to compound inequalities, individualize social problems and privatize disputes. These practices are routinely justified in the name of the 'community' or 'community safety'. Paradoxically, Aborigines are marginalized from the mainstream 'community' in Australia. Thus for Blagg (2001) the treatment of minority groups such as the Australian Aborigines who represent just under half of all juvenile admissions in police lock-ups begins to look distinctly sinister.

What is significant about this critique is that it can be extended to cover the experiences of other marginalized groups – particularly ethnic minorities – who are increasingly becoming the focus of crime control strategies in most parts of Western Europe and America (Tonry 1995; Mauer 1999). The forms of restorative justice outlined by Blagg seem unlikely to provide a progressive or transformative option for these minority groups and are more likely to encourage new forms of injustice (Crawford and Clear 2001). Rather than reduce the degree of punitiveness these measures signal the replacement of welfare provision, which has in the past been awarded to these socially and economically marginalized groups. In an increasingly diverse, multicultural society restorative justice programmes serve to impose the dominant value system on groups who may adhere to different or alternative sets of values. Those who are subject to different values, patterns of socialization, family structures and lines of authority may feel resentful and antagonistic towards shame-based restorative justice conferences. While restorative justice programmes may be effective for those who have reputations to lose, such as white-collar criminals and members of the respectable working class, they may have little meaning for those with a low social status or those who live on the margins of society. Finally, rather than promote informal modes of dispute resolution these state-sponsored programmes may operate to undermine existing local informal control processes, and rather than empower communities they can make them more passive and more reliant on state services.

In Kathleen Daly's (2001) evaluation of family-based conferences in New Zealand she found that many of the claims made in relation to these conferences, such as empowering the victim while eliciting remorse from offenders, were often unfounded. She found that just under a third of the young offenders said that the conference was not important to them, while over half said that they had not thought about what they would say to victims before the conference. Indicatively, over 40 per cent said that they were not sorry or were less sorry for the victim after the conference, while only 28 per cent of the victims interviewed believed that the offender was genuinely sorry. Some 18 per cent of victims left the conference upset and in 9 per cent of cases victims felt intimidated. It is clear from this account that in this type of conference, which mainly involves young people, a significant percentage of offenders do not take it seriously while others only engage in the process in order to reduce the penalty that they might receive. Clearly, many of these encounters are ineffective or counterproductive with many victims feeling short-changed or intimidated.

Richard Young's (2001) review of three police-led restorative justice conferences in Bethlehem, Pennsylvania in the USA, Canberra, Australia and the Thames Valley initiative covering the English counties of Oxfordshire, Berkshire and Buckinghamshire echoes some of the concerns raised by Blagg and he points out that there is a danger that the police can become 'judge and jury' in these cases. In opposition to the claims that these restorative justice conferences allow victims and offenders to come together to resolve their conflicts more informally these events are largely run by powerful professionals. Indeed, Young notes that in police-led conferences there is a tendency for the police to disclose their knowledge of offenders and that there is little possibility of challenging police behaviour. In a number of cases the conference scripts are not followed and instead the police 'improvise' and take a lead in directing proceedings. As in other reviews Young found evidence that proceedings tended to be over-controlled by professionals and were largely offender focused while the victims acted as little more than information providers. These observations raise serious questions about procedural fairness and accountability (Roche 2003). Not surprisingly, offenders often become defensive and are reluctant to speak openly. These conferences are more directive than enabling and in some cases facilitators pursue their own individual agendas and impose their own decisions. Young suggests that decisions reached were often unrealistic and unjust. In some cases the outcomes are much more punitive than they would have been in court, while in other relatively serious cases outcomes appeared extremely light. Thus, rather than empowering victims these conferences more often serve to empower the police. In effect these police-led conferences involve little more than a thinly disguised form of state-inflicted punishment (Young and Hoyle 2003).

In a similar vein David O'Mahoney and Jonathan Doak (2004) found in their study of police-led restorative cautioning pilots in Northern

Ireland evidence of net widening whereby a number of relatively minor offenders were drawn unnecessarily, in their view, into these schemes. Many of those who ended up in these programmes would not have been processed by the formal system either because they were too young or because their transgressions were not serious enough or because existing laws did not apply. On these restorative schemes very young offenders were subject to a very demanding process of adjudication. Thus:

> One of the greatest concerns arising from the pilots was that they appeared to draw in some very young and petty offenders who consequently experienced a very demanding process of accountability that in our opinion was disproportionate to the harm caused. Some 80% of cases that we examined were for offences concerning property worth less than £15. It was not uncommon to come across cases where a considerable amount of police time had been invested in arranging for a full conference for the theft of a chocolate bar or a can of soft drink. (O'Mahoney and Doak 2004: 495)

The consequence of intervening at this level is to formalize issues which were previously dealt with informally, and to inadvertently push offenders up the tariff. As Stanley Cohen explained in his *Visions of Social Control* (1985) these ostensibly innocuous interventions can have the effect of extending both the range and depth of social control producing a more complex, opaque and intensive system of regulation.

These and related evaluations of the different restorative justice programmes which have emerged over the past decade and a half amount to a major indictment of the claims and objectives of restorative justice. Alongside these reviews are a growing number of critiques which suggest that, rather than involving a more constructive and progressive option, the various forms of restorative justice involve the erosion of rights and legal safeguards, a blurring of civil and criminal proceedings and the construction of 'cheap justice' or second-class justice (Ashworth 2001). There have been various responses to this barrage of criticism by the advocates of restorative justice; however, these responses have been less than convincing (Braithwaite 1997; Morris 2002).

In this chapter the aim is to contribute to the growing scepticism associated with restorative justice in its various guises. It will be argued that the failings which have been identified by critics are not so much a result of poor implementation or a consequence of technical and organizational failures; rather it will be suggested that the limitations of restorative justice programmes stem more or less directly from the weak theoretical base on which they have been constructed. The implication is that no amount of tinkering with these programmes will solve the fundamental problems which have been identified by critics. In particular, the aim is to try to trace back the perceived limitations of restorative justice programmes to John Braithwaite's influential reintegrative shaming thesis which has provided one of the central pillars on which the 'new generation' restorative justice programmes centred around conferencing and shaming which emerged during the 1990s have been constructed. It is not, however, the intention to provide a comprehensive review of John Braithwaite's theory, although such a review is long overdue, but rather to examine certain aspects of the theory – particularly those relating to the processes of shaming, reintegration and recidivism.

Shaming

Arguably, the major difference between the development of informal justice during the 1980s and its representation in the form of restorative justice in the 1990s is the wide-scale adoption of the reintegrative shaming thesis elaborated by John Braithwaite in *Crime, Shame and Reintegration* (1989). In this book he elaborated the notion of shame and provided a new theoretical rationale which revived the flagging fortunes of the informal justice movement of the 1980s. For the most part Braithwaite's ideas and aspirations have been realized in the restorative justice conferences, which have over the last decade or so become part of the penal landscape around the world.

The two other theoretical approaches which had been influential in promoting informal justice in the 1980s – abolitionism and faith-based criminology – lacked the breadth and depth of analysis to turn ideas into specific programmes. Braithwaite's extensive writings made up that gap and in his work he acknowledges his debt to both abolitionism and faith-based approaches. In line with abolitionism he emphasizes informalism, anti-statism, bringing parties together to resolve disputes as well as recognizing the victim (Hulsman 1986; Christie 1982). In conjunction with faith-based criminology he places emphasis on forgiveness and remorse and consequently his approach contains a strong confessional element (Pepinsky and Quinney 1991).

The main point of departure, in Braithwaite's (1989) analysis, is the notion of reintegrative shaming. Shaming is seen as a powerful sanction which, he claims, can be more effective than the conventional forms of punishment centred around the strategies of retribution, deterrence, incapacitation and rehabilitation. It is important, he argues, to avoid a potentially stigmatizing impact of shaming whereby individuals may be propelled into further offending and deviant subcultures. Therefore, he argues that it is necessary to follow the shaming of offenders with strategies of reintegration. Thus the aim is to indicate the unacceptability of the offender's actions while encouraging him or her to repair the damage done and consequently be reintegrated into the community. In this way it is possible, he suggests, to be tough on crime but to do so in a way that encourages the offender to think about the consequences of their action and thereby reduce future offending. Consequently, crime can be reduced in the longer term. At the same time it aims to restore the dignity and security of victims by 'making good':

> The basic idea of reintegrative shaming theory is that locations in space and time where shame is communicated effectively and reintegratively will be times and places where there is less predatory crime – less crime that is a threat to freedom as non-domination. Reintegrative shaming prevents such offending; stigmatization increases the risk of crime for the stigmatized. Reintegrative shaming means communicating disapproval for the *act* with respect, with special efforts to avert outcast identities and to terminate disapproval with rituals of forgiveness and reconciliation. Stigmatization means communicating disapproval of a *person* with disrespect, where offenders are labeled with outcast identities (like 'criminal', 'junkie'), where there are no rituals to terminate disapproval. (Braithwaite and Braithwaite 2001: 39)

Through a reworking of labelling theory with its emphasis on the stigmatizing impact of criminal sanctions Braithwaite presents a deceptively simple distinction between stigmatizing and exclusionary forms of shaming on one hand, and inclusionary and reintegrative forms of shaming on the other. Where the latter are applied, he argues, the result is not only to maintain respect for the offender but also to put in place a procedure that can ultimately reduce crime through the more effective resolution of conflicts. It is on the basis of this distinction that some of the leading restorative justice programmes have been developed, while Braithwaite has also used it to rework classical approaches to criminological theory and to tie this theorization into the development of a political programme: namely republicanism. There are few theorists in the postwar period who have sought to provide a synthesis of conceptual, practical and political concerns in this way and it is the ability of Braithwaite to provide such an integrated approach that accounts in no small part for the power and influence of his work (Braithwaite and Pettit 1990). Interestingly, Braithwaite has stated that he would like to have called the term reintegrative shaming 'restorative shaming' in order to make the links between his theory and practice more transparent.

As a number of commentators have pointed out, there is something unusual about placing the notion of shaming at the centre of the analysis since it has been widely noted that shaming can be an extremely destructive emotion (Johnstone 1999, 2002; Whitman 1998). At the same time others, including Braithwaite, have pointed out that shaming as a social sanction has been in decline over the past hundred years or so and is widely viewed as a high-risk option which in certain circumstances can be extremely damaging both individually and socially (Braithwaite 1993). It therefore seems strange that an approach which is clearly committed to developing an inclusive and radical approach to crime control should place at the centre of its analysis a concept which in the past has been closely associated with authoritarian regimes.

James Whitman (1998) in a thoughtful article on shaming has identified a number of objections to the adoption of state directed shaming sanctions in modern western societies. First, he argues that shaming involves an ugly and politically dangerous complicity between the state and the crowd. Second, shame sanctions are undesirable because they promote a spirit of public indecency and brutality. Third, the use of shaming sanctions has historically only been seen to apply to a strictly delimited range of offences and offenders – sexual offences, commercial offences and minor or first-time offences. Fourth, in a rights-based society like our own it is important to uphold the rights of offenders and to maintain dignity and respect. Shaming carries the likelihood of taking away the dignity of the offender as a result of humiliation. In answer to the question; 'what is wrong with shame sanctions?', Whitman suggests that:

> They involve a dangerous willingness, on the part of the government, to delegate part of its enforcement power to a fickle and uncontrolled general populace. Even in their mildest American form, shame sanctions amount to a kind of posse-raising legal politics, with all the risks that it implies. They are at base a form of officially sponsored lynch justice, meted out by courts that have given up on the obligation of the state both to define what is criminal and to administer criminal sanctions itself.
> (Whitman 1998: 1088/9)

As Whitman suggests there may be different reasons historically why certain groups should have been the object of shame sanctions. It is also the case that among those groups to whom shame sanctions have been directed, the impact and effects can considerably vary. The dynamics of attempting to mobilize shame sanctions against sexual offenders and minors, for example, who may feel vulnerable and marginal, is very different than mobilizing such sanctions against white-collar and corporate criminals. As Mike Levi (2002) has argued, there are a variety of commercial criminals who are relatively immune from such sanctions, while at the same time he suggests that there are some business people for whom stigma and exclusion may well be suitable penalties. At the same time shaming sanctions directed towards the managers or employees in certain firms may well affect everyone working for that firm. The morally neutralizing effect of money, on the other hand, may allow corporate criminals to minimize the likelihood and effects of shaming and to reinvent themselves where necessary.

At the other end of the social spectrum there are also difficulties in applying shaming sanctions. As Harry Blagg (1997) has noted in relation to Australian Aboriginal people, they have a very different notion of shame from that which is promoted by the advocates of restorative justice, while the whole idea of 'representation' is highly contentious, particularly that contained within wholly exterior, adjudicatory structures such as courts where there is only limited scope for individuals to 'speak for' others. Given these different cultural, ethnic and class dimensions, not only in relation to the meaning of shame but also in relation to its effects, it suggests that the mobilization of what is seen as a natural, universal and transhistorical concept of shame is both naive and dangerous (Johnstone 2002).

Alison Morris (2001) has pointed out that shaming is not only a potentially problematic sanction but is likely to be counter-productive. Thus instead of placing the emphasis on shaming in restorative justice conferences she sees the process itself as being educative and its effectiveness allied to eliciting expressions of remorse. Thus rather than focusing on shaming she argues for what she calls 'reintegrative remorse'. Thus she writes:

> It is certainly possible that it is empathy which triggers remorse, and not shaming (disapproval). If this is so it would mean that the emphasis in conferencing (or in other restorative justice processes) should not be on processes of shaming (disapproval) but on processes which focus on the consequences of offending for others (for families and communities as well as for victims). In the meantime

the use of the words 'shame' and shaming' in the development and refinement of reintegrative shaming is best avoided. They are too readily and easily misunderstood and it is not that difficult in practice to slip from the intent of reintegrative shaming to the practice of stigmatic shaming or for intended reintegrative shaming to be perceived as stigmatic. (Morris 2001: 12)

As Alison Morris (2001) notes, shaming clearly carries a strong punitive and exclusionary component. If it were not a powerful mechanism of disintegration there would be no point in spending so much time and effort in trying to reintegrate those shamed. However, it might seem a little strange to the untrained eye that these two strategies of shaming and forgiveness or stigmatization and reintegration should be joined together and be presented as complementary strategies, particularly since the implementation of one would seem to be designed to negate the impact of the other. Thus in restorative justice conferences where the prearranged script is predictably going to strive for forgiveness and reintegration and this is known by all participants beforehand the potential power of the shaming process would seem to be largely undermined in advance.

The salvation of the notion of shaming from its potentially disastrous consequences, Braithwaite insists, is dependent upon its being followed by rituals of reintegration. Since these rituals of reintegration are aimed at overcoming the negative impact of stigmatization the critical question is the degree to which it is possible to uncouple the processes of shaming and reintegration.

Reintegration

As Ken Polk (1994) has argued, the negative impact of shaming is only likely to be partially alleviated by strategies of reintegration. As we have seen above many of the participants in restorative justice conferences are either relatively impervious to the shaming process or engage in the process for pragmatic reasons. These findings have three important implications for the reintegrative shaming thesis. The first is that only certain types of offenders are likely to be amenable to this type of sanction. The second is that there is no guarantee that those who do experience the effects of shaming will be reintegrated effectively. The third is that because reintegrative shaming is mainly directed towards minor offenders, rather than more serious and hardened offenders, it is likely to work best where it is needed least and to be least effective where it is needed most.

Although it is recognized by the advocates of restorative justice that reintegration is far from certain, the various dimensions of reintegration are not fully explored and many see reintegration as a single process. There are two problems with this conception. The first is that because the reintegrative shaming thesis is for the most part *offender focused* it tends to see reintegration as an issue only for the offender, but as has been suggested, because the shaming mobilized by restorative justice programmes can impact upon the victims as well as their friends and family, there are questions about how the reintegration of all the parties involved will be realized. Most of the time the advocates of restorative justice express the view that the apology or the admission of guilt is sufficient to satisfy the victim. However, in a significant number of cases no formal apology is forthcoming, the victim is not present at the hearing, while some sessions end in acrimony (Daly 2001). Despite all the rhetoric of bringing the victim back in and developing a victim-centred approach the victim plays a limited role in many of the restorative justice programmes. Recent research reports that there has been a considerable degree of dissatisfaction among conference victims both in relation to the way in which conferences are carried out and their aftermath (Strang 2002).

Parents and friends who are drawn into the dispute may understandably feel upset, stigmatized and marginalized. They may be reluctant participants and not understand a great deal about what is going on (Karp *et al.* 2004). Reintegrative shaming has little to say about their difficulties and restorative justice programmes provide little or no support to deal with the shame or guilt experienced by participants and have no powers to facilitate their reintegration into their community.

The second and related issue is who decides that reintegration has taken place? In many of the trivial cases that appear in restorative justice programmes, particularly those involving juveniles who are living in stable households, reintegration may be possible. But in more serious cases and particularly for those already subject to some degree of social exclusion, it is not always clear who decides and who takes responsibility for reintegration. Is it the offender, the court, the family or the communities who facilitate reintegration and decide whether such reintegration has been successful or not?

There are issues about the degree of community interest in restorative justice programmes, both in terms of participation and outcomes. Particularly in more disorganized and transitory areas interest is likely to be particularly low, while restorative justice programmes with their emphasis on interpersonal relations tend to limit the involvement of the wider community.

246

In cases where reintegration in whatever form is not completed successfully the consequences are potentially disastrous. Given the powerful and destructive nature of shame and stigmatization those offenders who are not fully reintegrated are likely to be, according to Braithwaite, propelled into future offending and driven towards criminal subcultures. As we have seen, a significant percentage of offenders who engage in restorative justice programmes exhibit cynicism or indifference and are unlikely to be affected by shaming processes, except negatively. Even in the more successful cases very few offenders are likely to become reintegrated on every level with the consequence that there will be a significant individual or social deficit in many of the cases that are processed.

Shame and trust

The reintegrative shaming thesis presented by Braithwaite is based to some extent on a family model of social relations. Braithwaite frequently alludes to family dynamics in which sanctions are issued in the context of ongoing relations of love and respect. What Braithwaite fails to recognize is that even within these 'happy families' there are points of exclusion and rejection. It is also the case that there exist significant asymmetrical power relationships within the family and that those on the receiving end of sanctions are dependent on the care and resources of those issuing sanctions. Even in this context transgressions may be seen to be so frequent or so serious that the parents end up by rejecting and dismissing the children. By the same token, children who can no longer take the abuse or neglect of parents may lose respect for and be unwilling to forgive the parents for their behaviour.

This scenario raises important issues about the nature of social relations and particularly the role of shaming and forgiveness. If we explore the dynamics of contemporary family relations we find that it is trust that plays a more central role than shaming (London 2003). When either party in a relationship engages in some form of wrongdoing against the other the most usual response is not the mobilization of shame but a suspension of trust. That is, the trust that exists between parties is fractured and as a result the other is held at a certain distance and treated with caution. The more the wrongdoing occurs the greater the distance and the greater the caution with which they are treated. Apologies and expressions of remorse may ameliorate the situation but words are rarely in themselves sufficient to repair the damage. What is normally required is demonstrative change in behaviour and/or attitudes in order to regain trust. At the point where trust breaks down completely the relationship is likely to be severed.

If we extrapolate the logic of this observation and apply it to the wider more impersonal social world where social bonds are looser and relations of domination and subordination are more complex we can see the centrality of trust. We give trust to others as a precondition of social interaction, but this trust is always conditional. Indeed, we may see trust as the glue of social relations. As in the family setting relations of trust underpin basic social exchanges but where transgressions occur in situations of 'lightly engaged strangers' we have less reason to be forgiving and are more likely to want to place offenders at some distance from ourselves and to view them with some caution, unless persuaded otherwise. If it is the case that trust is a more central and fundamental element of social interaction and regulation than shaming then it would have implications for what is to be restored following a crime or a wrongdoing and by what mechanism this restoration is to be effected. If the aim is to bring the victim and offender together the reinstatement of trust may be a more appropriate objective than inflicting shame on offenders. Even so, the likelihood of repairing a fractured relationship in a brief orchestrated encounter is slight. If the re-establishment of trust is to be the objective it is unlikely to be achieved through a 'talking cure' in which the parties express their remorse or anger.

Interestingly, in Heather Strang's assessment of the impact of restorative justice programmes on victims, she notes that reference to trust recurred repeatedly in conference discussions:

> It was particularly salient for young offenders' parents, who frequently commented that the biggest harm they had experienced was the loss of trust, the feeling of being 'let down', and how much they regretted the loss of their former confidence in their children. The young offenders themselves recognized this cost as well. (Strang 2002: 104–5)

The loss of trust in some cases such as sexual assault was not only directed towards the offender but involved a more general loss of trust.

It is important to note that unlike the family model that Braithwaite likes to use as a point of reference, crime victims and offenders in a large percentage of cases have no pre-existing relationship. Not only are they strangers but in many cases the offender has little or no interest in the lives or personalities of their victims. Victims in many cases are selected fairly randomly and it is the accessibility and attractiveness of the target which motivates the offender not the personality of the victim (Sparks 1981). This has obvious implications for any approach that aims to be restorative, since in a significant percentage of cases there is no relationship to restore. Also, within the restorative justice literature there is a rather crude distinction between victims and offenders who are often presented as if they constitute two quite distinct groups. However, as criminologists are discovering there is a significant overlap between victims and offenders, with many of those who are victims today being offenders tomorrow and vice versa.

Many of those who are processed by the criminal justice system, of course, will already have a history of marginalization, rejection and stigmatization. In some cases they will have been in care, expelled from schools or come from broken homes. These individuals do not accord with the idealized model which Braithwaite presents that sees each transgression based on a one-off event occurring in a context of unconditional trust and love. People have biographies and reputations. To some extent these reputations are shaped by gossip which Braithwaite sees as a largely positive force since it mobilizes social shaming. But stigmatized shaming without reintegration is potentially damaging and destructive according to Braithwaite's distinction between stigmatizing and reintegrative shaming and, therefore, it should follow that gossip is an undesirable social practice.

By the time most offenders are processed through the criminal justice system and appear in court they already have a criminal record. Although they may still be part of a community network the levels of trust accorded to them by significant others may be relatively low. The logic of this social and interpersonal distancing has implications for Braithwaite's suggestion that we should treat each transgression as an act rather than essentialize the offender as a 'criminal' or a 'junkie'. This suggestion begs the question why we routinely move from seeing a transgression as an individual discrete act, or a series of acts, to seeing it as part of someone's character or personality. Clearly, in our daily lives we make rough and ready distinctions between those who offend sporadically and those cases where offending is seen as part of a master status. Interestingly those who engage in crime make similar distinctions. As Jack Katz (1991) demonstrated in his analysis of persistent robbers there is significant difference between a person who commits one or two robberies and those that do it persistently. In these cases the internalization of violence and engagement with risk-taking becomes more embedded in the personality of the offender and increasingly becomes the way in which they define themselves

(Matthews 2002). Similarly, research on prostitution has shown the difference in terms of identity between those who perform social services for money on a temporary basis and those who identify themselves as prostitutes (Pheonix 1999). Braithwaite conveniently blurs these distinctions and overlooks the ways in which identities are shaped, biographies are interpreted and offending behaviour is categorized. Thus to treat all transgressions as if they were one-off *acts* is myopic to say the least and, as we have seen in relation to police-led conferences, there is an overriding temptation to bring the offenders' previous history into view (Young 2001). Similarly Kathleen Daly (2001) reports that in family-based conferences one in three victims saw the offender as a bad person rather than as a good person who had committed a bad act.

In many ways the initial plausibility of the reintegrative shaming thesis rests on a number of false dichotomies. One dichotomy which Braithwaite mobilizes in order to make the thesis appear more credible and to provide a justification for the development of restorative justice is to counterpoise restorative justice to what he calls retributive justice. The characterization of the existing criminal justice system as essentially 'retributive' is used by Braithwaite and others to depict it as unnecessarily punitive, while presenting restorative justice as relatively benign. This unrealistic dichotomy not only overlooks the ways in which restorative justice can be more punitive than court processes but also how restorative, reparative and compensatory strategies are a regular feature of the existing criminal justice system. At the same time it is worth remembering that within the formal criminal justice system there already exists a number of ways in which forgiveness plays a role in the process. The demeanour and attitude of the defendant towards the victim, the willingness to admit guilt and claims that the transgression was out of character are routinely rewarded in courts with lighter sentences. Mitigation, the deferral and suspension of sentences and the offer of a 'second chance' are also regularly applied in the criminal justice system. Moreover, a significant percentage of cases do not make it to court and are dealt with informally by warnings, 'no further action' and the like. The attrition rate in the criminal justice system is such that only a very small percentage of cases that come to the attention of the police ever make it to court and even fewer are sent to prison. In England and Wales, for example, it is estimated that only 2 per cent of known offences result in a conviction while only one in 300 result in a prison sentence (Barclay and Tavaras 1999). Interestingly, Braithwaite, in his revision of the reintegrative shaming thesis, portrays the criminal justice and prison system not so much as opposites to be overcome, but rather as a necessary backup to restorative justice programmes, which he suggests should be mainly used for minor and first-time offenders (Braithwaite and Braithwaite 2001).

Looking at attrition rates reminds us not only that very few of those who commit crime are actually convicted and that most are dealt with informally, but also reminds us that the relation between formalism and informalism is rarely a zero sum option but a matter of degree. To a large extent the role of the criminal justice system is to provide a backdrop against which conflicts can be negotiated and resolved. Arguably, the importance of the criminal justice system is not so much a function of the cases which it actually processes but its role in providing a point of reference for the informal resolution of disputes. Indicatively, the majority of divorce and fraud cases are settled out of court and the formal system of adjudication creates a form of 'shadow justice' (Mnookin and Kornhouser 1979; Harrington 1985). Thus comparing restorative justice only to the formal dimensions of the criminal justice system is to present a one-sided and distorted account of the processes involved.

Guilt and shame

The concerns which have been expressed about the value of shaming in relation to wrongdoing raise the question of the relation between shame and guilt. Social historians tend to make a distinction between shame-based societies such as Japan and guilt-based societies such as those of Western Europe and America. The debate therefore about guilt and shame operates on at least two levels. On one level, it is tied to notions of interdependency and communitarianism and, on another level, to the emotional dynamics of conferences. Japan is repeatedly cited in Braithwaite's *Crime, Shame and Reintegration* (1989) as an exemplar of how shaming can operate in a communitarian culture to produce an effective system of regulation. Thus:

> It is argued that societies that have low rates of common types of crime (such as Japan) rely more on this type of social control, working hard at reforming the deviant through reconstructing his or her social ties. Conversely, high crime societies (such as the US) rely upon stigmatization, thus doing little to prevent cycles of reoffending. (Braithwaite and Mugford 1993: 140)

The Japanese, Braithwaite informs us, maintain shaming rituals and the main mechanisms of social control remain in the hands of significant others. Its unique historical development has meant that regulation is more informal and more pervasive than in the more individualistic societies of the West (Komiya 1999). The attractiveness of Japan for Braithwaite is that he sees it as providing confirmation of his belief that more communitarian societies with high levels of interdependency will have lower crime rates. While this was the case in the 1980s, during the 1990s, when crime rates were plummeting in many 'individualistic' western societies, the crime rate in Japan steadily increased (Blumstein and Wallman 2000). In his defence Braithwaite would no doubt argue that the reason for the increase in crime in Japan is a result of the breakdown of the traditional family and community structures and the growing number of outsiders, particularly in expanding urban centres. However, this does not account for the surprising downturn of crime in the UK and USA. There are considerable problems about uncritically comparing crime rates in Japan and elsewhere because of differences of classification and accounting. When assessing the role of communitarianism and interdependency in Japan, some commentators have pointed out that the Mafia in Japan act as an alternative enforcement agency alongside the police contributing to security and insecurity, while some acts which would be counted as crimes in other countries are seen as expressions of 'mental illness' in Japan (Leonardson 2001). Interestingly, after extolling the virtues of Japanese society, Braithwaite admits that: 'as much as I admire the crime control achievements in Japan I would not want to live there because I would find the informal pressures of conformity oppressive' (Braithwaite 1989: 158). The majority of the population in most advanced western societies would probably share Braithwaite's view.

The difference, it is claimed, between shame and guilt is that 'guilt is felt as an action one has undertaken or omitted, whereas shame is felt about the self as a whole' (Harris et al. 2004: 193). If it is the case that one is seeking to develop a mode of adjudication in which the aim is to respond to the act rather than to the whole self it would seem that eliciting guilt would be more appropriate than mobilizing shame. Others depict guilt as a mainly internal process, while shaming is seen to be generated externally (Harris 2003). Braithwaite sees guilt and shame as overlapping processes but fails to examine the powerful mechanisms at work in the manufacture of guilt and how this is linked historically to religious doctrines, particularly Christianity, and how it has, in turn, been incorporated within the criminal justice system.

The importance of guilt in the criminal justice system is that it has both a subjective and objective dimension. Guilt can be proven whereas shame can only be mobilized. It is obviously important in cases where offenders deny the charges brought against them that some agreement about the guilt and culpability can be established, while the subjective experience of guilt is able to work whether formal guilt is established or not. The effects of guilt can come to the fore whether the case is proven or not, or indeed if anyone else knows whether a wrongdoing has occurred, and therefore it is arguably a more pervasive and powerful emotion than shaming. It has also been suggested that whereas guilt is more frequently linked to empathy and reparation, which are both among the main objectives of restorative justice programmes, shame can often provoke feelings of defensiveness, anger and rejection (van Stokkom 2004).

Social psychologists claim that when shame is not counterbalanced by pride or social support the person experiencing shame 'feels weak, inattentive, defective, lacking in control, degraded and exposed' (van Stokkom 2004: 342). This is not the ideal state for anyone being sanctioned, while the forms of reintegration which are offered to offenders are unlikely to undo these emotions. Shaming can also generate anger and resentment and, whatever the formalities of the restorative justice hearing, these emotions are likely to carry on some time after the event (Scheff and Retzinger 1991).

It is not difficult to mobilize shaming sanctions in late modern societies and in recent years we have seen evidence of such developments (Pratt 2000). The question which arises, however, is what is the effect of mobilizing a range of shaming sanctions in western guilt-based cultures? The most likely result, according to Tangney, is 'interminable rumination and self-castigation' (Tangney 1995: 1142). As van Stokkom (2004: 348) concludes in his review of the literature on guilt and shame: 'While guilt induction triggers responsibility, shame induction is destructive. This suggests that it might be far better for offenders to feel guilt rather than shame.'

When we begin to explore the emotional dynamics of both interpersonal relations and the emotions of court processes and conference programmes we find that we begin to encounter a series of familiar everyday terms such as guilt, trust, respect, dignity and embarrassment, which, while critical to the analysis, remain undertheorized. These meta-concepts provide the conceptual scaffold on which our understanding of interpersonal dynamics takes place and are clearly pertinent to any understanding of the likely effects of those forms of adjudication, which are designed to be restorative. While there has been some useful discussion of guilt and shame in the restorative justice literature it remains the case that many of the other key terms are poorly understood.

Recidivism

There is a growing chorus of liberal humanists who believe that society is becoming increasingly punitive and that part of the mission of restorative justice is to promote a more moderate and more compassionate response to offending (Matthews 2005). In this climate there is a serious danger that the justifications for restorative justice rest on these liberal humanistic concerns and that this in turn will descend into a form of moralizing. Braithwaite himself, although occasionally joining in with the calls for lighter sentences, avoids descending into pure moralizing by linking the reintegrative thesis to a crime reduction strategy. His argument is that the educational effect of restorative justice programmes with their emphasis on forgiveness and inclusion avoid the danger of propelling offenders into more serious crime. Consequently, one of the strengths of the reintegrative shaming thesis lies with its claim to reform offenders. A standard measure for the process of reform is recidivism.

While the measures of recidivism are lacking in conceptual or empirical certainty, they remain important social yardsticks since they aim to measure the effectiveness of different sanctions. A number of critics have noted that in relation to recidivism the results of restorative justice programmes are at best mixed and at worst disappointing. Lawrence Sherman (2001), for example, compared reoffending rates for four separate samples of offenders – young violent offenders under the age of thirty years, drink-driving offenders, juvenile property offenders where there was a personal victim and juvenile shoplifters. He found that while there were significantly lower rates for the young violent offenders than the court sample, differences were slight or insignificant for the other three groups. A recent study in Iceland, which is organized along communitarian lines, and which relies heavily on informal shaming as a means of social control, found that while the crime rate is relatively low, the rates of recidivism are not significantly different from those found in other countries. The implication of this finding is that the social forces which govern crime rates are not the same ones that drive recidivism rates (Baumer *et al.* 2002).

Despite the claims that restorative justice based on reintegrative shaming techniques would reduce reoffending, the results, to date, are far from convincing. Where restorative justice programmes have targeted young minor offenders one would expect a relatively low level of recidivism, but the contention that more serious offenders are going to be 'reformed' in a two- or three-hour conference is unrealistic. The only aspect of offending which is addressed in these sessions is empathy for others but this in itself is unlikely to have much effect even among minor offenders. Thus:

> As currently implemented, most restorative justice programs fail to incorporate the principles of effective intervention, particularly as they relate to risk, need and responsivity principles. In restorative justice the primary criterion for matching sanctions to offenders is the nature and extent of the harm caused by crime. The seriousness of the offence, however, is not consistently related to the offender's risk of recidivism. Thus restorative justice programs run the dual risks of producing an interaction effect in low-risk offenders and of underservicing high-risk offenders. (Levrant *et al.* 1999: 19)

The inability to develop effective programmes which will significantly reduce levels of reoffending among different groups of offenders stems in part from a rejection of rehabilitative measures on the one hand, and of identifying offenders primarily in relation to the offence for which they have been caught on the other. As an object of reintegrative shaming the impact and experience of offenders will invariably be mixed and uncertain. Consequently, behaviour will be changed in relatively few cases and individuals and communities will continue to suffer from the effects of the criminal behaviour of repeat offenders. Thus restorative justice is unlikely to make much impact on the level of crime or the rates of reoffending, particularly among more experienced and persistent offenders.

Although there are significant methodological issues about comparing the populations dealt with by courts and those dealt with by conferences, it would seem that the educational and shaming effect of conferences is much less effective in changing behaviour than Braithwaite predicted. This may be for a number of reasons. Either the external conditions that are conducive to recidivism are relatively impervious to different modes of adjudication or another less welcome explanation may be that restorative justice programmes do not have the educational and shaming effects which Braithwaite outlines. Indeed, they may not affect offenders in the ways expected. They may in fact create more cynicism, more alienation or more commitment to offending as a result of what might be perceived as receiving little more than a 'telling off' for engaging in crime.

Conclusion

It has been argued that the problems currently confronting restorative justice programmes are not so much a function of problems of implementation or organization but stem more or less directly from the theoretical base on which they rest. Abolitionism and faith-based criminology are largely removed from *Realpolitik* and do not possess the type of reflexivity and awareness of the changing nature of the state and governmentality to allow a full appreciation of the role and significance of restorative justice in late modernity (Rose 2000). As largely oppositional and anti-statist approaches, developing an understanding of the changing nature of the state and modes of adjudication is largely beyond their remit. The reintegrative shaming thesis, by providing a rationale for focusing on shaming and reintegration, provided an important rationale for the development of the new modes of informal justice which emerged in the 1990s and centred around different forms of conferencing. This new generation of informal justice, however, has run into similar problems as its predecessors experienced during the previous decade (Matthews 1988). The promise of the development of an alternative and competing mode of adjudication is fading as restorative justice practices are becoming increasingly absorbed within a more pluralistic criminal justice system whose range and depth has expanded (Santos 1987).

If we look at the evidence of various evaluations of restorative justice in its various forms, the most benign reading that we could put on it is that the results are mixed. Given that much of the earlier research on restorative justice was carried out by those who were generally sympathetic to this approach, the research has suffered from significant selection bias. There are also major methodological problems in comparing the courts and conferences given the individualized nature of law and justice in contemporary society. But even if advocates can take some comfort from some of these studies, there remains a dark side to restorative justice programmes and it is apparent that beneath the veneer of benign humanism there are other more sinister and disturbing processes at work. Besides the erosion of rights and welfare, the blurring of criminal and civil process, the responsibilization of citizens and the re-mobilization of risky shaming sanctions, there are also tendencies to provide a form of 'cheap justice' which fails to properly protect the weaker and poorer victims on the one hand while giving some of the more powerful and serious offenders little more than a 'slap on the wrist' on the other. The production of what appear to many observers as chaotic and arbitrary sanctions is allowed to stand partly because of the relatively low level of public involvement and accountability.

John Braithwaite provides an imaginative attempt to place restorative justice on a solid theoretical and political foundation. However, rather than distancing himself from abolitionism, faith-based criminology and versions of liberal humanism, he manages in his attempt to incorporate these positions into his grand scheme to produce a rather disjointed theory which, while carrying the trappings of these other theories, attempts to build his position on the notion of reintegrative shaming. The distinction, however, between stigmatizing and reintegrative shaming proves on closer inspection to be untenable and consequently it drifts towards a moralizing approach which falls back on pleas for more ostensibly benign and humane forms of punishment. Without convincing evidence that such strategies will reduce the level of recidivism he joins hands with the faith-based approaches which call for more forgiveness and compassion. But unlike them he does not seem to fully realize that the effective exercise of absolution is premised upon the mobilization of the threat or implementation of the most severe, exclusionary and draconian forms of punishment in a context of absolute power.

The marriage of the reintegrative shaming thesis and restorative justice practices is on the rocks. This is not the time and place, however, to apportion blame or to make judgments about whether the failure of the marriage has mainly been a function of the conceptual inadequacies of the reintegrative shaming thesis or the deficiencies in the implementation of restorative justice programmes. Both parties must carry a degree of responsibility. However, it is clear that no amount of mediation and counselling is going to overcome these problems. It might be time to start thinking about negotiating a divorce.

References

Ashworth, A. (2001) 'Is restorative justice the way forward for criminal justice?', *Current Legal Problems*, 54: 347–76.

Barclay, G. and Tavaras, C. (1999) *Digest: Information on the Criminal Justice System in England and Wales*. London: Home Office.

Baumer, E., Wright, R., Kristinsdottir, K. and Gunnlaugsson, H. (2002) 'Crime, shame and recidivism', *British Journal of Criminology*, 41: 40–59.

Blagg, H. (1997) 'A just measure of shame? Aboriginal youth and conferencing in Australia', *British Journal of Criminology*, 37: 481–501.

Blagg, H. (2001) 'Aboriginal youth and restorative justice: critical notes from the Australian frontier', in A. Morris and G. Maxwell (eds), *Restorative Justice for Juveniles*. Portland, OR: Hart Publishing, pp. 227–42.

Blumstein, A. and Wallman J. (2000) *The Crime Drop in America*. New York: Cambridge University Press.

Braithwaite, J. (1989) *Crime, Shame and Reintegration.* New York: Cambridge University Press.

Braithwaite, J. (1993) 'Shame and modernity', *British Journal of Criminology,* 33 (1): 1–18.

Braithwaite, J. (1997) 'Conferencing and plurality: reply to Blagg', *British Journal of Criminology,* 37 (4): 502–9.

Braithwaite, J. and Braithwaite, V. (2001) 'Revising the theory of reintegrative shaming', in E. Ahmed, N. Harris, J. Braithwaite and V. Braithwaite (eds), *Shame Management Through Reintegration.* New York: Cambridge University Press, pp. 39–57.

Braithwaite, J. and Mugford, S. (1993) 'Conditions of successful reintegration ceremonies', *British Journal of Criminology,* 34 (2): 139–71.

Braithwaite, J. and Pettit, P. (1990) *Not Just Deserts.* Oxford: Clarendon Press.

Christie, N. (1982) *Limits to Pain.* Oxford: Martin Robertson.

Cohen, S. (1985) *Visions of Social Control.* Cambridge: Polity Press.

Crawford, A. and Clear T. (2001) 'Community justice: transforming communities through restorative justice?', in G. Bazemore and M. Schiff (eds), *Restorative Community Justice.* Cincinnati, OH: Anderson Publishing, pp. 127–49.

Daly, K. (2001) 'Conferencing in Australia and New Zealand: variations, research findings and prospects', in A. Morris and G. Maxwell (eds), *Restorative Justice for Juveniles.* Portland, OR: Hart Publishing, pp. 59–84.

Daly, K. (2002) 'Restorative justice: the real story', *Punishment and Society,* 4(1): 55–79.

Harrington, C. (1985) *Shadow Justice? The Ideology and Institutionalisation of Alternatives to Court.* Westport, CT and London: Greenwood Press.

Harris, N. (2003) 'Reassessing the dimensionality of the moral emotions', *British Journal of Psychology,* 94: 457–73.

Harris, N., Walgrave, L. and Braithwaite, J. (2004) 'Emotional dynamics in restorative conferences', *Theoretical Criminology,* 8(2): 191–210.

Hulsman, L. (1986) 'Critical criminology and the concept of crime', *Contemporary Crisis,* 10(1): 63–80.

Johnstone, G. (1999) 'Restorative justice, shame and forgiveness', *Liverpool Law Review,* 21(2–3): 197–216.

Johnstone, G. (2002) *Restorative Justice: Ideas, Values Debates.* Cullompton: Willan.

Karp, D., Sweet, M., Kirshenbaum, A. and Bazemore, G. (2004) 'Reluctant participants in restorative justice? Youthful offenders and their parents', *Contemporary Justice Review,* 7(2): 199–216.

Katz, J. (1991) 'The motivation of persistent robbers', in M. Tonry (ed.) *Crime and Justice,* 14. Chicago, IL: University of Chicago Press, pp. 277–306.

Komiya, N. (1999) 'A cultural study of the low crime rate in Japan', *British Journal of Criminology,* 39(3): 369–89.

Leonardson, D. (2001) 'The impossible case of Japan', *Australian and New Zealand Journal of Criminology,* 35(2): 203–29.

Levi, M. (2002) 'Suite justice or sweet charity?', *Punishment and Society,* 4(2): 147–63.

Levrant, S., Cullen, F., Fulton, B. and Wozniak, J. (1999) 'Reconsidering restorative justice: the corruption of benevolence revisited?', *Crime and Delinquency*, 45(1): 3–27.

London, R. (2003) 'The restoration of trust: bringing restorative justice from the margins to the mainstream', *Criminal Justice Studies*, 16(3): 175–95.

Matthews, R. (ed.) (1988) *Informal Justice?* London: Sage.

Matthews, R. (2002) *Armed Robbery*. Cullompton: Willan.

Matthews, R. (2005) 'The myth of punitiveness', *Theoretical Criminology*, 9(2): 175–202.

Mauer, M. (1999) *Race to Incarcerate*. New York: Sentencing Project.

Mnookin, R. and Kornhauser, L. (1979) 'Bargaining in the shadow of the law', *Yale Law Journal*, 88: 950–97.

Morris, A. (2001) 'Revisiting reintegrative shaming', *Criminology Aotearoa/New Zealand*, No. 16. Institute of Criminology, Victoria University of Wellington, 10–12.

Morris, A. (2002) 'Critiquing the critiques: a brief response to critics of restorative justice', *British Journal of Criminology*, 42: 596–615.

O'Mahoney, D. and Doak, J. (2004) 'Restorative justice – is more better? The experience of police-led restorative cautioning pilots in Northern Ireland', *Howard Journal*, 43(5): 484–505.

Pepinsky, H. and Quinney, R. (1991) *Criminology as Peace-Making*. Bloomington, IN: Indiana University Press.

Pheonix, J. (1999) *Making Sense of Prostitution*. Basingstoke: Macmillan.

Polk, K. (1994) 'Family conferencing: theoretical and evaluative concerns', in C. Adler and J. Wundersitz (eds), *Family Conferencing and Juvenile Justice*. Canberra: Australian Institute of Criminology, pp. 123–40.

Pratt, J. (2000) 'Emotive and ostentatious punishment: its decline and resurgence in modern society', *Punishment and Society*, 2(4): 417–39.

Roche, D. (2003) *Accountability in Restorative Justice*. Oxford: Clarendon.

Rose, N. (2000) 'Government and control', *British Journal of Criminology*, 40: 321–39.

Santos, B. (1987) 'Law: a map of misreading. Toward a postmodern conception of law', *Journal of Law and Society*, 14(3): 279–302.

Scheff, T. and Retzinger, S. (1991) *Emotions and Violence: Shame and Rage in Destructive Conflicts*. Lexington, MA: Lexington Books.

Sherman, L. (2001) 'Two Protestant ethics and the spirit of restoration', in H. Strang and J. Braithwaite (eds), *Restorative Justice and Civil Society*. Cambridge: Cambridge University Press, pp. 35–55.

Sparks, R. (1981) 'Multiple victimisation: evidence, theory and future research', *Journal of Criminal Law and Criminology*, 72: 762–78.

Strang, H. (2002) *Repair or Revenge: Victims and Restorative Justice*. Oxford: Clarendon.

Tangney, J. (1995) 'Recent advances in the empirical study of shame and guilt', *American Behavioral Scientist*, 38(8): 1132–45.

Tonry, M. (1995) *Malign Neglect: Race Crime and Punishment in America*. New York: Oxford University Press.

Van Stokkom B. (2002) 'Moral emotions in restorative justice conferences: managing shame, designing empathy', *Theoretical Criminology*, 6(3): 339–60.

Young, R. (2001) 'Just cops doing "shameful" business? Police-led restorative justice and the lessons of research', in A. Morris and G. Maxwell (eds), *Restorative Justice for Juveniles*. Portland, OR: Hart Publishing, pp. 195–226.

Young, R. and Hoyle, C. (2003) 'Restorative justice and punishment', in S. McConville (ed.) *The Use of Punishment*. Cullompton: Willan, pp. 199–234.

Whitman, J. (1998) 'What is wrong with shame sanctions?', *Yale Law Journal*, 107: 1055–92.

Chapter 12

Balancing the ethical and the political: normative reflections on the institutionalization of restorative justice

Barbara Hudson

Introduction

Restorative justice is conceived both as a 'replacement discourse', decentring punishment of offenders as the focus of criminal justice processes and emphasizing instead reparation to victims and reintegration of offenders into their communities, and as a new resource for existing penal modes. It has been developed as a mode of penality with adherence to an ethic of restoration rather than retribution. As it has developed in policy and practice, restorative justice has become attractive to policy-makers in a multiplicity of jurisdictions as a new form of holding offenders to account, with potential for effectiveness in reducing reoffending as well as recompensing victims. It has become institutionalized in criminal justice to a degree that seemed unlikely twenty years ago.

As restorative justice processes have proliferated, criminal justice in western countries has undergone other changes, most notably giving a new primacy to 'risk management' rather than 'doing justice'. I will begin this chapter with some reflections on 'risk' in criminal justice, highlighting some developments which seem to me to have been particularly important in recent years, and then move on to considerations of what these developments in penal policy might mean for the institutionalization of restorative justice. In particular, I am concerned with the implications of institutionalizing restorative justice in the current penal environment for the aspirations of restorative justice to be a replacement discourse, inspired at least in part by the ideals of European abolitionists such as Christie (1982) and Hulsman (1986).

It is clear that in the 1990s, continuing into the 2000s, 'something happened' to the place and meaning of risk in criminal justice and to the place and meaning of restorative justice in criminal justice. Risk appeared as a more dominant theme in criminal justice policy and practice, but I will argue that what really happened was a change in the meaning of risk. Restorative justice also appears to have become more prominent, moving from the periphery to the centre of criminal justice: does this entail a change of meaning from replacement ideal to a new step on the penal ladder?

Obviously, as an English person my idea of 'what happened' is largely coloured by what happened in the UK (actually, by what happened in England and Wales). My perception of the extent to which what happened in England and Wales reflects international trends is in turn coloured overmuch by what happened in other English-speaking countries, notably the USA, Canada and Australia. Like other UK academics and, even more, penal policy-makers, my thinking is over-dominated by the USA. In many ways penal policy in the UK shares more with the USA than with Europe, a fact which I deplore. But I am also aware that the toughening of criminal justice, the expansion of penal policy and contraction of social policy, and the declining feelings of solidarity between different social groups that manifest themselves in Anglo-Saxon criminal justice practice have affected countries in Western Europe that have traditionally been among the most liberal and tolerant, such as the Netherlands and some of the Scandinavian nations. So I am confident that the trends I will mention affect all our countries to a greater or lesser extent.

Commentators on law and justice have continually pointed out the tension between the political and the ideal. Packer (1969) gives us his models of crime control and due process; Habermas (1996) analyses law's position of being 'between facts and norms', between social reality and ideals, while Derrida (2001) says that processes and institutions of justice must always incorporate a political moment and an ethical moment. I want to address three themes that illustrate important normative aspects of contemporary penality, and which exemplify these perennial tensions between facts and norms, between the politics and the aspirations of criminal justice. These three themes are:

- a move from risk management to risk control;
- the persistence of the white, male standpoint in law;
- the decline of 'community'.

These three issues all have implications for the institutionalization of restorative justice and the later sections of the chapter explore these implications, focusing on the ideal moment of restorative justice as a replacement discourse and the political moment of accommodation to existing penal rationales.

Risk management and risk control

In my recent work on risk and criminal justice (Hudson 2003) I have drawn on Clear and Cadora's distinction between risk management and risk control (Clear and Cadora 2001). Penal policy has not recently invented or adopted 'risk' as a penal goal: 'risk' is its *raison d'être*; penal policy is always targeted at the risk of crime. Rather, as Clear and Cadora point out, what happened in the last decades of the twentieth century was that risk management gave way to risk control.

Risk management means that the risk of crime is accepted as inevitable, but criminal justice policies and practices endeavour to reduce risks by good rehabilitative programmes and by good assessment to inform decision-making about custodial or community sentences, early release, extent of post-release supervision, etc. Risk management allows for the balancing of risks to potential victims with the rights of offenders to be free from unjustified restriction of liberty. Risk management accepts that there will be failures; so the inevitable failures will not lead to changes in policy. Risk control means the elimination of risk; the strategy of risk control is that of controlling offenders' lives to such a degree that they have no possibility of committing a further offence. Risk control policy means that no chances will be taken by releasing offenders, or by giving them freedom of movement if they are returned to the community or sanctioned within the community. Risk control politics means that any failure (i.e. reoffending) leads to calls for the tightening up of policies, and it means that such calls will probably be responded to positively by policy-makers.

The cases of Polly Klaas and Megan Kanka in the USA led to changes in parole regulations and the introduction of notification laws for sex offenders; in England the case of Sarah Payne produced calls for the introduction of public notification arrangements similar to those of Megan's law.[1] In the event, UK notification laws are not as extensive as in the USA (there is no public right to information on the location of a sex offender in a community), but the case has played a considerable part in the current proposals for previous convictions to be disclosed to juries, not just to be considered post-conviction in deciding sentences.[2] In these three cases, failure to keep the perpetrator in prison or under very strict control on release was seen as something that must not possibly be allowed to occur again. The responses to the cases show the policy of risk control, rather than risk management, in operation.

In a previous era, an equally notorious 'failure' of risk management led to public outcry, but not to the introduction of new laws or substantially changed procedures. Graham Young, described as the 'almost compulsive' poisoner (Walker 1985: 385), killed again on his release in 1971 after serving 9 years of a 15-year tariff term in Broadmoor, the English hospital/prison for mentally disordered criminals, imposed for killing members of his family. Not only had Young been released, he had been given the task of making the tea in his post-release job. In a short spell after release he poisoned 70 colleagues, although only one poisoning was fatal. Although opprobrium was heaped on those responsible for the decision to release him and for those planning his post-release life, the policy response was to try to improve risk management by improving assessment procedures rather than a turn to risk control by removing the possibility of release in such cases.[3] Although Young's victims were not young girls as in the Klaas, Kanka and Payne cases, it is highly unlikely that a similar case today would not be followed by calls for the ending of any early release of Broadmoor prisoners.

Less sensationally, but affecting a greater number of offenders, the move from risk management to risk control is demonstrated by changing approaches to persistent but non-dangerous offenders. Throughout the 1970s and 1980s, there was professional and policy consensus that non-violent offenders (except in particularly serious cases) should be dealt with by community penalties rather than imprisonment. Throughout Europe as well as the English-speaking world, the 'bifurcation' or 'twin-tracking' approach was dominant, with imprisonment for serious and violent offences, and more robust, constructive community penalties for non-violent offences. Although non-violent offenders did continue to be sent to prison (especially female offenders – see, for instance, Carlen 1999), there was a general decrease in the proportions of non-violent offenders in prison populations. Where proportions of non-violent offenders in prison populations remained significant, this was regarded as a focus for criticism. The non-politically partisan breadth of consensus on this is exemplified by Douglas Hurd, Conservative Home Secretary in the lead-in to the 1991 Criminal Justice Act which inscribed this bifurcation principle into England and Wales legislation. Hurd thought that prison was an expensive resource which tended to make 'bad people worse' and should be reserved for those who posed a serious, proximate risk of physical harm to the public if not incarcerated.

From about the mid-1990s, however, the distinction between violent and non-violent offenders and persistent and dangerous offenders was blurred – in England and Wales but also in other countries. While attitudes to dangerous offenders and to mentally disordered offenders more broadly emphasized risk control at the expense of patient/ offenders' rights, policies towards non-violent, non-dangerous persistent offenders also exhibited the logic of risk control. The metaphor of the 'revolving door' has often been invoked to demonstrate the futility of sentencing persistent offenders to short prison terms. In the 1970s and 1980s the consensus was that the door should stop revolving with persistent non-serious offenders on the outside; in the later 1990s and into the 2000s, it seems that the door should stop revolving with the non-violent but persistent offender on the inside. The twin-tracking of the early 1990s has given way to a merging of tracks so that offenders can be given sentences higher than proportionate to the current offence either because of assessments as dangerous or of possessing risk-of-reoffending characteristics, even if the offending risked is non-violent.

What I – following Clear and Cadora – am characterizing as a move from risk management to risk control is very close to what other commentators describe as a move from risk to precaution (Haggerty 2003). Haggerty's description of the risk logic is similar to Clear and Cadora's logic of risk management: the risked event is accepted as inevitable – its incidence and consequences can be minimized but not eliminated. His description of precaution is a logic which is tinged with emotion and apprehension as well as actuarial knowledge. Under precautionary logic, the risked event must on no account be allowed to happen, and the most far-reaching precautions are set in place to make sure it does not occur. While this precautionary logic is most clearly evident in measures to prevent terrorist attacks, Haggerty argues that it is becoming more general in crime control.

It is easy to demonstrate the penal rhetoric of risk control, but the sociological question is, of course, why risk management has been displaced by risk control and why this happened when it did. Analysts such as David Garland, Pat O'Malley and Jonathan Simon among others have examined its possible causes and its social effects (Garland 2000, 2001; O'Malley 2001; Simon 2001) and their arguments are too well-known to need repetition here. For explanation of the causes, I take elements of all of these authors: the importance of neoliberal economic policies and neoconservative social policies; the 'normalcy' of high crime rates; the emergence of new control technologies (such as electronically monitored curfews) and techniques (psychometric risk assessment); and the deeper analyses of the conditions of late modernity provided by Beck (1992), Giddens (1990) and Bauman (1989, 1991).

The persistence of the white, male perspective in law

European and other western democracies express strong commitment to equality. One manifestation of this commitment is that western countries now take far more seriously than hitherto the complaints of women and minority groups about the deficiencies of criminal law: the failure to secure convictions in rape cases; the failure to prosecute racial attacks and racial harassment; the failure to take adequate account of violence and threat of violence in cases of female killings of abusive partners. Ironically, it is in recognizing and attempting to respond more constructively and robustly to harms against women and minority citizens that the dependence of law on the subjectivity of the white, dominant male is most clearly revealed.

Our countries are concerned about the low rate of convictions in rape cases. Commissions, inquiries, improvements in police procedures, all kinds of innovations have been introduced, but the conviction rate remains low. Improvements in police responses to complainants, with specially trained police working in 'rape suites' which offer more comforting and comfortable environments than the traditional police interview room, as well as increased feminist consciousness that has developed over the last decades, have produced increases in reporting of rape, but these increases have not been matched by corresponding increases in convictions. Indeed, the latest UK research, commissioned by the Home Office, finds that the conviction rate has fallen to an all-time low of 5.6 per cent of reported cases in 2002, compared to a rate of 32 per cent in 1977 (Kelly *et al.* 2005). This lack of correspondence between increases in reporting rates and increases in convictions has, say the researchers, turned the justice 'gap' into a justice 'chasm'. Securing convictions in rape cases is bound to be difficult – these offences are committed out of sight and therefore there are unlikely to be eyewitnesses, and evidence is difficult to obtain. Proposals which might make convictions more likely (such as evidence of previous convictions as is now proposed in England and Wales) are problematic in terms of due process and troubling to those of us who continue to care about defendants' rights. The recommendations of this latest research include, instead, more vigorous case-building, through cooperation between police and prosecutors, making sure that all possible evidence is obtained and drawing on expert witnesses and victim support groups as well as the usual range of witnesses and evidence.

The root of difficulties in securing rape convictions is the way in which the offence of rape is constructed and conceptualized. At root, the idea of rape depends on the traditional gender stereotype of it being woman's role to manage male sexuality. Male sexuality is revealed as predatory, always ready for action, disruptive and disturbing. It is woman's task to control male sexuality, making clear that consent is present or absent, that saying yes once does not mean yes for any occasion, that by her appearance, lifestyle or relationship with the defendant she does not give out 'mixed signals'. Even with advances in thinking about women's roles in society and their rights to sexual independence, rethinking consent and emphasizing violence have not made it any easier for women successfully to obtain rape convictions other than in stereotypical 'stranger danger' cases (Lea *et al.* 2003). This powerful stereotype of 'real rape' means that cases demonstrating the 'realities of rape', in which perpetrators are likely to be known to the victims or the rape takes place within potentially sexual encounters (drinking in bars, for example), are invalidated and go unreported and unprosecuted (Kelly 2001).

Sympathy with abused women has made our judges and legal scholars troubled about the sentencing of abused women who kill their partners. Some progress has been made in western countries, mainly in admitting a wider range of expert witnesses into court proceedings (O'Donovan 1993). The Lavallee case in Canada was a landmark case in that the Canadian Supreme Court acknowledged that without the help of feminists working with abused women, courts could not understand the perspective of the 'battered woman' (Valverde 1996). The Supreme Court judgment describes the paradigm case of self-defence as a one-off, unpremeditated bar-room brawl between two men of more or less equal size (Martin *et al.* 1991). It also recognized that understandings of provocation and reasonable behaviour are also based on male behaviour patterns. In the UK, women are still receiving life sentences for killing partners after years of abuse, while men receive short custodial sentences or non-custodial sentences for killing when they discover their partners' infidelity or 'lose control' in response to nagging. The continued success of the 'nagging and shagging' defence clearly demonstrates the dependency of ideas of provocation and reasonable behaviour on the male perspective (Cooke 2001).

The Lavallee case marks perhaps the first judicial recognition of the 'maleness of law', a view of law hitherto associated almost only with feminist academics and lawyers (MacKinnon 1989; Naffine 1990 *inter alia*). The use to which the wider range of expert evidence is put is illustrative. Most judges would say that they need the evidence to help them understand so-called 'battered woman syndrome', the effect of long-term abuse which makes them feel powerless to leave, helpless to resist and so eligible for the mitigation of 'diminished responsibility'. This fits the well-established situation that any 'lenience' to women comes at the price of being seen as less rational, less reasonable, than males. Feminist critics and legal thinkers talk past each other. The lawyers are sympathetic, but point out that, after all, it is murder; the feminists focus on the abuse and oppression that preceded the killing.

In spite of declared commitment to racial/ethnic equality, minorities continue to be over-represented in prison populations, and black and Asian people are proportionately more frequently stopped by police than white citizens (Phillips and Bowling 2002). At the same time, minority communities continue to feel under-protected by law. Like sexualized/partner violence, taking racial attacks and harassment more seriously seems to have resulted in more reporting and more recording of incidents, but not in correspondingly more convictions. In the UK as elsewhere, there have been debates about whether there should be specific 'hate crime' legislation to deal with racially motivated crimes, or whether racial motivation should lead to an increased penalty for an 'ordinary' offence (Hamm 1993; Bjorgo and Witte 1993). Whether offences are 'really' racially motivated remains confused and contested, and minority ethnic groups remain dissatisfied with responses by police and the criminal justice system.

Investigation of the police response to the murder of Stephen Lawrence in England exposed the 'institutional racism' of law enforcement and criminal justice agencies, highlighting the tendency of police to regard African-Caribbeans as troublemakers rather than victims (Macpherson 1999). Other European countries have similar cases, and it is by no means only in England that minority persons fit more easily into the construction of the ideal suspect than the ideal victim (Christie 1986).

Michael Tonry (1995) demonstrated the impact of 'war on crime' and risk-oriented policies on black Americans. He said that while the outcome of mass imprisonment of black Americans was not intended, it was predictable. While not leading to mass imprisonment on the US scale, the risk control, war on crime, toughening up of asylum rules and other precautionary policies adopted in the UK and elsewhere in Europe are clearly discriminatory. The so called 'static' risk indicators (educational attainments, work record, contact with the criminal justice system as a juvenile, etc.) in risk-of-reoffending assessments are clearly racially correlated in racially stratified societies (Morris 1994).

The 'dynamic' risk factors in the new generation of risk assessments – attitudes to offending, attitudes to supervision, family and associates, personality traits etc. – are assumed by government departments who introduce them to be racially/ethnically neutral, but research suggests that they too are racially/ethnically correlated (Hudson and Bramhall 2005). Assessments of offenders reflect public stereotypes of different ethnic groups and demonstrate that the 'penal norm' continues to be the white male.

Decline of community

Thinking about the term 'community', it becomes immediately obvious that there is a big gap between the criminal justice literature and sociology/criminology which draws on wider social theory. The criminal justice literature positions restorative justice as a strategy which alongside community policing and community crime prevention makes up a programme of community safety and community justice (Clear and Karp 1999). Community governance of crime and public safety has been one of the dominant themes of the politics and policies of law and order in the 1990s (Crawford 1997).

The meaning of 'community' in criminal justice writing is elusive. Community is both goal (it is something to be created, for example safer community) and resource (communities provide resources for education, employment and other facilities supporting reduction of reoffending); it is a unity (*the* community) and it is fragmented (ethnic communities, religious communities). While penal policies tend to use phrases which imply a unified community, critics of crime control strategies not uncommonly point out that, in reality, policies are driven by particular communities, usually the business community (Crawford 1998). Even when the word 'communities' is substituted for 'community', the meaning remains unclear and shifting. Nonetheless, 'community' is one of the most prominent themes in recent criminal justice policy and politics.

On the other hand, contemporary social theory argues that late-modern societies are no longer communities. The citizens of late modernity, it is argued, no longer believe in 'society' as an inclusive, diverse community (Rose 1996). As late-modern persons, we engage in personal strategies of 'private prudentialism' (O'Malley 1992) and defensive individualism; our penal policies are derived more from criminologies of the 'other' than criminologies of the 'self' (Garland 2001), and our engagement with our societies is defined by fear and hostility towards strangers. This combination of defensive individualism, instrumentality in associations, hostility to outsiders and intense, selective loyalties has been described as 'new tribalism' (Maffesoli 1996). Rather than the inclusivity of 'society' with the ideal of accommodation of heterogeneous groups, we restrict our self-chosen and self-defined 'community' to ever-narrowing circles of people who look like ourselves and who behave like ourselves.

Decline of community is evident in the way in which western democracies tend to talk about crime and criminals. The widely used metaphor 'war on crime' itself implies that criminals are external to the community – the enemy within society but outwith community. Criminals are represented as monsters, as creatures 'whose features are essentially different from ours and shocking to the well-behaved' (Melossi 2000: 311). They are entirely different from us, their actions are 'impossible to imagine oneself doing, on the edge of human comprehension and sympathy' (Young 1999: 114). The 'monster' framework is no longer restricted to extreme, rare, outrageous and incomprehensible cases such as the Belgian Dutroux, the German Internet-arranged cannibalistic murder case, or to terrorists such as those in Beslan or those beheading captives in Iraq. 'Monstruum' is also applied to young people committing burglaries and robberies and perpetrators of other routine offences. Dehumanizing labels such as super-predator, rat-boy and other such epithets indicate the monstruum designation. In the UK, the vogue term at the time of writing seems to be 'feral' children. Feral describes beasts who threaten our communities, not fellow-members.

The communitarian rhetoric which underlies so much recent criminal justice politics incorporates elements of the monstruum mentality: people who do not recognize the community's moral rules are not recognized as fellow-citizens deserving of rights and social inclusion. Rights entail responsibilities is the mantra *du jour*, and those who behave irresponsibly are said not to deserve the protection of rights. Communities, it is argued, have rights to protect themselves and be protected against the irresponsible, the evil and the feral: by neighbourhood watch, by zero-tolerance policing, by Anti-Social Behaviour Orders (ASBOs), by preventive incarceration and by divided, gated communities.

Jonathan Simon (2001) has argued that the contrast between the more inclusionary, constructive punishments used for some kinds of offenders and the exclusionary, 'life-trashing' regimes used for others can best be understood by noticing that the toughest war on crime tactics are used against groups that the citizens of our constricted, separated communities 'fear and loath'. Drive-by shootings and crack cocaine are

Simon's prime examples; we can also add the recent criminalization of activities associated with asylum seekers and the aggressive policing of Muslims in the UK and much of western Europe. What we see is crime control and penal policies which reflect the divisions and apprehensions of the times. Rehabilitative, inclusive policies aimed to reintegrate offenders into communities do not extend to those who are radically 'other' than the dominant legal subjectivity; and at the same time inclusionary policies are impossible if there is no real community, embracing diversity and forgiving of transgression, to be integrated into. At best, offenders and others beyond the moral or national/ethnic bounds of community can expect resentment, suspicion, and never-ending surveillance.

The political and the ethical

These three examples – the move from risk management to risk control, the persistence of white, male perspectives in criminal justice and the decline of approaches to crime control that reflect diverse, inclusive communities – illustrate the perennial coexistence of the political and the ethical, social realities and normative aspirations in law and criminal justice. Risk management is the general goal of criminal justice. Risk management represents recognition of the twin tenets of liberalism: J. S. Mill's insistence that security is the one universal, non-substitutable good, and the principle that restriction of liberty should only be permitted in response to harm or demonstrable risk of harm. This aspiration to balance security and liberty, using law to give people security in their freedoms as well as in the inviolability of their persons and their property, is represented today by legal scholars and jurists who champion human rights as the anchoring value for criminal justice and who insist that, although potential victims' rights to safety might count for more than offenders' rights to liberty, these rights are the same category of thing and therefore must be held in balance rather than the one being everything and the other nothing (Ashworth 2002; Dworkin 1978). This aspiration to balance liberty and security for all through a system of rights inscribed through the rule of law – the task of justice – is the ideal or ethical moment of criminal law, the normative foundation of law.

The political moment, on the other hand, is the accommodation of this aspiration to balance rights and security to the politics of risk and safety as it plays out in our late-modern societies. The contemporary division of people into 'them' and 'us' is the identification of some groups (them) as those who pose risks to others – the rough, the different, the unknown – while other groups (us) are those who bear the risks. The risk systems which deal with the respectable and affluent are based on a system of sharing risks and pooling costs; the risk systems which deal with the poor, with outsiders, are based on risk elimination through restriction of movement and possibilities of action. The affluent join together in associations where risks are pooled; the poor and the 'other' are dealt with by imposed orders of precaution.

In the case of the response to racialized and sexualized offences, and the response to female and minority offenders, the ideal, the ethical moment is the aspiration to equality. As feminist and radical race critics argue, however, legal equality is predicated on sameness: persons and groups will only get equality of treatment to the extent that they can demonstrate that they are 'the same' as the norm of legal subjectivity, the white male. Women who kill in response to the same provocations as men, with the same lack of premeditation, will be able to draw on the same defences and mitigations as men, but they do not have available to them a defence that is based on the behaviours of women; black people who have the same lifestyles as white people, who use the same expressions of remorse and resolve, will have the same risk assessment scores, but there is no attempt to develop assessment techniques which give discursive space for minority offenders to work through their own experiences and attitudes. While there is gradually increasing recognition that 'equality' of penal treatment does not mean the same penal treatment, there is little systematic working through penal processes and sanctions to make sure that they are race- and gender-appropriate.

In these areas, the ethical moment is undermined by the closures of law and its philosophical groundings to subjectivities other than that of the white male, and by the politics of race and gender. Moreover, aspirations to do justice for women and for minorities are also constrained by the wider politics of law and order. The effect of this is that it is usually easier to obtain positive responses to those demands that mean more criminalizations and tougher penalties than to those demands which might seek to change the conceptual building blocks of criminal justice or to open the law up to outsider perspectives.

In the complex relationships between law, criminal justice and the idea of community, the ethical aspect is the aspiration to give effect to the moral norms of a community, to reflect its standards and concerns – the Durkheimian function, as sociologists would say. This important symbolic function is especially important in categories of crime that have traditionally been over-tolerated and under-penalized, for example racial and sexual aggression (Hudson 1998). As well as reflecting existing values, law and community are mutually constitutive: the experience of living together and having to solve conflicts, decide rules and procedures, and evolve shared cultures is the source of moral and political obligation (Matravers 2000).

The political moment of law and criminal justice is seen in the effects of criminalizations, penalties and processes in constructing and reinforcing barriers of inclusion and exclusion, membership and non-membership. Communitarian strands in present criminal justice and crime prevention policies – especially strong in the UK – strengthen these effects, which are already to some degree inevitable in any process of criminal labelling. As well as endeavouring to be less reliant on divisive, exclusionary crime prevention strategies, politicians, the media and others concerned with crime and punishment should be restrained from using dehumanizing labels, or labels which tend to strip people of membership status. A government-sponsored crime prevention TV campaign in the UK a few years ago, which depicted people stealing from cars as hyenas, is the sort of approach to be eschewed. Penal policies should always be based on the idea of offenders as fellow-citizens, not as animals or monsters.

At its best, criminal justice should give strong, clear messages that certain forms of behaviour are wrong, but should still deal with perpetrators of those behaviours as members of the community, and should make reintegration into the community the goal of all its penalties and procedures (Duff 2001).

Restorative justice: the ethical and the political

Restorative justice clearly has its ethical and its political aspects. Its ethical moment is its defining aspirations: to restore relationships between victims, offenders and their communities, and to be a 'replacement discourse' which decentres retributive punishment of offenders in favour of a more healing, relational approach which provides benefits for all parties to the conflict rather than imposing burdens on just one party. The political moment of restorative justice is its harnessing by criminal justice systems as merely another penal option. Restorative cautions; conferences and meetings which are mandatory for certain offenders and offences as in the new referral orders in England and Wales (Crawford and Newburn 2003); restorative justice procedures as part of court-imposed sanctions and as part of imprisonment programmes – displacing neither court nor imprisonment – are expressions of this accommodation of restorative justice to the political moment of penal policy.

There are many ways in which the ethical aspects of restorative justice can be undermined by the political, and I am sure that other contributors to this volume are more aware of them than I am. So in this section I will just mention a few that seem important to me. The first relates to the exaggerated risk-of-reoffending focus of current criminal justice. I would be concerned if restorative justice oversells itself in terms of its effectiveness in preventing reoffending. John Braithwaite claims in his comprehensive 1999 review that 'restorative justice has more incapacitative keys to turn than retributive justice', because it can mobilize friends and family to help the offender refrain from future crime (Braithwaite 1999: 67). There seems to me a difference between his invocation here of 'Uncle Harry' as an agent of incapacitation and, for example, the 'befriending circles' in some Canadian projects to help the reintegration of sex offenders, supporting them in their attempts not to reoffend. In the befriending circles, volunteer members meet regularly with the offender, come to the offender's aid in times of crisis, and once a week the circle has a meal together. Although both the befriending circles and Braithwaite's 'Uncle Harry' scenario aim at prevention of reoffending, I think that it is important to see the involvement of community members as helping to promote the balance of offender/potential victims' rights (as seems to be the tenor of the Canadian example) rather than selling itself to tough-on-crime governments as a more effective strategy of incapacitation (Hudson 2002a).

Another way in which the ethics of restorative justice can be undermined is if it becomes too much identified with one particular party: whether victims, offenders or communities. Although all definitions of the aims of restorative justice include all three parties, some theorists and some projects emphasize one at the expense of one or more of the other elements. For example, some emphasize the impact of meeting victims on offenders, and though it almost never happens that victims cannot refuse to participate, they may sometimes feel that they are being used instrumentally rather than as claimants on justice. This is most likely in schemes which are seen as part of a punishment programme, for example projects in prisons, rather than processes to name harms and determine outcomes. Other schemes might protect victims' rights and interests – as they should – but at the expense of offenders' rights: victim vetoes over offenders' supporters or representatives, for example, or processes where the only objective is to make the offender appreciate the victims' perspective. Braithwaite (1999) observed that he had yet to see a scheme where providing rehabilitative measures to offenders was taken as seriously as providing reparation to victims. In yet other schemes, the community is the primary focus. Again, this is most likely when schemes are part of a penal process, it being part of the sanction to make some reparation to communities. Some diversion schemes, as well as restorative justice as an element in punishment, can be like this if offenders (usually young offenders) are able to avoid a court appearance if they undertake some work for the community.

Risks of the ethics of restorative justice being undermined by the politics of crime and punishment as it becomes institutionalized are most acute when it becomes integrated into the criminal justice system, when it finds its place and moves from marginal, experimental projects to becoming part of the standard criminal justice repertoire. In the UK, restorative justice is being inserted into the repertoire of responses to offending at various points, but it looks like a tool in the penal repertoire rather than a replacement discourse. David Blunkett, the former British Home Secretary, commends restorative justice almost as a silver bullet:

> The Government supports restorative justice because it can help victims, putting them at the centre of the justice process and can reduce re-offending, as well as meeting a range of other objectives... (Home Office 2003)

Restorative justice, as represented by this Home Office statement, promises to allow the expression of victims' feelings, reduce reoffending and control crime without significant extra cost (Hudson 2004). While one can readily understand (indeed one expects) politicians to harness new ideas and new forms of justice to their law and order objectives, restorative justice advocates and practitioners should resist the temptation of offering their new justice modality as the silver bullet, the cure-all that can restore relationships, control reoffending, reintegrate offenders, provide reassurance and redress to victims, construct safe communities and demonstrate community norms, as well as providing appropriate punishment. The comprehensiveness of Braithwaite's (1999) review is worrying exactly because it makes claims in relation to a wide range of conventional penal aims as well as restorative justice's own ideals and objectives.[4]

The problem of the relationship between restorative justice and 'mainstream' justice is a matter of debate among restorative justice theorists themselves. Two crucial points are contested. The first point concerns the articulation between restorative justice and criminal justice. Braithwaite's idea of the 'enforcement pyramid' suggested restorative justice as the first rung on a penal ladder, a soft approach to be backed up by the big stick of formal punishment including imprisonment, for those who reoffend, refuse to accept the terms of restorative measures or who generally prove themselves to be 'beyond rehabilitation' (Braithwaite 1997). James Dignan has argued against this, suggesting that restorative justice should be the principle of all penal procedures (Dignan 2002). If it is to operate as a replacement discourse rather than be one rung on the penal ladder, then Dignan's approach must prevail. Braithwaite's approach risks positioning restorative justice as diversion – either as a first chance for first offenders, or as alternative justice for minor offences. The latter role would leave it open to all the critiques of earlier forms of informal justice, that it was second-class justice for crimes that weren't serious enough for expensive, formal state justice (see Matthews in this volume; McEvoy and Mika 2002).

The other point that is still contested and that concerns the positioning of restorative justice either as diversion, first chance or replacement is the question of whether restorative justice really has radically different aims to conventional penal modes, or performs or incorporates some of the same functions. Those who advocate restorative justice for more serious offences insist that it is not diversion but more effective justice (Daly 2002; Hudson 2002b). The argument has centred mainly on retribution, with some seeing it as part of restorative justice and others seeing it as incompatible with the aims of restorative justice. Daly argues that restorative justice must incorporate an element of retribution to mark the 'wrongness' which distinguishes crime from other forms of harm. Theorists such as Dignan continue to position restorative justice as a replacement discourse, and so the whole point is its difference from conventional criminal justice. For Dignan, as for Hulsman, naming the harm and establishing the wrong are elements of the restorative justice process; cases do not deal with already defined acts which need to be acknowledged with appropriate retribution as well as other ingredients of the restorative package. As with incapacitation, claiming retribution as part of restorative justice may be necessary for its institutionalization but is not compatible with restorative justice as replacement discourse and marks a break with the abolitionist aspirations of its original theorists.

Restorative justice *could* retain its alternative normative qualities in relation to my three themes of risk, sex- and race-conscious justice and diverse inclusivity of communities. Clifford Shearing (2001) argues that 'risk logic' is quite different from 'retribution logic' and advocates restorative justice because it follows the former rather than the latter. His illustrations ('parables' as he calls them) and arguments fit the template of risk management rather than risk control or elimination and I would argue that to retain its normative possibilities restorative justice must avoid crossing the line between risk management and risk control in either its claims or its practices.

I have examined the possibilities of restorative justice in relation to sexualized and racialized crimes (Hudson 1998; Hudson 2002b). The argument for the use of restorative justice in these kinds of cases is that it can provide much stronger messages about the wrongness of the behaviour than are provided by the very small rates of convictions secured by formal criminal justice, and that it can allow a greater range of discourses, explaining the harms from women's and minority perspectives, and making sure the message is understood by offenders and their representatives by telling victims' stories directly, without refraction through incomprehensible legal language. Restorative justice can contribute to the growth of disapproval of these behaviours and reassure victims that the strength of community feeling supports them. These processes can be particularly effective in responding to, for example, domestic violence in minority communities, dispelling the myth that persists in some quarters that minority communities regard physical chastisement of women as acceptable. It can, therefore, serve the aspirations of moving beyond a justice which is dependent on white male subjectivity, and it can also serve the aim of creating and reinforcing community values with respect to sexual and racial behaviours. Restorative justice can establish the 'wrongness' of acts but at the same time offer an opening for reintegration of offenders into their communities; it can censure wrongs without labelling offenders as monsters, beyond community. It can only realize these difficult objectives, however, if it avoids incorporation of the most regrettable incapacitative and exclusionary trends of contemporary penal politics and strategy.

Balancing the ethical and the political

In my recent and continuing work, I have been interested in the writings on justice by Habermas and Derrida. Both writers say that justice cannot be based entirely on ethical or political principles and demands. Habermas (1996) says that law must constantly move between the two poles of incorporating ideals (which it needs for its legitimacy) and inhabiting social realities (which it needs for its effectiveness).

Derrida (2001) says something similar when he argues that justice and other social institutions must always contain an ethical moment and a political moment. They must contain an aspiration to unconditionality (all strangers will be treated without hostility) and acknowledgment of conditionality (we must take steps to protect ourselves against those who may pose actual threats). Without the political/conditional, justice would be based on abstract, unchallengeable principles: its abstraction would mean that it was inoperable in the actual world; its unchallengeableness would mean that dissent would be excluded. Without the ethical, ideals of justice would not be present to provide any restraint to the politics of risk, the politics of race/gender oppression, the politics of community, the politics of exclusion and elimination of the different or risky.

In participating in or responding to the institutionalization of restorative justice, then, the point is not to insist on some sort of inflexible purity (overemphasis of the ethical), nor to offer restorative justice as an effective element of all possible penal strategies (overemphasis of the political). The essential point – as with most questions of criminal justice – is the balance between the ethical and the political.

Notes

1 Polly Klaas, aged 12, was taken at knifepoint from her bedroom in her home in Petaluma, California, on 1 October 1993; two friends who were sleeping over were tied up and gagged. Polly was strangled, and it was alleged that she had been sexually molested. Police were led to her body two months later by the killer. The killer was a man with previous convictions who was on parole at the time of the murder. The case was a driving force behind the California law which prescribes a life jail term for people convicted of a third felony crime. Megan Kanka, aged seven, was abused and strangled in New Jersey in 1994. Her killer was a previously convicted sex offender who had been released and allowed to move into the Kankas' neighbourhood without the community being notified. The argument for the passage of the new law was that the community would have been more vigilant had it been aware that he was living among them.

2 The person convicted for the murder of Sarah Payne had a previous conviction for sexual assault. If he had been acquitted, it is thought that subsequent disclosure of this previous offence would have led to public uproar.

3 Young received a life sentence in 1972 and died in custody in 1990.

4 This review is somewhat untypical of his most recent work on restorative justice, where he returns to a position which is closer to the idea of restorative justice as a replacement ideal rather than a process which can accomplish the goals of formal criminal justice (Braithwaite 2002).

References

Ashworth, A. (2002) *Human Rights, Serious Crime and Criminal Procedures*, The Hamlyn Lectures. London: Sweet and Maxwell.

Bauman, Z. (1989) *Modernity and the Holocaust*. Cambridge: Polity Press.

Bauman, Z. (1991) *Modernity and Ambivalence*. Cambridge: Polity Press.

Beck, U. (1992) *Risk Society: Towards a New Modernity*. London: Sage.

Bjorgo, T. and Witte, R. (1993) *Racist Violence in Europe*. Basingstoke: Macmillan.

Braithwaite, J. (1997) 'On speaking softly and carrying sticks: neglected dimensions of republican separation of powers', *University of Toronto Law Journal*, 47: 1–57.

Braithwaite, J. (1999) 'Restorative justice: assessing optimistic and pessimistic accounts', in M. Tonry (ed.), *Crime and Justice: A Review of Research*, Vol. 25. Chicago, IL: University of Chicago Press, pp. 1–127.

Braithwaite, J. (2002) *Restorative Justice and Responsive Regulation*. Oxford: Oxford University Press.

Carlen, P. (1999) *Sledgehammer: Women's Imprisonment at the Millennium*. Basingstoke: Macmillan.

Christie, N. (1982) *Limits to Pain*. Oxford: Martin Robertson.

Christie, N. (1986) 'The ideal victim', in E. Fattah (ed.), *From Crime Policy to Victim Policy*. Basingstoke: Macmillan, pp. 17–30.

Clear, T. and Cadora, E. (2001) 'Risk and community practice', in K. Stenson and R. R. Sullivan (eds.), *Crime, Risk and Justice: The Politics of Crime Control in Liberal Democracies*. Cullompton: Willan, pp. 51–67.

Clear, T. R. and Karp, D. R. (1999) *The Community Justice Ideal: Preventing Crime and Achieving Justice*. Chicago, IL: Westview Press.

Cooke, R. (2001) 'Snap decisions', *Guardian*, 30 October: 8.

Crawford, A. (1997) *The Local Governance of Crime*. Oxford: Clarendon Press.

Crawford, A. (1998) 'Community safety and the quest for security: holding back the dynamics of exclusion', *Policy Studies*, 19, 34: 237–53.

Crawford, A. and Newburn, T. (2003) *Youth Offending and Restorative Justice*. Cullompton: Willan.

Daly, K. (2002) 'Sexual assault and restorative justice', in H. Strang and J. Braithwaite (eds), *Restorative Justice and Family Violence*. Melbourne: Cambridge University Press, pp. 62–88.

Derrida, J. (2001) *Cosmopolitanism and Forgiveness*, trans. M. Dooley and M. Hughes. London: Routledge.

Dignan, J. (2002) 'Restorative justice: limiting principles', in A. von Hirsch, J. Roberts, A. Bottoms, K. Roach and M. Schiff (eds), *Restorative Justice and Criminal Justice: Competing or Reconcilable Paradigms?* Oxford: Hart Publishing, pp. 135–56.

Duff, R. A. (2001) *Punishment, Communication and Community*. Oxford: Oxford University Press.

Dworkin, R. (1978) *Taking Rights Seriously*. Cambridge, MA: Cambridge University Press.

Garland, D. (2000) 'The culture of high crime societies: some preconditions of recent "law and order" policies', *British Journal of Criminology*, 40(3): 347–75.

Garland, D. (2001) *The Culture of Control: Crime and Social Order in Contemporary Society*. Oxford: Oxford University Press.

Giddens, A. (1990) *The Consequences of Modernity*. Cambridge: Polity Press.

Habermas, J. (1996) *Between Facts and Norms*, trans. W. Rehg. Cambridge: Polity Press.

Haggerty, K. D. (2003) 'From risk to precaution: the rationalities of personal crime prevention', in R. V. Ericson and A. Doyle (eds), *Risk and Morality*. Toronto: University of Toronto Press, pp. 194–214.

Hamm, M. (1993) *Hate Crime: International Perspectives on Causes and Control*. Cincinnati, OH: Academy of Criminal Justice Sciences/Anderson.

Home Office (2003) *Restorative Justice: The Government's Strategy*. Online at: www.homeoffice.gov.uk

Hudson, B. (1998) 'Restorative justice: the challenge of sexual and racial violence', *Journal of Law and Society*, 25(2): 237–56.

Hudson, B. (2002a) 'Victims and offenders', in A. von Hirsch, J. Roberts, A. Bottoms, K. Roach and M. Schiff (eds), *Restorative Justice and Criminal Justice: Competing or Reconcilable Paradigms?* Oxford: Hart Publishing, pp. 177–94.

Hudson, B. (2002b) 'Restorative justice and gendered violence: diversion or effective justice?', *British Journal of Criminology*, 42(3): 616–34.

Hudson, B. (2003) *Justice in the Risk Society*. London: Sage.

Hudson, B. (2004) 'The culture of control: choosing the future', *Critical Review of International Social and Political Philosophy*, 7(2): 49–75.

Hudson, B. and Bramhall, G. (2005) 'Assessing the "Other": constructions of "Asianness" in risk assessments by probation officers', *British Journal of Criminology*, 45(5): 721–40.

Hulsman, L. (1986) 'Critical criminology and the concept of crime', in H. Bianchi and R. van Swaaningen (eds), *Abolitionism: Towards a Non-repressive Approach to Crime*. Amsterdam: Free Press, pp. 113–26.

Kelly, L. (2001) *Routes to (In)justice: A Research Review on the Reporting, Investigation and Prosecution of Rape Cases*. London: Her Majesty's Crown Prosecution Service Inspectorate.

Kelly, L., Lovett, J. and Regan, L. (2005) *A Gap or a Chasm? Attrition in Reported Rape Cases*, Home Office Research Study 293. London: Home Office.

Lea, S. J., Lanvers, U. and Shaw, S. (2003) 'Attrition in rape cases: developing a profile and identifying relevant factors', *British Journal of Criminology*, 43(3): 583–99.

McEvoy, K. and Mika, H. (2002) 'Restorative justice and the critique of informalism in Northern Ireland', *British Journal of Criminology*, 42(3): 534–62.

MacKinnon, C. (1989) *Toward a Feminist Theory of the State*. Cambridge, MA: Harvard University Press.

Macpherson, W. (1999) *The Stephen Lawrence Inquiry*, Cmnd 4262-1. London: Stationery Office.

Maffesoli, M. (1996) *The Time of the Tribes*. London: Sage.

Martin, D., MacCrimmon, M., Grant, I. and Boyle, C. (1991) 'A forum on Lavallee *v*. R.: women and self-defence', *British Columbia Law Review*, 25: 23.

Matravers, M. (2000) *Justice and Punishment*. Oxford: Oxford University Press.

Melossi, D. (2000) 'Social theory and changing representations of the criminal', *British Journal of Criminology*, 40(2): 296–320.

Morris, N. (1994) 'Dangerousness and incapacitation', in R. A. Duff and D. Garland (eds), *A Reader on Punishment*. Oxford: Oxford University Press, pp. 238–60.

Naffine, N. (1990) *Law and the Sexes*. Sydney: Allen and Unwin.

O'Donovan, K. (1993) 'Law's knowledge: the judge, the expert, the battered woman, and her syndrome', *Journal of Law and Society*, 20(4): 427–37.

O'Malley, P. (1992) 'Risk, power and crime prevention', *Economy and Society*, 21: 252–75.

O'Malley, P. (2001) 'Risk, crime and prudentialism revisited', in K. Stenson and R. R. Sullivan (eds), *Crime, Risk and Justice: The Politics of Crime Control in Liberal Democracies*. Cullompton: Willan, pp. 89–103.

Packer, H. (1969) *The Limits of the Criminal Sanction*. Stanford, CA: Stanford University Press.

Phillips, C. and Bowling, B. (2002) 'Racism, ethnicity, crime and criminal justice', in M. Maguire, R. Morgan and R. Reiner (eds), *The Oxford Handbook of Criminology*, 3rd edn. Oxford: Oxford University Press, pp. 579–619.

Rose, N. (1996) 'The death of the "social"? Refiguring the territory of governance', *Economy and Society*, 26(4): 327–46.

Shearing, C. (2001) 'Punishment and the changing face of governance', *Punishment and Society*, 3(2): 203–20.

Simon, J. (2001) 'Entitlement to cruelty: neo-liberalism and the punitive mentality in the United States', in K. Stenson and R. R. Sullivan (eds), *Crime, Risk and Justice: The Politics of Crime Control in Liberal Democracies*. Cullompton: Willan, pp. 125–43.

Tonry, M. (1995) *Malign Neglect – Race, Crime and Punishment in America*. New York: Oxford University Press.

Valverde, M. (1996) 'Social facticity and the law: a social expert's eyewitness account of law', *Social and Legal Studies*, 5(2): 201–08.

Walker, N. (1985) *Sentencing: Theory, Law and Practice*. London: Butterworths.

Young, J. (1999) *The Excusive Society*. London: Sage.

Chapter 13

Epilogue

Ivo Aertsen, Tom Daems and Luc Robert

As editors, we had two options to conclude this book. Either we could abruptly stop the book here – if that option was taken, our job was done – or we could try to facilitate a reading of this book by pinpointing a number of important topics and issues. The second option seemed more attractive to us. Without claims of presenting an exhaustive overview of overarching themes, questions dealt with, answers provided or points taken, this Epilogue offers readers a number of issues which are addressed in the chapters, at times in quite divergent ways. Reading (and re-reading) the contributions allowed us to identify a number of common questions not directly tackled, yet of importance for anyone thinking about or working in the field of restorative justice (hereafter RJ).

In a book about institutionalizing RJ, it is of paramount importance to know what key concepts signify. Therefore, in the first section, we briefly explore the semantics of RJ. Next, drawing on one of the adages in criminology – 'good ideas become bad practices' – we touch upon the problem of the 'gap', the chasm between ideas and their implementation. Furthermore, societal changes since the 1970s have affected and changed the field of punishment. How can we look at institutionalizing RJ in these times of penal ambiguities? Here questions of democratized or elitist penal policy-making and a possible instrumentalization of RJ are addressed. A final section poses a number of questions related to the internationalization of RJ policies (particularly in the EU) and explores the question of an equilibrium between politics and ethics in institutionalizing RJ.

The semantics of RJ

The central theme of this book, institutionalizing RJ, serves as a kind of centripetal force aligning all contributions (see Introduction). The thread of the book nevertheless varies depending on the author's approach (analytical, normative), theoretical affiliation and stance towards RJ. One of the interesting points of entry to approach the variation among the contributions in this volume relates to the semantics at play. Semantics, from the Greek *semantikos* or 'significant meaning' (as derived from *sema*, sign), always refers to some kind of meaning of something that is written.

The question then arises: 'Why ask what?' Why would one delve into the question of semantics? A focus on semantics constitutes one way of extricating and bringing to light, in the words of Isaiah Berlin (1999: 10), 'the hidden categories and models in terms of which human beings think (that is, their use of words, images and other symbols), to reveal what is obscure or contradictory in them, to discern the conflicts between them'. To explore the semantics of a key concept, then, is to unveil the meaning of the basic conceptualizations underlying each of the contributions.

A discussion of semantics is important for at least two other reasons. First of all, the conceptual content of RJ influences the theoretical base of each of the contributions and reflects the categories and models by which the author interprets the world. Secondly, the meaning accorded to basic concepts greatly affects the subsequent analysis. The conceptual framework consisting of the key concepts already demarcates and delimits points of discussion.

Of course, to solely focus on the *term* RJ would leave out important considerations. Some of the contributions deploy a different terminology to refer to what is supposedly known as RJ. Others mention terminologically closely related concepts to RJ, such as Aboriginal justice. A conflation in meaning poses particular dangers. A third distinction can be made by looking at the content of RJ itself. Although the same concept is used, it refers to different yet to some extent overlapping provinces of meaning.

The first category entails a *different terminology* for RJ. Jacques Faget singles out a number of reasons why, in French-speaking countries and particularly in France, the concept of RJ is relatively unknown.

Other concepts in French-speaking countries have also proven to be without 'success'. The preferred concept is that of mediation and, more specifically in the sphere of criminal justice, penal mediation. The reasons cited are of a linguistic, historical and political, institutional and conceptual nature. Notwithstanding these reasons, Faget poses that '[e]ven though the words to designate them are different, there exist, at least in western countries, social practices that share the same philosophy.' It leads him to conclude that RJ, rather than being considered as non-existent in France, suffers from an invisible and 'phantomlike presence'.

As Faget argues, the concept of penal mediation functions as a terminologically imperfect substitute for RJ. On the representational level, penal mediation implies an overlap but not an identity in meaning with RJ. This difference should be seen in its historical–political context: the political system, which originated after the French Revolution, condemns all forms of communitarianism. In this 'society of individuals', practices such as community conferencing or sentencing circles – 'community mobilizations' – are therefore absent. Due to this demarcation, penal mediation seems to be the only practice corresponding to the criteria of the restorative model listed by Faget.

While different concepts can refer to a very similar (though not identical) content, the logic can also be turned around: similar concepts can have significantly different meanings. In this case, one can speak of *conceptual confusion*. Different yet comparable concepts such as Aboriginal justice and RJ can suggest an evident and extensive overlap, while there are significant differences in the content of each of the terms and the meanings they comprise. Here the dangers of homogenization and identification lurk, with a range of possible consequences attached to them. These dangers are situated, at least in part, on the level of ideas about the relationship of concepts and the context in which they emerged and developed. For example, according to 'histories of RJ', RJ supposedly is strongly aligned with and related to premodern forms of justice and with a revival of indigenous justice practices. As John Pratt shows, there are 'undeniable resonances between justice in the premodern world and contemporary RJ', but 'the claims about RJ having its roots there are at best tenuous – and are frequently quite mistaken.' Such claims constitute 'a serious misreading of history and social relations' and bring with them a kind of 'epistemological violence' (Matthews). These 'origin myths' of RJ (Daly 2002: 62) have contributed to an overstated relationship between Aboriginal justice and RJ.

Other conceptual confusions relate to the institutionalization of RJ, particularly in countries with Aboriginal communities. For example, in

Canada, as Kent Roach writes, the institutionalization of RJ may have some unintended consequences for Aboriginal justice practices. 'In the case of Aboriginal justice initiatives, it may pressure programmes that for good reasons focus on the rehabilitation of the offender to take on victim issues in order to qualify as restorative justice programmes that are eligible for funding or diversion.' While 'attempts to squeeze Aboriginal community justice initiatives into the mould of restorative procedures may also threaten such initiatives', there also exists the risk of excluding other groups (such as African-Canadian women) on the basis of restricting RJ practices to Aboriginal offenders.

These problems also go back to the 'very imprecise nature of what RJ actually is'; it is a kind of 'umbrella term' (Pratt). Perhaps the divergent meanings of RJ – *conceptual diffusion* – can best be illustrated by contrasting two conceptualizations of RJ. On the one hand, Roger Matthews starts his analysis by drawing a distinction between theory and practice. He identifies RJ with what he calls 'the 'new generation' of restorative justice programmes that emerged in the 1990s. These all apply some form of conferencing. John Blad, on the other hand, sees RJ as a 'form of justice', comprising both continuously developing restorative practices and theories. Drawing on Berger and Luckmann, Blad defines restorative practices as 'patterns of interaction, potentially routines, of a secondary nature, to be applied when things go wrong in everyday social interaction'. He even mentions the 'necessity and development of a *restorative culture* to guide and accompany the use of restorative interaction patterns'. These interaction patterns have themselves crystallized into two kinds of practices. Informal RJ practices are being mobilized in peer mediation, neighbourhood conflict mediation, civil and administrative law, while formal RJ practices such as victim–offender mediation and family group conferences are embedded in reactions to breaches of criminal law. As this illustrates, the demarcation of the content of RJ and its meaning is not without problems.

As can be seen in different conceptualizations of RJ, both by using other concepts and by deploying different demarcations of the term RJ, the definitions of RJ seem to relate closely to the context in which they arise. Ideas on RJ depend, always, at the very least to some extent, on the social setting (the history, politics, culture of a particular place in a particular time). Ian Hacking (2000: 10) denotes this as 'the matrix within which an idea, a concept or kind, is formed'. This raises questions concerning the commonality of RJ. These sketchy comments on semantics seem to suggest that the final and conclusive definition of RJ does not exist. RJ, in the words of Kent Roach, 'means different things to different people'.

In the course of RJ's institutionalization, it can be expected that the processes of defining and redefining RJ will intensify. The more people, organizations and resources are involved, the higher the stakes and the more intense the struggles to define and redefine RJ.

The problem of the gap: from intentions to consequences

The observation that there is a chasm between ideas and their implementation should be far from shocking. It has been noted time and time again that this gap is self-evident and inevitable (Abel 1980b; Blomberg and Cohen 2003; Daly 2003). The interesting task, then, is not to reveal a chasm between restorative theory and practice (this chasm will always be there) but rather to ask – and attempt to answer – the question: 'What accounts for this apparently permanent gap?' (Blomberg and Cohen 2003: 9). As Blomberg and Cohen (2003) suggest, there are at least three answers to this question. Firstly, things can go wrong at the implementation stage, i.e. the original intentions are not well understood, or there might be a lack of sufficient resources or appropriate staff. Secondly, the gap is there because the intentions are undermined by bureaucratic convenience or professional self-interest. Thirdly, and more fundamentally, the original intentions themselves are for a variety of reasons suspect (see also Cohen 1985: Chapter 3).

None of the authors touches directly upon this question yet throughout the book attentive readers can find clues of why there is either a lack of institutionalization of RJ or why institutionalization is not occurring along the lines of the 'good intentions'. Here we have a closer look at the chapters by John Blad and Roger Matthews. In his chapter on RJ in the Netherlands John Blad explains the grim situation by relying on arguments that can largely be classified under the first two categories. For example, he argues that better training of HALT functionaries and a more explicit RJ discourse in the public realm might result in HALT becoming more fully restorative in the future. Moreover, notwithstanding its apparent 'success', the restorative mediation project he discusses was discontinued because '[…] the founding organizations [Victim Support and Probation Service] felt that the project was not satisfactorily embedded in their organization and that the administration of the project had been suboptimal. Budget cuts imposed by government decisions, necessitating hard choices with regard to what is to be the "core business", figured in the background.' In addition, he is critical about the lack of a formal relation to criminal procedure in five of the seven projects of family group conferencing because this reveals, so he argues, '[...] that there has *not* been an *intention* to develop a restorative *justice* programme.' Somewhat further into his chapter he writes that 'divided and dividing organizational interests [...] were the cause for the malfunctioning of the restorative [conferencing] project in Utrecht.' Also his lament of there being no sufficiently receptive 'restorative culture' and especially his discussion (under the subheading 'obstacles') of impediments to transforming the criminal justice system clearly demonstrate how Blad's explanations of the gap are largely falling within the ambit of 'poor' implementation, 'malign' bureaucracy and 'unreceptive' organizations and professionals.

The explanation provided by Roger Matthews is of a totally different kind. It belongs firmly to category three: the intentions themselves are suspect. The following quote from his chapter leaves the reader little room for doubt:

> [...] the failings which have been identified by critics are not so much a result of poor implementation or a consequence of technical and organizational failures; rather it will be suggested that the limitations of restorative justice programmes stem more or less directly from the weak theoretical base on which they have been constructed.

Matthews explicitly states that the ideas themselves are in need of revision. Here he clearly adopts a different position to that of John Blad. In the remainder of his chapter Matthews delivers a piercing critique of the theory of reintegrative shaming which, so he argues, provides a questionable basis for developing restorative programmes. His different definition of the problem has of course implications for a potential solution: instead of being preoccupied with better staffing and smoother running of RJ programmes we should ask ourselves serious questions about the theoretical building blocks of these programmes. His suggestion is therefore much more radical: maybe we should start thinking about negotiating a divorce?

We leave it to the reader to judge the power of these and other explanations that can be found throughout the book. Here we briefly touch upon two other topics that are related to the gap: the *bottom-up* modification of original intentions, and the ambivalence surrounding the consequences. For the first topic we have a closer look at the chapter by Robert Mackay; for the second we rely on the chapter by Adam Crawford.

The chapter by Robert Mackay can be read in different ways. From a policy perspective the discussion by Mackay gives the reader an insider's look at how a policy community attempts to develop a set of RJ principles that can guide and monitor processes of institutionalization. From a more sociological perspective though, the exercise of Mackay reveals how original intentions tend to become modified because of the *anticipation* of resistances on the way to official policy relevance. In other words, intentions may lose their purity because those who embody them are eager to make them more attractive and less hostile to the outside world in general, and the existing criminal justice system and its practitioners in particular. In this way, RJ advocates (as do participants in other social movements that are striving towards policy relevance) make use of *discursive manoeuvres*: '[...] the formation of certain movements in theory (for example, the production of conceptual compromises or new alignments), which are produced not so much by conceptual logic as by political desire' (Garland 1985: 172).

The discussion of the topics in the chapter by Mackay and the detailed exposé of argument and contra-argument, definition and redefinition, vision and revision, gives us an interesting glimpse of what part these manoeuvres play in RJ discussions. Mackay highlights the importance of policy relevance by referring to 'the rapid growth of restorative justice practice', the 'strong need for guidance at a time when the urge to experiment is strong' and by insisting that 'it is [...] imperative that those who wish to promote restorative justice practice are in a position to inform governments about how practice should be developed in their jurisdictions.'

A drive to enhance the attractiveness of RJ for policy-makers in the criminal justice system is particularly present in the discussion of human rights. Mackay writes that: 'In the current climate of law and international opinion, any theoretical justification of restorative justice that did not take into account and attempt to exemplify the discourse of fundamental rights would be incongruent.' A little further in the chapter he emphasizes a 'core concern' for RJ: '[...] if restorative justice is not based in human rights then it will lose credibility and legitimacy', and he continues: 'There is already a growing body of critical opinion suggesting that restorative justice does not uphold human rights. There is a heavy onus on restorative justice advocates to scotch this line of critique.' This is also conveyed in the statement that: 'If RJ is to be taken seriously by courts and prosecutors and by the public we will need to recognize some of their concerns.' In other words, becoming an attractive partner for policy-makers inevitably means dealing with, and adequately addressing, the (for RJ advocates) tricky issues of (human) rights and proportionality.

In this process it might be necessary to revise and redefine core concepts and working principles. The difficulty and sensitivity of this task is amply illustrated in Mackay's chapter when participants in the debate utter criticisms to the proposed (re-)formulations: is the purity of RJ falling prey to the underlying philosophy and the overt practices of the existing criminal justice system? Yet it also means, Mackay insists, that RJ advocates need to learn to speak with 'one voice' when addressing policy-makers. In his chapter Mackay lists three reasons why one should be cautious about being too relaxed about continuing lack of agreement. In other words, between the lines one can read a call for what David Garland once referred to as *pragmatic compromises*, i.e. modifications of intentions in order to efface '[...] theoretical difference in the name of practical unity' (Garland 1985: 172). The formulation of the guidelines therefore is not only an interesting exercise for policy-makers; the discussion of the relevant issues and the semantics, rephrasing and redefining of core concepts that form part of restorative theory also demonstrate how advocates, by means of 'pre-emptive strikes', mould their own intentions in an attempt to close the gap. This means that restorative intentions are not only (as has often been argued) perverted or co-opted from a *top-down* perspective (see further); they also are modified by RJ advocates themselves in an ongoing attempt to influence everyday penal practice and to redirect the existing criminal justice system in a restorative way.

Lastly, the consequences are much more ambivalent than they seem at first sight. What do 'good' and 'bad' mean in the context of institutionalizing RJ and is it fruitful (and *überhaupt* possible) to think and speak in terms of this dichotomy?[1] In Chapter 6 Adam Crawford offers some interesting thoughts in this respect. Referral orders in England and Wales are coercive measures yet at the same time '[...] coercion provides the capacity to move certain restorative justice values to the very heart of the youth justice system.' In the end, so he argues, referral orders circumvent a frequent stumbling block for many RJ initiatives, i.e. small, self-selective caseloads and a lack of referrals.[2] The loss of voluntariness, so he suggests, is the price paid for this. Should RJ advocates consider paying this price? Crawford seems to hint at this when he writes: '[...] one of the positive lessons for restorative justice may be that despite the coercive context, and possibly partly as a consequence of it, change in the direction of delivering a more deliberative process can be realized.'

Crawford builds upon a line of thinking that he explored more in detail with Tim Newburn. Crawford and Newburn (2003) took issue with some polemical critiques that swiftly discarded referral orders;

their coercive nature is invariably interpreted as an insuperable obstacle towards genuine restorative youth justice reform. These critiques are wrong, they argue, because they fail to take into account the way in which the orders have been implemented. Too often, Crawford and Newburn (2003: 234) argue:

> [...] those writing about the state of criminal justice generally, and youth justice in particular, tend in their work to elide policy prescription and professional practice. Accounts of contemporary developments either tend to rely on a reading of formal instruments or formal statements (legislation, green and white papers, consultation documents, press releases, speeches by government ministers, etc.) or they focus on the minutiae of practice. Relatively seldom, it seems, is attention paid to both. Rarer still, is the attempt to examine the dissonance between the two.

On the one hand, the worries of the critics are understandable because the new referral orders form part of a questionable package of more repressive measures. In other words, there is a contagious effect at work here: the coercive nature of the orders becomes (too) quickly associated with the other measures in the package. However, to apply one of the basic assumptions of Luhmannian sociology in this context, 'the parts are more than the whole'. In this respect Crawford and Newburn highlight how practitioners 'on the ground' (they refer to them as 'the primary street-level bureaucrats' (p. 236)) have tended to administer the orders in a constructive way. Official intentions and policies can be transformed, subverted and redirected in practice. Whatever the reader's opinion on the sensitive topic of 'coercion *versus* voluntariness' might be, Crawford and Newburn's plea for more attention to be paid to the empirical details of policy implementation and the reception (and potential transformation) of ideas in practice entails an important lesson for those who tend to fall prey to an infamous mantra – 'to condemn more and to understand less'.

RJ, democracy and the state

Criminology is a small discipline but it deals with big questions. Some of them go straight to the heart of political organization. This should not come as a surprise: processes of law making and law enforcement materialize through deliberative democratic structures and a vast range of executive state agencies. Since punishment has traditionally been monopolized by the state, it can be expected that changes in the state will reconfigure the field of punishment. This is exactly what is happening today. Since the 1970s, 'the old certainties of "the welfare state" are under attack and welfare systems are undergoing transformation' (Rose 1996: 327).[3] These transformations of the welfare state seem to go the furthest in Anglo-Saxon countries. Yet continental European welfare states are also facing tremendous challenges and are struggling with financial, institutional and cultural problems (Rosanvallon 1992).

These developments have important consequences in the study of punishment. The existing modalities of criminal justice – 'penal welfarism' – have been questioned (e.g. Garland 1996; Loader and Sparks 2002). Developments such as globalization, increases in (reported) crime rates and the growing influence of managerialist discourses have influenced and affected the capacities of the state to govern crime control and punishment.

Most analyses identify two responses. On the one hand, governments are seeking to (re)assert their authority over the areas of crime and punishment. This can be seen in a range of 'strategies of denial', giving way to a so-called 'new punitiveness' (see Chapter 3 by John Pratt). Opposed to the exclusionary and defensive reactions of the state, there exist a number of 'adaptive strategies' (Garland 1996). These constitute ways of governing crime and crime control at a distance, i.e. through strategies which involve (or enlarge the involvement of) individuals, communities and (quasi-autonomous and private) organizations (Crawford 1999; Rose 2000). The state increasingly relies on the capacities of individuals, organizations and communities and is not the sole nor the most important actor (pre)occupied with the governance of crime.

RJ programmes can be seen as ways to govern at a distance, a 'responsibilizing strategy', in which 'central government is operating upon the established boundaries which separate the private from the public realm, seeking to renegotiate the question of what is properly a state function and what is not' (Garland 1996: 453). Especially given claims of some early RJ scholars about the theft of conflicts by professional thieves (Christie 1977), as well as claims relating to RJ as a 'replacement discourse' (Dignan 2003), attention should go to the influence of the state in institutionalizing RJ. In this section we discuss two themes. For the first theme 'state, democracy and elitist policy-making' we have a closer look at the chapters by John Pratt, Michael Tonry and Hans Boutellier. For the second topic 'instrumentalization of RJ' we rely on the chapters by John Blad, Hans Boutellier, Kent Roach and Pat O'Malley.

State, democracy and elitist policy-making

The chapters by John Pratt (3) and Michael Tonry (1) are different in many respects yet in a certain way they seem to be built on a similar normative premise – implicit in the chapter by Pratt, explicit in the one by Tonry: the need for a strong and multi-layered state apparatus with a proper place for expertise. Pratt's analysis of modern penality, which is strongly inspired by the work of German sociologist Norbert Elias (see Pratt 2002), tells us something striking about the social conditions that were necessary to have a humane and moderate penal system: processes of centralization, professionalization and bureaucratization made it possible for a penal elite to take criminal policy into their own (presumably qualified) hands. The state assumed monopolistic control over penal affairs and an administrative gulf was created between bureaucratic authorities and the general public. The latter became detached from, and indifferent to, the administration of punishment. From the 1970s, however, this arrangement of penal power broke down under the influence of profound social change in general and neoliberal attacks directed at the state in particular. It was this breakdown of modern penality that created the fertile soil for restorative justice to emerge *and* for the 'new punitiveness' to take off.

In Chapter 3 Pratt identifies a link between RJ and weak, absent or non-functioning central states. He even seems to suggest that RJ *necessarily* presupposes a weak state. The (modest) rise of RJ with concomitant (powerful) punitive trends leads him to a rather grim projection for the future: '[...] the empowerment of the public at a time when the sense of threat and insecurity are heightened as a result of law and order concerns seems likely to balance the scales in favour of the new punitive trends, in a penal realm that has lost its sense of stability, permanence and direction.' Pratt's social analysis of contemporary penality does not contain a pronounced normative position yet between the lines one can read, so it seems to us, a need to contain and channel the unleashed human sentiments by means of strong governmental structures.

It is at this point that Pratt and Tonry partly touch upon common ground. Tonry is in favour of a system of *inter alia* 'relatively non-politicized criminal justice policy-making processes', 'non-partisan professional criminal justice practitioners' and 'constitutional systems characterized by strong separation of powers traditions' because, according to Tonry, these are preconditions for more constructive and less punitive-oriented criminal justice policies to develop. In this respect he also mentions the inadequate American constitutional arrangements for dealing with 'raw public emotion' and he is highly critical about politically selected judges and prosecutors because they are much more receptive to changes in public attitudes. Moreover, he laments the lower degrees of confidence in the USA in elite or expert opinion (see also Tonry 2004). Yet there is also a crucial difference between the positions of both authors: according to Pratt *only* a weak, absent or non-functioning state enables RJ to develop; Tonry's list of factors that are conducive to the institutionalization of RJ suggests the opposite.

Despite their disagreements, it is interesting to note that both seem to be in favour of a strong state apparatus where penal policy-making and the administration of punishment is shielded from unleashed emotions, sentiments and immediate popular concerns. Does this imply a renewed belief in the state, bureaucracy and elitist policy-making? If this is the case, then it raises a set of questions that the reader may find worthwhile to explore further.

Firstly, how do you reconcile this position with a strong line of criticism towards state, bureaucracy and elitist policy-making that underpinned the development of the informal justice movement in the 1960s and 1970s and that also inspired the RJ movement of the 1990s? Twenty-five years ago Richard Abel (1980a: 439) wrote tellingly that 'critics on both sides of the political spectrum now attack centralized power, mushrooming bureaucracy, and the lack of direct democratic control.' Some years later Stan Cohen (1985: 31) grouped these (and other attacks) under the notion of a 'destructuring impulse': '[...] a sustained assault on the very foundations of the control system whose hegemony has lasted nearly two centuries'. This vehement critique encompassed a desire to move away from 'the state', 'the expert' and 'the institution'. Advocates in the RJ movement share many of these old (but still lively) concerns about the ways in which states exercise their power to punish.

Secondly, and related to the first question: Is the state really the ideal partner to fight these alleged punitive tendencies? There are two reasons why one might need to be cautious about this. First, as Pratt himself highlights, the story of modern penality with its strong penal bureaucracy and enlightened experts is not a fairytale either: it was capable of inflicting great brutalities and privations on the recipients of punishment – particularly prisoners; victims were routinely ignored; and it functioned so to speak detached from public debate and scrutiny. There is by now a large body of revisionist literature on punishment and social control that questions the role of the state in penal history (see, for example, Cohen and Scull 1983). Second, at times when states are curbing civil rights in the war against terror and crimes by the state are a daily reality for millions of people around the globe, the suggested move 'back to the state' may need some more qualification.

Thirdly, is it really the case that, as Pratt suggests, institutionalizing RJ is incompatible with strong, present or functioning modern (welfare) states? RJ developments in continental Europe in general, and at the level of the EU in particular, seem to suggest that this statement needs some qualification (see further – section 4). Or maybe continental Europeans speak in different terms about RJ than Anglo-Saxons in the USA, New Zealand and Australia? This leads us again to the opening theme of this chapter: the question of semantics. What is it that we are talking about?

Fourthly, does this (implicit) response to the contemporary predicament fully take into account the challenges of our times? Modern penality, for example, completely ignored victims of crime. Notwithstanding its flaws and the well-documented questionable developments, RJ at least *attempts* to provide an answer to some of the most pressing puzzles of our penal times, i.e. how to deal with victims, harm and emotions (Daems 2004). Moreover, distancing oneself from RJ will not do away with the existing social arrangements, feelings of insecurity and the growing attention for victims of crime. Abandoning serious intellectual and practical engagement with (parts of) RJ theory may leave the so-called 'new punitiveness' as the only available option.

The state- and expert-centred approach in the chapters of Pratt and Tonry stands in sharp contrast with the political philosophy that underpins Chapter 2 by Hans Boutellier. One of the core arguments of Boutellier is that crime has been transformed into a security issue. During the 1990s security and unsafety became a number one theme and the current crime control situation is largely an honest *response* to this changed situation. Boutellier takes issue with constructionist positions that, in his view, tend to explain away the underlying problems: safety is a 'realistic factor', he writes. In his view, findings from surveys and the attention that is devoted to the topic in the media and the political arena serve as 'evidence' for this. Politicians merely fulfil their duty when they respond to these concerns: 'After all, meeting the needs of the citizens is ultimately the most important legitimating force in a constitutional democracy.' The 'cry for safety', Boutellier argues, should be taken seriously – not only by politicians but also by criminologists.

While Tonry and Pratt are anxious about politicians, judges and prosecutors responding too readily to public concerns, moral panics and collective emotions, Boutellier seems to evaluate this in more positive terms, as a manifestation of direct democracy. The buffers of specialist bodies and administrative agencies against the forces of emotionalism do not feature in Boutellier's contribution. The *bottom-up* approach of Boutellier is also illustrated by his definition of crime: 'Criminal behaviour is [...] not so much a deviation from the norm enforced from above as a denial of a fundamental principle of a humanist culture, the recognition of the other and of the other's freedom.' For Boutellier the 'vital context' provides a window of opportunity for RJ to develop. Some readers probably will question his realism[4] and others will disagree with his views on democracy, yet the provocative nature of his vision puts a challenging question in the spotlight: to what extent can punishment be 'democratized' and what role can RJ play in this?

Instrumentalization of RJ

In this subsection, we briefly touch upon the problem of the instrumentalization of RJ. It would lead us too far to explore all the questions revolving around the issue of instrumentalization. What *can* be done, though, is to present some arguments and views as they figure in the contributions. For example, Blad, Boutellier and Roach broach the question of institutionalizing RJ in its relationship to the state. They suggest RJ is becoming an 'instrument' in the hands of the state. Where Blad problematizes a move towards a co-optation of RJ practices, thereby suggesting that 'the bad state' is (ab)using and distorting the rationales of RJ, Boutellier rather sees the use of RJ as part of a larger strategy to be pursued and embraced. Roach adds to the debate by posing some questions following an instrumental institutionalization of RJ in Canadian sentencing. For him, an instrumental use of RJ can lead to a deepening of existing inequalities or give rise to new problems.

To avoid this, as Pat O'Malley iterates, it could be a fruitful exercise to look at programmes such as drug harm minimization (DHM). O'Malley's argument starts from another framework: 'post-social' government, in which the main accent is put on individuals, communities and organizations. 'The' state does not (any longer) appear to be of relevance.

According to Blad, among the obstacles to institutionalizing RJ are 'the high level of institutionalization, division of labour and bureaucracy within the criminal justice system itself'. The core ideas of RJ, as a consequence, are 'being received and perceived by highly developed agencies with strongly institutionalized other rationalities' than restoration. 'As a consequence, the core idea of restorative justice is suppressed in the shaping of restorative practices and cannot come to a full realization.'

Blad illustrates this tendency to *define in* restorative practices. In the Netherlands, all the initiatives for RJ practices are taken by 'collaborators of criminal justice agencies or para-legal organizations' (e.g. police, probation service), perceived by their own organizations as 'marginal experimenters who can be relieved of their "core business" for the time being to prove that their initiatives may contribute to that core business which in itself does not become redefined.' He criticizes the *instrumentalism* in organizations who initiate restorative programmes as a kind of supplementary aid to their core task. The state and its institutions are presumed to be particularly strong.

Boutellier, on the other hand, seems to embrace the instrumentalization of RJ practices. He presents a 'soccer model', in which criminal law plays the role of goalkeeper. The defence line is constituted by 'the connection between the criminal justice system and the world of social and public policy.' It is here that Boutellier sees a lot of potential for RJ. Drawing on his metaphor of the soccer team, he restricts restorative practices to the defence line. Along with the goalkeeper, Boutellier seems to suggest that the defence line belongs to a sphere in which the state holds enough authority and power to steer and enable if possible and row if necessary.

The upper part of the soccer team is driven by a 'vitality, the experience of most citizens that they have the right – and duty – to define and form their life in their own way.' The role of the state seems to be restricted to the enabling of the 'vital drive' of individuals. Only when particular boundaries are surpassed is a defensive strategy adopted. The criminal justice system and its partnerships are then set in motion. RJ becomes of 'use', both as better suited to respond to the needs of those involved and because, if treated as an equal moral subject, 'the moral appeal to the offender is stronger'. 'The contrast between the prominent normative function of criminal justice and its limited instrumental possibilities needs to be supplemented by other forms of conflict management.'

There are, however, a number of problems involved in this 'top-down' institutionalization. For example, in Canada, RJ has been institutionalized at sentencing. To some extent, the Canadian example might shed a different light on Boutellier's instrumental model of RJ. In Canada, the inscription of RJ purposes at sentencing followed among others from a concern with the overrepresentation of Aboriginal offenders in Canadian prisons. Some of the problematic (unintended) effects are: a too easy identification of RJ purposes of sentencing with Aboriginal justice initiatives – as Roach demonstrates, the associations made between RJ and Aboriginal justice are being used to exclude other groups from restorative approaches; and a problematic application of RJ in cases of disadvantaged groups. Institutionalizing RJ as an instrument of government can deepen particular societal divides along the lines of ethnicity, gender and class.

While these contributions all make reference to the state and its institutions, Pat O'Malley starts from a different angle. Closely tied to a line of thinking developed in writings on 'governmentality', his analysis lacks the crucial position others accord to the state. Social changes, including the demise of the welfare state, have brought us into a 'post-social' era, in which a 'downsized state' goes hand in hand with appeals to the responsibilities of individuals and communities (e.g. O'Malley 1996).

In his thought-provoking contribution, O'Malley looks at the points of articulation and difference between RJ and DHM programmes. RJ could find important points of inspiration in other, yet similar programmes. Among the major differences, O'Malley identifies the 'victim–offender binary' of RJ, which 'prioritizes rectification of past wrongs by one party'. Another problem he singles out goes back to RJ's 'assumption of communal consensus', which 'creates a potential for 'totalitarian' domination in which one set of values and experiences are to be the subject of condemnation, denial and apology'. Among the political and ethical dangers, this might bring forth an ignoring or suppression of social diversity and social conflicts 'of a sort that is important for "the community" to recognize'. DHM strategies avoid these pitfalls. Therein, the preferred discourse speaks of 'stakeholders', which 'allows conflicts of interest to be centred rather than an assumption that one party is necessarily in the right and the other to be blamed', and, secondly, 'it allows for a diversity of values and stakes within the network of those concerned', which avoids some of the problems RJ faces.

The comparison of differences, then, leads readers to the suggestion that RJ should look at other programmes in order to overcome some of the challenges it faces. It also shows that instrumentalization, particularly from a posited weak state, is absent. At least, as O'Malley notes, appealing to the interests each member of the community holds can lead to a democratization of risks and bring about a move 'from dispute resolution toward the possibility of dispute management', itself more susceptible to dealing most 'justly' with conflicts. O'Malley's paper brings to the fore another telling question: if programmes are mobilized without (reference to) the state (or positing a 'minimal state'), does this automatically preclude any kind of instrumentalization?

4. Politics, ethics and internationalization

Can and should the institutionalization of RJ be seen from, and furthered by means of, a consistent policy orientation?

There are reasons to believe that developing a consistent policy for RJ at state level is a realistic perspective. In the first chapter of this book, Michael Tonry reminds us how decisive penal policy within a country can be, and how states can adopt very different policies. It is illustrated that penal policy is something that can be made. Finland has taught us how a consistent policy can emerge from a broad agreement among policy-makers, practitioners and academics (taking into account the influence of other, for example, historical factors as well) (Lappi-Seppälä 2001). In this respect, the impact of an elite or expert culture is clear, whereas at other moments a more popular criminal justice culture will prevail.

RJ, because of its multitude of possible objectives and variety of underlying ideologies, can lend itself to an expert steered policy approach while it can also become part of trends towards 'popular punitiveness'. However, we should avoid thinking in terms of dichotomies; rather a mingling of elements from both tendencies might be expected in many countries, which makes it more appropriate to speak in terms of a continuum. Where can we locate, for example, England/Wales and Belgium on the scale – two countries with pronounced RJ practices and policies? A challenge for research is to carry out comparative studies to reconstruct the implementation processes of RJ in different states, and to identify influencing factors (see, for a similar approach, the study of victim policy developments in Canada and England/Wales by Paul Rock (1986, 1990)).

In this line of thinking, research should also focus on policy-making at an international and supranational level. In Europe, criminal justice policy-making escapes the narrow boundaries of nation states, and recently this has also been the case with respect to RJ issues. In the 1980s and 1990s the Council of Europe played a key role in developing victim policies and mediation practices within its (now) 46 member states, although to varying degrees (see, for example, on the influence of Recommendation R(99)19 on mediation in penal matters: Pelikan 2004). A more decisive impact can be expected from the EU Council Framework Decision of 15 March 2001 on the standing of victims in criminal proceedings. This legal instrument, through Article 10, obliges EU member states to promote RJ practices, and to ensure that their outcomes can be taken into account in judicial decision-making processes. Because of the legally binding force of the Framework

Decision for national governments, its consequences are much more far-reaching than soft law regulations at the level of the Council of Europe or the UN (Aertsen and Peters 2003). Not only is the *promotion* of RJ practices entering the political agenda of European countries, but also the *harmonization* of RJ practices and policies can be expected in the near future (Commission of the European Communities 2004). This input of international and supranational regulations and policies is placing the institutionalization of RJ in a new light, *in concreto* in a more internationalizing context. This new development should invite further analysis of the precise location of RJ politics of the European institutions on the expert–popular continuum. It is clear at which end of the continuum the Council of Europe with its strong tradition of expert involvement in crime policies has to be situated. However, EU politics might evolve in a more popular direction.

It follows from these arguments that there *are* prospects for the institutionalization of RJ at the highest political levels. Less clear is the ideological direction in which the institutionalization will be oriented, and which kind of RJ practices will emerge in the end. This RJ policy approach, and the belief in its potential, has to be confronted with a more critical approach, as presented by several of the authors in this volume. In particular, the question should be raised whether social-political developments in contemporary societies as discussed by several authors allow thinking in terms of manageable, persistent and sustainable policies. From a wider, more diversified and less definable cultural context, assessing the chances and likelihood for RJ to become institutionalized is a tricky exercise for policy-makers nowadays. However, the undefined nature of broader socio-cultural developments does not preclude finding useful reference points for the assessment exercise. For example, according to Boutellier, only two of the symptoms of the new crime complex are in direct contrast with the aims of RJ: the reappearance of punitive sanctions and expressive criminal justice, and the rediscovery of the prison.[5]

Another question, from a normative point of view, is to what degree a more uniform and centralized institutionalization of RJ – as it becomes more and more policy driven – is desirable, or under which conditions this might be done. In justice matters, as we have been reminded in this volume, the tension between the political and the ethical is present all the time. As Barbara Hudson concludes, RJ clearly also has its ethical and political aspects. The ethical moment refers to the aspiration of participation, communication and restoration. The political moment is reflected in its instrumentalization and possible 'harnessing' by criminal justice systems. The point made by many commentators is that the institutionalization of RJ is dominated by the political moment, i.e. is taking place almost exclusively from the political angle. Indications of this imbalance are – according to Hudson – the overemphasis on the effects on reoffending, one-sidedness in practices (focus on victim, offender or community) and becoming part of the exclusionary and punitive nature of criminal justice. The latter represents a real challenge for RJ when it aims to integrate fundamentally new principles inside penal procedures and not just to function as a diversionary tool.

In order to form a necessary counterbalance to the growing impact of the political dimension, one should ask then what are the conditions and ways of conceiving the progressive institutionalization of RJ from an ethical point of view? RJ practitioners are aware of the importance of the ethical dimension and the presence of values and principles in daily work. Many umbrella organizations have, after ample discussion and consultation, adopted ethical codes and examples of good practice. This book presents one such exercise, from the UK, which demonstrates the evolving character of these types of reflections. Mackay's chapter starts from a concern with the one-sidedness in practice (offender orientation), the ambivalent relationship with criminal justice and the need to safeguard RJ values. Also Mackay pleads for a balance when he concludes that system integrity can only be realized in the context of a mutual recognition of an ethical framework on law and RJ on the one hand and a socio-political agenda on the other.

In several countries deontological committees on the practice of mediation and RJ have been established which transcend traditional tasks of supervision and sanctioning; they also tend to provide fora for discussion about principles and day-to-day practice. Principles and permanent reflection on these matters are stressed in initial and in-service training.[6] In particular, there seems to be a broad consensus among mediators working in the field of criminal justice that the communicative and process-related aspects in mediation constitute a value on their own and are at least as important as the final outcome. Definitions of victim–offender mediation, as they appear in manuals, official statements and legislation, provide evidence for this orientation (Miers and Willemsens 2004) and contribute to the institutionalization of RJ from a principled and ethical point of view. Definitions and principles of mediation and other RJ practices also have found a prominent place in international soft law, such as the already mentioned Council of Europe Recommendation on mediation in penal matters and the UN Draft Basic principles on the use of RJ programmes (Van Ness 2003). These manifestations of attention to principles and ethics in RJ do not necessarily imply, of course, that practice always and everywhere is done according to these principles. But at least, based on these observations, we should not exclude the potential of practitioners and practice-oriented policies to work towards a balanced approach.

A necessary condition to achieve this is establishing sufficient autonomy in the way RJ programmes are organized and supervised. Here again, support can be found in the Council of Europe Recommendation where the fifth general principle states: 'Mediation services should be given sufficient autonomy within the criminal justice system'. The Explanatory Memorandum on this principle points out the 'different rationale' of the mediation process compared to the traditional criminal justice system. It has been argued therefore (for example in the case of Belgium), that RJ agencies, analogous to the processes they aim to facilitate, should be organized themselves on a neutral basis. This means that, while cooperating with the criminal justice system and other agencies, RJ programmes should not *depend* on the rationales of the partner organizations. Instead, as Aertsen argues in this volume, an ongoing interaction and constructive confrontation between different rationales should be made possible by a particular mode of local institutionalization of RJ. Steering committees and local protocols of cooperation play an important balancing role in this respect. In order to evaluate the viability of these and other similar ideas, much more qualitative research on both RJ processes and the institutional context of RJ agencies is needed.

Notes

1 Chapter 11 by Roger Matthews can also be read as a critique to this tendency of thinking in dichotomies and exclusive categories.
2 See, for example, Chapter 5 by John Blad where he discusses the 'complex and time-consuming' character of a conferencing project in Utrecht that led to an insufficient number of referrals and, subsequently, to the failure of the project.
3 Rose (1996: 327–8) lists the following changes: '[...] the privatization of public utilities and welfare functions, the marketization of health services, social insurance and pension schemes, educational reforms to introduce competition between schools and colleges, the introduction of new forms of management into the civil service modelled upon an image of methods in the private sector, new contractual relations between agencies and service providers and between professionals and clients, a new emphasis on the personal responsibilities of individuals, their families and their communities for their own future well-being and upon their own obligation to take active steps to secure this.'

4   Note how Boutellier's realism differs from an earlier version of (left) realism. The springboard for the emergence of left realist criminology, Jock Young (1997: 474) writes, was '[...] the injunction to "take crime seriously", an urgent recognition that crime was a real problem for a large section of the population, particularly women, the most vulnerable sections of the working class, and the ethnic minorities.' In Boutellier's realism it is not 'crime' but 'safety' that moves to the centre of attention. Moreover, he injects an extra emotional shot into his realism when he adds that it is the *cry* for safety and protection that should be taken seriously.

5   Here the question can be asked whether these two remaining symptoms are really in contrast with RJ. Many will argue that RJ practices – certainly for more serious crimes – precisely provide a forum for both expressing and channelling punitive feelings. Moreover, even the prison setting does not exclude RJ approaches.

6   See, for example, a document from the European Forum for Victim–Offender Mediation and Restorative Justice drafted at the end of an EU-funded AGIS project on training models and experiences in European countries (Willemsens and Delattre 2004).

References

Abel, R. L. (1980a) 'Taking stock', *Law and Society Review*, 14(3): 429–43.

Abel, R. L. (1980b) 'Redirecting social studies of law', *Law and Society Review*, 14(3): 805–29.

Aertsen, I. and Peters, T. (2003) 'Des politiques européennes en matière de justice restauratrice', *Journal International de Victimologie/International Journal of Victimology*, 2 (October). (http://www.jidv.com/VICTIMOLOGIE_Sommaire_JIDV_2003,2(1).htm)

Berlin, I. (1999) 'The purpose of philosophy', in I. Berlin (ed.), *Concepts and Categories: Philosophical Essays*. London: Pimlico, pp. 1–11.

Blomberg, T. G. and Cohen, S. (2003) 'Introduction', in T. G. Blomberg and S. Cohen (eds), *Punishment and Social Control*, enlarged 2nd edn. New York: Aldine de Gruyter, pp. 1–13.

Christie, N. (1977) 'Conflicts as property', *British Journal of Criminology*, 17(1): 1–15.

Cohen, S. (1985) *Visions of Social Control: Crime, Punishment and Classification*. Cambridge: Polity Press.

Cohen, S. and Scull, A. (1983) *Social Control and the State: Historical and Comparative Essays*. Oxford: Blackwell.

Commission of the European Communities (2004) *Green Paper on the approximation, mutual recognition and enforcement of criminal sanctions in the European Union*. Brussels: COM(2004)334 final.

Crawford, A. (1999) *The Local Governance of Crime: Appeals to Community and Partnerships*. Oxford: Oxford University Press.

Crawford, A. and Newburn, T. (2003) *Youth Offending and Restorative Justice: Implementing Reform in Youth Justice*. Cullompton: Willan.

Daems, T. (2004) 'Is it all right for you to talk? Restorative justice and the social analysis of penal developments', *European Journal of Crime, Criminal Law and Criminal Justice*, pp. 132–49.

Daly, K. (2002) 'Restorative justice. The real story', *Punishment and Society*, 4(1): 55–79.

Daly, K. (2003) 'Mind the gap: Restorative justice in theory and practice', in A. von Hirsch, J. V. Roberts, A. Bottoms, K. Roach, and M. Schiff (eds), *Restorative Justice and Criminal Justice: Competing or Reconcilable Paradigms?* Oxford: Hart Publishing, pp. 219–36.

Dignan, J. (2003) 'Towards a systemic model of restorative justice', in A. von Hirsch, J. V. Roberts, A. Bottoms, K. Roach, and M. Schiff (eds), *Restorative Justice and Criminal Justice: Competing or Reconcilable Paradigms?* Oxford: Hart Publishing, pp. 135–56.

Garland, D. (1985) *Punishment and Welfare: A History of Penal Strategies*. Aldershot: Gower.

Garland, D. (1996) 'The limits of the sovereign state: strategies of crime control in contemporary society', *British Journal of Criminology*, 36(4): 445–71.

Hacking, I. (2000) *The Social Construction of What?* Cambridge, MA: Harvard University Press.

Lappi-Seppälä, T. (2001) 'Sentencing and punishment in Finland: the decline of the repressive ideal', in M. Tonry and R. S. Frase (eds), *Sentencing and Sanctions in Western Countries*. New York: Oxford University Press, pp. 92–150.

Loader, I. and Sparks, R. (2002) 'Contemporary landscapes of crime, order, and control: governance, risk, and globalization', in M. Maguire, R. Morgan and R. Reiner (eds), *The Oxford Handbook of Criminology*, 3rd edn. Oxford: Oxford University Press, pp. 83–111.

Miers, D. and Willemsens, J. (2004) *Mapping Restorative Justice: Developments in 25 European Countries*. Leuven: European Forum for Victim–Offender Mediation and Restorative Justice.

O'Malley, P. (1996) 'Post-social criminologies: some implications of current political trends for criminological theory and practice', *Current Issues in Criminal Justice*, 8(1): 26–38.

Pelikan, C. (2004) 'The impact of Council of Europe Recommendation No. R(99)19 on mediation in penal matters' in Council of Europe, *Crime Policy in Europe: Good Practices and Promising Examples*. Strasbourg: Council of Europe Publishing, pp. 49–74.

Pratt, J. (2002) *Punishment and Civilization: Penal Tolerance and Intolerance in Modern Society*. London: Sage.

Rock, P. (1986) *A View from the Shadows*. Oxford: Clarendon Press.

Rock, P. (1990) *Helping Victims of Crime: The Home Office and the Rise of Victim Support in England and Wales*. Oxford: Clarendon Press.

Rosanvallon, P. (1992) *La crise de l'Etat-providence*. Paris: Editions du Seuil.

Rose, N. (1996) 'The death of the social? Re-figuring the territory of government', *Economy and Society*, 25: 327–56.

Rose, N. (2000) 'Government and control', *British Journal of Criminology*, 40: 321–39.

Tonry, M. (2004) *Thinking about Crime: Sense and Sensibility in American Penal Culture*. Oxford: Oxford University Press.

Van Ness, D. (2003) 'Proposed basic principles on the use of restorative justice: recognising the aims and limits of restorative justice' in A. von Hirsch, J. Roberts, A. E. Bottoms, K. Roach and M. Schiff (eds), *Restorative Justice and Criminal Justice. Competing or Reconcilable Paradigms?* Oxford: Hart Publishing, pp. 157–76.

Willemsens J. and Delattre, R. (2004) *Recommendation on the Training of Mediators in Criminal Matters*. Available on line at http://www.euforumrj.org.

Young, J. (1997) 'Left realist criminology: radical in its analysis, realist in its policy', in M. Maguire, R. Morgan and R. Reiner (eds), *The Oxford Handbook of Criminology*, 2nd edn. Oxford: Oxford University Press, pp. 473–98.

Index

Note: RJ is used as an abbreviation for restorative justice

Aboriginal cultures 2, 22, 58, 244
  Canada 51–2, 53, 184
Aboriginal justice initiatives
  Australia 237–8
  Canada 169, 172, 176–82, 189, 284–5
Aboriginal Legal Services of Toronto 179, 180–81, 185
academic role in developing RJ
  Belgium 74–5
  Netherlands 109
  see also principles of practice in RJ
actuarial justice 218, 219–21, 222, 223, 233
African-Canadians 169, 182–5
agreements 160, 197
  see also restorative agreements; youth offender contracts
Albrecht, Hans-Jörg 6, 206
alternative to custody movement 48–9

Ancient Greeks, dispute resolution 51, 53
Anti-Social Behaviour Act 2003 (UK) 140, 141
ASBOs (anti-social behaviour order) 125, 140–41, 142
Audit Commission, *Misspent Youth* 122, 124
Australia
  Aboriginal justice initiatives 237–8
  conferences 237–8, 239
  harm minimization 223, 226–7

Baskin, D 76–7
Beck, Ulrich 32, 216–17
Belgium 68–75, 152
  adult criminal law 70–73
  institutionalization of RJ 77–8, 84, 85
  security policies 81–2
  victim–offender mediation 69–73, 74, 76, 77–8, 82
Berger, PL and Luckman, T 94–7
Blad, John 285, 286–7, 295–6
Blagg, Harry 238, 244

Blair, Tony 120
Blunkett, David 275
boot camps 19
Borde 2003 182–3
borstal movement 47–8
Boutellier, Hans 294–5, 296
Braithwaite, J 49, 51, 58, 62, 81, 274
   reintegrative shaming thesis 241–3,
     245, 247–52, 255, 256–7

Canada 167–90
   Aboriginal justice initiatives 169,
     172, 176–82, 189, 284–5
   Aboriginal justice practices 51–2, 53
   befriending circles 274
   developing restorative
     jurisprudence 167–9
   imprisonment rates 17, 170, 179
   legal framework for RJ 17, 167,
     170–73, 175, 185
   penal policy trends 4, 17
   RJ and disadvantaged groups 169,
     182–5, 186
   sentencing reforms 168–9, 170–77,
     296
   youth justice 185–8
Catholic University of Leuven 70, 71,
   73, 74
cautions
   juvenile offenders 121, 122, 124,
     125–6, 188
   and mediation 159
   Northern Ireland 239–40
Children, Young Persons and their
   Families Act 1989 (NZ) 58
civil law matters
   England and Wales 125, 140–41
   Netherlands 100–101
claims mediation 104–5
CLCJ (Comité de liaison des
   associations de contrôle judiciaire)
   156–7
Clear, T and Cadora, E 263, 265
community decline 269–71
community justice 269, 272
   historical examples 49–53, 54

community mediation 76–7, 99–100
community participation in RJ 132,
   133–8, 229
   partisanship 136–7
   representativeness 134–5
   sentencing circles 176–7
   and victim involvement 137–8,
     202–3
community penalties 18–21, 264, 275
community safety 37, 38–9, 238, 269
community service 20–21, 70
community-based governance 222
concepts of RJ 44–5, 46, 124–5, 167–8,
   285–6
   institutionalization 75–7, 82–9,
     94–8
   theory and practice 286–90
     see also principles of practice
      in RJ
conducing conditions for RJ initiatives
   1–2, 22
conferences 238, 244–5, 255, 273
   Australia 237–8, 239
   Belgium 70
   Canada 186, 187, 189–90
   England and Wales 237, 239
   Netherlands 100–101, 103–4, 113
   USA 237, 239
   see also family group conferencing
conflicts of interest 229
constraining conditions for RJ
   initiatives 1–2, 22–3
contemporary crime complex 25,
   26–30
conviction rates 250, 266–7
Council of Europe 298, 299, 300, 301
Crawford, Adam 289–90
Crime and Disorder Act 1998 (UK)
   30, 120–21, 124, 125–6, 139
crime policies *see* penal policies
crime prevention 16, 28–9, 36–7, 38, 81
crime rates 3–4, 6–7, 31, 32, 60
   Canada 17
   England and Wales 122
   Finland 8, 11
   France 9, 10

Netherlands 31
USA 3, 7–8
criminal behaviour 40–41
criminal justice systems 250–51
deficit 25–6, 35–6
and elitism 54–5, 292
and guilt 252–3
managerialism in 29, 110–111, 121,
132, 134
politics and ethics 262, 271–3,
275–6, 277–8
and rise of pressure groups 57,
59–60
transformation of 106–111
see also legal framework for RJ;
prisons
criminals *see* offenders
cultural attitudes to offenders 5,
13–15, 22
Canada 17
England and Wales 12, 122
France 11–12, 14–15
Germany 14–15
USA 12, 13–14, 22
see also new punitiveness
Cunneen, Chris 218–19, 223
curfews 125, 143

Daly, Kathleen 238–9, 244
day fines 18–19
death penalty 1, 14, 34–5, 50, 52
abolition 56
Dignan, James 276
disadvantaged groups and RJ 238
Canada 169, 182–5, 186
dispersal orders 141–2
dispute resolution
and harm minimization 229
informal 251
pre-modern world 49–53
state controlled 54
diversity 229, 297
doli incapax, abolished 125, 142–3
drugs
harm minimization policies 223–30
USA 12

education 78, 244, 254
see also schools
electronic monitoring 21
England and Wales
community penalties 18–19, 20–21
conferences 237, 239
conviction rates 250
crime prevention 16
crime rates 122
cultural attitudes to offenders 12,
122
imprisonment rates 4, 121, 123, 139
legal framework for RJ 16–17,
125–30
penal policy trends 6, 15–17, 54
penal reform 47–9
see also youth justice in England
and Wales
equality 266, 272
ethics
and politics 262, 271–3, 277–8,
300–301
in RJ 261, 273–7
see also principles of practice in RJ
ethnic minorities 57–8, 182–5, 238,
244, 268–9
see also Aboriginal justice
initiatives; disadvantaged
groups and RJ
European Convention of Human
Rights (ECHR) 16, 142
European Forum for Restorative
Justice 75
European Union 197, 200–201, 206,
298–9
evangelical criminology 45–9, 62
exclusion 218, 219, 220, 225, 273
expressive aspects of RJ *see* sentiment

Faget, Jacques 284
family group conferencing
England and Wales 196
Netherlands 100–101, 103–4, 113,
286–7
New Zealand 237, 238–9, 250
see also conferences

family model of social relations
247–8
fear and anxiety 59
fostered by the media 15, 32
and rising crime 5, 16, 27, 31
Feeley, M and Simon, J 219–20, 223
final warnings 125, 126, 137
Finland
community penalties 18
imprisonment rates 5, 8, 10–11
penal policy trends 4, 8, 10–11
Fitzpatrick, P 85–7
formal RJ practices, Netherlands
101–5, 285
France 151–65, 283–4
autonomous mediation practices
154–5, 162–3
cultural attitudes to offenders
11–12, 14–15
imprisonment rates 9, 10, 11
institutionalization of penal
mediation 155–61, 164–5
invisible presence of RJ 151–2
judicial and restorative models
160–64
mediation practices 152–4
freedom and security 32–4, 41

Garland, David, *The Culture of
Control* 4–6, 12, 25–30, 36–7, 225
gender issues 177, 184, 266–8, 272,
277
Germanic peoples, community justice
49–50, 53
Germany
community penalties 18, 21
cultural attitudes to offenders
14–15
imprisonment rates 8–9, 11
penal policy trends 4, 8–9, 11
Giddens, Anthony 33, 216
Gladue 1999 171–2, 173, 178–80, 184
globalization 220–21
governments
alternative modes of governance
57

legitimacy 31–2, 35, 46, 64
post-social 222–3
and security 31–2, 34–7
see also Labour government (UK);
states
Graham, J and Bowling, B 122–3
guilt and shame 251–3

habitualization 94–5
Haggerty, KD 265
HALT programme 102, 104, 286
Hamilton 2004 183–4
harm minimization
drug users 223–6
and RJ 226–30, 233, 297
Henry, S 87–8
homicide rates 6–7
Hudson, Barbara 299–300
human rights 142, 201, 211, 271, 288
Human Rights Act 1998 (UK) 142
Hurd, Douglas 264–5

Iceland 254
identity politics 33
imprisonment rates 3–4, 6–12
Canada 17, 170, 179
England and Wales 4, 121, 123,
139
Finland 5, 8, 10–11
France 9, 10, 11
Germany 8–9, 11
Netherlands 28
New Zealand 61
USA 4, 7–8, 10, 28
INAVEM (Institut d'aide aux
victimes et de la médiation) 156–7
inclusion 225–6, 273
indigenous rights issues 58–9
indiginous justice practices 2, 22,
51–3, 58, 284
informal RJ practices, Netherlands
98–100, 105–6, 285
institutionalization, theories of 75–7,
82–9, 94–8
instrumentalization of RJ 78, 295–8
integral plurality 85–6

interactive settings 87–8
internalization 95–6
International Crime Victim Survey
    (ICVS) 13–14
interpersonal dynamics 83, 253
intervention, early 139–42, 240

Japan 4, 251–2
Jennes, Diamond 52
judges 17, 83
juridification of social conflicts 158
justice 41, 95, 106, 271
Juvenile Justice Act 1965 (Belgium)
    69, 70
juvenile mediation initiatives
    Belgium 69–70, 72, 78
    HALT programme (Netherlands)
        102, 104
    see also family group conferencing

Kanka, Megan 263
Klaas, Polly 263

Labour government (UK) 15, 16, 145
    youth justice 120, 122, 124–5
Lauwaert, K 102, 104, 107
Law Commission of Canada 181–2
Lawrence, Stephen 268
lay participation in RJ 127, 133–7,
    230–32
legal framework for RJ 113, 197,
    200–201, 210
    Belgium 72, 74
    Canada 17, 167, 170–73, 175, 185
    England and Wales 16–17, 125–30
    France 157
    USA 13, 292–3
    see also states
legal pluralism 77, 84–7
legitimation practices 95, 210
Llewellyn, Jennifer 174
local partnerships, Belgium 72, 84, 89

Mackay, Robert 196, 198–205, 206–9,
    287–9, 300
managerialism
    in criminal justice systems 29,
        110–111, 121, 132, 134
    and RJ 131–2
Maori community 58
Matthews, Roger 285, 286, 287
mediation for redress
    Belgium 71–4, 77–8, 82–3, 85, 89
    see also reparation
mediators 206–8, 300
    see also professionalization, of RJ
        practices
Moore, Sally 84–5
moralism 13–14, 16, 19, 22
morality and offenders 40–41, 42
Morris, Alison 244–5
Moses 1992 176–7
multi-agency strategies
    crime management 26, 29, 30,
        36–9, 291
    local partnerships (Belgium) 72
    restorative practices 103–4

neighbourhood conflict mediation,
    Netherlands 99–100, 105
neoliberalism 220–23
Netherlands 93, 98–111
    civil law matters 100–101
    community penalties 19, 20, 21
    crime rates 31
    family group conferencing
        100–101, 103–4, 113, 286–7
    imprisonment rates 28
    informal restorative practices
        98–100, 105–6, 107–8
    penal policy trends 4
    restorative mediation 102–3
    transforming the criminal justice
        system 106–111
new informalism 85–7
new punitiveness 46, 60, 63, 291, 292,
    294
    youth justice 122, 144–5
    see also vigilantism
New Zealand
    family group conferencing 237,
        238–9, 250

imprisonment rates 61
progress with RJ 58, 63, 113
referenda 61
NGOs (non-governmental
organizations) 207
Belgium 70, 71, 74
France 156
non-judicial processes 44–5
see also informal RJ practices
Northern Ireland 63, 239–40
notification laws 263
Nova Scotia, youth justice 187

offenders 5, 14–15, 40–41, 42
Aboriginal 177, 178
exclusion 218, 219, 220, 225
juvenile see Canada, youth justice;
juvenile mediation initiatives;
youth justice in England and
Wales
represented as monsters 60, 270,
273
restorative outcomes 44–5, 180–81
and sentencing 174–5, 264–5
see also cultural attitudes to
offenders; harm minimization;
rehabilitation; reintegrative
shaming
O'Mahoney, D and Doak, J 239–40
O'Malley, Pat 295, 297
organizational models 83–8
origins of RJ 49–52, 59
myths 52–3, 284

parent involvement 127, 246
participation and RJ 79–80, 82–3, 98,
202–3
lay participation 127, 133–7,
230–32
victims 137–8, 175, 202–3, 246
partisanship, community involvement
in RJ 136–7
Payne, Sarah 263
peer mediation 100, 105
penal mediation
Belgium 70–71, 74, 77, 78, 82

see also France
penal policies 1, 9–10, 23, 36–7, 298–9
changes 262–5
and community decline 269–71
community penalties 18–21, 264, 275
populism 28, 60–62
protection of citizens 27
and risk 263–6
see also security
RJ an additional resource 261,
273–4, 275–7
youth justice in England and
Wales 120–24
see also new punitiveness;
punishment
penal policy trends 3–17, 54–6
Canada 17
England and Wales 6, 15–17, 54
Finland 8, 10–11
France 9, 10, 11
Germany 8–9, 11
USA 6, 7–8, 10, 12–15, 27
penal reform 47–9, 56, 61
see also youth justice in England
and Wales
penal-welfarism 25
Platt, Tony 47
police level mediation, Belgium 72,
77, 78
police-led restorative practices
239–40, 250
politics
and actuarial justice 219–21, 222,
223
and ethics 262, 271–3, 277–8,
298–301
and RJ 221–3
Pratt, John 284, 292–3, 294
precautionary logic 265
primary institutions 96–7, 98
principles of practice in RJ 194–214,
288–9, 300–301
importance of remorse 205–6
and the legal system 200–201
need for a code 196–8, 209, 210,
211–12

neutrality and impartiality 206–8
priority of process or outcome 205
proportionality in agreements
    203–5, 211
rights and responsibilities 201
UK case study 194–5, 198–210,
    212–14
voluntariness 130, 171, 199, 202
Prisoners and Victims Claims Bill
    (NZ) 62
prisons 72–3, 77, 104
privacy 27, 37
private justice 87–8
professionalization 54–5, 230–32, 292
    of RJ practices 78, 137, 157, 181–2
prospects for RJ 62–4, 277, 299–301
Proulx 2000 173–4
public empowerment 57, 63, 292
    drug users 225
punishment 45, 107, 111, 290–91
    centralization 54, 55
    pre-modern world 50–53
    and RJ 111–14
    shaming 61, 140–41
    see also imprisonment rates;
        sentencing

Quebec 152, 156

race issues 182–5, 268–9, 272, 277
rape cases 266–7
recidivism 110, 130–31, 254–5, 274
referenda 61
referral orders in England and Wales
    126–43, 202, 273
    lay participation 133–7
    and levels of intervention 139, 142
    and managerialism 131–3
    role of practitioners 138–9
    victim involvement 137–8
    in the youth justice system
        126–31, 289–90
rehabilitation 171–2, 176–7, 188
reintegrative shaming 237–57
    guilt and shame 251–3
    recidivism 254–5

reintegration 245–7
restorative justice in practice
    237–41, 255–7
    shaming 241–5
    and trust 247–51
remorse 205–6, 244
reoffending *see* recidivism
reparation
    financial payments 185, 186
    in sentencing 171, 175, 185–6
reparation orders 126, 137
replacement discourse 261, 262, 273,
    276, 291
reprimands 125–6
resocialization ideal 26–7
responsibilities 142–4, 201, 221–2
    harm minimization 224–5, 228
restorative agreements 112, 202–6
    see also reparation; youth offender
        contracts
restorative culture, Netherlands 106,
    109, 285, 287
restorative detention, Belgium 73, 77
Restorative Justice Consortium (RJC)
    194, 196, 210
    Statement of Principles 194, 196
restorative outcomes
    Canada 168–9, 180–81
    UN Basic Principles 174, 186
retribution 27, 276
rights 27, 37
    ethnic rights groups 57–8
    human 142, 201, 211, 271, 288
    indigenous 58–9
    offenders 240, 243, 270
    victims 57, 201, 274
risk management and control 30,
    263–6, 271–2, 277
risk and RJ 216–33, 262
    actuarial justice 218, 219–21, 222,
        223, 233
    expert domination 230–32
    harm minimization 223–30, 233
    politics and RJ 221–3
    risk and uncertainty 216–18
risk society 25, 30, 32–5, 59, 216–17,
    233

Roach, Kent 285, 296
Roman justice 50–51
Rudin, Jonathan 180–81

SACRO 211
safety *see* security
sanctions
    criminal 143, 242
    in restorative practices 109, 112, 113
    in sentencing 170–71, 172
    see also reintegrative shaming; shaming punishments
Scandinavia
    community penalties 18, 21
    penal policy trends 4, 56
schools
    peer mediation 100, 105
    and security management 38, 39
Scotland, Children's Hearings system 194, 211
secondary institutions 96–7, 98, 105
security
    community safety 37, 38–9
    and crime 25, 27, 30–32, 34, 294
    and freedom 32–4, 41, 271, 295
    and politics 34–7
    and RJ 80–82
semantics of RJ 283–6, 289, 294
semi-autonomous social fields 84–5, 86
sentencing
    reforms in Canada 113–14, 168–9, 170–77, 178–80
    for risk reduction 218, 219, 220
sentencing circles 176–7, 180
sentiment
    in non-judicial processes 45, 131–2
    and penal policies 60–62, 293
sex offenders 177, 243–4, 263–4, 274
shaming punishments 61, 140–41
    see also reintegrative shaming
Shearing, Clifford 63, 228, 276–7
Sherman, Lawrence 254
Simon, Jonathan 270–71
social change 32–3, 59
social control 96–7

South Africa 63, 228
stakeholders 227, 229
Standards for Restorative Justice, review 194, 196
states
    and institionalization of RJ 57–9, 64, 290–95
    see also governments; legal framework for RJ
Strang, Heather 248
Supreme Court of Canada 171–4
    Gladue 1999 171–2, 178–80, 184
    Lavallee 267

tabloid media, England and Wales 15, 16
tagging 21
Thatcher, Margaret 57
three-strikes-and-you're-out laws 1, 60, 218
Tonry, Michael 268, 292–3, 294, 298
Toronto *see* Aboriginal Legal Services of Toronto
trust 247–51

underclass 220, 221
United Nations Basic Principles 174, 180, 186, 200–201, 211, 300
United States of America (USA)
    community penalties 18–19, 20–21
    conferences 237, 239
    crime rates 3, 7–8
    imprisonment rates 4, 7–8, 10, 28
    juvenile courts 47
    legal framework for RJ 13, 292–3
    penal policy trends 6, 7–8, 10, 12–15, 27

victim support 73, 109–110
victim-offender mediation 41–2, 300–301
    Belgium 69–73, 74, 76, 77–8, 82
    Netherlands 102–3, 104
    see also penal mediation; youth offender panels
victimization 5, 27, 31, 34, 227–30

victims 294
  and offenders 248–9, 274–5
  participation in RJ 137–8, 175, 202–3, 246
  restorative outcomes 169, 181, 186, 188, 246
  see also reparation
  rights 57, 201, 274
vigilantism 46, 51, 62
violent crime 160, 177, 178, 264, 267
vitality in contemporary society 33–4, 35
voluntariness 130, 171, 199, 202
Von Hirsch, A 26

Wagga Wagga conferences 237–8
welfare states
  and crime management 32, 54–6
  decline 57, 62, 79, 221, 291
Whitman, James 14, 243–4
Wynne, Brian 231–2

Young, Graham 264
Young, Richard 239
Youth Criminal Justice Act (YCJA) 2002 (Canada) 169, 185–8, 189–90
youth custody 121, 122, 123, 139

youth justice *see* Canada, youth justice; juvenile mediation initiatives; youth justice in England and Wales
Youth Justice Board (YJB) 125, 126, 141
Youth Justice and Criminal Evidence Act 1999 (UK) 120–21, 124, 127
youth justice in England and Wales 59, 120–45
  community involvement 133–8, 139
  legal framework 125–31
  levels of intervention 139–42
  managerialism 131–3
  penal policy 121–5
  rights and responsibilities 142–4
  role of practitioners 138–9
  victim involvement 137–8
youth offender contracts 127–8, 129, 143
youth offender panels 59, 127–30, 131–9, 142, 143
  community involvement 133–8
Youth Offending Teams (YOT) 125–6, 127, 133, 206